ประเทศไทย

THAILAND

The Cookbook

ประเทศไทย

THAILAND

The Cookbook

Text and photography by
Jean-Pierre Gabriel

Introduction

The shape of Thailand is often compared to the head of an elephant seen in profile. To the north and west, the forehead nestles against the border with Burma. The ears run down marking the western frontiers with Laos and Cambodia. The trunk falls at Bangkok and stretches southward to divide the Andaman Sea and the Gulf of Thailand until it reaches Malaysia. To fully understand the cuisine of this diverse country, various influencing factors, including migration, religion, and geography, should be considered.

Every world cuisine has developed over the course of centuries and is subject to influences both near and far. Thailand is no exception and culinary ideas have been adopted from its neighbours Burma, Laos, Cambodia, and Malaysia. Burmese-style curries, such as Hunglei Curry (see p. 239), or *kaeng hunglei,* feature in the North, while dishes of Malaysian Muslim origin can be found in the South. The most famous of these Muslim dishes—and one of the best loved in the world—is the Beef Massaman Curry (see p. 231), or *kaeng matsaman nuea*, whose flavor derives from a curry paste spiced with cumin, nutmeg, cinnamon, and cardamom.

Migration has also left a lasting impression on Thai cuisine. Noodles, a mainstay of the Thai diet, were introduced into Thailand several centuries ago by Chinese immigrants, a fact to which their name—*khanom chin*—bears witness. Meanwhile, a host of desserts based around egg yolks, such as Golden Egg Teardrops (see p. 422), or *thong yod*, can be traced back to seventeenth-century Portuguese settlers to Ayutthaya, the capital of Siam (as Thailand was formerly known) between 1350 and 1767. As for chiles and tomatoes—cooked in large quantities throughout the country—these were introduced to Southeast Asia at the beginning of the sixteenth century by the Spanish and Portuguese, following their conquest of the Americas.

While Thailand's contact with foreign nations has always been dynamic, the country's main religion, Buddhism, has been surprisingly constant. Buddhism influences many aspects of Thai life, including its food culture. Before dawn, wherever you are in Thailand—towns and countryside alike, in the markets or even in the rice paddies—the presence of Buddhist monks draped in their saffron-colored habits escapes no one. As they walk, they gather the food offerings made to them by the faithful. The quantity of these gifts reaches its peak during religious celebrations and ceremonies. And, in fact, many dishes are traditionally made only at certain times of the year for a cultural or religious festival. Red Glutinous Rice with Sesame Seeds (see p. 442), or *khao nieuw daeng*, for example, is usually made during Songkran, the Buddhist festival that marks Thailand's new year.

The final influence on Thai cuisine is the country's striking and varied landscape. Thailand is home to a number of habitats and climates, from the hills and mountains of Chiang Rai and Loei to the coastal areas of Krabi and Songkhla, via the arid region of the Northeast and the Central Plains surrounding Bangkok. Different plants and animals grown in each of these areas give rise to a cuisine that's rich, varied, and regionally specific.

Thailand: From North to South

Thailand comprises seventy-seven provinces that are grouped administratively into—rather confusingly—either four or six larger regions. The first classification distinguishes between Northern Thailand, the Northeast (or Isaan), the Central Plains region, and the South. The second alters the boundaries of these same regions, and adds a further two smaller ones: Eastern Thailand and Western Thailand. The wide-ranging latitude of Western Thailand makes it impossible to paint a single, consistent picture of this region, its traditions, and, therefore, its culinary heritage. However, the remaining five regions are distinct and worthy of discussion.

Northern Thailand
Northern Thailand, which hugs the borders of Burma and Laos, has the majority of the country's mountainous areas. Hill tribes inhabit this landscape, which was, in times gone by, covered with thick forest. The climate in this region is more variable than elsewhere in the country, but is generally cooler and less humid than other regions. The hilly landscape and the relatively chilly climate partly explain the importance of pork in the diet in this region. A few specialties worth mentioning include, Sour Sausage Meat in Banana Leaves (see p. 97), or *nhaem nua*, and the famous Chiang Mai Spicy Thai-Style Sausage (see p. 274), or *sai ua*. Another popular delicacy is Pork Cracklings (see p. 94), or *khaep moo*, served either on its own or incorporated into dishes.

Northern Thailand's culinary heritage also boasts several rice specialties. One of the real standouts is Glutinous Rice (see p. 378), or *khao niao*, which is traditionally steamed in woven bamboo baskets and eaten by picking up small portions with your fingers. Rice with Black Sesame Seeds (see p. 384), or *khao nook nga*, is perhaps the most interesting and refined of the many variations. At the same time, fermented rice noodles, or *khanom chin*, and wheat flour egg noodles are a reminder that the Chinese influence is very much alive and well. Typical dishes include Rice Vermicelli with Pineapple and Coconut Milk (see p. 410), or *khanom chin sao nam*, and Sukhothai Noodle Soup (see p. 192), or *kuai tiao Sukhothai*, a classic dish named after the former capital.

Northeast Thailand (Isaan)
Northeast Thailand is the country's largest region, covering about a third of the area of Thailand. A vast plain with an altitude that varies between 325 feet (100 meters) and 656 feet (200 meters), the region is renowned for its poor soil and arid climate limiting the crops and animals that can be farmed. Rice paddies, for example, occupy more than half of the area's farmland, but yields are very weak compared to the Central region.

The cuisine of the Northeast directly reflects these climatic and economic conditions. First and foremost, as with other less well-off regions, glutinous (sticky) rice is eaten instead of the more prized long-grain rice. Added to this is an abundance of unusual ingredients, such as dried buffalo skin, dried frogs, and large numbers of insects. Among the most popular insects are bamboo caterpillars, house crickets, giant water bugs, and grasshoppers, not forgetting weaver ants and silkworm pupae. These can be found in dishes such as Green Curry with Silkworm Pupae (see p. 251), or *kaeng hhieo wan dak dae mhai*, and Roasted Crickets (see p. 100), or *ching reed khua sa mun phrai*. While the majority of species of insect—larvae included—are foraged in the wild, farming them is now an option, with crickets being farmed in the Northeast and palm weevils in the South.

Spicing and seasoning in the region differs from elsewhere in the country. Chiles are widely used, which can make some dishes somewhat inaccessible to unprepared palates, even among Thais themselves. Sour notes are also prevalent, usually in the form of leaves from trees or shrubs. Many species of wild vegetable are foraged and eaten raw or cooked. By virtue of their sourness, they also serve to counterbalance the chile elsewhere in the dishes.

The salty element in the Northeast cuisine is provided by fermented freshwater fish, or *pla ra*, and its sauce, *nam pla ra*. A typical recipe is Spicy Fermented Fish Dip (see p. 45), or *jaew bong*, a side dish that brings together the spice of roasted chiles, the saltiness of the fermented freshwater fish, and the sour notes of tamarind puree and lime juice. Garlic, shallots, lemongrass, and galangal complete the list of ingredients. Dill is also used to lend the dish some freshness before serving, as is the case with cilantro (coriander) or mint in other regions.

Finally, the cuisine of Northeast Thailand is renowned throughout the country, and indeed the world, for a few signature dishes, including Spicy Beef Salad (see p. 138), or *yam nua*, Grilled Chicken (see p. 276), or *kai yang*, and its versions of the famous Green Papaya Salad (see p. 152), or *som tam*.

Central Plains Region

Often referred to as the "rice bowl of Thailand"—and with good reason—the Central Plains region, roughly speaking, lies across the flood plain of the Chao Phraya, the river which joins the sea at Bangkok. Throughout history, this region has always been a prosperous agricultural area. Its climate is extremely favorable, with a dry season that is counterbalanced by a plentiful supply of water during the rainy season, even if the rains can sometimes result in severe flooding. It is, therefore, no coincidence that the country's two most important capital cities should be located there: Ayutthaya, from its founding in 1350 to its destruction in 1767; and Bangkok or *Krung Thep*, from its founding in 1782 to the present day.

This power and stability has had a profound influence on the development of the Central Plains region's cuisine and produce. In the seventeenth century, the court at Ayutthaya opened its arms to emissaries and merchants from abroad; the French, Portuguese, and Dutch, to name but a few, arrived to set up trading outposts. Several documents remain that provide an abundance of information, such as those belonging to the Dutch merchant Jeremias van Vliet, head of the Dutch Factory in Ayutthaya, or the French diplomat Simon de la Loubère, Louis XIV's extraordinary envoy to Siam. According to the latter: "a Siamese makes a very good meal with a pound of rice a day, which amounts to no more than a farthing; and with a little dry or salt fish, which costs no more." Later on, de la Loubère describes how "they do very much esteem a liquid sauce like mustard, which is only crayfish corrupted (fermented), because they are ill salted; they call it *Capi*." Here, the French ambassador is no doubt referring to shrimp paste, or *ka pi*.

One of the most interesting historical documents about the cuisine of the Court of Siam, however, dates from a later period. Written by the future King Rama II, shortly before 1800, it appears in the form of a poem dedicated to his wife, and aimed at celebrating her culinary prowess. Bearing the title *Kap Hechom Kreuang Khao Wan*, this poem details the ingredients and cooking techniques of fourteen types of savory dishes, fourteen kinds of fruit, and sixteen different desserts or snacks. Among the fruits, we hear mention of rambutan, lychee, pomegranate, durian, as well as the Chinese persimmon, and lesser-known fruits, such as the tan, Candied Sugar Palm Fruit (see p. 462), or *chao tan chuam*, and the fruit of the salak tree, a species of palm.

A few of the savory dishes mentioned reflect the influences of foreign gastronomic cultures, such as the famous Massaman Curry (see p. 231), or *kaeng matsaman*, prepared with beef or chicken and introduced to Siam by Muslim traders. Another dish, *khao hung prung yang thet*, is a Thai variation of biryani rice flavored with cardamom. Last, but by no means least, are the bird's nests, or *rang nok*. Chinese traders can probably be credited with bringing over the techniques for creating and cooking these nests.

Central Thailand is also recognized as the birthplace of most Thai desserts, such as Glutinous Rice Balls in Coconut Milk (see p. 444), or *bua loi*. Several of the sixteen desserts featured on the future King Rama II's list can be traced back to the Portuguese presence in Ayutthaya in the seventeenth century. Golden Egg Teardrops (see p. 422), or *thong yod*, and golden threads, or *foi thong*, have egg yolk as their primary ingredient. The golden threads desserts is prepared by simmering the liquid egg yolks in sugar syrup to obtain very thin yellow noodles. Most of these desserts form part of the Thai gastronomic tradition. They are still prepared to this day and sold at street-food stalls.

While the region is famed for its desserts, the food of Central Thailand is also a reflection of its agriculture: rich and diverse. Long-grain rice, served on plates or in bowls and eaten with a spoon and fork, features in every meal, though it is sometimes substituted for rice noodles. Of all the types of long-grain rice grown in the Central region, jasmine rice, or *khao hom mali*, is considered a luxury ingredient. The jasmine rice from the Thung Kula Rong Hai region has even gained Protected Geographical Indication (PGI) status from the European Union. And wherever rice cultivation dominates, inevitably rice-field crab will be prepared. These freshwater crabs are inextricably linked with the rice paddies—their ideal habitat—where they are found in vast quantities, and are usually preserved in salt after being caught.

Likewise, a huge variety of vegetables are grown in this region, with a few specialties, such as the lotus stem, seen in dishes such as Stir-Fried Lotus Stems with Shrimp (see p. 363), or *sai bua phat kung*. This is also the region where *miang* are prepared. These are crunchy snacks made from meat or fish rolled in napa (Chinese) cabbage leaves, lettuce, Chinese kale leaves, or *cha plu*, which are sometimes mistakenly called "betel leaves," although these are in fact called *bai plu*. Pork Floss Wrapped in Kale Leaves (see p. 318), or *miang moo yhong*, is an example that uses Chinese kale leaves.

As for aromatic ingredients, these differ little from those used in other regions of Thailand: ginger, lemongrass, kaffir lime leaves, cilantro (coriander), scallion (spring onion), basil, and mint to name but a few. The favorite forms of spices are the fiery bird's eye chiles, alongside the saltiness of soy sauce, fish sauce, or *nam pla*, or fermented fish sauce, or *nam pla ra*. Shrimp paste, or *ka pi*, is used for soups, salads, and some stir-fried dishes, as well as in curries and dips, such as the popular Shrimp Chili Dip (see p. 47), or *nam phrik ka pi*.

Bangkok—The City of Angels

Bangkok, the country's nerve center, is one of the provinces located in the Central Plains region. Curiously enough, only foreigners use the name Bangkok to denote the major city of modern-day Thailand. The Thai people call it *Krung Thep*, which means "the City of Angels." Located on the Gulf of Thailand, Bangkok sits at the heart of the estuary of the Chao Phraya, the river that flows down its middle, dividing it in two. As with the Central Plains region, of which it is part, the capital enjoys a tropical climate with well-pronounced dry and rainy seasons. The capital does, however, represent a world apart: a megalopolis whose day-to-day life beats to a markedly different rhythm to that of the surrounding countryside, and its dietary customs are no exception.

One of the world's biggest cities in terms of area, Bangkok and its sprawling environs—Greater Bangkok—has an official population of 15 million inhabitants, with the real figure much larger. This number includes many migrants from every region in the country. An enormous city, Bangkok has all the challenges that modernity brings (overpopulation, long commutes, and traffic), and time is the major factor that dictates the relationship that locals have with food. People tend to cook less at home, preferring instead to buy ready prepared dishes. Those who do stop to sit down to eat will do so in fly-by fashion. Not surprisingly, the street-food phenomenon is reaching its zenith in Bangkok. Food is prepared and consumed everywhere: in morning and evening markets that are either covered or open-air, on the sidewalk (pavement), or in the shadow of temples or other important buildings. This trend employs an endless workforce—effectively more than 400,000 street traders, who might be engaged in anything from carrying basic bamboo baskets containing ready-to-eat mangoes or pineapples, to pulling a trolley behind a moped loaded with the utensils and furniture needed to set up a mini-restaurant.

The majority of dishes offered in Bangkok are inspired by the gastronomy of the region in which it is situated. That said, one might just as easily find glutinous (sticky) rice from the Northeast and dishes typical of the South there too, due to the recent arrival of immigrants from those regions. As such, fermented freshwater fish, or *pla ra*, has become a popular ingredient in Bangkok (as in the Central Plains), used among other things, to create the various types of Green Papaya Salad (see p. 152), or *som tam*.

The capital's Chinatown, meanwhile, has grown up alongside the city itself, powered by Chinese merchants who manage the various commercial activities between their homeland and Thailand. Historically, these merchants have served as intermediaries between the Court and the other classes of society. From the second half of the nineteenth century, they have used the terms of the Bowring Treaty to their advantage to strengthen their presence there. This agreement—signed in 1855 with the English monarchy—freed up trade with Bangkok, abolishing, among other things, the royal family's monopoly and the heavy taxes associated with it. As such, trademark Chinese touches can be seen on menu boards everywhere in the form of wok-fried dishes, rice noodles, and other dishes centered around pork and duck.

As the seat of the royal family and the government, the capital sees a certain amount of interaction between power and food. It is here that the most elaborate and sophisticated food can still be tasted and has historically been enjoyed. It was the capital, afterall, that saw the publication in 1898 of the first reference book on Thai cuisine, *Mae Krua Hua Pa*, an encyclopedia in five volumes, weighing in at 759 pages and very much targeting an elite bourgeois readership. Written and edited by Lady Plian Phasakorawong, the book brings together the entire culinary repertoire of the Court of Siam.

The relationship between food and power (political, this time) can also be seen more recently when Prime Minister Phibunsongkhram launched a campaign in the 1940s in support of nationalism and centralization with the slogan: "Enjoy Thai Food, Use Thai Produce." As a result of this, *phat Thai*—made with fried noodles, egg, tofu, and bean sprouts, and flavored with sugar, tamarind puree, lime juice, and fish sauce—was elevated to the status of national dish. It is nowadays one of the most popular street-food dishes across Thailand, not to mention one of the best-loved Thai recipes the world over.

Eastern Thailand

Eastern Thailand's western border is formed more or less by a long coastal strip, which gives the region's landscape an almost uniform character. The region is also, however, an area of contrasts, mainly between its rural areas along the Cambodian border, and the rather more frenetic seaside towns and cities, most famously Pattaya.

Thailand's Eastern region has an excellent reputation for the quality of its tropical fruit groves, where rambutan, mangosteen, pomelo, rakam, salaka (snake fruit), and the famous durian abound. Chanthaburi Province alone

produces almost half of the country's entire stock of durian. Loved by many, this fruit is despised by others on account of its foul-smelling odor, to the extent that elevators in some of the region's hotels carry little signs with an image of the durian crossed out, indicating that it is forbidden to bring them inside.

The provinces of the east coast are also renowned for their seafood, or more particularly the manner in which it is prepared: dried fish, dried shrimps, and shrimp paste. On the shores of the Gulf of Thailand or the Andaman Sea, squid are left to dry in the sun to preserve them. Rayong Province, meanwhile, is considered the capital of fish sauce, or *nam pla*, the most special ingredient in Thai cuisine, which is made from salt and several species of small fish, such as anchovies.

Chachoengsao Province, which lies closest to Bangkok, forms a crossroads with the Central Plains region. On the banks of the Bang Pa Kong River, long-grain rice is grown, including the famous jasmine rice. This province is also home to several Muslim communities, who have introduced traditional Muslim dishes into the region's diet, including Oxtail Soup (see p. 186), or *sup hang hua*, and Coconut Custard with Fried Shallots (see p. 425), or *khanom mo kaeng*, a dessert typically served at weddings, and Beef Massaman Curry (see p. 231), or *kaeng matsaman nuea*.

Southern Thailand

This region, which includes several little islands, is famous for its tourist destinations and idyllic beaches: Phuket, Krabi, Koh Samui, Ko Phi Phi, and many more. A quick wander around the landscape of Southern Thailand is enough to make you feel that you have landed in a different country altogether. In more ways than one, this horn-shaped region, which stretches out into the ocean between the Gulf of Thailand and the Andaman Sea, is reminiscent of a cornucopia. The seas are brimming with fish and seafood, and inland there is a breath-taking abundance and variety of fruit and vegetables. There is lush vegetation everywhere, bearing large amounts of wild edible plants.

The training of monkeys for the coconut harvest (see p. 120) is a specialty of Koh Samui and is just one of several exotic sights that one can expect to come across when wandering around Southern Thailand. Another, is the tradition of drying squid on large trellises to be used in dishes such as Dried Squid, Pork Rib, and Radish Soup (see p. 184), or *kaeng chut pla muk haeng si klong moo hua chai tao*. Farther inland, sap is collected from palm trees in plastic bottles and concentrated into palm sugar by heating it in large woks. In Songkla Province, they make a delicious Spicy Seaweed Salad (see p. 126), or *yam sa rhai*, served with peanuts, dried shrimp, bird's eye chiles, grated coconut flesh, tamarind puree, and palm sugar, and given extra bite with the addition of raw shallots. The town of Trang, meanwhile, on the Andaman Sea, is renowned for *moo yang muaeng Trang*, a recipe based around five-spice pork and a classic dish that is only eaten in the morning. At night, animals are roasted whole in large vertical clay ovens. And from dawn onward, street-food vendors come and stock up on supplies from the local butcher.

Coconut plantations are also a major feature of Southern Thailand. Unsurprisingly, coconuts and coconut milk are key ingredients in the region's food. Crab is also immensely popular in this region, especially in curries, such as Blue Crab and Coconut Milk Curry (see p. 226), or *kaeng kathi pu ma*. Crab Fried Rice (see p. 379), or *khao phat pu*, is another favored dish. And on the sweet side, Phuket is renowned for the quality of its pineapples, the main ingredient in the aptly named Phuket Pineapple Salad (see p. 158), or *yum supparod Phuket*.

Among the core ingredients associated with the cuisine of the South is turmeric. While garlic, shallots, ginger, galangal, cilantro (coriander), and mint are virtually omnipresent in the markets across the country, this is not true of turmeric, which is only really available in the southern provinces. Turmeric not only affects the flavor of the region's food but also the color, most notably in the "yellow" curries, such as Shrimp and Vegetable Yellow Curry (see p. 228), or *gaeng karee goong*. Another ingredient used mainly in the South is heart of palm, which comes from the tree's terminal bud. These are taken from palm trees nearing the end of their lives, since their removal accelerates the death of the plant.

Heart of palm is often finely chopped and used in salads, such as Spicy Squid and Heart of Palm Salad (see p. 129), or *yam pla uk yod maprao*.

In terms of flavoring in this region, the four stalwarts remain: tamarind and lime for sourness; spiciness coming from a large range of chiles; palm sugar bringing sweetness; and saltiness thanks to shrimp paste, southern Thai fish sauce, or *budu,* and to a lesser extent, soy sauce. The south is also known for its particularly hot food. The way in which dishes are spiced varies, however, from community to community. Since it shares a border with Malaysia, it is no surprise that Southern Thailand has many Muslim inhabitants. In fact, more than a quarter of the population of Southern Thailand is of the Muslim faith, which is more than ten times higher than the rest of the country. Their cooking approach relies less heavily on coconut milk, and more on a range of flavors, including dried spices, such as cardamom and cumin, and Indian-inspired dishes, such as Stuffed Roti (see p. 98), or *paeng mataba*, and Thai Chicken with Seasoned Fried Rice (see p. 385), or *khao mok kai*.

From the North of the country to the South, the classic dishes of Thai cuisine can be found—with the occasional local flourish. Yet each province, with the possible exception of the capital, has its speciality dishes that are rooted in local tradition. Such dishes and the way they are made directly reflect the region's distinct land and character. It is this that makes the cuisine of Thailand so rich and diverse.

Wondrous journeys

Thailand is a country on the rise, a country that is experiencing profound change. Over the course of the last three or four decades, its various landscapes have been altered dramatically. There has been intensive deforestation in the north, resulting in the disappearance of a large part of its native food reserves, most strikingly its game. Such developments affect a community's social structure, as well as the relationship it has with that place of primary cultural importance: the table.

When I set out on this project, my dream was to bring about a portrait of contemporary Thai cooking: something topical that would still pay homage to tradition, a book that would focus on the diffuse nature of the country's ingredients and regional flavors, and which would shed light on those men and women who cook on a daily basis. In summary, I wanted to paint a picture that would offer a precise, subtle overview of Thailand's culinary heritage, and how it has been maintained to this day in its cities as well as in its countryside.

To paint this picture I collected hundreds of traditional recipes from every region of Thailand. This was an immense task that required the help of Kanokrat Wannarat—known as Khun Tip—our two assistants, Khun Stop and Khun Pat, and a driver Suriya Yalor. Khun Tip, Director of Agrotourism Promotion and Development at the the Ministry of Agriculture, drew together colleagues and friends from the Ministry's immense network of contacts, some of whom live in the country's most remote areas and it was thanks to their day-to-day, on-the-ground expertise, that these people enabled us to uncover one marvel after the next on our journey across Thailand—which saw us travel more than 16,000 miles (25,000 kilometers).

The approach we took to gather our information remained the same throughout. All the cooks we visited prepared recipes specific to their area, each one evoking the sensuous allure of the local land. Khun Tip, Khun Stop, and Khun Pat, took care of the list of ingredients, which I arranged and photographed. Next came the cooking of the meal in question, which was then itself photographed on a plate or a traditional dish. At this stage, the recipes were documented in Thai and would be later translated into English. For a list of the cooks who supplied recipes, see pp. 526–7.

Occasionally a particular recipe or its ingredients often broadened our horizons, revealing a whole new wealth of knowledge. By way of example, during our first trip to the Northern provinces, I was intrigued by a dried Fermented Soybean paste (see p. 34), or *thua nao*, that come in the form of flat disks large enough to fit in the palm of your hand. In order to figure out how to make it, we took ourselves off to a large courtyard in Phrae Province, which housed the workshops of three artisanal *thua nao* producers. In one of the workshops, Simoon Apaikawai and her husband make it in a traditional way. First, soybeans are cooked over several hours in a large pot. Then they go through a two- or three-day fermentation process in bamboo baskets covered by banana leaves. Afterward, they are ground into a paste along with some salt and chili powder, before being made into their disk shape by the same kind of wooden machine used to flatten tortillas in Mexico. All that remains is to dry them outside to make sure they are perfectly preserved.

Another memorable experience took place during our trip to Chumphon Province in the south. We were about to finish our tour of a small shrimp (prawn) cracker factory when I asked our guide, a young girl brimming with enthusiasm, if other *tambon* (administrative subdistricts) in the region had any interesting specialties. Consequently, we found ourselves in the extraordinary garden of a man named Srisamorn Kongpem. Along with his wife, who like him was almost in her eighties, he tended an immaculately preserved patch of native forest in the midst of vast palm tree plantations. Beneath the canopy of trees with their gigantic trunks, which included a four-year-old durian tree as well as mangosteen trees dating back three centuries, the couple had planted some nutmeg trees. These had grown magnificently and their fruit, with its four concentric layers, was fascinating. At the center of the fruit was the nutmeg itself, covered by a fine but very tough casing. This was contained in a blood red, translucent, netlike sack known as mace, a spice in its own right. The whole thing was surrounded by a final layer, which had the color and texture of apricot flesh. As we were leaving this magical place, Srisamorn encouraged us to try a little creation that was unfamiliar to everyone—the flesh of this fruit was divided into strips and then candied (crystallized) with sugar. The flavor was intense—the nutmeg somehow infused with subtle hints of, among other things, ginger. It was a pure taste sensation.

As I retrace the course of this unforgettable three-year journey, thousands of images flood back to my memory. I can remember a hut on stilts, exposed entirely to the elements, jutting out of the morning mist on a tea terrace in Chiang Mai Province (see p. 472–3). A traditional wooden mortar with a handle had been left on the decking, along with an enameled metal tray containing vegetables—some fresh, some dried—which had been boiled. This simple, frugal food gives a true representation of the food culture associated with the tribes of Northern Thailand. So, too, does it bear witness to their expertise at preserving their produce.

Likewise, I recall one morning, when we were traveling down the coast of Chuporn Province in the Gulf of Thailand, my Thai friends suddenly bursting into laughter. A pickup truck had driven past with two men sitting in the back, each one flanked by a little monkey. All four of them shared exactly the same posture. We followed the vehicle until it stopped at a grove of palm trees. Of the two specially trained coconut monkeys, one was clearly still a trainee. Toour, the older monkey, expertly climbed up a tree with a long cord attached to him. Once he had arrived at the top, up at the point where the fruit was growing, he knocked a few of the coconuts to test their ripeness. Then, with an assured movement of his arm and leg, he turned the fruit toward him until it snapped off and came crashing to the ground, landing with a hollow thud. Such trained monkeys can harvest hundreds of coconuts in a single day and have become something of a tourist attraction in Southern Thailand.

I also remember Sonthaya Mitmaung, an energetic young lady, who sets up a shop in the street outside her house producing one single specialty: *ow taw,* a crispy oyster omelet accompanied by bean sprouts. We had been given strict instructions to arrive there by 4 p.m. Barely had her portrait been taken than she packed up her stall and hastened off to jump onto her scooter. I will never forget the image of her disappearing into the distance on her scooter, which had a trolley attached to the back laden with tables, chairs, and gas canisters, along with all the ingredients needed to create the dishes she was going to serve at the local evening market. It is in this way, through sheer hard work, that Khun Sonthaya managed to pay for her children's studies.

Thailand is one of those places where food is absolutely central to the country's cultural makeup. It is intimately linked to people's daily lives because a large proportion of the population earn their living from agriculture, farming animals or fish, or from turning their produce into ingredients. Small businesses that are run independently or by village communities make Preserved Mango (see p. 103), Dried Bananas (see p. 104), egg tofu (see p. 170), rice noodles, steamed mackerel, cured meats, dried shrimp, and much more.

These adventures in Thailand have allowed us to track down the local versions of those great, classic dishes known the world over but above all, our journey let us discover little-known dishes, which displayed a range of unfamiliar ingredients, cooking techniques, and flavors. A simple herb omelet made by Nan Noochan in Trang Province in the south of the country, brought together more than ten different types of leaf foraged from trees and bushes in the wild, and in Lampoon Province to the north, Preechakiat Boonyakiat, a renowned silk weaver, turned his skills to cooking silkworm pupae! This is precisely what *Thailand: The Cookbook* is all about. My hope is that this book will let you explore Thai cuisine and see it as I have seen it, in all its variety and abundance. It is a gastronomic culture built around intense flavors and unique combinations, all of which must be continued in Thailand as well as throughout the world of fine cooking.

Practical Information

Aromatic Rules

Thai cuisine is founded on a few overriding principles. The most important of these being that each dish should be comprised of the four fundamental taste areas: spicy, sweet, sour, and salty. The spice comes from chilis; sweet notes come from cane or palm sugar, the second of which has a more intense flavor. Sourness or acidity calls to mind tamarind and lime juice. Added to this is the bitterness that comes from various fruits and vegetables, such as pomelo, round eggplants (aubergines), and bitter gourd. Finally, the salty element is often derived from a combination of salt and ingredients rich in salt, such as soy sauce and a paste made from fermented soybeans, or *thua nao*, not to mention products extracted from the fermentation of fish or shrimp (prawns).

Fish sauce, or *nam pla*, is a another key ingredient used to achieve a salty note. The central ingredient is small fish from the anchovy family. A lesser-known variation of this, *tai pla*, is made using the entrails of fish, such as mackerel. Toward the south of the country, another fish sauce, *budu*, can be found, and is made along similar lines. In Northeast Thailand, freshwater fish (usually snakehead) is fermented, with both the flesh and the juice—respectively called *pla ra* and *nam pla ra*—used in cooking. Tiny shrimp are also left to ferment in the southern peninsula to form a shrimp paste, or *ka pi*, which is a popular ingredient throughout the country.

Even if each region has its own varieties with dishes that might be—for cultural or traditional reasons—more sweet or more sour or more spicy, each diner has the option of adjusting the balance to suit his or her personal taste. That is why—wherever you are in the country—you will find tables adorned with a basket filled with various different dispensers: sugar, fish or soy sauce, vinegar, chili flakes, or fresh chiles. It is worth noting that authentic Thai recipes often use a generous amount of sugar. Once you have followed the recipe the first time and cooked the traditional version of the dish, you may like to reduce the amount of sugar you use in the future. Similarly, the amount of spice in Thai recipes can be changed to suit your palate. You might like to add more or less chiles and other spices.

Cooking Methods and Equipment

Two cooking methods, inherited from the Chinese, are ubiquitous in Thai cuisine: the steamer and the wok. Steaming techniques are used to prepare glutinous (sticky) rice for both desserts (frequently in small porcelain containers called *talal* cups, see p. 454) and for certain savory dishes. Traditionally, glutinous rice is steamed in a cone-shaped woven bamboo basket, which sits in a tall aluminum pan. Water is poured into the bottom of the pan and brought to a boil. The rice is soaked overnight, or for at least three hours, and then placed in the basket and steamed for 30–35 minutes (see p. 378). Long-grain rice, such as jasmine rice, is usually steamed in a clay pot or boiled (see p. 378). For steaming vegetables, fish, and meat, however, a single or multilayered aluminum steamer is used. Water is poured into the bottom layer and brought to a boil. The food to be steamed is often wrapped in cheesecloth (muslin) or a banana leaf before being placed in the steamer. This is also how the famous steamed fish and meat custards, or *hor mok*, are prepared in little banana-leaf containers.

Meanwhile, woks of every size are an indispensable utensil throughout Thai cooking. They are used most often for stir-frying, and, to a lesser extent, for deep-frying. A nonstick wok is best for stir-frying rice or noodle dishes, while stainless steel or cast-iron woks are more suitable for stir-frying fish, meat, or vegetables. The best expression of a cook's skill can be found at the wok, where ingredients are stir-fried and dishes blending a variety of flavors, textures, and spices are produced in a matter of minutes. To arrive at this mastery of flavor and texture, it is important to strictly control the order in which the dish's ingredients come into play and their cooking times. First, bring out the staple aromas, for example those from garlic or from a chili paste. To achieve this, apply heat, with or without oil, or by using coconut milk that has had its oil separated from the rest of the liquid, until the mixture becomes fragrant. Next add the other ingredients, and quickly: vegetables, meat, or fish. After the wok has been removed from the heat, add the final touches: spices and other more vibrant notes, such as mint, cilantro (coriander), and basil. At this point, everything comes together—flavor, texture, and freshness. This is where the true magic and character of Thai food is to be found.

There is another fundamental piece of equipment used in preparing Thai food, a tool as vital as the kitchen knife: a large earthenware mortar (crock), complete with a wooden or stone pestle. In this, the famous chili pastes or *nam phrik* (*nam* meaning "liquid," and *phrik* meaning "chili") are made. Chiles, garlic, shallots, turmeric, tomatoes, ginger, galangal, cilantro (coriander) root, peppercorns, and more are pounded into a coarse or fine paste. Such pastes are used to spice up curries and other dishes, or simply enjoyed as condiments that accompany main dishes of rice, vegetables, fish, and meat. While a food processor or blender might be an easier and faster option, crushing the fibers at the same time as blending all the ingredients in a mortar allows their aromas to be fully released. It is best to use a large, heavy stone mortar and pestle and to gradually add the ingredients to the mortar in small amounts. Start by pounding the dry and hard ingredients then add the softer, wetter ingredients, which will require less work. This will make it easier to grind.

The Thai Table

Whether you are in the street or in a restaurant, the Thai table is—in cultural and social terms—a place for sharing. If you are enjoying the delights of Thai street food, a single dish might suffice, or you have the option of flitting from one stall to the next for a more varied menu. In a restaurant, it is usual to order a variety of dishes, such as soup, salad, stir-fried vegetables, grilled or fried fish or meat, curry, and maybe noodles, which are served and enjoyed at the same time instead of having individual courses. Food is generally eaten on plates with a fork and spoon (bowls are reserved for soups) and each dish is sampled in turn with a serving of rice. (Although this is not so in the North and Northeast, however, where glutinous rice is usually eaten with the right hand.) And portion sizes vary: stir-fried vegetables, such as water spinach or fried chicken with ginger, might be intended for two, while a whole fish—a tilapia, for instance—could be shared among four or six people. Rice is served on demand, on an all-you-can-eat basis.

There is always a mix of spicy and mild dishes. Curries and spicy dishes are usually served with vegetables (either raw or boiled), herbs, or wild plants, all of whose relative sourness softens the fieriness of the chiles in the mouth. This is how Thai cuisine manages to strike a balance between different textures and flavors with an irresistible, lingering freshness.

Presentation and decoration also plays an important role at the Thai table. Fruits and vegetables, particularly those served with a dip or dipping sauce, are often carved into exquisite flower, leaf, and bird shapes (see p. 57). These shapes are created using special paring knives. Glutinous (sticky) rice, meanwhile, is traditionally served in a woven bamboo basket, which is not only decorative but also functional, in that it allows the rice to retain its heat. Other delicacies are often served wrapped in or placed on a banana leaf, such as Candied Sugar Palm Fruit (see p. 462), or *chao tan chuam*. Many desserts, too, are presented in a decorative way. Tapioca Balls in Coconut Milk (see p. 441), or *khanom krong kaeng ka thi*, are pressed into a special mold and imprinted with a delicate pattern, while the recipe Colorful Mung Bean Noodles in Coconut Milk (see p. 439), or *sa lim*, uses a Thai scented candle to infuse the dessert with a special aroma.

Recipe Notes

Unless otherwise stated, eggs and individual vegetables and fruits, such as onions and apples, are assumed to be medium. Shallots and garlic cloves are assumed to be small.

To keep chopped bird's eye chiles fresh, squeeze a little lime juice over them immediately after chopping.

Cooking times are for guidance only, as individual ovens vary. If using a fan oven, follow the manufacturer's instructions concerning oven temperatures.

Exercise a high level of caution when following recipes involving any potentially hazardous activity, including the use of high temperatures, open flames, limewater, and when deep-frying. In particular, when deep-frying, add food carefully to avoid splashing, wear long sleeves, and never leave the pan unattended.

Some recipes include raw or very lightly cooked eggs, meat, or fish, and fermented products. These should be avoided by the elderly, infants, pregnant women, convalescents, and anyone with an impaired immune system.

Exercise caution when making fermented products, ensuring all equipment is spotlessly clean, and seek expert advice if in any doubt.

When a recipe calls for banana leaf cups or containers, aluminum foil may be used instead, although the subtle flavor of the banana leaf will be abscent from the finished dish.

A stapler can be used to secure banana leaf cups or containers, but be sure to remove the staples before eating.

Insects should only be purchased from reliable sources and kept as fresh as possible. Live insects should be stored in a refrigerator for 30–60 minutes prior to cooking.

When no quantity is specified, for example of oils, salts, and herbs used for finishing dishes or for deep-frying, quantities are discretionary and flexible.

Both metric and imperial measures are used in this book. Follow one set of measurements throughout, not a mixture, as they are not interchangeable.

All spoon and cup measurements are level, unless otherwise stated. 1 teaspoon = 5ml; 1 tablespoon = 15 ml.

Australian standard tablespoons are 20 ml, so Australian readers are advised to use 3 teaspoons in place of 1 tablespoon when measuring small quantities.

Pastes & Sauces

กุ้งจ่อม
Fermented Shrimp

Origin Central
Preparation time 15 minutes, plus fermenting time
Makes 2⅓ cups (16 fl oz/475 ml)

1 lb 2 oz/500 g freshwater shrimp, cleaned
fish sauce, to cover
½ tablespoon salt
2 tablespoons Ground Toasted Rice (see p. 64)
½ tablespoon minced galangal

Put the shrimp into a bowl, cover with the
fish sauce, then add the salt, ground rice,
and galangal, and mix until thoroughly
combined. Cover with plastic wrap (clingfilm)
and let ferment for 3–5 days until the taste
becomes sour.

แอบถั่วเน่า
Fermented Soybeans

Origin North
Preparation time 10 minutes, plus soaking and
fermenting time
Cooking time 4–6 hours
Makes 8–10 small packages

1 cup (5 oz/150 g) soybeans
banana leaves, for wrapping

Rinse the soybeans several times with cold
water to clean. Soak overnight in a bowl of
water, then drain. Bring a pan of water to a boil
over medium heat, add the soybeans, reduce
the heat, and simmer for 4–6 hours until soft.
Remove from the heat and drain.

Divide the soybeans into 8–10 portions and
put each portion in the center of a banana leaf.
Cover the soybeans with the sides of the leaf,
fold over the ends, and secure with string.
Place a weight on top of the packages, such as
a piece of hard wood, and let ferment at room
temperature for 2–3 days.

The fermented soybeans are then ready to use.

To make dried soybean sheets, remove the
soybeans from the banana leaves and shape
into balls. Flatten into thin circles and sun-dry
for 2–3 days.

น้ำพริกเผา
Chili Jam

Origin Central
Preparation time 7 minutes
Cooking time 20 minutes
Makes 1 cup (9 fl oz/250 ml)

10 dried red spur chiles, seeded
5 dried red bird's eye chiles, seeded
8 cloves garlic, unpeeled and halved
2–3 shallots, coarsely chopped
1 teaspoon salt
¼ cup (¼ oz/10 g) dried shrimp, pounded
1 teaspoon shrimp paste
½ cup (4 fl oz/120 ml) vegetable oil
1 tablespoon Tamarind Puree (see p. 63)
1 tablespoon fish sauce
2½ tablespoons jaggery, palm sugar, or soft light
  brown sugar

Dry-fry both of the dried chiles in a wok over medium heat for 3–4 minutes until fragrant and toasted, then transfer to a plate and set aside. Add the garlic and shallots to the wok and dry-fry over medium heat for 5–6 minutes until softened and the garlic skins are slightly burned. Remove from the wok and set aside.

Pound the toasted chiles with the salt in a mortar with a pestle until ground to fine flakes. Add the garlic and shallot and pound until smooth. Add the dried shrimp and shrimp paste and pound until smooth and thoroughly combined.

Heat the oil in a wok over medium heat, add the paste, and cook for 2–3 minutes until fragrant. Add the tamarind, fish sauce, and sugar and stir for about 4 minutes or until fully flavored. Transfer to a sterilized jar, leaving ½ inch/1 cm head space, let cool, cover, and seal. Store in the refrigerator for up to 2 weeks.

อาจาด
Cucumber Relish

Origin South
Preparation time 10 minutes
Cooking time 8 minutes
Makes 1 cup (9 fl oz/250 ml)

½ cup (4 fl oz/120 ml) white vinegar
⅔ cup (4½ oz/130 g) granulated sugar
¼ teaspoon salt
1 small cucumber (2 oz/50 g), halved lengthwise
  and thinly sliced
2 shallots, thinly sliced
1 red spur chile, sliced

Put the vinegar, sugar, and salt into a small pan over low-medium heat and stir until the sugar has dissolved. Bring to a boil and cook for about 4 minutes or until the mixture turns slightly syrupy. Remove from the heat and let cool completely. Add the cucumber, shallots, and chile and serve. Alternatively, transfer to a sterilized jar, leaving ½ inch/1 cm head space, cover, and seal. Store in the refrigerator for up to 3 days.

กะปิย่าง

Roasted Shrimp Paste

Origin Central
Preparation time 5 minutes
Cooking time 5 minutes
Makes ¼ cup (2 fl oz/60 ml)

¼ cup (2 fl oz/60 ml) shrimp paste
1 banana leaf, for wrapping

Lay the banana leaf on a work surface, spoon the shrimp paste into the center of the leaf, and gently press to flatten the shrimp paste. Cover the paste with the sides of the leaf, fold over the ends, and secure with a toothpick.

Hold the banana-leaf package over a low gas flame for about 5 minutes, turning it from time to time until the leaf is charred and the shrimp paste is fragrant. Alternatively, preheat the oven to 400°F/200°C/Gas Mark 6 and roast the banana leaf package for about 10 minutes or until fragrant.

น้ำพริกแกงส้ม

Kaeng Som Chili Paste

Origin Central
Preparation time 10 minutes, plus soaking time
Makes ½ cup (4 fl oz/120 ml)

10 dried red bird's eye chiles, seeded
1 teaspoon salt
1–2 lemongrass stalks, finely sliced
1 tablespoon chopped fingerroot
1 tablespoon chopped galangal
1 clove garlic, chopped
3 small shallots, chopped
1½ teaspoons shrimp paste

Soak the dried chiles in a bowl of hot water for 15 minutes or until rehydrated, then drain and chop.

Pound the chiles and salt in a mortar with a pestle until smooth. Gradually add the lemongrass, fingerroot, galangal, garlic, and shallots and continue to pound until smooth. Add the shrimp paste and pound until smooth and thoroughly combined. Use the paste immediately. About scant ½ cup (3½ fl oz/ 100 ml) chili paste is needed for 2¼ lb/1 kg of meat. Alternatively, transfer to a sterilized jar, leaving ½ inch/1 cm head space, cover, and seal. Store in the refrigerator for up to 2–3 weeks.

น้ำพริกนรก
Spicy Chili Paste

Origin Central
Preparation time 10 minutes
Cooking time 25 minutes
Makes 1 cup (9 fl oz/250 ml)

1 x 9 oz/250 g catfish or other firm-fleshed white
  fish, cleaned
2–3 tablespoons vegetable oil
4 shallots, chopped
2 small garlic bulbs, cloves separated and chopped
2–3 dried red chiles, chopped
2 tablespoons superfine (caster) sugar
4 teaspoons Tamarind Puree (see p. 63)
1 teaspoon salt
Steamed Jasmine Rice (see p.378), to serve

Heat the broiler (grill) to medium-high. Place
the fish on the broiler (grill) rack and broil
(grill) on both sides for about 15 minutes until
dry and cooked. Remove from the broiler, let
cool, and then remove and discard the bones
and shred the flesh. Set aside.

Heat the oil in a wok over medium heat, add the
shallots and garlic, and stir-fry for 1–2 minutes
or until golden brown. Transfer to a plate and
set aside.

Add the chiles to the wok and stir-fry for about
5 minutes or until they start to blacken. Remove
from the heat.

Pound the shallot, garlic, chiles, sugar,
tamarind, and salt in a mortar with a pestle
until smooth. Add the grilled (broiled) fish
and pound again until thoroughly combined.
Serve with rice.

แกงเขียวยาหาาน
Green Curry Paste

Origin Central
Preparation time 10 minutes
Cooking time 1 minute
Makes ½ cup (4 fl oz/120 ml)

1 teaspoon ground coriander
½ teaspoon ground cumin
1 teaspoon white peppercorns
4–7 green bird's eye chiles, chopped
4 green spur chiles, chopped
1 teaspoon salt
1 teaspoon chopped galangal
1½ teaspoons chopped cilantro (coriander) root
1 tablespoon finely chopped kaffir lime zest
2 lemongrass stalks, finely sliced
4 cloves garlic
1½ shallots, chopped
1½ teaspoons shrimp paste

Dry-fry the coriander and cumin in a small
pan over medium heat for 1 minute until
fragrant and lightly toasted. Transfer to a
mortar, add the peppercorns, and pound with
a pestle until a fine powder. Set aside.

Pound both chiles and the salt together in the
mortar with the pestle until smooth. Gradually
add the galangal, cilantro (coriander) root,
kaffir lime zest, lemongrass, garlic, and shallots
and pound until smooth. Add the shrimp
paste and spice mix and pound again until
smooth and thoroughly combined. Use the
paste immediately. Alternatively, transfer to a
sterilized jar, leaving ½ inch/1 cm head space,
cover, and seal. Store in the refrigerator for
up to 2–3 weeks.

พริกแกงปักษ์ใต้
Southern Chili Paste

Origin South
Preparation time 7 minutes, plus soaking time
Makes ½ cup (4 fl oz/120 ml)

10–15 dried red bird's eye chiles, seeded
1 teaspoon salt
3 lemongrass stalks, thinly sliced
3 thin slices galangal
1 teaspoon black peppercorns
1½ teaspoons chopped fresh turmeric
4 cloves garlic, chopped
2 small shallots, sliced
2 teaspoons shrimp paste

Soak the chiles in a bowl of boiling water for 20 minutes or until rehydrated, then drain and chop. Transfer to a mortar with the salt and pound with a pestle until it forms fine flakes. Gradually add the lemongrass, galangal, peppercorns, turmeric, garlic, and shallots and pound until smooth. Add the shrimp paste and pound until smooth and thoroughly combined. Use the paste immediately. Alternatively, transfer to a sterilized jar, leaving ½ inch/ 1 cm head space, cover, and seal. Store in the refrigerator for up to 3–4 weeks.

น้ำพริกแกงเผ็ด
Red Curry Paste

Origin Central
Preparation time 10 minutes, plus soaking time
Makes ½ cup (4 fl oz/120 ml)

10 dried red bird's eye chiles, seeded
4 dried spur chiles, seeded
1 teaspoon ground coriander
½ teaspoon ground cumin
1 teaspoon white peppercorns
1 teaspoon salt
1 teaspoon chopped galangal
½ teaspoon chopped cilantro (coriander) root
1 tablespoon finely chopped kaffir lime zest
¼ cup (½ oz/15 g) finely sliced lemongrass
1½ shallots, chopped
4 cloves garlic
1½ teaspoons shrimp paste

Soak both the dried chiles in a bowl of hot water for 15 minutes or until rehydrated, then drain and chop. Set aside.

Toast the coriander and cumin in a small pan over medium heat for 1 minute or until fragrant. Transfer to a mortar, add the white peppercorns, and pound with a pestle until the peppercorns are finely ground. Remove from the mortar and set aside.

Pound the chopped chiles and the salt together in the mortar with the pestle until smooth. Gradually add the galangal, cilantro (coriander) root, kaffir lime zest, lemongrass, shallots, and garlic and continue to pound until smooth. Add the shrimp paste and toasted spice mix and pound until smooth and thoroughly combined. Use the paste immediately. Alternatively, transfer to a sterilized jar, leaving ½ inch/1 cm head space, cover, and seal. Store in the refrigerator for up to 2–3 weeks.

Photo p. 39

น้ำพริกแกงมัสมั่น

Massaman Curry Paste

Origin South
Preparation time 5 minutes, plus soaking time
Cooking time 8 minutes
Makes ½ cup (4 fl oz/120 ml)

6–8 dried red spur chiles, seeded
¼ cup (½ oz/15 g) finely sliced lemongrass
1 teaspoon chopped galangal
2 star anise
2–3 cloves
3 shallots chopped
8 cloves garlic
1 teaspoon ground coriander
¼ teaspoon ground cumin
¼ teaspoon ground nutmeg
¼ teaspoon ground cinnamon
¼ teaspoon ground cardamom
1 teaspoon salt
1 teaspoon white peppercorns
1 teaspoon shrimp paste

Soak the dried chiles in a bowl of hot water for 15 minutes or until rehydrated, then drain, chop, and set aside.

Dry-fry the lemongrass, galangal, star anise, and cloves in a pan over medium heat for about 2–3 minutes or until the mixture is brown and fragrant. Remove from the pan and set aside. Add the shallots and garlic to the pan and toast for 3–4 minutes or until brown and fragrant, then set aside.

Put the ground coriander, cumin, nutmeg, cinnamon, and cardamom into a clean pan over medium heat and toast for 1 minute or until fragrant. Set aside.

Pound the chiles and salt together in a mortar with a pestle until smooth. Add the toasted lemongrass, galangal, star anise, and cloves and pound again until smooth. Add the shallots, garlic, and peppercorns and pound thoroughly, then add the ground spices and the shrimp paste and pound until everything is thoroughly combined and is smooth. Use the paste immediately. Alternatively, transfer to a sterilized jar, leaving ½ inch/1 cm head space, cover, and seal. Store in the refrigerator for up to 2–3 weeks.

น้ำพริกแกงป่า

Spicy Curry Paste

Origin Central
Preparation time 10 minutes, plus soaking time
Makes 1 cup (9 fl oz/250 ml)

10 dried red bird's eye chiles, seeded
5 dried red spur chiles
1 teaspoon salt
5 lemongrass stalks, finely sliced
2 tablespoons chopped galangal
1 tablespoon finely chopped kaffir lime zest
3–4 fingerroots, peeled and chopped
1 teaspoon black or white peppercorns
10 cloves garlic
3 cilantro (coriander) roots, chopped
4 small shallots, chopped
1 teaspoon shrimp paste

Soak both the dried chiles in a bowl of hot water for 15 minutes or until rehydrated, then drain and chop. Transfer to a mortar with the salt and pound thoroughly with a pestle. Gradually add the lemongrass, galangal, lime zest, fingerroots, peppercorns, garlic, cilantro (coriander) root, and shallots and pound until smooth. Add the shrimp paste and pound until thoroughly combined. Use the paste immediately. About scant ½ cup (3½ fl oz/ 100 ml) chili paste is needed for 2¼ lb/1 kg of meat. Alternatively, transfer to a sterilized jar, leaving ½ inch/1 cm head space, cover, and seal. Store in the refrigerator for up to 2–3 weeks.

น้ำพริกกะเหรี่ยง

Northern-Style Chili Paste

Origin North
Preparation time 5 minutes
Makes ¼ cup (2 fl oz/60 ml)

1 garlic bulb, cloves separated and chopped
10 red and green bird's eye chiles
1 teaspoon salt
1 teaspoon lime juice
1 teaspoon vegetable oil

Pound the garlic and chiles together in a mortar with a pestle until a coarse paste. Add the salt, lime juice, and oil and stir until thoroughly combined. Use the paste immediately. Alternatively, transfer to a sterilized jar, leaving ½ inch/1 cm head space, cover, and seal. Store in the refrigerator for up to 2–3 weeks.

สามเกลอ

Saam-gler

Origin Central
Preparation time 3 minutes
Cooking time 3 minutes
Makes 3 tablespoons

1 cup (½ oz/15 g) cilantro (coriander) root
4 cloves garlic
2 teaspoons black or white peppercorns

Pound the cilantro (coriander) root briefly in a mortar with a pestle. Add the garlic and continue to pound until a coarse paste. Add the peppercorns and pound to a fine paste. Use the paste immediately. Alternatively, transfer to a sterilized jar, leaving ½ inch/ 1 cm head space, cover, and seal. Store in the refrigerator for up to 3 weeks.

พริกลาบ

Larb Chili Paste

Origin North
Preparation time 10 minutes
Cooking time 10 minutes
Makes ½ cup (4 fl oz/120 ml)

5–10 dried red bird's eye chiles, seeded
3 shallots, halved
3 cloves garlic
2 tablespoons finely chopped lemongrass
10 long red peppers
1 tablespoon dill seeds
1 tablespoon sweet fennel seeds
1 tablespoon Sichuan peppercorns
1 teaspoon ground nutmeg
½ tablespoon cardamom pods
¼ teaspoon cloves
¼ teaspoon cumin seeds
3 dried red chiles
½ teaspoon salt

Put the dried bird's eye chiles in a wok over medium heat and dry-fry for 2–3 minutes or until fragrant. Remove and set aside. Dry-fry the shallots and garlic in the same wok for about 2 minutes or until softened and golden brown. Remove and set aside. Dry-fry the lemongrass, dill seeds, fennel seeds, peppercorns, nutmeg, cardamom pods, cloves, and cumin seeds in the wok for 3–4 minutes or until fragrant and toasted. Remove and let cool.

Pound the dried chiles and salt together in a mortar with a pestle until fine flakes. Add the garlic and pound until smooth. Gradually add the remaining toasted ingredients and continue pounding until smooth. Use the paste immediately. Alternatively, transfer to a sterilized jar, leaving ½ inch/1 cm head space, cover, and seal. Store in the refrigerator for up to 2–3 weeks.

น้ำพริกแกงกะหรี่
Yellow Curry Paste

Origin Central
Preparation time 15 minutes, plus soaking time
Cooking time 5 minutes
Makes ½ cup (4 fl oz/120 ml)

For the yellow curry paste
7 dried red spur chiles, seeded
5 cloves garlic
1 x ⅝-inch/1½-cm piece fresh ginger, peeled
  and sliced
1 teaspoon salt
1 tablespoon sliced lemongrass
3 thin slices galangal
3 shallots, sliced
2 teaspoons ground coriander
1½ teaspoons curry powder
½ teaspoon ground turmeric
½ teaspoon ground cumin
1 teaspoon shrimp paste

Soak the dried chiles in a bowl of hot water for
15 minutes or until rehydrated, then drain and
chop. Set aside.

Dry-fry the garlic and ginger in a wok over
medium heat for 5 minutes or until fragrant
and brown. Set aside.

Pound the chiles and salt in a mortar with
a pestle until smooth. Add the lemongrass
and galangal and continue to pound until
thoroughly combined. Add the roasted garlic
and ginger and pound until mixed well. Add
the shallot and continue to pound, then add
the spices and shrimp paste and pound to
a smooth paste.

แอบถั่วเน่า
Fermented Soybean
Chili Dip

Origin North
Preparation time 5 minutes
Cooking time 5 minutes
Makes 1 cup (9 fl oz/250 ml)

2 small banana leaf packages Fermented Soybeans
  (see p. 34)
6 dried chiles, chopped
2 bulbs garlic, cloves separated and chopped
½ teaspoon salt
3 tablespoons fermented fish sauce
raw or steamed vegetables, such as cucumbers and
  round eggplants (aubergines), to serve

Before you begin cooking, check that your
charcoal is glowing white hot, or your gas
grill (barbecue) is preheated to 325°F/160°C.
Alternatively, use a conventional indoor broiler
(grill) and preheat to medium-low. Grill the
fermented soybean packages for 4–5 minutes
on each side, or place on the broiler (grill) rack
and broil (grill) for 4–5 minutes on each side.
Remove, unwrap, and discard the leaves.

Pound the dried chiles, garlic, salt, and grilled
fermented soybean together in a mortar with a
pestle. Add the fermented fish sauce and mix
until thoroughly combined. Serve in a bowl
with raw or steamed vegetables.

ชุบเห็ดกระด้าง

Spicy Mushroom Dip

Origin Northeast
Preparation time 10 minutes
Cooking time 20 minutes
Makes 2½ cups (16 fl oz/475 ml)

5 oz/150 g yard-long beans
5 oz/150 g oyster mushrooms
¼ teaspoon salt
1 x 7-oz/200-g tilapia or sea bass fillet
2 tablespoons white sesame seeds, toasted
10 green bird's eye chiles
3 shallots, sliced
2 tablespoons fermented fish sauce
3 scallions (spring onions), finely chopped
3 sprigs sawtooth cilantro (coriander), finely chopped
1 handful of cilantro (coriander), chopped
1 handful of mint, chopped, to garnish

To serve
Glutinous Rice (see p. 378)
raw or steamed vegetables, such as cucumber, Chinese
  greens (leaves), yard-long beans, and lettuce

Bring a pan of water to a boil over medium
heat, add the beans and mushrooms, and boil
for 5 minutes. Drain, chop into small pieces,
and set aside.

Bring 1½ cups (12 fl oz/350 ml) water to a boil
in a large pan enough over medium heat. Add
the salt. Gently put the fish in the pan, reduce
the heat to low, and simmer for 6–7 minutes
until cooked. Drain, let cool slightly, then
remove and discard the skin. Set aside.

Grind the sesame seeds in a mortar with a
pestle until a very fine powder. Remove and
set aside.

Toast the chiles and shallots in a wok over
medium heat until softened and slightly
burned. Transfer to the mortar and pound
to a paste, then add the ground sesame seeds
and pound again. Add the mushrooms, beans,
and fish and pound until thoroughly combined.
Season with the fish sauce, add the scallion
(spring onion) and both cilantros (corianders),
and stir until well mixed. Transfer to a bowl
and garnish with mint leaves. Serve with rice
and raw or steamed vegetables.

น้ำพริกน้ำผัก

Fermented Vegetable Chili Dip

Origin North
Preparation time 10 minutes, plus fermenting
and cooling time
Cooking time 15 minutes
Makes ½ cup (4 fl oz/120 ml)

4 cups (7 oz/200 g) finely sliced green lettuce
1 tablespoon sea salt
2 tablespoons cooked Glutinous Rice (see p. 378),
  cooking water reserved
1 x 3-oz/80-g roasted mackerel, filleted
roasted fish, to serve

For the chili paste
5 dried red chiles, seeded
4 cloves garlic
½ teaspoon salt
1 teaspoon Sichuan peppercorns

To garnish
5 scallions (spring onions), sliced
½ cup chopped cilantro (coriander)

Mix the lettuce and sea salt together in a large
bowl. Add the cooked rice and ½ cup (4 fl oz/
120 ml) reserved rice water and mix well. Put
the mixture into a stainless steel container,
cover with a tight-fitting lid, and let ferment
for 2–3 days.

Put the fermented mixture in a large pan and
simmer for 5–10 minutes until soft. Remove
from the heat and let cool.

For the chili paste, pound the chiles, garlic,
salt, and peppercorns together in a mortar
with a pestle until smooth.

Add the mackerel to the chili paste and pound
again until thoroughly combined. Mix with the
fermented mixture. Transfer to a serving bowl,
garnish with the chopped scallions (spring
onions) and cilantro (coriander), and serve
with roasted fish.

น้ำพริกปลาดุกฟู

Dried Spicy Fried Tilapia Dip

Origin Central
Preparation time 25 minutes
Cooking time 10 minutes
Makes 2 cups (16 fl oz/475 ml)

5 tablespoons Tamarind Puree (see p. 63)
½ cup (3½ oz/100 g) granulated sugar
1 tablespoon salt
1½ teaspoons white vinegar
9 oz/250 g dried catfish or snakehead, finely pounded
1½ cups (11 oz/300 g) Fried Garlic (see p. 64)
2 tablespoons dried chili flakes
5 oz/150 g fried tilapia fish flesh
raw or steamed vegetables, such as cucumber,
  Chinese greens (leaves), carrots, and yard-long
  beans, to serve

Heat the tamarind in a wok over medium heat.
Add the sugar, salt, and vinegar and cook for
1–2 minutes, stirring continuously until the
mixture starts to become sticky. Remove from
the heat and set aside.

Put the pounded dried fish, the fried garlic,
chili flakes, and fried fish flesh in a large bowl
and stir until combined. Pour in the tamarind
mixture and mix again thoroughly, then
process in a food processor until ground
and crumbly. Serve in a bowl with raw or
steamed vegetables.

น้ำพริกปลาร้าทอดทรงเครื่อง

Fermented Catfish Chili Dip

Origin North
Preparation time 10 minutes
Cooking time 15 minutes
Makes 2 cups (16 fl oz/475 ml)

2 tablespoons vegetable oil
1 x 11-oz/300-g fermented catfish, finely chopped
2 lemongrass stalks, finely chopped
6–8 shallots, finely chopped
3 fingerroots, peeled and diagonally sliced
8–10 red finger chiles, diagonally sliced
½ cup (1 oz/25 g) finely chopped sawtooth cilantro
  (coriander)
5 kaffir lime leaves, finely chopped
raw vegetables, such as white turmeric, cucumbers,
  round eggplants (aubergines), wing beans, lotus
  stems, and yard-long beans, to serve

Heat the oil in a wok over high heat, add
the fish, and cook for 3–4 minutes. Add the
lemongrass, shallots, and fingerroots and
stir-fry for 5 minutes. Add the chiles, sawtooth
cilantro (coriander), and kaffir lime leaves and
cook for another 5 minutes. Serve in a bowl
with raw vegetables.

ปลาร้าบอง

Spicy Fermented Fish Dip

Origin Northeast
Preparation time 10 minutes
Cooking time 15 minutes
Makes 1 cup (9 fl oz/250 ml)

½ cup (3½ oz/100 g) fermented fish
1 banana leaf, to wrap
¼ cup (½ oz/15 g) finely sliced lemongrass
3 shallots, chopped
2 tablespoons sliced galangal
5 cloves garlic, chopped
1½ tablespoon dried chili flakes
¼ cup (2½ oz/65 g) peeled and seeded sour
  tamarind pods
1 tablespoon granulated sugar
6 kaffir lime leaves, finely sliced, plus extra to garnish
raw vegetables, such as mustard greens, Chinese
  greens (leaves), and cucumbers, to serve

Preheat the broiler (grill) to medium. Wrap
the fermented fish in a banana leaf, place
on the broiler (grill) pan, and broil (grill) for
3–4 minutes until the banana leaf is brown and
fragrant. Alternatively, cook the wrapped fish
in a pan. Unwrap the fermented fish, remove
and discard the fish bone, and set aside.

Dry-fry the lemongrass, shallots, galangal,
and garlic in a wok over medium heat for
5–6 minutes until brown and fragrant. Remove
and pound thoroughly in a mortar with a pestle.
Set aside in the mortar.

Toast the chili flakes in the wok over medium
heat for about 1 minute or until fragrant.
Remove and set aside.

Chop the fermented fish and tamarind on
a cutting (chopping) board until a smooth
chopped mixture forms. Add to the mortar
and pound until combined. Add the sugar,
chili flakes, and kaffir lime leaves and pound
again until thoroughly combined. Transfer to
a bowl and garnish with the remaining lime
leaves. Serve with raw vegetables.

น้ำพริกปลาทูย่าง

Broiled Mackerel Dip

Origin Central
Preparation time 5 minutes
Cooking time 20 minutes
Makes 1 cup (9 fl oz/250 ml)

3 x 9¾-oz/275-g horse mackerel (or 4½-oz/
  130-g smoked mackerel fillet)
3 banana leaves, for wrapping
10 red and green finger chiles
10 cloves garlic
5 small shallots, coarsely chopped
¼ teaspoon salt
1½ teaspoons granulated sugar
2 tablespoons fish sauce
2 tablespoons lime juice

To serve
Steamed Jasmine Rice (see p.378), to serve
raw vegetables such as cucumber, Chinese greens
  (leaves), wing beans, or carrots

Preheat the boiler (grill) to medium-high.

Individually wrap the mackerel in a banana
leaf and secure with a toothpick. Place the
packages on the boiler (grill) rack and broil
(grill) for 5–6 minutes on each side, until
cooked. Unwrap the fish from the banana
leaves and discard the skin, bones, and the
leaves. Set aside the fish flesh.

Toast the chiles in a wok over medium heat
for 4 minutes or until soft and the skin slightly
burned. Transfer to a plate. Add the garlic and
shallots to the wok and toast for 6–7 minutes
or until soft and slightly burned.

Put the chiles, shallots, and garlic in a mortar
and pound with a pestle until smooth. Add the
fish and pound until smooth, then add the salt,
sugar, fish sauce, lime juice, and 4 tablespoons
warm water. Gently mix together. Serve in a
bowl with rice and raw vegetables.

แจ่วกุ้ง

Spicy Shrimp Dip

Origin Northeast
Preparation time 10 minutes
Cooking time 7 minutes
Serves 2 cups (16 fl oz/475 ml)

2 tablespoons vegetable oil
11 oz/300 g uncooked freshwater shrimp, cleaned
5–7 red bird's eye chiles
3 cloves garlic
1-inch/2.5-cm piece galangal, peeled and sliced
1 tablespoon Ground Toasted Rice (see p. 64)
1 teaspoon fish sauce
1 teaspoon lime juice
1 teaspoon fermented fish sauce
2 tablespoons sliced scallions (spring onions)
2 tablespoons chopped cilantro (coriander)
1 tablespoon chopped sawtooth cilantro (coriander)
2 tablespoons chopped dill
3 tablespoons peppermint leaves
raw or steamed vegetables, such as carrots, cucumber,
  napa (Chinese) cabbage, and round eggplants
  (aubergines), to serve

Heat the oil in a wok over medium heat. Add
the shrimp and stir-fry for 1–2 minutes until
cooked. Set aside.

Finely pound the chiles, garlic, and galangal in
a mortar with a pestle. Add the shrimp, toasted
rice, fish sauce, lime juice, and fermented fish
sauce and mix thoroughly. Add the scallions
(spring onions), both cilantros (corianders), dill,
and peppermint leaves and mix well. Serve in
a bowl with raw vegetables.

ยำกุ้งจ่อม

Spicy Fermented Shrimp Dip

Origin Northeast
Preparation time 10 minutes
Cooking time 5 minutes
Makes 1½ cups (12 fl oz/350 ml)

1 cup (7 oz/200 g) Fermented Shrimp (see p. 34)
1 tablespoon sliced red and green bird's eye chiles
2 tablespoons sliced shallots
1 x ¾-inch/2-cm piece fresh ginger, peeled and sliced
2 tablespoons thinly sliced round yellow eggplants
  (aubergines)
1 tablespoon thinly sliced lemongrass
1 tablespoon sliced kaffir lime leaves

To serve
Glutinous Rice (see p. 378)
raw or steamed vegetables, such as cucumbers
  and round eggplants (aubergines)

Put the fermented shrimp in a pan and cook
over low heat for 3–4 minutes. Bring to a boil,
then remove from the heat, add the remaining
ingredients, and mix together until thoroughly
combined. Serve in a bowl with rice and raw
or steamed vegetables.

Shrimp Chili Dip

น้ำพริกกะปิ

Origin Central
Preparation time 10 minutes
Makes 2 cups (16 fl oz/475 ml)

1 clove garlic, chopped
4–5 red or orange spur chiles, chopped
4–5 red or green bird's eye chiles, chopped, plus
   extra whole chiles to garnish
1 round eggplant (aubergine), sliced
2 tablespoons shrimp paste
3 tablespoons lime juice
1 tablespoon fish sauce
3 tablespoons jaggery, palm sugar, or soft light
   brown sugar
1 handful of pea eggplants (aubergines), to garnish

To serve
grilled fish
raw and steamed vegetables, such as such as carrots,
   cucumber, napa (Chinese) cabbage, and round
   eggplants (aubergines), to serve

Pound the garlic and both chiles together
in a mortar with a pestle. Add the eggplant
(aubergine) and pound to a smooth paste.
Add the shrimp paste and mix until thoroughly
combined. Season with the lime juice, fish
sauce, and sugar. Transfer to a bowl and
garnish with pea eggplants (aubergines) and
extra bird's eye chiles. Serve with grilled fish
and raw or steamed vegetables.

Fresh Shrimp Chili Dip

น้ำพริกกุ้งสด

Origin South
Preparation time 5 minutes
Cooking time 10 minutes
Makes 1 cup (9 fl oz/250 ml)

4 oz/100 g uncooked jumbo shrimp (king prawns),
   peeled, deveined, and diced
1 tablespoon vegetable oil
6 cloves garlic
4 red bird's eye chiles, sliced
2 red spur chile, cut into ¾-inch/2-cm pieces
2 shallots, halved
2 teaspoons shrimp paste
¼ teaspoon salt
2 tablespoons jaggery, palm sugar, or soft light
   brown sugar
4 tablespoons lime juice
2 teaspoons Tamarind Puree (see p. 63)
2 tablespoons fish sauce

To serve
Steamed Jasmine Rice (see p.378), to serve
raw or steamed vegetables, such as such as carrots,
   cucumber, napa (Chinese) cabbage, and round
   eggplants (aubergines), to serve

Bring 4 tablespoons water to a boil in a small
pan. Add the shrimp (prawns) and stir for
1 minute. Once the shrimp start to turn pink,
remove from the heat and keep stirring until
fully cooked. Set aside and reserve the
cooking liquid.

Heat the oil in a wok over low-medium heat,
add the garlic, both chiles, and shallots, and
stir continuously, for 5–6 minutes until the
shallots have turned dark brown.

Pound the shallot mixture in a mortar with a
pestle. Add the shrimp paste and salt and keep
pounding until a fine paste. Season with the
sugar, lime juice, tamarind, fish sauce, and
1½ tablespoons of the reserved cooking liquid,
and stir. Add the cooked shrimp. Serve in a
bowl with rice and raw or steamed vegetables.

กะปิหลน

Shrimp Paste and Coconut Milk Dip

Origin Central
Preparation time 15 minutes
Cooking time 25 minutes
Makes 1 cup (9 fl oz/250 ml)

⅔ cup (5 fl oz/150 ml) coconut milk
1½ tablespoons jaggery, palm sugar, or soft light
  brown sugar
1 tablespoon fish sauce
1½ teaspoons Tamarind Puree (see p. 63)
2 oz/50 g shrimp (prawns), peeled, deveined,
  and ground (minced)
2 kaffir lime leaves, torn
4–5 green finger chiles, sliced

For the chili paste
4–6 dried red bird's eye chiles, seeded
2 cloves garlic
2 lemongrass stalks, chopped
1 x ½-inch/1-cm piece galangal, peeled and chopped
1 fingerroot, peeled and chopped
1 tablespoon chopped shallot
1 tablespoon Roasted Shrimp Paste (see p. 36)

To serve
raw or steamed vegetables, such as pumpkin, wing
  beans, round eggplants (aubergines), cucumber,
  and yard-long beans
1 hard-boiled egg, quartered

To make the chili paste, pound the chiles and garlic in a mortar with a pestle until smooth. Gradually add the lemongrass, galangal, fingerroots, and shallot and pound thoroughly until smooth. Add the shrimp paste and pound to a smooth paste. Set aside.

Heat the coconut milk in a wok over medium heat for 3–4 minutes until the oil separates from the coconut milk. Add the chili paste and stir for 1–2 minutes until fragrant and the paste and coconut milk are mixed well. Simmer for 1–2 minutes, then add the sugar, fish sauce, and tamarind and mix well until the sugar has dissolved. Add the shrimp (prawns), kaffir lime, and green chiles. Cook for another 2 minutes or until thickened. Serve in a bowl with raw or steamed vegetables and the boiled egg.

ปลาร้าหลน

Fermented Fish Chili Dip

Origin Central
Preparation time 5 minutes
Cooking time 10 minutes
Makes 2½ cups (16 fl oz/475 ml)

½ cup (4 fl oz/120 ml) fermented fish sauce
1 cup (9 fl oz/250 ml) coconut milk
3 shallots, sliced
1 x ¾-inch/2-cm piece fingerroot, peeled and sliced
3 kaffir lime leaves, torn
3–5 green, red, and yellow finger chiles, sliced
1–2 tablespoons jaggery, palm sugar, or soft light
  brown sugar
½ teaspoon fish sauce
7 oz/200 g ground (minced) pork
1 cup (4 oz/120 g) bamboo shoots, boiled and chopped
  into small pieces
4 round eggplants (aubergines), chopped
2 cups (16 fl oz/475 ml) coconut cream
1 cup (6½ oz/185 g) chopped yard-long beans, about
  1 inch/2.5cm long

To serve
Steamed Jasmine Rice (see p.378), to serve
raw or steamed vegetables, such as bamboo shoots,
cabbage, carrots, and cucumber

Heat the fermented fish sauce and coconut milk in a wok over low heat and simmer for 3–4 minutes until any pieces of fish melt. Strain the mixture through cheesecloth (muslin) into a heatproof bowl and return to the wok. Add the shallots, fingerroot, kaffir lime leaves, chiles, sugar, and fish sauce and bring to a boil. Add the pork and boil for 3–4 minutes, stirring occasionally, until the pork is cooked. Add the bamboo shoots and eggplants (aubergines), then pour in the coconut cream. Add the yard-long beans, stir, and turn off the heat. Serve in a bowl with rice and raw or steamed vegetables.

น้ำพริกมะขาม

Spicy Tamarind Dip

Origin South
Preparation time 10 minutes
Cooking time 15 minutes
Makes 2 cups (16 fl oz/475 ml)

scant 1 cup (3½ fl oz/100 ml) vegetable oil
7 oz/200 g ground (minced) pork side (belly)
1 cup (7 oz/200 g) jaggery, palm sugar, or soft light
  brown sugar
raw or steamed vegetables, such as cucumber, round
  eggplants (aubergines), and yard-long beans, to serve

For the chili paste
10 red bird's eye chiles
7 oz/200 g young tamarind pods
3 cloves garlic
2 shallots
½ cup (3½ oz/100 g) shrimp paste

To make the chili paste, finely pound the chiles,
tamarind, garlic, and shallots in a mortar with
a pestle. Add the shrimp paste and pound until
smooth and thoroughly combined.

Heat the oil in a wok over medium heat, add
the chili paste, and stir-fry for 1–2 minutes
until fragrant. Add the pork and sugar and
cook for about 7 minutes or until the pork is
cooked. Serve in a bowl with raw or steamed
vegetables. Alternatively, transfer to a sterilized
jar, leaving ½ inch/1 cm head space, cover, and
seal. Store in the refrigerator for up to 1 week.

Photo p. 49

ต่ามะเขือยาว

Eggplant Dip with Pork

Origin North
Preparation time 20 minutes
Cooking time 30 minutes
Makes 1½ cups (12 fl oz/350 ml)

2 tablespoons vegetable oil
7 oz/200 g long green eggplants (aubergines),
  quartered crosswise
3–4 red or green spur chiles
7 cloves garlic
2 shallots
2¾ oz/70 g ground (minced) pork
½ teaspoon shrimp paste
¼ teaspoon salt
1½ teaspoons fish sauce
2 hard-boiled eggs, coarsely chopped
raw or steamed vegetables, such as Chinese greens
  (leaves), cucumber, carrots, and yard-long beans,
  to serve

To garnish
1 tablespoon Fried Garlic (see p. 64)
1 small handful of mint leaves

Brush a griddle or stove-top grill pan with the
oil, then grill the eggplant (aubergines) over
medium heat for 10–13 minutes until softened
and the skin is burned. Let cool, then remove
the skin and set aside.

Dry-fry the chiles in a wok or pan over
medium-high heat for 15 minutes until the
chiles have softened and the skins are burned.
Remove from the wok or pan, let cool, then peel
off the skins and set aside.

In the same wok, dry-fry the garlic and shallots
for 5–6 minutes until softened and slightly
burned. Remove from the heat and set aside.

Bring ⅓ cup (2½ fl oz/75 ml) water to a boil
in a small pan, add the pork, and blanch for
1–2 minutes until cooked. Remove from the
heat, drain, and set aside.

Pound the garlic, shallots, and shrimp paste
in a mortar with a pestle. Add the chiles,
eggplant, pork, salt, and fish sauce, and use
a spoon to gently mix until thoroughly
combined. Add the eggs and gently mix.
Transfer to a bowl and sprinkle with the Fried
Garlic and mint leaves. Serve with raw or
steamed vegetables.

น้ำพริกอ่อง

Pork and Tomato Chili Dip

Origin North
Preparation time 10 minutes, plus soaking time
Cooking time 10 minutes
Makes 2 cups (16 fl oz/475 ml)

10 dried red chiles, seeded
5 shallots, chopped
10 cloves garlic, sliced
2 teaspoons salt
14 oz/400 g ground (minced) pork
25 cherry tomatoes
4 tablespoons vegetable oil
1½ tablespoons fish sauce
2½ tablespoons granulated sugar
raw or steamed vegetables, such as carrots, mustard
  greens, Chinese greens (leaves), and cucumbers,
  to serve

To garnish
2 tablespoons chopped fresh cilantro (coriander)
2 tablespoons finely chopped scallions (spring onions)

Soak the dried chiles in a bowl of hot water
for 15 minutes or until rehydrated, then drain
and chop.

Pound the chiles, shallots, garlic, and half the
salt in a mortar with a pestle until smooth. Add
the pork and pound again until well mixed.
Add the tomatoes and gently press into the
mixture, then coarsely pound until combined.

Heat the oil in a wok over medium heat. Add
the pounded tomato mixture and stir-fry for
about 4 minutes or until fragrant. Add a small
amount of water and season with the fish sauce,
sugar, and the remaining salt. Stir until well
mixed. Cook for another 6–7 minutes, stirring
occasionally, until the tomatoes are cooked
and the dip is fully flavored.

Transfer to a bowl and garnish with the cilantro
(coriander) and scallions (spring onions). Serve
with raw or steamed vegetables.

ข้าวตังหน้าตั้ง

Spicy Dip with Rice Crackers

Origin Central
Preparation time 40 minutes
Cooking time 10–15 minutes
Makes 2 cups (16 fl oz/475 ml)

1 teaspoon chopped cilantro (coriander) root
1 clove garlic
1 teaspoon white peppercorns
1½ cups (12 fl oz/350 ml) coconut milk
3½ oz/100 g ground (minced) pork
8 uncooked shrimp (prawns), peeled, deveined,
  and finely chopped
2 shallots, finely sliced
2 tablespoons granulated sugar
1 tablespoon fish sauce
2 tablespoons Tamarind Puree (see p. 63)
¼ cup (1½ oz/40 g) roasted peanuts
rice crackers, to serve

Finely pound the cilantro (coriander) root,
garlic, and peppercorns in a mortar with
a pestle, then set aside.

Heat a scant 1 cup (7 fl oz/200 ml) coconut
milk in a wok over low heat. Add the pounded
cilantro root mixture and stir until the coconut
oil separates and becomes fragrant. Add the
pork and shrimp (prawns) and stir-fry for
1–2 minutes until the nearly cooked. Add the
shallots and remaining coconut milk and stir-
fry for 3–4 minutes. Season with the sugar, fish
sauce, and tamarind. Add the peanuts and stir
thoroughly. Serve in a bowl with rice crackers.

Spicy Frog Dip

Origin Northeast
Preparation time 15 minutes
Cooking time 10 minutes
Makes 2 cups (16 fl oz/475 ml)

4 green bird's eye chiles
4 slices galangal
2 lemongrass stalks, cut into 1-inch/2.5-cm pieces
1 tablespoon fermented fish sauce
3½ oz/100 g frog meat, skin removed
3 cups (3½ oz/100 g) young tamarind leaves
  or sorrel leaves
½ teaspoon fish sauce

To garnish
2 cilantro (coriander) leaves, sliced
2 scallions (spring onions), sliced
3 young Vietnamese cilantro (coriander) leaves, sliced

To serve
raw or steamed vegetables, such as yard-long beans,
  round eggplants (aubergines), and winged beans

Dry-fry the chiles in a wok over medium heat
for 3–4 minutes until fragrant and toasted, then
transfer to a plate and set aside.

Bring 2 cups (16 fl oz/475 ml) water to a boil in a
large pan over medium heat. Add the galangal,
lemongrass, fermented fish sauce, and frog
meat and cook for 5 minutes or until the meat
is cooked. Add the young tamarind leaves,
stir, and remove from the heat. Remove the
frog meat with a slotted spoon and set aside.
Reserve the broth (stock).

Pound the chiles in a mortar with a pestle to
form fine flakes, then add the boiled frog meat
and pound coarsely. Add 2–3 tablespoons
of the frog broth and the fish sauce and mix
well. Transfer to a bowl and garnish with the
cilantro (coriander), scallion (spring onion),
and Vietnamese cilantro leaves. Serve with
raw or steamed vegetables.

Pickled Bamboo Shoot Dip

Origin North
Preparation time 5 minutes
Cooking time 10 minutes
Makes 1½ cups (12 fl oz/350 ml)

4 oz/120 g ground (minced) pork
1 cup (4 oz/120 g) pickled bamboo shoots
  (sour and salty version)
2–3 cloves garlic, chopped
5–7 green bird's eye chiles
3 scallions (spring onions), finely sliced
1 teaspoon chopped cilantro (coriander)
salt

To serve
½ cup (2 oz/50 g) pork cracklings
raw or steamed vegetables, such as cucumber,
  cabbage, and lettuce

Blanch the ground (minced) pork in a pan
of boiling water for 1 minute or until cooked.
Drain and set aside.

Blanch the bamboo shoots in another pan of
boiling water for about 2 minutes to reduce the
sourness and saltiness. Drain and set aside.

Dry-fry the garlic and chiles in a wok over
medium heat for 4–5 minutes until softened
and slight burned. Transfer to a mortar and
pound thoroughly. Add the bamboo shoots
and pound until just before the bamboo breaks
into small pieces. Add the blanched pork and
coarsely pound until thoroughly combined.
Season to taste. Transfer to a bowl and garnish
with the scallions (spring onions) and cilantro
(coriander). Serve with pork cracklings and
raw or steamed vegetables.

Photo p. 52

แจ่วมะเขือเทศ

Spicy Tomato Dip

Origin Northeast
Preparation time 5 minutes
Cooking time 10 minutes
Makes 1 cup (9 fl oz/250 ml)

2 tomatoes
2 lemongrass stalks, finely sliced
5 red bird's eye chiles, sliced
2 shallots, finely sliced
2 thin slices galangal, chopped
3 cloves garlic, chopped
1 tablespoon fermented snakehead fish flesh
1 teaspoon Tamarind Puree (see p. 63)
1 teaspoon lime juice
3 kaffir lime leaves, finely sliced

To serve
Steamed Jasmine Rice (see p.378), to serve
raw or steamed vegetables, such as cucumber and
  round eggplants (aubergines)

Heat the broiler (grill) to medium-high. Put
the tomatoes onto the broiler (grill) rack and
grill (broil) for 5–6 minutes until softened and
the skins are charred.

Dry-fry the lemongrass, chiles, shallots,
galangal, and garlic in a wok over medium
heat for 4–5 minutes until fragrant and lightly
toasted. Transfer to a mortar and pound with a
pestle until smooth. Add the broiled (grilled)
tomatoes and gently press with the pestle
until combined. Add the fermented fish flesh,
tamarind, lime juice, and kaffir lime leaves and
stir until well mixed. Serve in a bowl with rice
and raw or steamed vegetables.

น้ำพริกข่า

Galangal Chili Dip

Origin North
Preparation time 5 minutes
Cooking time 5 minutes
Makes ½ cup (4 fl oz/120 ml)

1 x 1½-inch/4-cm piece galangal, peeled and chopped
3 cloves garlic
7 dried red chiles, seeded
½–1 teaspoon salt

To serve
raw or steamed vegetables, such as mushrooms,
  cucumber, and napa (Chinese) cabbage

Preheat the broiler (grill) to high.

Crush the galangal and garlic in a mortar
with a pestle, then remove and set aside.

Put the dried chiles onto the broiler (grill)
rack and broil (grill) for a few minutes until
slightly burned. Transfer to the mortar, add
the crushed galangal and garlic, and pound
until thoroughly combined. Season with the
salt. Serve in a bowl with raw or steamed
vegetables.

พริกค่ำสมุนไพร

Roasted Chili Dip

Origin Central
Preparation time 10 minutes, plus soaking time
Cooking time 8–10 minutes
Makes 2 cups (16 fl oz/475 ml)

2 cups (16 fl oz/475 ml) coconut milk
¼ cup (2 oz/50 g) jaggery, palm sugar, or soft light
  brown sugar
2 teaspoons salt
5 kaffir lime leaves, chopped
5 bitter orange leaves, coarsely sliced, to garnish
raw or steamed vegetables, such as cucumber and
  round eggplants (aubergines), to serve

For the chili paste
2 oz/50 g dried red chiles, seeded
2 garlic bulbs, cloves separated
5 shallots, chopped
1½ cups (3½ oz/100 g) finely chopped lemongrass
4-inch/10-cm piece red galangal, peeled and finely
  chopped
¼ oz/10 g bastard cardamom leaves
3½ oz/100 g dried shrimp
⅓ cup (2¼ oz/60 g) shrimp paste

To make the chili paste, soak the dried chiles
in a bowl of hot water for 15 minutes or until
rehydrated, then drain. Pound the chiles,
garlic, shallots, lemongrass, red galangal, and
cardamom leaves together in a mortar with a
pestle until smooth. Add the dried shrimp and
shrimp paste and pound again until combined.

Bring the coconut milk to a boil in a wok over
medium heat and boil for 4–5 minutes or until
a grainy texture. Add the chili paste, sugar,
salt, and kaffir lime leaves and simmer for
3–4 minutes. Transfer to a bowl and garnish
with the bitter orange leaves. Serve with raw
or steamed vegetables.

น้ำพริกระกำ

Spicy Salacca Dip

Origin Central
Preparation time 10 minutes
Makes 1½ cups (12 fl oz/350 ml)

6 cloves garlic, chopped
5 shallots, chopped
10 red and green bird's eye chiles, chopped
2 tablespoons shrimp paste
6 salacca (snake fruit), peeled and pitted
2 tablespoons jaggery, palm sugar, or soft light
  brown sugar
¼ cup (2 fl oz/60 ml) fish sauce
raw or steamed vegetables, such as carrots and
  cucumber to serve

Pound the garlic, shallots, chiles, and shrimp
paste in a mortar with a pestle. Add the snake
fruit and pound again until combined. Add the
sugar, and fish sauce, and mix well. Serve in
a bowl with raw or steamed vegetables.

น้ำพริกมะม่วง

Spicy Green Mango Dip

Origin Central
Preparation time 5 minutes
Cooking time 5 minutes
Makes 1 cup (9 fl oz/250 ml)

5–10 green bird's eye chiles, chopped
3 cloves garlic, chopped
1 tablespoon jaggery, palm sugar, or soft light
  brown sugar
2 teaspoons Roasted Shrimp Paste (see p. 36)
½ cup (3 oz/80 g) shredded unripe green (sour) mango
  or green apple, plus extra to garnish
2 tablespoons dried shrimp, coarsely pounded
2½ teaspoons fish sauce
1 tablespoon lime juice
vegetables, such as cauliflower and cucumber, to serve

Pound the chiles and garlic in a mortar with a
pestle until smooth. Add the sugar and shrimp
paste and continue to pound until combined.
Add the mango or apple, dried shrimp, fish
sauce, lime juice, and 2 tablespoons warm
water and gently mix. Garnish with shredded
mango or apple and serve with raw vegetables.

Photo p. 55

น้ำจิ้มซีฟู้ด

Seafood Dipping Sauce

Origin South
Preparation time 5 minutes
Makes ¾ cup (6 fl oz/175 ml)

6–7 cloves garlic
10 red and green bird's eye chiles
½ cup (¾ oz/20 g) coarsely chopped cilantro (coriander)
3 tablespoons fish sauce
2 tablespoons jaggery, palm sugar, or soft light
  brown sugar
2 tablespoons lime juice
broiled (grilled) or steamed seafood, to serve

Pound the garlic in a mortar with a pestle,
add the chiles, and pound into fine pieces.
Add the cilantro (coriander) and pound until
smooth. Add the fish sauce, sugar, lime juice,
and 1 tablespoon water and stir with a spoon
until the sugar has dissolved. It should be
sweet, sour, salty, and hot. Serve in a bowl
with broiled (grilled) or steamed seafood.
Alternatively, transfer to a sterilized jar, leaving
½ inch/1 cm head space, cover, and seal. Store
in the refrigerator for up to 2 weeks.

Photo p. 59

กะปิคั่ว

Shrimp Paste Dipping Sauce

Origin Central
Preparation time 10 minutes
Cooking time 5 minutes
Makes 1¼ cups (10 fl oz/300 ml)

1½ tablespoons Red Curry Paste (see p. 40)
2 lemongrass stalks, thinly sliced
1 x ¾-inch/2-cm piece fingerroot, peeled and julienned
1 shallot, sliced
1½ tablespoons Roasted Shrimp Paste (see p. 36)
¼ oz/10 g salted mackerel
1 tablespoon vegetable oil
scant 1 cup (7 fl oz/200 ml) coconut milk
2 tablespoons jaggery, palm sugar, or soft light
  brown sugar
1 teaspoon fish sauce
1 tablespoon Tamarind Puree (see p. 63)
7 green bird's eye chiles, crushed
4 kaffir lime leaves, torn
raw or steamed vegetables, such as carrots, napa
  (Chinese) cabbage, cucumbers, and yard-long
  beans to serve

To garnish
1 green chile
1 cilantro (coriander) sprig
1 red bird's eye chile, seeded and finely sliced
  lengthwise

Pound the curry paste with the lemongrass,
fingerroot, shallot, shrimp paste, and salted
mackerel in a mortar with a pestle until smooth.

Heat the oil in a wok over medium heat, add the
pounded paste, and stir-fry for about 3 minutes
until fragrant. Add the coconut milk and stir
continuously until thickened. Add the sugar,
fish sauce, and tamarind to taste and stir until
thoroughly combined.

Add the crushed chiles and kaffir lime leaves,
stir, and remove from the heat. Transfer to a
bowl and garnish with the green chile, cilantro
(coriander) sprig, and sliced red chile. Serve
with raw or steamed vegetables.

Photo p. 57

น้ำพริกถั่วดิน
Peanut Chili Sauce

Origin North
Preparation time 10 minutes
Makes 2 cups (16 fl oz/475 ml)

5–6 cloves garlic
10 red and green bird's eye chiles, chopped
1 cup (5 oz/150 g) roasted peanuts
1½ tablespoon lemon juice
2 tablespoons fish sauce
½ cup (4 oz/120 g) jaggery, palm sugar, or soft light
  brown sugar
raw or steamed vegetables, such as cucumbers, round
  eggplants (aubergines), and yard-long beans, to serve

Pound the garlic, chiles, and peanuts in a
mortar with a pestle until smooth. Season with
the lemon juice, fish sauce, and sugar. Serve
in a bowl with raw or steamed vegetables.

น้ำจิ้มสะเต๊ะ
Thai-Style Satay Sauce

Origin South
Preparation time 5 minutes
Cooking time 8 minutes
Makes 1 cup (9 fl oz/250 ml)

1 tablespoon vegetable oil
1 tablespoon dry curry paste (see p. 233)
scant 1 cup (7 fl oz/200 ml) coconut milk
⅔ cup (5 oz/100 g) roasted peanuts, finely crushed
3 tablespoons jaggery, palm sugar, or soft light
  brown sugar
¼ teaspoons salt
½ teaspoon Tamarind Puree (see p. 63)

Heat the oil in a wok over medium heat. Add
the chili paste and sauté for 30 seconds until
it sizzles and becomes fragrant. Gradually
add the coconut milk, stir, and let boil for
2–3 minutes. Add the peanuts, sugar, salt, and
tamarind, and stir for 3–4 minutes. Remove
from the heat and transfer to a bowl. Serve.

น้ำจิ้มไก่
Sweet Chili Dipping Sauce

Origin Central
Preparation time 5 minutes
Cooking time 10 minutes
Makes ¾ cup (6 fl oz/175 ml)

½ cup (4 fl oz/120 ml) white vinegar
½ cup (3½ oz/100 g) granulated sugar
½ teaspoon salt
1 red chile, coarsely pounded
2 tablespoons peanuts, coarsely chopped (optional)
Grilled Chicken or Fried Spring Rolls, to serve
  (see p. 276 and p. 95)

Mix the vinegar, sugar, salt, 4 tablespoons
water, and the red chile together in a pan,
then bring to a boil and keep boiling for
2 minutes. Reduce the heat to low and simmer
for another 3–5 minutes until it becomes a
syrupy consistency. Remove from the heat
and let cool. Garnish with peanuts, if using,
and serve immediately. Alternatively, transfer
to a sterilized jar, leaving ½ inch (1 cm) head
space, let cool, cover, and seal. Store in the
refrigerator for up to 1 week.

น้ำจิ้ม
Very Spicy Thai Dipping Sauce

Origin North
Preparation time 10 minutes
Makes 1¼ cups (10 fl oz/300 ml)

20 cloves garlic, chopped
30 red bird's eye chiles, chopped
½ cup (4 oz/120 ml) fish sauce
½ cup (4 oz/120 ml) lime juice
grilled meat or fish, to serve

Pound the garlic and chiles together in a mortar
with a pestle until smooth. Transfer to a bowl,
add the fish sauce and lime juice, and mix well
until thoroughly combined. Serve with grilled
meat or fish.

Photo p. 61

น้ำพริกซอกไข่

Spicy Sauce with Boiled Eggs

Origin North
Preparation time 10 minutes, plus soaking time
Cooking time 5 minutes
Makes ¼ cup (2 fl oz/60 ml)

5 dried chiles, seeded
5 cloves garlic
1 tablespoon lemon juice
2 tablespoons fish sauce
3 small shallots, chopped
salt and black pepper
2 hard-boiled eggs, cut into quarters, to garnish
raw or steamed vegetables, such as yard-long beans,
  cucumber, and ferns, to serve

Soak the chiles in a bowl of hot water for
15 minutes or until rehydrated, then drain
and chop.

Transfer to a mortar with the garlic and pound
thoroughly with a pestle until smooth. Season
with the lemon juice and fish sauce, sprinkle
with the shallots, and mix well until combined.
Transfer to a bowl, season to taste, and garnish
with the boiled eggs. Serve with raw or
steamed vegetables.

Photo p. 62

น้ำมะขามเปียก

Tamarind Puree

Origin Central
Preparation time 15 minutes
Makes 2½ cups (18 fl oz/550 ml)

scant 2 cups (1 lb 2 oz/500 g) sour tamarind pods,
  peeled and seeded

Mix 2 cups (16 fl oz/475 ml) warm water
with the tamarind pods in a large bowl, then
knead together by hand. Strain the mixture
through cheesecloth (muslin) into a large
bowl. Use immediately. Alternatively, transfer
to a sterilized jar, leaving ½ inch (1 cm) head
space, let cool, cover, and seal. Store in the
refrigerator for up to 1 week.

น้ำจิ้มแจ่ว

Barbecue Sauce

Origin Northeast
Preparation time 3 minutes
Makes ¾ cup (6 fl oz/175 ml)

2 tablespoons fish sauce
1 tablespoon lime juice
1 tablespoon Tamarind Puree (see below left)
1 tablespoon jaggery, palm sugar, or soft light
  brown sugar
1 tablespoon dried chili flakes
1 teaspoon Ground Toasted Rice (see p. 64)
1 shallot, sliced
1 scallion (spring onion), finely sliced
grilled meat, to serve

Mix the fish sauce, lime juice, tamarind, sugar,
and chili flakes together in a bowl until the
sugar has dissolved. Transfer to a bowl and
sprinkle with the toasted rice, shallot, and
scallion (spring onion). Serve with grilled meat.
Alternatively, transfer to a sterilized jar, leaving
½ inch (1 cm) head space, cover, and seal.
Store in the refrigerator for up to 2–3 weeks.

สารสกัด ใบเตย

Pandan Extract

Origin Central
Preparation time 7 minutes
Makes 2 cups (16 fl oz/475 ml)

20 pandan leaves, sliced

Put the pandan leaves and 2 cups (16 fl oz/
475 ml) water into a food processor and blend.
Pour the mixture through a fine strainer (sieve)
or cheesecloth (muslin) into a bowl. Use the
extract immediately. Alternatively, transfer to a
sterilized jar, leaving ½ inch (1 cm) head space,
cover, and seal. Store in the refrigerator for up
to 1–2 weeks.

ข้าวคั่ว

Ground Toasted Rice

Origin Northeast
Preparation time 5 minutes
Cooking time 8–10 minutes
Makes ⅓ cup (3 oz/85 g)

½ cup (3 oz/85 g) glutinous (sticky) rice

Dry-fry the rice in a wok over medium heat for about 8–10 minutes, stirring continuously, until golden brown and fragrant. Let cool, then pound in a mortar with a pestle until a fine powder. Use immediately. Alternatively, transfer to an airtight container and store for up to 1–2 months.

น้ำพริกมะเขือเทศ

Tomato Chili Sauce

Origin North
Preparation time 5 minutes
Cooking time 5 minutes
Makes ½ cup (4 fl oz/120 ml)

5 green bird's eye chiles, chopped
2 shallots, chopped
2 cloves garlic, sliced
5 tomatoes, halved
2 lemongrass stalks, chopped
1 teaspoon salt
raw or steamed vegetables, such as cucumber, napa
  (Chinese) cabbage, and small bitter melon, to serve

Dry-fry the chiles, shallots, and garlic in a wok over medium heat for 3–4 minutes until softened and slightly burned. Remove from the heat and set aside.

Heat a broiler (grill) to medium-high heat. Put the tomatoes onto the broiler (grill) rack and broil (grill) for 6–7 minutes until softened and the skin slightly burned.

Pound the chiles, shallots, and garlic in a mortar with a pestle until smooth. Add the lemongrass and pound again until smooth. Add the broiled (grilled) tomatoes and salt, and gently press with the pestle until combined. Serve with raw or steamed vegetables.

Photo p. 65

หอมแดงเจียว

Fried Shallots

Origin Central
Preparation time 5 minutes
Cooking time 11 minutes
Makes 5 tablespoons

1½ cups (12 fl oz/350 ml) vegetable oil
5 shallots, peeled and finely sliced lengthwise

Heat the oil in a wok over medium heat, add the shallots, and stir-fry for 10–11 minutes until the shallots start to brown. Remove from the heat and use as an ingredient or a garnish.

กระเทียมเจียว

Fried Garlic

Origin Central
Preparation time 5 minutes
Cooking time 5 minutes
Makes 5 tablespoons

1½ cups (12 fl oz/350 ml) vegetable oil
2 garlic bulbs, cloves separated, peeled, and sliced

Heat the oil in a wok over medium heat, add the garlic, and stir-fry for 4–5 minutes until the garlic starts to brown. Remove from the heat and use as an ingredient or a garnish.

Snacks & Drinks

คั่วถั่วเน่าเมอะ
Roasted Fermented Soybean Dip

Origin North
Preparation time 5 minutes
Cooking time 5 minutes
Serves 4

4 shallots, chopped
4 lemongrass stalks, sliced
3 red and green long chiles, chopped
2 tablespoons grated galangal
3 tablespoons vegetable oil
3 cloves garlic, chopped
2 eggs, beaten
1 cup (3½ oz/200 g) Fermented Soybeans (see p. 34)
½ cup (4 oz/120 g) chopped dill (optional)
Glutinous Rice (see p. 378), to serve

Pound the shallots, lemongrass, chiles, and galangal in a mortar with a pestle until smooth.

Heat the oil in a wok over medium heat. Add garlic and the pounded paste and stir-fry for 1–2 minutes until fragrant. Pour in the beaten eggs, add the fermented soybeans with the dill, if using, and stir-fry for another 2–3 minutes until the eggs are cooked. Serve with rice.

เต้าหู้ทอดน้ำจิ้ม
Deep-Fried Tofu with Dipping Sauce

Origin Central
Preparation time 5 minutes
Cooking time 10 minutes
Serves 2

5 cups (2 pints/1.2 liters) vegetable oil, for deep-frying
3½ oz/100 g tofu, cut into triangles 2 inches/5 cm long
    and ½ inch/1 cm thick

For the dipping sauce
1 cup (9 fl oz/250 ml) vinegar
¾ cup (5 oz/150 g) granulated sugar
½ tablespoon salt
2 red bird's eye chiles, coarsely pounded
¼ cup (1½ oz/40 g) roasted peanuts, coarsely pounded

To make the sauce, put the vinegar, sugar, and salt in a small pan and mix well until combined. Bring to a boil over medium heat, then remove from the heat and set aside. Add the chiles and mix well, then add the peanuts and transfer to a small serving bowl.

Heat the oil for deep-frying in a wok or deep fryer to 350°F/180°C, or until a cube of bread browns in 30 seconds. Deep-fry the tofu for 10 minutes until crispy and golden brown. Remove with a slotted spoon and drain on paper towels. Serve immediately with the dipping sauce.

ข้าวจี่ น้ำมาจั้มแจ่วบอง
Roasted Rice with Spicy Paste

Origin Northeast
Preparation time 15 minutes, plus soaking time
Cooking time 20 minutes
Serves 4

3 eggs, beaten
½ teaspoon salt
2 cups (12 oz/350 g) cooked Glutinous Rice (see p. 378)

For the spicy paste
10 cloves garlic, chopped
7 shallots, chopped
1 tablespoon sliced galangal
3 lemongrass stalks, sliced
1 tablespoon dried chili flakes
7 kaffir lime leaves, chopped
7 oz/200 g fermented fish, rinsed and ground (minced)
1 tablespoon lime juice

Soak several bamboo skewers 4–6 inches/
12–15 cm long in a bowl of cold water for
30 minutes to prevent them from burning
during cooking.

Before you begin cooking, check that your
charcoal is glowing white hot, or your gas
grill (barbecue) is preheated to 375°F/190°C.

Whisk the eggs and salt together in a small
bowl, then set aside.

Using your hands, shape the glutinous rice
into oval patties and thread onto the soaked
skewers. Grill the patties for 4–5 minutes
on each side until the surface of the rice has
become crispy.

Remove from the grill, brush one side of
the rice with the egg mixture, and return to
the grill for 1–2 minutes until the egg dries.
Turn over and repeat with the other side.
Do this 5–6 times until there is a thick, crispy
coating of egg.

For the spicy paste, put the garlic, shallots,
galangal, lemongrass, chili flakes, and kaffir
lime leaves in a pan over medium heat and
cook for 10 minutes. Transfer to a mortar
and pound thoroughly with a pestle. Add the
ground (minced) fermented fish and mix well.
Season with the lime juice and serve with rice.

ข้าวตังโบราณ
Old-Style Rice Crust

Origin Central
Preparation time 5 minutes
Cooking time 30 minutes
Serves 2

½ tablespoon vegetable oil
1½ cups (9½ oz/275 g) cooked rice
1 clove garlic, chopped
1 tablespoon fish sauce
2 tablespoons granulated sugar
1 tablespoon chopped cilantro (coriander)

Put a wok or a pan over medium heat, add the
oil, and spread across the pan, making sure
that the inside surfaces are fully coated. Add
the rice to the wok and spread over the whole
surface to make a thin layer. Gradually move
the wok around to let the rice cook evenly for
20–25 minutes until the rice becomes golden
brown and crispy. Be sure to keep moving the
wok to prevent the rice at the bottom of the wok
from burning. Remove from the heat.

Mix the garlic, fish sauce, and sugar together
thoroughly in a bowl, then stir in the cilantro
(coriander). Dip a brush into the sauce and
spread it over the rice crust, then let dry.
Gently remove the rice crust from the wok
or pan and serve.

Photo p. 76

กะหรี่ปั๊บ

Basic Puff Pastry

Origin Central
Preparation time 10 minutes, plus resting time
Serves 10

For the outer layer pastry
scant 3⅔ cups (1 lb/450 g) all-purpose (plain) flour
2 tablespoons superfine (caster) sugar
½ teaspoon salt
⅓ cup (2½ fl oz/75 ml) vegetable oil
5½ tablespoons (2¾ oz/70 g) butter

For the inner layer pastry
scant 1¼ cups (5 oz/150 g) all-purpose (plain) flour
¼ cup (2 fl oz/50 ml) vegetable oil

To make the outer layer pastry, sift the flour
into a large bowl. Dissolve the sugar and salt
in ⅔ cup (5 fl oz/150 ml) cold water and add to
the flour. Add the vegetable oil and butter and
knead until a dough forms. Cover with plastic
wrap (clingfilm) and let rest in the refrigerator
for 10 minutes.

Meanwhile, to make the inner layer pastry, sift
the flour into another large bowl, add the oil,
and knead until a dough forms.

To shape the dough, divide the inner and outer
doughs into 20 small pieces.

On a lightly dusted work surface, roll out the
outer layer dough balls into rectangles, then
put the inner layer dough balls in the middle
and cover with the outer layer.

Lightly dust the work surface again and roll the
dough balls into rectangles (from the middle
to the top and from the middle to the bottom,
5–6 inches/12–15 cm long). Roll them up into
tube shapes and place lengthwise on the work
surface. Roll them out again into a rectangle
(from the middle to the top and from the middle
to the bottom, 7–8 inches/18–20 cm long), then
roll them up tightly into tubes and cut in half.
Place the halves vertically on the work surface
and press down on them with a rolling pin and
roll out to form thin flat disks. The pastry is now
ready to use.

กะหรี่ปั๊บไส้ไก่

Chicken Curry Puffs

Origin Central
Preparation time 30 minutes, plus resting time
Cooking time 25–30 minutes
Serves 10

2 tablespoons vegetable oil
1 tablespoon chopped cilantro (coriander) root
3 cloves garlic, chopped
1 teaspoon white peppercorns
14 oz/400 g boneless, skinless chicken breast, diced
2 tablespoons curry powder
2 onions, diced
2 potatoes, diced
1 tablespoon soy sauce
⅓ cup (2¾ oz/70 g) superfine (caster) sugar
1–2 teaspoons salt
1 quantity Basic Puff Pastry (see left)

Heat the oil in a wok over medium heat, add
the cilantro (coriander) root, garlic, and white
peppercorns, and sauté for 30 seconds. Add
the diced chicken and stir-fry for 3–4 minutes.
Add the curry powder, onions, potatoes, soy
sauce, sugar, salt, and a little water and stir-fry
for another 3–4 minutes until the potatoes have
softened and are cooked. Let cool.

Place the filling on the pastry disks, brush
the edges of the pastry with a little water, and
fold the bottom edge of the pastry over to
enclose the filling. Press down to seal, then
crimp the edge.

Heat the oil for deep-frying in a wok or deep
fryer to 350°F/180°C, or until a cube of bread
browns in 30 seconds. Deep-fry the pastry
packages in batches for 8–10 minutes or until
golden brown. Remove with a slotted spoon
and drain on paper towels. Serve.

Mung Bean Puffs

Origin Central
Preparation time 30 minutes, plus resting time
Cooking time 35–40 minutes
Serves 10

1½ cups (3¼ oz/90 g) split mung beans
scant ½ cup (3½ fl oz/100 ml) coconut cream
½ cup (3½ oz/100 g) granulated sugar
1 teaspoon salt
1 quantity Basic Puff Pastry (see p. 77)

Soak the mung beans in a bowl of water for 30 minutes, then drain.

Bring a pan of water to a boil over medium heat, add the mung beans, and cook for 30 minutes until cooked, then drain. Transfer to a mortar and pound with a pestle until a smooth paste.

Put the mung bean paste, coconut cream, sugar, and salt in a pan and heat over medium heat. Cook, stirring occasionally, for about 5 minutes until thick and sticky. Let cool, then form the mung bean filling into small balls.

Place the filling on the pastry disks, brush the edges of the pastry with a little water and fold the bottom edge of the pastry over to enclose the filling. Press down to seal, then crimp the edge.

Heat the oil for deep-frying in a wok or deep fryer to 350°F/180°C, or until a cube of bread browns in 30 seconds. Deep-fry the pastry packages in batches for 8–10 minutes or until golden brown. Remove with a slotted spoon and drain on paper towels. Serve.

Taro Puffs

Origin Central
Preparation time 30 minutes, plus resting time
Cooking time 20 minutes
Serves 10

1 x 11-oz/300-g taro, halved
scant ½ cup (3½ fl oz/100 ml) coconut cream
1¾ cups (14 oz/400 g) jaggery, palm sugar, or soft light brown sugar
1 teaspoon salt
1 quantity Basic Puff Pastry (see p. 77)

Bring a pan of water to a boil over medium heat, add the taro, then reduce the heat and simmer for 10–15 minutes until cooked. Drain, let cool, then peel and dice. Transfer to a mortar and pound with a pestle until a smooth paste.

Put the taro paste, coconut cream, sugar, and salt into a pan and heat over medium heat. Cook, stirring occasionally, for about 5 minutes until thick and sticky. Let cool, then form the taro filling into small balls.

Put the filling on the pastry disks, brush the edges of the pastry with a little water, and fold the bottom edge of the pastry over to enclose the filling. Press down to seal, then crimp the edge.

Heat the oil for deep-frying in a wok or deep fryer to 350°F/180°C, or until a cube of bread browns in 30 seconds. Deep-fry the pastry packages in batches for 10 minutes or until golden brown. Remove with a slotted spoon and drain on paper towels. Serve.

ไข่ต้มราดน้ำย่า

Hard-Boiled Eggs with Spicy Sauce

Origin Central
Preparation time 5 minutes
Cooking time 5 minutes
Serves 5

3 tablespoons lime juice
1 tablespoon fish sauce
½ tablespoon sugar
5 hard-boiled eggs, halved lengthwise
1 shallot, sliced
4 red and green finger chiles, chopped

Mix the lime juice, fish sauce, and sugar together in a small bowl. Place the halved eggs on a serving plate with the egg yolks facing up. Top with the shallot and chiles and serve with the sauce on the side.

ไข่ลูกเขย

Egg in Tamarind Sauce

Origin Central
Preparation time 10 minutes
Cooking time 20–25 minutes
Serves 4

1 cup (9 fl oz/250 ml) vegetable oil
10–15 shallots, thinly sliced
6 hard-boiled chicken or duck eggs
½ cup (4 fl oz/120 ml) Tamarind Puree (see p. 63)
¾ cup (5 oz/150 g) jaggery, palm sugar, or soft light
  brown sugar
2 tablespoons fish sauce
1 red spur chile, seeded and finely sliced
1 handful of cilantro (coriander), chopped, to garnish
cooked jasmine rice, to serve

Heat the oil in a wok over low-medium heat, add the shallot, and sauté for 8–10 minutes until golden brown. Remove the shallot with a slotted spoon and drain on paper towels. Set aside.

Sauté the whole eggs in the same oil in the wok over medium heat for 6–8 minutes until the eggs are evenly golden brown. Remove from the wok and set aside. Reserve 1 tablespoon of oil in the wok.

Add the tamarind, sugar, fish sauce, and about 4 tablespoons water to the wok and stir until the sugar has dissolved, then cook for 5 minutes or until the mixture turns syrupy. Remove from the heat and set aside.

Halve the eggs lengthwise. Place on a serving plate with the egg yolks facing up, then gently pour the sauce over the eggs and sprinkle with the crispy shallots, chile, and cilantro (coriander). Serve with cooked jasmine rice.

ไข่ยัดไส้สับปะรด

Pineapple Stuffed Omelet

Origin Central
Preparation time 7 minutes
Cooking time 15 minutes
Serves 5

3 eggs
½ teaspoon salt
3½ tablespoons vegetable oil
1 clove garlic, crushed
1 x 4-oz/120-g pork shoulder, ground (minced)
¼ cup (1½ oz/40 g) diced onions
½ carrot, cut into ¼-inch/6-mm dice
1 tomato, cut into ½-inch/1-cm dice
1–2 bird's eye chiles, chopped
1½ teaspoons sugar
1 tablespoon oyster sauce
½ teaspoon soy sauce
½ cup (3 oz/80 g) diced pineapple
sliced cucumber, to serve

Break the eggs into a bowl and add half the salt. Beat with a fork and set aside.

For the stuffing, heat 2 tablespoons of the oil in a wok over medium heat. Add the garlic and sauté for 30 seconds until fragrant, then add the ground (minced) pork and stir-fry for 2–3 minutes. Add the onions, carrot, tomato, and chiles and stir-fry for another 1 minute. Add 2–3 tablespoons water, then season with the sugar, oyster sauce, soy sauce, and remaining salt. Stir for 1–2 minutes, add the pineapple and stir-fry for 1 minute. Set aside.

For the omelet, heat another wok over medium heat, add 1½ tablespoons oil, and roll the oil around the wok. Reduce the heat to low, then add the beaten eggs. Roll the eggs around the wok to create a thin omelet. Move and roll the wok for 3–4 minutes until the omelet is cooked and starts to come away from the wok.

Spoon the stuffing mixture into the center of the omelet and gently fold the omelet bottom edge up, then fold the left and right sides into the middle, and finish by folding the top side down to create a square package. Place a serving plate upside down over the package, press firmly, and then quickly and carefully turn the wok upside down to transfer the omelet to the plate. Use a knife to cut across the middle of the omelet. Serve with cucumber slices.

ไข่ป่าม

Grilled Eggs in Banana Leaves

Origin North
Preparation time 15 minutes
Cooking time 15 minutes
Serves 5

2¼ lb/1 kg banana leaves, cut into 6-inch/
  15-cm-diameter circles
5 eggs
2 red bird's eye chiles, chopped
2 tablespoons soy sauce
2 tablespoons chopped cilantro (coriander)
½ teaspoon salt

Prepare the banana-leaf cups. For each cup, place 2 banana leaf circles back to back with the shiny surface face outward on both sides. From the outside of the circle, fold up about 1¼ inches/3 cm of banana leaf and then fold in on itself to create a corner. Secure with a toothpick or use a stapler. Repeat until there are 4 corners. Set aside.

Heat the broiler (grill) to low. Put the eggs, chiles, soy sauce, cilantro (coriander), and salt into a large bowl and mix well until combined. Add 1–3 tablespoons water while mixing the eggs to make the texture softer. Carefully pour the egg mixture into the banana leaf cups.

Put the containers on the broiler (grill) rack and broil (grill) for 15 minutes or until the eggs are cooked through.

Photo p. 81

ไข่กระทะ

Pan-Fried Eggs

Origin Northeast
Preparation time 5 minutes
Cooking time 10 minutes
Serves 2

2 tablespoons vegetable oil
2 tablespoons ground (minced) pork
2 eggs
2 scallions (spring onions), sliced
4 tablespoons julienned Chinese pork sausage
4 tablespoons julienned cooked white pork sausage
2 teaspoons Fried Garlic (see p. 64)
2 tomatoes, thinly sliced
2 tablespoons sliced onion

To serve
2 small baguettes
selection of dipping sauces

Preheat the oven to 350°F/180°C/Gas Mark
4. Heat the oil in a large skillet or frying pan
over medium heat. Add the ground (minced)
pork and cook for 3–4 minutes until browned.
Remove from the pan with a slotted spoon and
drain on paper towels.

Break the eggs into the pan, then add the
scallions (spring onions), Chinese sausage,
white pork sausage, garlic, tomato, and sliced
onion and cook for 2–3 minutes or until the egg
is cooked as desired.

Slice the baguette in half lengthwise and
fill with the egg, sausages, scallions (spring
onions), garlic, tomato, onions, and the fried
pork. Toast in the oven for 2 minutes, then
serve with the dipping sauces.

ไข่เจียวสมุนไพรชาววัง

Herb Omelet

Origin South
Preparation time 5 minutes
Cooking time 4–6 minutes
Serves 2

3 eggs, beaten
3½ oz/100 g ground (minced) pork or chicken
5 cloves garlic, chopped
2 scallions (spring onions), chopped
1 handful of cilantro (coriander), chopped
2 shallots, chopped
¼ teaspoon salt
7 red bird's eye chiles, chopped
¼ teaspoon white pepper
1 teaspoon soy sauce
1 teaspoon oyster sauce
½ cup (4 fl oz/120 ml) vegetable oil
Steamed Jasmine Rice (see p.378), to serve

Whisk the eggs with all the ingredients, except
the oil, in a large bowl until combined.

Heat the oil in a skillet or frying pan over
medium-low heat. Add the egg mixture and
cook for 3–4 minutes or until the underside
starts to set and the meat is browned. When
almost cooked, carefully flip the omelet over
and cook for 1–2 minutes to quickly color the
other side. Serve on its own or with rice.

หอยทอด

Fried Mussels

Origin Central
Preparation time 10 minutes
Cooking time 12 minutes
Serves 1

10–15 live mussels
2 tablespoons arrowroot flour
3 tablespoon rice flour
1 tablespoon all-purpose (plain) flour
⅛ teaspoon salt
¼ teaspoon baking powder
¼ cup (2 fl oz/50 ml) vegetable oil
1 egg, beaten
3 cloves garlic, chopped
½ cup (2 oz/50 g) bean sprouts
½ teaspoon granulated sugar
1 tablespoon light soy sauce
3 tablespoons water
½ teaspoon ground pepper
1 tablespoon finely sliced scallion (spring onion)

For the sauce
¼ cup (2 fl oz/50 ml) chili sauce
1½ teaspoons granulated sugar
¼ teaspoon salt
1 tablespoon white vinegar

For the sauce, mix the chili sauce, sugar, salt, vinegar, and 1–2 tablespoons water together in a pan over low heat. Heat for 1 minute or until the mixture starts to boil, then remove from the heat and let cool.

Clean the mussels in cold water. Blanch them in a pan of boiling water for 1 minute or until the mussels open and are cooked halfway through. Drain and discard the shells as well as any mussels that haven't opened and set aside.

Mix the arrowroot flour, rice flour, all-purpose (plain) flour, salt, baking powder, and ¼ cup (2 fl oz/50 ml) water together thoroughly in a bowl. Add the mussels and set aside.

Heat 3½ tablespoons oil in a pan over medium heat. Add the mussel and flour mixture to the pan, separate the mussels, and cook for 1 minute. Pour the beaten egg over the mussel mixture. Use a spatula to spread it evenly across the surface of the mixture. Divide the resulting "egg pancake" and mussel mixture underneath into portions and cook for another 4–5 minutes until the bottom of the mussel mixture starts to turn golden brown. Turn the portions over and cook for another 3–4 minutes until golden brown. Transfer to a serving plate and set aside.

Heat ½ tablespoon oil in the same wok over medium heat. Add the chopped garlic and quickly sauté for about 30 seconds until fragrant. Add the bean sprouts, sugar, and soy sauce and stir-fry for about 30 seconds. Remove from the heat and place on top of the mussels.

Sprinkle with finely sliced scallions (spring onions) and pepper and serve with the sauce.

ลูกชิ้นปลาอินทรีย์

Mackerel Fish Balls

Origin Central
Preparation time 10 minutes, plus soaking time
Cooking time 1 hour
Makes 30 balls

1 x 9-oz/250-g Spanish mackerel or clown fish,
  skinned and filleted
¼ teaspoon ground black pepper
1 teaspoon salt
2 teaspoons all-purpose (plain) flour
about ¼ cup (1½ oz/40 g) ice cubes, crushed

Put the fish into a food processor and process
until it is a fine, smooth texture, then transfer
to a large bowl. Add the black pepper, salt,
and flour and knead with your hands for
5–10 minutes. While kneading, slowly add the
ice cubes until the texture is sticky and firm.

Using a spoon, shape the fish mixture into small
½-inch/1-cm-diameter balls and soak in a bowl
of warm water (about 110–120°F/45–50°C) for
30 minutes. To harden the fish balls, maintain
the water temperate by refreshing it with warm
water as needed.

Fill a large bowl with ice-cold water. Set aside.

Bring a medium pan of water to a boil over
medium heat. Add the fish balls and cook for
5 minutes until they float to the surface. Remove
with a slotted spoon and transfer to the bowl of
ice-cold water. Transfer to an airtight container
and store in the refrigerator for up to 1–2 weeks
or freeze for a up to a month.

แจงลอน

Grilled Fish Patties

Origin Central
Preparation time 30 minutes
Cooking time 10 minutes
Makes 8–10

5 tablespoons coconut milk
2 tablespoons jaggery, palm sugar, or soft light
  brown sugar
1 lb 2 oz/500 g king mackerel fillets, skin removed
2½ teaspoons Red Curry Paste (see p. 38)
⅔ cup (2 oz/50 g) dry unsweetened (desiccated)
  coconut
2 teaspoons fish sauce
1 handful of sweet basil leaves

Soak 8–10 bamboo skewers in a bowl of cold
water for 30 minutes. This prevents the skewers
from burning during cooking.

Before you begin cooking, check that your
charcoal is glowing white hot, or your gas
grill (barbecue) is preheated to 400°F/200°C.
Alternatively, use a conventional indoor
broiler (grill) heated to medium.

Mix the coconut milk and sugar together in a
bowl until the sugar has dissolved. Set aside.

Put the fish and chili paste into a food processor
and process until smooth. Transfer the mixture
to a bowl and add the coconut milk and sugar
mixture, the dry unsweetened (desiccated)
coconut, fish sauce, and basil leaves, and using
your hands, knead the mixture for 10 minutes
until it becomes firm and sticky.

Using your hands, mold 2 tablespoons of the
fish mixture into an oval patty, then thread the
patty onto a soaked skewer. Squeeze and make
sure the fish is firmly attached to the skewer
and mold into an oval shape. Put 3–4 patties on
1 stick. Repeat until all of the fish mixture has
been used.

Grill the patties for 6–7 minutes on each side
until puffed up and brown. If using an indoor
broiler, put the broiler (grill) rack about
4 inches/10 cm away from the heat source, then
put the skewers on the rack and broil (grill) for
6–7 minutes on each side. Serve.

ค้างคาวเผือก

Taro Pyramids

Origin Central
Preparation time 10 minutes
Cooking time 40 minutes
Serves 4

For the dough
14 oz/400 g taro, peeled and cubed
scant ½ cup (2 oz/50 g) wheat starch, plus extra
  for dusting
¼ cup (2 fl oz/50 ml) coconut cream

For the batter
scant ½ cup (2 oz/50 g) wheat starch, plus extra
  for dusting
1 egg, beaten
2½ tablespoons superfine (caster) sugar
¾ cup (3½ oz/100 g) rice flour
½ cup (4 fl oz/120 ml) limewater (see p.509) or
  club soda (soda water)
½ teaspoon salt

For the filling
1 clove garlic
2 cilantro (coriander) roots
1 teaspoon white pepper
2 tablespoons vegetable oil, plus extra for deep-frying
4 oz/120 g ground (minced) pork
3¼ oz/90 g ground shrimp (prawns)
1¼ oz/35 g shiitake mushrooms, finely sliced
2 heaping teaspoons granulated sugar
1½ teaspoons soy sauce

To serve
Cucumber Relish (see p. 35)

To make the dough, steam the taro for about
30 minutes or until cooked. Drain and grind
or pound in a mortar with a pestle until smooth,
then let cool. When cool, put the taro in a large
bowl, add the wheat starch and coconut cream,
and mix until thoroughly combined.

For the batter, mix the wheat starch, rice flour,
salt, sugar, and egg in a bowl. Gradually add
the limewater or club soda (soda water) and
¾ cup (6 fl oz/175 ml) water, a small amount at
a time. Mix until no lumps are left. Set aside.

For the filling, pound the garlic, cilantro
(coriander) root, and pepper in a mortar with
a pestle until smooth. Heat the oil in a wok over
medium heat, add the pounded paste, and stir-
fry for 1 minute or until fragrant. Add the pork,
shrimp, and mushrooms and stir-fry for another
3–4 minutes until well cooked. Add the sugar
and soy sauce and stir until combined, then
remove from the heat.

Scoop out a tablespoon of the taro mixture
and flatten it with your hand. Put a teaspoon
of the filling in the center and fold and pinch
the edges together to enclose the filling into a
pyramid shape. Repeat until all the dough and
filling are used.

Heat enough oil for deep-frying in a large wok
or deep fryer to 350°F/180°C or until a cube
of bread browns in 30 seconds. Deep-fry the
taro pyramids in batches for 5–7 minutes or
until crispy and golden brown. Remove with a
slotted spoon and drain on paper towels. Serve
with cucumber relish.

ชุนเปี๊ยะ
Pork Roll

Origin South
Preparation time 15 minutes
Cooking time 15 minutes
Serves 4

8 oz/225 g minced pork
2 tablespoons pork liver, cut into small pieces
2 tablespoons crabmeat
1 tablespoon soy sauce
½ large onion, chopped
1 tablespoon sesame oil
1 tablespoon granulated sugar
1 large sheet tofu skin (bubble tofu)
1 cup (4 oz/120 g) tempura flour
2 cups (16 fl oz/475 ml) vegetable oil

For the dipping sauce
4 dried chiles
2 cloves garlic
1 cup (5¾ oz/165 g) diced pineapple
3 tablespoons granulated sugar
2 tablespoons white vinegar
1 teaspoon salt

To make the sauce, pound the chiles, garlic, and pineapple in a mortar with a pestle. Heat a pan over medium heat, add the chile and pineapple mixture, sugar, vinegar, and salt and simmer, stirring, until thick and sticky.

Put the pork, pork liver, crabmeat, soy sauce, onion, sesame oil, and sugar into a large bowl and mix with your hands until combined.

Place the tofu sheet on a work surface and put the filling at one end, leaving a ¾-inch/2-cm border. Brush the borders with a little water then roll up, tucking in the ends as you go, to form a roll. Brush the end with more water and press to seal. Set aside covered in a damp dish towel to prevent it from drying out.

Pour 1½ cups (12 fl oz/350 ml) water into a large bowl, add the tempura flour, and stir until the flour has dissolved.

Heat the oil for deep-frying in a wok or deep fryer to 350°F/180°C or until a cube of bread browns in 30 seconds. Dip the tofu roll into the tempura batter and deep-fry for 7–10 minutes until golden brown. Remove with a slotted spoon and drain on paper towels. Serve, cut into slices, with the dipping sauce.

ปอเปี๊ยะทอด
Thai Summer Rolls

Origin South
Preparation time 20 minutes
Cooking time 5 minutes
Makes 15 rolls

1 tablespoon vegetable oil
1 cup (4 oz/120 g) shredded jicama
2 tablespoons oyster sauce
20 spring roll wrapper sheets
2 cups (4 oz/120 g) shredded lettuce
2 cups (4 oz/120 g) boiled bean sprouts
1 cup (½ oz/15 g) crispy pork rind, coarsely chopped
2 tablespoons Fried Shallots (see p. 64)
20 cooked shrimp (prawns)
3½ oz/100 g roasted pork, sliced

For the sauce
1 cup (9 fl oz/250 ml) Tamarind Puree (see p. 63)
5 dried chiles, soaked
3 shallots
1 tablespoon soy sauce
½ cup (3½ oz/100 g) jaggery, palm sugar, or soft light brown sugar
7 cloves garlic
1 tablespoon Fermented Soybeans (see p. 34)

Heat the oil in a wok over medium heat, add the jicama and oyster sauce, and sauté for 30 seconds. Remove from the heat and set aside.

To make the sauce, pound all the ingredients together in a mortar with a pestle until smooth. Heat the sauce in a wok over medium heat, bring to a boil, then reduce the heat and simmer until thickened.

Lay a spring roll wrapper out on a work surface so that one of the corners faces you. Put a little of the lettuce, bean sprouts, pork skin, fried shallots, and jicama in the center of the wrapper and add a little sauce. Fold the bottom corner of the wrapper up and over the filling. Fold the left and right corners in to create a package. Roll the package up toward the top corner and brush a little water on the top edges of the wrapper to stick the package together. Repeat until you have used up the filling. Cut the rolls in half and serve with the remaining sauce.

Photo p. 87

Pork and Shrimp Golden Packages

Origin Central
Preparation time 10 minutes, plus chilling time
Cooking time 20–25 minutes
Makes 30 packages

1 scallion (spring onion) or baby leek, 8–12 inches/
  20–30 cm long
5 oz/150 g shrimp (prawns), peeled, deveined,
  and ground (minced)
3½ oz/100 g ground (minced) pork
1 tablespoon Saam-Gler (see p. 41)
3 tablespoons soy sauce
2 teaspoons granulated sugar
½ cup (2 oz/50 g) water chestnuts, diced
30 spring roll wrapper sheets, about 5 inches/13 cm
  in diameter
4 cups (1⅔ pints/950 ml) vegetable oil, for deep-frying
Sweet Chili Dipping Sauce (see p. 60), to serve

Fill a small heatproof bowl with boiling water. Fill another bowl with cold water. Set aside.

Cut the scallion (spring onion) or baby leek lengthwise into ¼-inch/5–7-mm-wide strips. Create as many strips as there are spring roll wrapper sheets. Put the strips into the bowl of boiling water for 30 seconds, then transfer to the bowl of cold water to cool. Drain and pat dry with paper towels, then set aside.

To make the filling, put the shrimp (prawns), pork, saam-gler, soy sauce, sugar, and water chestnuts into a large bowl and mix well. Cover with plastic wrap (clingfilm) and chill in the refrigerator for at least 10 minutes before wrapping.

Lay a spring roll wrapper on a work surface. Put 1 teaspoon of the filling in the center of the wrapper. Lift the edges of the wrapper up to create a package and tie with a strip of scallion (spring onion) or leek. Knot the strip twice to secure. Repeat until all the filling is used.

Heat the oil for deep-frying in a wok or deep fryer to 350°F/180°C or until a cube of bread browns in 30 seconds. Deep-fry the packages in batches for 5–7 minutes until golden brown and crispy. Remove from the wok with a slotted spoon and drain on paper towels. Serve with sweet chili dipping sauce.

Photo p. 89

Pork and Shrimp on Pineapple

Origin Central
Preparation time 10 minutes
Cooking time 20 minutes
Serves 5

8 cloves garlic
5 cilantro (coriander) root stems
½ teaspoon white pepper
3 tablespoons vegetable oil
¾ cup (5 oz/150 g) jaggery, palm sugar, or soft light
  brown sugar
1½ teaspoons salt
3½ oz/100 g ground (minced) pork
3½ oz/100 g uncooked shrimp (prawns), peeled,
  deveined, and ground (minced)
1 cup (5 oz/150 g) roasted peanuts, crushed
1 pineapple, peeled, cored, and cut into 1¼ x ½-inch/
  3 x 1-cm pieces
1 handful of cilantro (coriander) leaves
1 red spur chile, finely sliced

Finely pound the garlic, cilantro (coriander)
root, and pepper in a mortar with a pestle.

Heat the oil in a wok over low-medium heat,
add the garlic paste, and sauté for 2–3 minutes
until golden and fragrant. Add the sugar and
salt and cook for another 2–3 minutes until
the sugar softens. Add the pork and shrimp
(prawns) and cook for another 4 minutes. Stir
in the peanuts and cook for 8–9 minutes until
everything starts to become sticky. Remove
the wok from the heat and let cool.

When cool enough to handle, shape the
mixture into ¾-inch/2-cm-diameter balls
and place each ball onto an individual piece
of pineapple. Top each ball with a cilantro
(coriander) leaf and a slice of chile, then serve.

Cracker Salad

Origin North
Preparation time 10 minutes
Serves 2

5 large black sesame seed rice paper crackers
3 tablespoons spicy fish paste
1 cup (2 oz/50 g) pork crackling
2 tablespoons Fried Garlic (see p. 64)
2 tablespoons sliced shallots
2 tablespoons shredded carrot
2 tablespoons chopped yard-long bean
1 tablespoon lime juice
1 tablespoon vegetable oil
1 tablespoon fish sauce

Break the crackers into small pieces and put
into a deep bowl, add the paste, pork, garlic,
shallot, carrot, and yard-long bean, and gently
mix together until combined. Season with the
lime juice, oil, and fish sauce and serve.

จิ๋มจุ่ม

Thai-Style Hot Pot

Origin Northeast
Preparation time 20 minutes, plus soaking and
marinating time
Serves 2

2¼ oz/60 g dried glass noodles
11 oz/300 g tenderloin steak (beef sirloin), thinly sliced
1 tablespoon oyster sauce
1 teaspoon granulated sugar
1 tablespoon soy sauce
3½ oz/100 g uncooked jumbo shrimp (tiger prawns)
1 egg, beaten
½ head green or white cabbage, cut into chunks
3½ oz/100 g water spinach
1 bunch of sweet basil
1½ cups (4 fl oz/120 ml) Barbecue Sauce, to serve
  (see p. 63)

For the soup
4 cups (1⅔ pints/950 ml) chicken broth (stock)
3 kaffir lime leaves
1 lemongrass stalk, chopped
2 small shallots, halved
2–3 sawtooth cilantro (coriander) leaves
3 slices galangal

Soak the noodles in a bowl of water for
10 minutes, or prepare according to package
directions. Drain, cut, and set aside.

Put the beef in a bowl, add the oyster sauce,
sugar, and soy sauce, and mix well. Cover with
plastic wrap (clingfilm), and let marinate for
10–15 minutes.

Put the beef and shrimp (prawns) in a shallow
serving dish and pour the beaten egg over
them. Set aside.

Drain the noodles (vermicelli), and put onto a
serving plate with the cabbage, water spinach,
and basil leaves and set aside.

To make the soup, mix the chicken broth
(stock), kaffir lime leaves, lemongrass, shallots,
cilantro (coriander), and galangal together in
a large bowl. Pour into a hot pot and bring
to a boil.

To serve, bring the hot pot to the table. Use
chopsticks to dip small portions of the meat,
shrimp, or vegetables into the hot pot until
cooked. Remove from the hot pot, dip into
the barbecue sauce, and eat.

แหนมทอดใบมะกรูด

Deep-Fried Pork with Crispy Kaffir Lime Leaves

Origin North
Preparation time 20 minutes
Cooking time 8–10 minutes
Serves 2

vegetable oil, for deep-frying
½ cup (2¼ oz/60 g) all-purpose (plain) flour, cornstarch
  (cornflour), or tapioca flour
3 cups (5 oz/150 g) fresh breadcrumbs
7 oz/200 g sour pork sausage, cut into bite-size pieces
2 eggs, beaten
5 kaffir lime leaves

To serve
selection of condiments, such as sliced ginger, shallots,
  garlic, roasted peanuts, red bird's eye chiles, and
  scallions (spring onions)

Heat the oil for deep-frying in a wok or deep
fryer to 350°F/180°C or until a cube of bread
browns in 30 seconds.

Meanwhile, spread the flour and breadcrumbs
out on separate large plates. Dredge the pork
sausage in the flour, then dip in the beaten egg,
and coat in the breadcrumbs.

Deep-fry the coated sausage pieces for about
5 minutes or until golden brown and crispy.
Remove with a slotted spoon and drain on
paper towels. Set aside.

Deep-fry the kaffir lime leaves for 30 seconds
until crispy, then remove and drain on paper
towels. Set aside.

Put the sausage on a serving plate, garnish
with the deep-fried kaffir lime leaves, and
serve with a selection of condiments.

หมูปิ้ง

Grilled Pork Skewers

Origin Central
Preparation time 20 minutes, plus marinating time
Cooking time 10–12 minutes
Makes 10–15 skewers

15 cloves garlic, peeled
7 cilantro (coriander) roots
2–3 tablespoons white peppercorns
4½ lb/2 kg pork sirloin, rinsed and sliced into
  1-inch/2.5-cm strips
1 teaspoon salt
1 tablespoon dark soy sauce
1 cup (7 oz/200 g) jaggery, palm sugar, or soft light
  brown sugar
⅓ cup (2½ fl oz/75 ml) vegetable oil

Finely pound the garlic, cilantro (coriander)
roots, and peppercorns in a mortar with a
pestle. Transfer to a large bowl and add the
pork, salt, soy sauce, and sugar and mix well.
Cover with plastic wrap (clingfilm) and let
marinate in the refrigerator for 2–4 hours.

Meanwhile, soak 10–15 bamboo skewers in a
bowl of cold water for 30 minutes. This prevents
the skewers from burning during cooking.

Before you begin cooking, check that your
charcoal is glowing white hot, or your gas
grill (barbecue) is preheated to 400°F/200°C.

Using your hands, mold some of the pork
mixture onto a soaked wooden skewer, making
sure that the mixture is firmly attached to the
skewer and molds into an oval shape. Repeat
until all the mixture is used.

Brush the oil over the pork skewers, then grill
for 10–12 minutes until cooked. Serve.

Photo p. 93

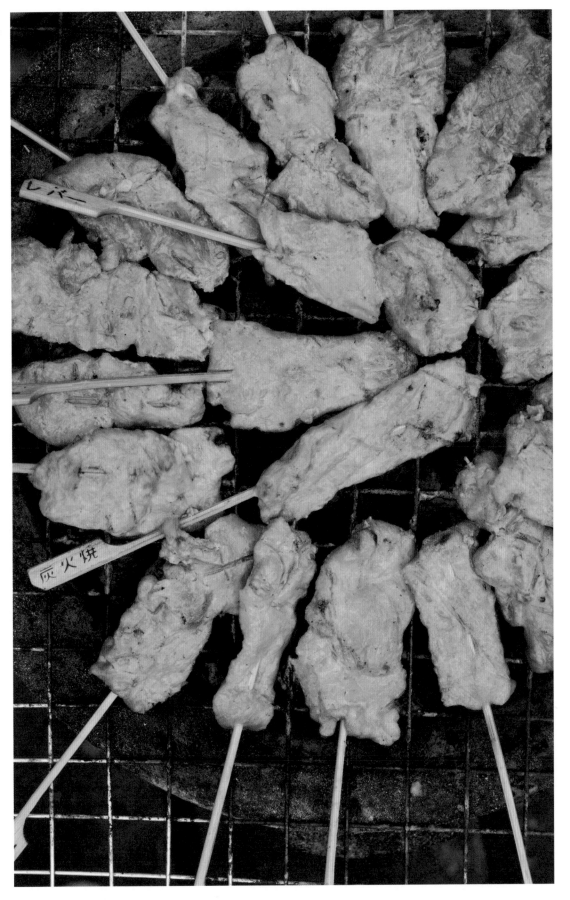

Pork Cracklings

Origin North
Preparation time 5 minutes, plus drying and standing time
Cooking time 35 minutes
Serves 4

1 lb 2 oz/500 g pork skin
2 tablespoons soy sauce
2 teaspoons salt
3 cups (1¼ pints/750 ml) vegetable oil

Bring a large pan of water to a boil over medium heat. Add the pork skin and boil for 30 minutes. Strain and cut into 1-inch/2.5-cm-long pieces. Mix the cooked pork skin, soy sauce, and salt together in a bowl, then sun dry for 4 hours or until dry.

Heat the oil for deep-frying in a wok or deep fryer to 350°F/180°C, or until a cube of bread browns in 30 seconds. Deep-fry the pork skin for 5 minutes, then remove with a slotted spoon and drain on paper towels overnight.

The next day, heat the oil for deep-frying in a wok or deep fryer to 350°F/180°C, or until a cube of bread browns in 30 seconds. Deep-fry the pork skin for about 5 minutes or until puffed. Remove with a slotted spoon and drain on paper towels. Let cool, then serve.

Thai-style Pork Satay

Origin South
Preparation time 15 minutes, plus marinating time
Cooking time 10–15 minutes
Makes 25 skewers

1 x 14-oz/400-g pork tenderloin (fillet) or loin
1 teaspoon finely pounded galangal
1 tablespoon finely pounded lemongrass
1 teaspoon ground turmeric
1 teaspoon coriander seeds, ground and toasted
1 teaspoon cumin seeds, ground and toasted
2 teaspoons ground white pepper
1 cup (9 fl oz/250 ml) coconut cream
2 teaspoons granulated sugar
1 teaspoon salt

To serve
Thai-Style Satay Sauce (see p. 60)
Cucumber Relish (see p. 35)

Slice the pork into pieces 1 inch/2.5 cm wide, 3 inches/1¼-cm long, and ⅜ inch/8 mm thick.

Put the pork, galangal, lemongrass, turmeric, ground coriander and cumin, white pepper, scant ½ cup (3½ fl oz/100ml) coconut cream, sugar, and salt in a large bowl and mix well. Cover with plastic wrap (clingfilm) and let marinate for 30 minutes.

Meanwhile, soak 25 bamboo skewers, about 6 x 7 inches/15 x 18 cm long, in cold water for 30 minutes. This prevents the skewers from burning during cooking.

Before you begin cooking, check that your charcoal is glowing white hot, or your gas grill (barbecue) is preheated to 400°F/200°C. Alternatively, use a conventional indoor broiler (grill) heated to medium. Thread a piece of pork onto each soaked skewer, then cook the pork, turning the skewers and basting frequently with the remaining coconut milk for 10–15 minutes until the pork is cooked. Serve with satay sauce and cucumber relish.

ปอเปี๊ยะ

Fried Spring Rolls

Origin Central
Preparation time 15 minutes, plus soaking time
Cooking time 40 minutes
Makes 10–12 rolls

2¾ oz/70 g dried glass noodles
10 dried shiitake mushrooms, soaked
¼ cup (1¼ oz/30 g) tapioca flour
5 cups (2 pints/1.2 liters) vegetable oil, for deep-frying,
  plus ¼ cup (2 fl oz/50 ml) for stir-frying
7 oz/200 g ground (minced) pork
1 tablespoon Saam-Gler (see p. 41)
3 cups (9¾ oz/275 g) finely shredded cabbage
1 tablespoon oyster sauce
1 tablespoon granulated sugar
1 teaspoon soy sauce
½ teaspoon salt
10–12 spring roll wrappers, 8 inches/20 cm in diameter
Sweet Chili Dipping Sauce (see p. 60), to serve

Soak the noodles in a bowl of water for
10 minutes, or prepare according to package
directions, then drain and cut into 1½-inch/
4-cm lengths. Set aside.

Squeeze out the water from the mushrooms,
discard the stems, and finely slice. Set aside.

Dissolve the tapioca flour in ½ cup (4 fl oz/
120 ml) water over low heat, then set aside.

Heat 2 tablespoons of the oil in a skillet or
frying pan over medium heat, add the pork,
and cook for 3–4 minutes until browned and
any liquid has evaporated. Strain and set aside.

Heat another 2 tablespoons oil in a wok over
medium heat, add the saam-gler, and cook
for 1 minute or until fragrant. Add the shiitake
mushrooms and sauté for 1–2 minutes until
fragrant. Reduce the heat to low, add the
cabbage, and stir-fry for 1½ minutes. Remove
the wok from the heat, add the noodles, pork,
oyster sauce, sugar, soy, and salt, and stir until
thoroughly combined. Avoid overcooking,
which will make the mixture soggy. Let cool.

Lay a spring roll wrapper on a work surface
so that one of the corners faces you. Put
2 tablespoons of the filling in the center of the
wrapper and fold the bottom of the wrapper
up and over the filling. Fold the left and right
sides in to create a package. Roll the package
up toward the top corner and brush the tapioca
mixture on the top edges of the wrapper to
stick the package together. Repeat until all the
filling is used. Cover the wrapper with a damp
dish towel to stop it from drying out.

Heat the oil for deep-frying in a wok or deep
fryer to 375°F/190°C, or until a cube of bread
browns in 30 seconds. Deep-fry the spring
rolls in batches for 7–10 minutes until golden
brown, then remove with a slotted spoon and
drain on paper towels. Serve with sweet chili
dipping sauce.

แหนมเนื้อ

Sour Sausage Meat in Banana Leaf

Origin Northeast
Preparation time 15 minutes, plus fermenting time
Serves 8

5½ lb/2.5 kg ground (minced) buffalo or beef
2 garlic bulbs, cloves separated and finely chopped
½ cup (3½ oz/100 g) cooked Glutinous Rice (see p. 378)
⅓ cup (3½ oz/100 g) salt
10 bird's eye chiles
1 banana leaf, for wrapping (optional)

To serve
Glutinous Rice (see p. 378)
selection of condiments, such as sliced ginger,
  shallots, peanuts, bird's eye chiles, and scallions
  (spring onions)

Put the ground (minced) meat, garlic, rice, and salt in a large bowl and mix together with clean, damp hands until the mixture is sticky and can be molded. Divide the mixture into portions, place the meat in the center of a banana leaf, and top with a chile. Cover the meat with the sides of the leaf, fold over the ends, and tightly seal with string. Alternatively, add the whole chiles to the meat, then pack the meat mixture into a large plastic food bag and seal.

Let ferment for 7–10 days at room temperature. The meat will taste sour when ready. Serve as patties with rice and a selection of condiments. Aternatively, store in an airtight container in the refrigerator for up to 1 week.

Photo p. 96

หมี่พันลับแล

Steamed Spring Rolls

Origin North
Preparation time 15 minutes, plus soaking time
Cooking time 25 minutes
Makes 30 rolls

5 oz/150 g dried rice vermicelli
2 tablespoons soy sauce
1 tablespoon lime juice
1 tablespoon Chili Jam (see p. 35)
1½ teaspoons granulated sugar
¼ cup (2 oz/50 g) bean sprouts
3 tablespoons finely chopped cilantro (coriander)
1 tablespoon Fried Garlic (see p. 64)
30 rice crepes or rice paper spring roll wrappers
plum sauce, to serve

Soak the vermicelli in a bowl of cold water for 5 minutes, then drain.

Put all the ingredients except the rice crepes in a large bowl and mix together until thoroughly combined.

Lay a rice crepe on a work surface. Put 1–2 tablespoons of the filling in the center of the crepe and spread out thinly. Don't overfill because it might tear. Fold the bottom of the crepe up and over the filling. Fold the left and right sides in to create a package. Roll the package up toward the top of the crepe and brush a little water on the top edges of the crepe to stick the package together. Repeat until all the filling is used.

Steam the rolls in a steamer for about 5 minutes or until cooked. Serve with plum sauce.

Stuffed Roti

Origin South
Preparation time 30 minutes, plus standing time
Cooking time 25–30 minutes
Serves 4

For the roti pastry
½ cup (4 fl oz/120 ml) ghee or vegetable oil, plus extra for greasing
2 cups (9 oz/250 g) all-purpose (plain) flour
1 egg, beaten
2 tablespoons milk
¼ teaspoon salt
¼ teaspoon granulated sugar

For the stuffing
½ tablespoon butter
½ cup (4 fl oz/120 ml) vegetable oil
1½ teaspoons Saam-Gler (see p. 41)
1 teaspoon curry powder
2 onions, sliced
11 oz/300 g ground (minced) chicken
¼ teaspoon salt
½ tablespoon granulated sugar
1 egg, beaten
3 scallions (spring onions), chopped

To serve
½ cup (4 fl oz/120 ml) Cucumber Relish (see p. 35)

Grease a baking sheet with vegetable oil and set aside.

To make the roti pastry dough, put the flour into a large bowl and set aside. Whisk half the beaten egg, the milk, salt, sugar, and ½ cup (4 fl oz/120 ml) water in another bowl until the sugar and salt have dissolved. Pour into the flour and mix and knead until the ingredients start to combine. Add 1 tablespoon ghee or vegetable oil and continue kneading until a smooth dough forms. Split the dough into small equal portions. Coat your fingers with ghee or oil and shape the dough portions into small balls. Place the dough balls on the greased baking sheet and repeat until all the dough is used. Cover the dough with plastic wrap (clingfilm) or cheesecloth (muslin) and let stand for 2–10 hours before cooking.

Meanwhile, prepare the stuffing. Heat the butter and 1 tablespoon oil in a pan over medium heat. Add the saam-gler and curry powder and cook for 1 minute until fragrant. Add the onions and sauté for 1 minute, then add the chicken and stir-fry for 2 minutes or until the chicken is cooked. Season with the salt and sugar and stir-fry until fully flavored. Remove from the heat and set aside.

Place a dough ball on an oiled work surface. Dip your hand in ghee or oil, then press and flatten the dough into a very thin and wide sheet. It should be almost translucent. Put 3–4 tablespoons of the stuffing into the center of the dough sheet, then pour about 1½ teaspoons of beaten egg onto the filling and sprinkle with a little scallion (spring onion). Cover the filling with the sides of the dough sheet, then fold over the ends to form a square package. Repeat until all the dough and filling is used.

Heat ½ tablespoon oil or ghee in a large skillet or frying pan over medium-low heat, add the roti one at a time, and cook for about 2 minutes on each side or until golden brown and crispy. Transfer to a serving plate and repeat with the remaining roti. Serve with the cucumber relish.

Roasted Crickets

จิ้งหรีดคั่วสมุนไพร

Origin Northeast
Preparation time 5 minutes, plus chilling time
Cooking time 10 minutes
Serves 4

7 oz/200 g live crickets
1 lemongrass stalk, finely sliced
3 pandan leaves, finely sliced
salt

Put the crickets in an airtight container and chill in the refrigerator for 30 minutes, then remove and transfer to the freezer for 30 minutes. Remove the crickets from the freezer and wash 3 or 4 times in water.

Heat a wok over medium heat, add the crickets, and roast for 6–7 minutes. Add the lemongrass and pandan leaves and season with salt. Stir-fry for 2–3 minutes. Serve.

Photo p. 101

Fried Crickets with Herbs

แมงสะดิ้งทอดสมุนไพร

Origin Northeast
Preparation time 10 minutes, plus chilling time
Cooking time 10 minutes
Serves 4

1 lb 2 oz/500 g live small house crickets
3 cups (1¼ pints/750 ml) vegetable oil
⅓ cup (1½ oz/40 g) finely sliced fresh ginger
1½ oz/40 g galangal, finely sliced
½ cup (1½ oz/40 g) finely sliced lemongrass
3 garlic bulbs, cloves separated and finely sliced
1 cup (5 oz/150 g) peanuts (optional)
8 young kaffir lime leaves
1 teaspoon salt

Put the crickets in an airtight container and chill in the refrigerator for 30 minutes, then remove and transfer to the freezer for 30 minutes.

Blanch the crickets in a pan of boiling water for 1–2 minutes, then rinse under cold running water, drain, and set aside.

Heat the oil for deep-frying in a wok or deep fryer to 350°F/180°C, or until a cube of bread browns in 30 seconds. Deep-fry the ginger, galangal, lemongrass, and garlic for 1 minute or until golden brown and crispy. Remove with a slotted spoon and drain on paper towels.

Deep-fry the peanuts, if using, in the oil for about 1 minute or until toasted. Remove with a slotted spoon and drain on paper towels.

Deep-fry the kaffir lime leaves in the oil for 20–30 seconds. Remove with a slotted spoon and drain on paper towels.

Make sure the oil is at the correct temperature, then deep-fry the crickets for about 5 minutes or until golden brown and crispy, then remove with a slotted spoon and drain on paper towels.

Mix the crickets, ginger mixture, garlic, and peanuts together and season with the salt. Garnish with the kaffir lime leaves and serve.

Photo p. 99

ไข่เจียวไข่มดแดง

Omelet with Red Ant Eggs

Origin Northeast
Preparation time 5 minutes
Cooking time 7 minutes
Serves 2

3 eggs
2 tablespoons sliced shallots
1 cup (4 oz/120 g) red ant eggs
1 teaspoon fish sauce
3–4 tablespoons vegetable oil
3 cloves garlic, sliced

Break the eggs into a bowl, add the shallots, red ant eggs, and fish sauce, and beat thoroughly with a fork.

Heat the oil in a wok over medium heat, add the garlic, and sauté for 1 minute. Pour the egg mixture into the wok and roll the egg around the wok to create an omelet. Continue moving and rolling the wok for 2–3 minutes until the omelet becomes yellow and starts to come away from the wok. When almost cooked, carefully flip the omelet over and cook for 1–2 minutes to color the other side. Serve.

ค้าเป้งมดแดง

Roasted Big Red Ants

Origin Northeast
Preparation time 5 minutes
Cooking time 5 minutes
Serves 2

1 cup (3 oz/80 g) big red ants (queen caste)
1 tablespoon salt
1 tablespoon fish sauce
2 lemongrass stalks, sliced
10 kaffir lime leaves, sliced
2–3 pandanus leaves, sliced

Put the ants in an airtight container and chill in the refrigerator for 30 minutes, then remove and transfer to the freezer for 30 minutes.

Roast all the ingredients in a skillet or frying pan over medium heat for 3–5 minutes until dry. Let cool and serve.

ผักกาดดอง

Pickled Cabbage

Origin Northeast
Preparation time 10 minutes
Serves 2

2½ cups (1 lb 2 oz/500 g) rice
14 oz/400 g choy sum (flowering Chinese cabbage), cut into 2-inch/5-cm lengths
2 tablespoons salt
2 tablespoons cooked Glutinous Rice (see p. 378)
3 slices ginger (optional)

Mix 4 cups (1⅔ pints/950 ml) water and the rice together in a large bowl. Stir until the water turns milky white. Strain through cheesecloth (muslin) and reserve 1 cup (9 fl oz/250 ml) rice water. Strain the rice water again and set aside.

Put the choy sum and salt in a large bowl and rub the salt all over the cabbage. Squeeze and knead for 2–3 minutes until the cabbage has softened. Add the rice and massage the mixture until well mixed. Transfer to a large sterilized jar and fill with the reserved rice water, leaving a ¼ inch/5 cm head space. Add the ginger, if using, cover with a lid, and let stand overnight at room temperature. The next day, drain and serve.

มะม่วงแผ่น
Dried Mango

Origin Central
Preparation time 30 minutes, plus drying time
Serves 5

4½ lb/2 kg ripe mangoes, peeled, pitted, and
  cut into thin slices
1 teaspoon salt

Put the mango and salt in a food processor
and blend until smooth. Transfer to a wok and
heat over medium heat for about 20 minutes
until sticky. Remove from the heat and let cool
slightly, then shape the mango mixture into
small balls. Flatten the balls into disks about
2 inches/5 cm in diameter. Put the mango disks
on a tray and sun-dry for 24 hours. Turn over
and let dry for another 48 hours. Store the dried
mango in sterilized airtight jars. They must be
stored away from moisture, so when filling the
jars, make sure your hands are dry.

มะม่วงน้ำปลาหวาน
Green Mango with Sweetened Fish Sauce

Origin Central
Preparation time 5 minutes
Cooking time 7 minutes
Serves 4

⅓ cup (2½ oz/65 g) jaggery, palm sugar, or soft light
  brown sugar
⅓ cup (2½ fl oz/75 ml) fish sauce
10 shallots, finely chopped
10 bird's eye chiles, finely chopped
3 tablespoons dried shrimp, pounded
2 sour green mangoes, peeled and thinly sliced

Mix the sugar and fish sauce together in a
wok, then heat over medium heat, stirring
constantly, for 5–6 minutes until thick. Add the
shallot, chiles, and dried shrimp and mix well.
Transfer to a small serving bowl and serve
with the sliced green mango.

มะม่วงแช่อิ่ม
Preserved Mango

Origin Central
Preparation time 15 minutes, plus soaking and
drying time
Cooking time 3 days
Serves 6–8

1½ cups (12 oz/350 g) sea rock salt
2¼ lb/1 kg sour green mango, peeled, seeded,
  and sliced
4 cups (1⅔ pints/950 ml) limewater (see p.509)
4 cups (1¾ lb/800 g) superfine (caster) sugar

Pour 5 cups (2 pints/1.2 liters) water into a large
bowl, add the rock salt, and stir until the salt has
dissolved. Add the mango slices to the salted
water, cover with plastic wrap (clingfilm), and
let soak for 24 hours.

The next day, remove the mango from the
salted water with a slotted spoon and soak
in the limewater for 1 hour. Rinse under cold
running water and let dry.

Bring 3½ cups (1¾ pints/800 ml) water and
3½ cups (1 lb 8 oz/700 g) sugar to a boil in
a large pan and keep boiling for 3–4 minutes.
Remove from the heat and let cool.

Put the sliced mango in a large bowl, pour
the sugar syrup over the fruit, and cover
with plastic wrap. Let soak overnight in the
refrigerator.

The next day, remove the mango with a slotted
spoon and set aside.

Bring the sugar syrup to a boil over medium
heat and gradually add the remaining ½ cup
(3½ oz/100 g) sugar. Boil until thick and sticky.
Remove from the heat and let cool. When cool
pour into an airtight container and add the
mango. Cover and set aside for 2–3 days. Store
in the refrigerator for up to 1 month.

กล้วยตาก

Dried Bananas

Origin Central
Preparation time 10 minutes, plus drying time
Cooking time 20 minutes
Makes 10

10 small ripe bananas, peeled and sliced into circles
½ cup (4 oz/120 g) honey

Line a baking sheet with cheesecloth (muslin). Arrange the bananas on the lined baking sheet, cover with more cheesecloth to prevent any bugs from settling on the bananas, and let dry in the sun for 3–5 days. Turn the baking sheet once a day so the bananas dry evenly.

Preheat the oven to 325°F/160°C/Gas Mark 3 and line a large baking sheet with wax (greaseproof) paper.

Mix the dried bananas with the honey in a large bowl. Transfer to the lined baking sheet and bake in the oven for about 20 minutes. Let cool, then transfer to a sterilized airtight jar and store for up to 3–4 weeks.

ปาท่องโก๋

Thai-Style Chinese Cruller

Origin Central
Preparation time 20 minutes, plus resting time
Cooking time 10 minutes
Serves 2

1 cup (4 oz/120 g) all-purpose (plain) flour, plus ⅓ cup (2 oz/50 g) flour, for dusting
½ teaspoon active dry (fast-action) yeast
½ teaspoon baking powder
2 teaspoons superfine (caster) sugar
a pinch of salt
1 tablespoon vegetable oil, plus extra for deep-frying

To serve
coffee, hot chocolate, congee, or sweetened condensed milk

Put the flour, yeast, baking powder, sugar, and salt into a large bowl and mix well. Add 5 tablespoons water and knead for 10 minutes or until the dough is mixed well. Add the 1 tablespoon oil and knead for another 2–3 minutes. Cover the dough with plastic wrap (clingfilm) and let rest for 2–10 hours.

Knead the dough on a floured work surface. Roll into a tube shape and gently press with a rolling pin to create a ¼-inch/5-mm thick rectangle sheet. Cut the rectangle in half lengthwise, then cut crosswise to create ¾ x 3¼-inch/2 x 8-cm strips. Take 2 dough strips. Moisten the middle of one strip with some water, then press the other strip on top where the water is. Stretch them out slightly. Repeat until all the dough strips are used.

Heat the oil for deep-frying in a wok or deep fryer to 350°F/180°C or until a cube of bread browns in 30 seconds. Deep-fry the dough for 1–2 minutes on each side or until the dough has puffed up and turned golden brown. Remove with a slotted spoon and drain on paper towels.

Serve with coffee, hot chocolate, congee, or sweetened condensed milk.

มันบั้ง

Grilled Yuca Root with Coconut Syrup

Origin Central
Preparation time 10 minutes, plus soaking time
Cooking time 35–40 minutes
Serves 4

1 x 1½-lb–2¼-lb/700-g–1-kg yuca root (cassava),
  peeled and cut crosswise into 4-inch/10-cm
  long pieces
scant 1 cup (7 fl oz/200 ml) coconut milk
1 cup (7 oz/200 g) jaggery, palm sugar, or soft light
  brown sugar
¼ teaspoon salt

Soak the yuca root (cassava) in a bowl of cold water for 15 minutes, then drain and set aside.

To make the coconut syrup, heat the coconut milk in a pan over medium heat. When it starts to boil, add the sugar and salt and stir until the sugar has dissolved. Reduce the heat slightly and lightly boil for 4–5 minutes. Remove from the heat and set aside.

Before you begin cooking, check that your charcoal is glowing white hot, or your gas grill (barbecue) is preheated to 350°F/180°C. Alternatively, use a conventional indoor broiler (grill) heated to medium-high.

Steam the yuca root over high heat for about 10 minutes or until it starts to cook. Be careful not to overcook, otherwise the root can become too soft.

Remove the yuca root from the steamer and grill over a medium charcoal fire for about 10 minutes on each side or until the cassava turns brown. If using an indoor broiler, put the broiler (grill) rack about 4 inches/10 cm away from the heat source, then put the yuca root on the rack and broil (grill) for about 10 minutes on each side.

Put the grilled yuca root on a cutting (chopping) board and flatten each piece by pressing it with another board or a plate. Repeat until all the yuca root pieces have been flattened.

Dip the yuca root into the coconut syrup for 2–3 minutes until well coated, then place back onto the grill or under the broiler and cook each side for 3–5 minutes until the syrup coating dries. Transfer to a serving plate, pour over the remaining syrup, and serve.

Photo p. 105

ทับทิมกรอบ

Water Chestnut Rubies and Emeralds in Coconut Milk

Origin Central
Preparation 20 minutes, plus soaking time
Cooking time 15 minutes
Serves 4

1 cup (9 fl oz/250 ml) cream soda syrup or green
   sugar syrup
1 cup (9 fl oz/250 ml) grenadine or red sugar syrup
¾–1½ cups (3½–7 oz/100–200 g) tapioca flour
3½ cups (14 oz/400 g) peeled and diced water chestnuts
1 cup (7 oz/200 g) superfine (caster) sugar
1 pandan leaf, tied in a knot
1 cup (9 fl oz/250 ml) coconut milk
ice cubes, crushed to serve

Put the cream soda syrup, grenadine, and tapioca flour in separate bowls. Divide the water chestnuts between the bowls of red and green sugar syrup and let soak for about 10 minutes or until the chestnuts absorbs the color. Remove with a slotted spoon and transfer to the bowl of tapioca flour. Shake the bowl until the water chestnuts are well coated with starch.

Have a bowl of ice water ready. Bring 5 cups (2 pints/1.2 liters) water to a boil in a pan, add the coated water chestnuts, and let sit for 3–4 minutes until the water chestnuts float to the surface and the flour has become transparent (jellylike). Transfer to the bowl of ice water and set aside.

Bring 1 cup (9 fl oz/250 ml) water and the sugar to a boil in a pan over medium heat. Boil until the mixture turns syrupy, then remove from the heat, let cool, and set aside.

Heat the pandan leaf and coconut milk in a pan over low-medium heat for 3–4 minutes or until it reaches a boil. Remove from the heat, let cool, and set aside.

Drain the water chestnuts and spoon into a serving bowl. Add the sugar syrup, and infused coconut milk, and crushed ice cubes and serve.

Photo p. 107

น้ำดอกอัญชัน

Butterfly Pea Juice

Origin Central
Preparation time 3 minutes
Cooking time 10 minutes
Serves 10

3½ oz/100 g butterfly pea flowers, washed
5 cups (2¼ lb/1 kg) superfine (caster) sugar
1 teaspoon salt
3 tablespoons lemon juice
ice cubes, to serve

Bring 12⅔ cups (5 pints/3 liters) water to a boil in a pan over medium heat, add the butterfly pea flowers, and boil for about 5 minutes. Add the sugar, salt, and lemon juice and stir for about 5 minutes until the sugar and salt have dissolved. Remove the pan from the heat and let cool slightly. Once cool, strain through cheesecloth (muslin) into a heatproof pitcher (jug) and let cool completely. Serve with ice cubes.

น้ำแก้วมังกรปั่น

Dragon Fruit Frappé

Origin Central
Preparation time 5 minutes
Cooking time 3 minutes
Serves 4

4 dragon fruits, peeled and chopped
8 ice cubes
2 tablespoons honey
2 teaspoons lime juice

Put the dragon fruits into a blender, add the ice cubes, honey, and lime juice and blend until smooth. Serve.

Photo p. 109

น้ำเสาวรส
Passion Fruit Juice

Origin Northeast
Preparation time 5 minutes
Cooking time 5 minutes
Serves 4

1 cup (7 oz/200 g) superfine (caster) sugar
2¼ lb/1 kg passion fruit, halved
1 teaspoon salt
ice cubes, to serve

Bring 1½ cups (12 fl oz/350 ml) water to a boil in a large pan over medium heat. Add the sugar and stir until the sugar has dissolved and the mixture has become syrypy, then remove from the heat.

Strain the passion fruit through a piece of cheesecloth (muslin) into a large heatproof pitcher (jug) and discard the residue. Add the salt and ½ cup (4 fl oz/120 ml) sugar syrup and stir well. Serve cold with ice cubes.

Photo p. 111

น้ำส้มจี๊ด
Kumquat Juice

Origin Central
Preparation time 10 minutes
Cooking time 5 minutes
Serves 6–8

2¼ lb/1 kg kumquats
5 cups (2¼ lb/1 kg) superfine (caster) sugar
1 tablespoon salt
ice cubes, to serve

Wash the kumquats and squeeze the juice into a large pan. Pour in 8½ cups (3½ pints/2 liters) water and stir until mixed. Add the sugar and salt, then bring to a boil over medium heat. Remove from the heat, strain through a piece of cheesecloth (muslin) into a large heatproof pitcher (jug), and let cool. Serve cold with ice cubes.

น้ำใบบัวบก
Asiatic Pennywort Juice

Origin Central
Preparation time 30 minutes
Serves 4

¾ oz/20 g Asiatic pennywort leaves, washed thoroughly
2 tablespoons sugar syrup (see left)
ice cubes, to serve

Put the leaves in a blender, add about 1 cup (9 fl oz/250 ml) recently boiled water, and process until smooth. Strain through a piece of cheesecloth (muslin) into a large heatproof pitcher (jug) to remove the residue.

Carefully pour 1 cup (9 fl oz/250 ml) boiling water over the residue into the pitcher and squeeze the cheesecloth to extract the liquid. Discard the residue. Add the sugar syrup to the juice, stir well, and let cool. Serve cold with ice cubes.

น้ำตะไคร้
Lemongrass Juice

Origin Central
Preparation time 10 minutes
Cooking time 15 minutes
Serves 6–8

7⅓ cups (1 lb 2 oz/500 g) chopped lemongrass stalks
1½ cups (11 oz/300 g) superfine (caster) sugar
⅛ teaspoon salt
ice cubes, to serve

Bring 8½ cups (3½ pints/2 liters) water to a boil in a large pan over medium heat. Add the lemongrass, and simmer for 8–10 minutes. Remove from the heat and strain the lemongrass juice through a piece of cheesecloth (muslin) into a large heatproof pitcher (jug). Add the sugar and salt and stir until dissolved. Pour the lemongrass juice into a clean pan and bring to a boil over medium heat, then remove from the heat and let cool. Serve cold with ice cubes.

Photo p. 112

น้ำใบเตยพร้อมดื่ม

Pandan Juice

Origin Northeast
Preparation time 5 minutes
Cooking time 10 minutes
Serves 4–6

5 x 1¼-oz/30-g pandan leaves, washed and cut
  crosswise into 2–3-inch/5–7.5-cm strips
¼ cup (2 oz/50 g) granulated sugar
a pinch of salt
ice cubes, to serve (optional)

Bring 6 cups (2½ pints/1.4 liters) water to a boil
in a large pan over medium-high heat. Add the
pandan leaves, reduce the heat to medium-
low, and boil for 5 minutes. Add the sugar and
salt and boil for another 2–3 minutes until the
sugar and salt have dissolved. Remove from
the heat and adjust the sweetness to taste. Pour
the mixture through a fine strainer (sieve) into
a heatproof pitcher (jug). Serve hot or cold with
ice cubes.

น้ำกระเจี๊ยบ

Roselle Juice

Origin North
Preparation time 5 minutes
Cooking time 20 minutes
Serves 6–8

7 oz/200 g fresh roselle (or ¾ oz/20g dried roselle),
  cleaned
1 cup (7 oz/200 g) granulated sugar
4 teaspoons salt
ice cubes, to serve

Bring 8½ cups (3½ pints/2 liters) of water to a
boil in a large pan. Add the roselle, reduce the
heat, and simmer gently until the water turns
dark red. Remove the roselle with a slotted
spoon, add the sugar and salt, and bring back
to a boil. Boil for 10 minutes, then remove
from the heat and flavor to taste. Pour into a
heatproof pitcher (jug) and let cool. Serve cold
with ice cubes.

Photo p. 115

น้ำมะขามเปียกพร้อมดื่ม

Tamarind Juice

Origin Northeast
Preparation time 5 minutes, plus soaking time
Cooking time 7 minutes
Serves 4

⅓ cup (3 oz/80 g) peeled and seeded sour
  tamarind pods
¼ teaspoons salt
1¼ cups (9 oz/250 g) granulated sugar
ice cubes, to serve

To make the tamarind puree, soak the
tamarind pods in 1½ cups (12 fl oz/350 ml)
warm water for 15–20 minutes. Use your
hand to squeeze the tamarind and water to
mix and remove the tamarind flesh until you
have quite a thick puree. Strain the tamarind
mixture through a fine strainer (sieve) into a
cup. Set aside.

Bring 4 cups (1⅔ pints/950 ml) water to a
boil in a pan over medium heat. Add the
tamarind puree, salt, and sugar and stir until
the sugar has dissolved, then boil for 4–5
minutes. Remove from the heat. Serve hot
or cold with ice cubes.

น้ำเต้าหู้

Sweetened Soy Milk

Origin Central
Preparation time 10 minutes, plus soaking time
Cooking time 10 minutes
Serves 6

½ cup (5½ oz/160 g) soybeans, peeled
½ cup (3½ oz/100 g) superfine (caster) sugar

Rinse the soybeans until the water becomes
clear, then soak in 3 cups (1¼ pints/750 ml)
water for at least 6 hours. Drain and discard
the soaking water.

Finely pound the soybeans in a mortar with
a pestle, then transfer to a large bowl, pour
in 7 cups (3 pints/1.7 liters) water, and stir
well. Strain through a piece of cheesecloth
(muslin) into a pan, discarding the residue
left in the cheesecloth.

Bring the soy milk to a boil over medium
heat, stirring continuously for 5 minutes. Add
the sugar, reduce the heat to low, and stir for
5–10 minutes or until the sugar has dissolved.
Remove from the heat and serve hot or cold.

Salads

ยำไข่ต้ม
Spicy Egg Salad

Origin Central
Preparation time 10 minutes
Serves 2

4 hard-boiled eggs, peeled and quartered lengthwise
2 shallots, sliced lengthwise
5 red and green bird's eye chiles, finely chopped
2½ tablespoons fish sauce
2 tablespoons lime juice
1½ tablespoons superfine (caster) sugar
1 handful of cilantro (coriander), leaves only

Place the eggs on a serving plate and set aside.

Stir the shallot, chiles, fish sauce, lime juice, and sugar in a large bowl until the sugar has dissolved. Pour the mixture over the eggs, garnish with cilantro (coriander) leaves, and serve.

ส้มตำไข่เค็ม
Spicy Salted Egg Salad

Origin Central
Preparation time 15 minutes
Serves 2

5–6 red bird's eye chiles
3–4 cloves garlic
1 yard-long bean, cut into 3-inch/1¼-cm pieces
3 small tomatoes
1 cup (6 oz/175 g) julienned green papaya
2 tablespoons dried shrimp
1–2 tablespoons lime juice
1 tablespoon jaggery, palm sugar, or soft light brown sugar
1 tablespoon fish sauce
2 salted duck eggs, cut into quarters lengthwise
2 tablespoons roasted peanuts, to garnish

Coarsely pound the chiles and garlic in a mortar with a pestle. Add the yard-long bean, tomatoes, papaya, and dried shrimp and mix together. Season with the lime juice, sugar, and fish sauce and mix well. Add the egg and gently stir with a spoon. Transfer to a serving dish, sprinkle with the peanuts, and serve.

ข้าวยำเกาะยอ

Thai Rice Salad

Origin South
Preparation time 30 minutes, plus soaking time
Cooking time 30 minutes
Serves 6

7 great morinda leaves, chopped
2 cups (14 oz/400 g) jasmine rice, rinsed and drained
2¼ lb/1 kg uncooked shrimp (prawns), peeled and
  deveined
3 cups (8½ oz/240 g) grated fresh coconut
11 oz/300 g rice vermicelli
⅔ cup (5 fl oz/150 ml) coconut milk
½ teaspoon salt
1 tablespoon granulated sugar

For the dressing
1 cup (9 fl oz/250 ml) budu (Southern Thai fish sauce)
¼ cup (2 oz/50 g) jaggery, palm sugar, or soft light
  brown sugar
3 lemongrass stalks, chopped
5 kaffir lime leaves, chopped
2 galangal roots, pounded

Side dishes
2 tablespoons dried chili powder
1 tablespoon ground white pepper
2¼ lb/1 kg sour green mango, julienned
1 handful of skunk vine leaves (optional)
3 cups (11 oz/300 g) finely sliced yard-long beans
10 lemongrass stalks, finely sliced
15 kaffir lime leaves, finely sliced
25 betel leaves, finely sliced

To make the dressing, bring the fish sauce and
1 cup (9 fl oz/250 ml) water to a boil in a pan
over medium heat. Add the sugar, lemongrass,
lime leaves, and galangal and return to a
boil. Reduce the heat to low and simmer for
5 minutes, then remove from the heat. Strain
the liquid through cheesecloth (muslin) into a
clean pan and discard the residue. Return to
the heat and bring to a boil. Reduce the heat
and simmer for another 5–7 minutes or until
thickened and reduced by half. Set aside.

For the rice salad, put the morinda leaves
in a blender and process. Strain through
cheesecloth into a bowl or pitcher (jug). Pour in
2½ cups (1 pint/600 ml) water and stir to mix.

Put the rice into a pan and pour in enough of
the morinda water to cover. Bring to a boil over
medium heat, then simmer for 20 minutes.

Meanwhile, cook the shrimp (prawns) in a pan
of boiling water for 1–2 minutes or until pink.
Drain, pound in a mortar until smooth, then
toast this paste in a wok for 5–7 minutes until
dry. Set aside.

Dry-fry the grated coconut in a clean wok for
3–4 minutes, stirring constantly, until golden
brown. Remove from the heat and set aside.

Soak the vermicelli in a bowl of water for
10 minutes, or according to package directions,
then drain and set aside.

Bring the coconut milk to a boil in a wok over
medium heat. Add the salt, sugar, and noodles
and stir-fry for 3–5 minutes until dry.

Mix all of the rice salad ingredients together
and serve with the dressing and side dishes.

ย่าสาหร่าย
Spicy Seaweed Salad

Origin South
Preparation time 20 minutes, plus soaking time
Cooking time 5 minutes
Serves 20

12 oz/350 g dried Gracilaria seaweed
1 cup (9 fl oz/250 ml) coconut cream
1⅓ cups (12 fl oz/350 ml) Tamarind Puree (see p. 63)
scant 2¼ cups (1 lb 2 oz/500 g) jaggery, palm sugar, or soft light brown sugar
1½ teaspoons salt
½ cup (3½ oz/100 g) shrimp paste
4⅓ cups (1 lb 7 oz/650 g) roasted peanuts, coarsely chopped
scant 1 cup (3½ oz/100 g) dried shrimp, coarsely chopped
1 lb 2 oz/500 g coconut meat, roasted
3½ oz/100 g red and green bird's eye chiles
2⅓ cups (12 oz/350 g) sliced shallots
betal leaves, to serve

Soak the seaweed in a bowl of water for 1 hour, then drain and set aside.

Mix the coconut cream, tamarind, sugar, salt, and shrimp paste together in a large pan. Bring to a boil over medium heat, then remove from the heat and let stand until warm. Add the soaked seaweed, the peanuts, dried shrimp, coconut, chiles, and shallot and mix together. Put a tablespoon of the salad into the center of a betal leaf. Repeat until all the salad is used. Serve.

ลาบปลา
Spicy Fish Salad

Origin Northeast
Preparation time 15 minutes
Cooking time 10 minutes
Serves 8–10

1 x ¼-lb/1-kg sea bass or sea bream, cleaned and filleted
⅓ cup (1¼ oz/30 g) dried chili flakes
2 teaspoons Ground Toasted Rice (see p. 64)
4 shallots, chopped
½ cup (1½ oz/40 g) chopped scallions (spring onions)
⅓ cup (1 oz/25 g) chopped cilantro (coriander)
1 cup (2 oz/50 g) chopped sawtooth cilantro (coriander)
1 tablespoon fish sauce
1½ tablespoons fermented fish sauce
1 tablespoon finely minced galangal
½ cup (2½ oz/65 g) pea eggplants (aubergines), grilled (broiled) and pounded
1 cup (¾ oz/20 g) chopped mint leaves

Finely chop the fish, then cook in a large skillet or frying pan for 2–3 minutes. Set aside.

Mix the chili flakes, ground rice, shallots, scallion (spring onion), cilantro (coriander), and sawtooth cilantro (coriander) together in a bowl. Add the fish, fish sauce, fermented fish sauce, galangal, and eggplant (aubergine), and mix well. Sprinkle with the mint leaves, and serve.

Photo p. 127

ยำปลาทู

Spicy Mackerel Salad

Origin Central
Preparation time 10 minutes
Cooking time 5 minutes
Serves 2

½ cup (4 fl oz/120 ml) vegetable oil
2 x 5 oz/150 g steamed salted horse mackerel
  or 5 oz/150 g smoked mackerel
3 shallots, finely sliced lengthwise
7 red and green bird's eye chiles, chopped
3 lemongrass stalks, finely sliced
1 x ¾-inch/1.5-cm piece fresh ginger, peeled and
  julienned
1½ tablespoons lime juice
2 tablespoons fish sauce
1 handful of peppermint leaves, to garnish

Heat the oil in wok over medium heat. Add
the horse mackerel and fry for 2–3 minutes on
each side. Remove from the wok and let cool.
Remove the skin and bones from the mackerel
and put the flesh into a large bowl. Gently
crumble into small pieces. Add the shallot,
chiles, lemongrass, ginger, lime juice, and fish
sauce and mix well. Transfer to a serving plate
and sprinkle with the mint leaves. Serve.

ยำปลาหมึกยอดมะพร้าว

Spicy Squid and Heart of Palm Salad

Origin South
Preparation time 15 minutes
Cooking time 5 minutes
Serves 4

11 oz/300 g squid, cleaned and cut into 1½-inch/
  4-cm pieces
3½ oz/100 uncooked shrimp (prawns), peeled and
  deveined, tails still intact
5 oz/150 g heart of palm, julienned
½ cup (3 oz/80 g) julienned sour green mango
1 cup (3½ oz/100 g) shredded carrots
1 onion, sliced lengthwise
¼ cup (¼ oz/10 g) chopped cilantro (coriander)
5 scallions (spring onions), sliced lengthwise

For the dressing
2½ tablespoons fish sauce
2 tablespoons lime juice
1½ tablespoons granulated sugar
10 red bird's eye chiles, finely chopped

Blanch the squid in a pan of boiling water
for 2–3 minutes or until cooked. Drain and
set aside.

Blanch the shrimp (prawns) in another pan
of boiling water for 1–2 minutes or until pink,
then drain and set aside.

For the dressing, mix the fish sauce, lime juice,
sugar, and chiles together in a large bowl
until the sugar has dissolved. Add the squid,
shrimp, heart of palm, mango, carrot, onion,
cilantro (coriander), scallion (spring onion)
and mix well. Serve.

Photo p. 128

พล่าปลาหมึกกรอบ
Deep Fried Squid Salad

Origin Central
Preparation time 15 minutes
Cooking time 5 minutes
Serves 2

⅔ cup (3 oz/75 g) all-purpose (plain) flour
2 cups (16 fl oz/475 ml) vegetable oil, for deep-frying
11 oz/300 g squid, cut into ½-inch/1-cm thick rings
2 tablespoons Chili Jam (see p. 35)
2 tablespoons lime juice
2 tablespoons fish sauce
½ teaspoon granulated sugar
1 shallot, sliced
3 kaffir lime leaves, finely sliced
5 red bird's eye chiles, chopped
2 lemongrass stalks, finely sliced
peppermint leaves, to garnish

Whisk the flour and ⅓ cup (2½ fl oz/75 ml) cold water together in a bowl with a wire balloon whisk, until thoroughly combined. Set aside.

Heat the oil for deep-frying in a wok or deep fryer to 350°F/180°C or until a cube of bread browns in 30 seconds. Dip the squid into the batter, then carefully put the squid in the hot oil and deep-fry for 4–6 minutes until golden and crispy. Remove with a slotted spoon and drain on paper towels.

Mix the chili jam, lime juice, fish sauce, sugar, shallot, kaffir lime leaves, chiles, and lemongrass together in a bowl. Add the squid and mix well. Transfer to a serving plate, garnish with peppermint leaves, and serve.

ยำถั่วพู
Spicy Wing Bean Salad

Origin Central
Preparation time 10 minutes
Cooking time 10 minutes
Serves 4

12 uncooked jumbo shrimp (king prawns), peeled and deveined, with tails still intact
20 wing beans
¼ cup (1 oz/25 g) finely sliced dried squid
¼ cup (1½ oz/40 g) cashew nuts
peppermint leaves, to garnish

For the spicy sauce
3 shallots, sliced
1 tablespoon dried chili flakes
2 tablespoons fish sauce
1 tablespoon granulated sugar
3 teaspoons lime juice
1 tablespoon Chili Jam (see p. 35)

Cook the shrimp (prawns) in a pan of boiling water for 1–2 minutes or until they turn pink, then drain and set aside.

Fill a bowl with ice cold water and set aside.

Blanch the wing beans in a pan of boiling water for 30 seconds, then drain and transfer to the ice water for 1 minute. Drain and slice into ¼-inch/5-mm-thick slices and set aside.

To make the sauce, mix all the ingredients together in a large bowl until thoroughly combined. Add the shrimp, squid, cashew nuts, and wing beans and mix well. Transfer to a serving plate, garnish with peppermint leaves, and serve.

ย่าสาทในบาง

Spicy Heart of Palm Salad

Origin South
Preparation time 10 minutes
Cooking time 6–8 minutes
Serves 3

3½ oz/100 g ground (minced) pork
3½ oz/100 g squid, sliced
3½ oz/100 g uncooked shrimp (prawns), peeled
  and deveined
1 cup (3½ oz/100 g) julienned carrots
10 red bird's eye chiles, finely chopped
4–5 shallots, sliced
⅓ cup (2 oz/50 g) chopped Chinese celery stalk
3½ oz/100 g heart of palm, julienned
2 tablespoons fish sauce
2 tablespoons lime juice
1 teaspoon jaggery, palm sugar, or soft light
  brown sugar
lettuce leaves, to serve

Blanch the ground (minced) pork in a pan of
boiling water for 2–3 minutes or until cooked,
then drain and set aside.

Blanch the squid in another pan of boiling
water for 2–3 minutes, then drain and set aside.

Blanch the shrimp (prawns) in a pan of boiling
water for 1–2 minutes or until they turn pink,
then drain and set aside.

Mix the pork, squid, shrimp (prawns), carrots,
chiles, shallots, celery, and heart of palm
together in a large bowl. Add the fish sauce,
lime juice, and sugar and mix well until the
sugar has dissolved. Serve on lettuce leaves.

พล่ากุ้งนาง

Spicy Giant Freshwater Shrimp Salad

Origin Central
Preparation time 5 minutes
Cooking time 4–6 minutes
Serves 2

4 uncooked giant freshwater shrimp (prawns)
3 shallots, finely sliced
1 tablespoon fish sauce
1 tablespoon lime juice
1 tablespoon Chili Jam (see p. 35)
3–5 red bird's eye chiles, finely chopped
2 cilantro (coriander) sprigs, finely chopped

Preheat the broiler (grill) to high. Put the
shrimp on the broiler (grill) rack and broil
(grill) for 2–3 minutes on each side or until
cooked. Let cool slightly, then remove the
shells and press the juices out of the head.
Put the shrimp into a bowl, add the remaining
ingredients, and mix together until thoroughly
combined. Serve.

ยำทะเล

Seafood Salad

Origin Central
Preparation time 15 minutes
Cooking time 7 minutes
Serves 4

5 oz/150 g squid, sliced into ¾-in/2-cm-thick rings
5 oz/150 g uncooked shrimp (prawns), peeled
  and deveined
1 onion, sliced
1 cup (5¾ oz/165 g) julienned sour green mango
1 carrot, thinly sliced
1 tablespoon sliced red and green bird's eye chiles
2 tomatoes, sliced
1 handful of cilantro (coriander), chopped, plus extra
  sprigs to garnish
½ cup (2¾ oz/70 g) Chinese celery stalk, chopped
  into 1¼-inch/3-cm lengths
2 scallions (spring onions), chopped
1 lemongrass stalk, finely sliced (optional)
5 kaffir lime leaves (optional)
lettuce leaves, to serve

For the dressing
1½ tablespoons lime juice
2 tablespoons fish sauce
1 tablespoon granulated sugar
¼ cup (2 fl oz/60 ml) chicken broth (stock) or water

Blanch the squid in a pan of boiling water for
2–3 minutes, then drain and set aside.

Blanch the shrimp (prawns) in another pan of
boiling water for 1–2 minutes, then drain and
set aside.

For the dressing, put the lime juice, fish sauce,
and sugar into a small bowl, add the chicken
broth (stock) or water and stir until the sugar
has dissolved.

Put the shrimp, squid, onion, mango, carrot,
chiles, tomatoes, cilantro (coriander), celery,
scallions (spring onions), lemongrass, kaffir
lime leaves, if using, and the dressing in a large
bowl and stir 3–4 times until all the ingredients
are coated with the dressing. Serve on a bed
of lettuce leaves and garnish with cilantro
(coriander) sprigs.

Photo p. 134

ยำดอกแค

Spicy Salad with Shrimp and Pork

Origin Central
Preparation time 10 minutes
Cooking time 10 minutes
Serves 4

11 oz/300 g uncooked shrimp (prawns), peeled and
  deveined, with tails still intact
7 oz/200 g ground (minced) pork
1 lb 2 oz/500 g vegetable hummingbird flowers,
  stamen removed
10 shallots, chopped

For the dressing
10 red and green bird's eye chiles, chopped
1 clove garlic, chopped
2 tablespoons fish sauce
2 tablespoons lime juice
1 tablespoon granulated sugar

Blanch the shrimp (prawns) in a pan of boiling
water for 1–2 minutes or until pink, then drain
and set aside.

Blanch the ground (minced) pork in another
pan of boiling for 2–3 minutes or until cooked,
then drain and set aside.

Blanch the vegetable hummingbird flowers in
another pan of boiling water for 1 minute, then
drain and set aside.

For the dressing, pound the chiles and garlic in
a mortar with a pestle, then add the fish sauce,
lime juice, and sugar and mix well. Transfer
to a large serving bowl, add the shrimp, pork,
and vegetable hummingbird flowers and mix
well. Stir in the chopped shallots and serve.

Photo p. 133

ยำวุ้นเส้น

Glass Noodle Salad

Origin Central
Preparation time 10 minutes, plus soaking time
Cooking time 5 minutes
Serves 4

1 lb 2 oz/500 g glass noodles
2 oz/50 g pork tenderloin, sliced
2 oz/50 g squid, sliced into ¾-in/2-cm-thick rings
2 oz/50 g fish balls
2 oz/50 g ground (minced) pork
4 fried fish balls
7 slices Chinese fish cake
1 cup (3½ oz/100 g) sliced onion
10 red bird's eye chiles, very finely chopped
1 tablespoon granulated sugar
2 tablespoons lime juice
1½ tablespoons fish sauce
1 tablespoon chopped cilantro (coriander)
¼ cup (1 oz/30 g) sliced Chinese celery stalks
   (cut into 1-inch/2.5-cm pieces)

Soak the noodles in a bowl of water for
10 minutes, then drain and blanch in a pan
of boiling water for 1 minute or prepare
according to package directions, until cooked.
Drain and set aside.

Blanch the sliced pork in a pan of boiling water
for 1–2 minutes, then drain and set aside.

Blanch the fish balls in a pan of boiling water
for 1–2 minutes, then drain and set aside.

Blanch the squid in another pan of boiling
water for 2–3 minutes, then drain and set aside.

Blanch the ground (minced) pork in a pan of
water for 2–3 minutes, then drain and set aside.

Put the noodles in a large bowl, then add the
sliced pork, fish ball, squid, ground pork, fried
fish balls, sliced fish ball, onion, chiles, sugar,
lime juice, fish sauce, cilantro (coriander), and
Chinese celery and mix together. Serve.

ยำกุ้งเสียบ

Spicy Shrimp and Mango Salad

Origin South
Preparation time 10 minutes
Cooking time 5 minutes
Serves 2

5 red bird's eye chiles
4 shallots, sliced
1 tablespoon sliced lemongrass
4 teaspoons chopped cilantro (coriander) leaves
2 teaspoons chopped scallion (spring onions)
4 kaffir lime leaves, thinly sliced
2 tablespoons julienned sour green mango
½ carrot, shredded
2 tablespoon roasted cashew nuts
1 cup (3½ oz/100 g) dried shrimp

For the dressing
2 tablespoons lime juice
2 teaspoons fish sauce
2 teaspoons sugar

To garnish
5 dried red chiles, fried
2 tablespoons Fried Shallot (see p. 64)

To make the dressing, mix all the ingredients
together in a bowl and set aside.

For the salad, mix all the ingredients together
in a large bowl, add the dressing, and mix until
combined. Garnish with the dried chiles and
fried shallot and serve.

ยำผักชี

Cilantro Salad

Origin North
Preparation time 15 minutes, plus soaking time
Cooking time 5 minutes
Serves 2

1 cup (2 oz/50 g) finely sliced cilantro (coriander)
1 cup (2 oz/50 g) pork crackling, cut into small pieces
3 tablespoons Fried Garlic (see p. 64)
3 tablespoons Fried Shallots (see p. 64)
salt

For the chili paste
7 dried red chiles
7 cloves garlic
4 ginger slices
5 shallots, chopped
2 slices galangal
2 lemongrass stalks
3 cilantro (coriander) roots
1 teaspoon shrimp paste
2 tablespoons vegetable oil

For the chili paste, soak the dried chiles in a bowl of warm water for 15 minutes or until rehydrated, then drain and chop.

Pound the chiles, garlic, ginger, shallots, galangal, lemongrass, cilantro (coriander) root, and shrimp paste thoroughly in a mortar with a pestle.

Heat the oil in a wok over medium heat, add the chili paste, and stir-fry for 2 minutes or until fragrant, then remove from the heat.

Put the cilantro (coriander) and the pork crackling in a bowl and mix well. Add the chili paste and a pinch salt, and mix well. Sprinkle with the fried garlic and shallots and serve.

ยำป่าถั่วป่าเขือ

Spicy Yard-Long Bean and Pork Salad

Origin North
Preparation time 10 minutes
Cooking time 15 minutes
Serves 3

1 cup (3½ oz/100 g) water spinach
1 cup (3½ oz/100 g) chopped yard-long beans
2–3 round eggplants (aubergines), chopped
1 cup (6½ oz/180 g) lablab (hyacinth) beans
¼ cup (2 fl oz/60 ml) vegetable oil
10 cloves garlic, chopped
7 oz/200 g ground (minced) pork

For the chili paste
10-15 dried bird's eye chiles, chopped
5 shallots, chopped
10 cloves garlic, chopped
½ teaspoon salt
1 tablespoon shrimp paste

To garnish
2 neem tree tips
10 shallots, finely chopped
2 tablespoons chopped cilantro (coriander)
2 tablespoons chopped scallions (spring onions)
white sesame seeds (optional)

For the chili paste, soak the dried chiles in a bowl of warm water for 15 minutes or until rehydrated, then drain and chop. Pound the chiles, shallot, garlic, salt, and shrimp paste in a mortar with a pestle until smooth.

Blanch the water spinach in a pan of boiling water for 30 seconds, then transfer to a large bowl of cold water. Drain and set aside.

Blanch the yard-long beans in a pan of boiling water for 1 minute, then transfer to the bowl of cold water. Drain and set aside.

Boil the eggplants (aubergines) and lablab beans in separate pans of boiling water for 2–3 minutes, then drain. Coarsely chop the blanched and boiled vegetables and set aside.

Heat the oil in a wok over medium heat. Add the garlic and chili paste and stir-fry for 1 minute. Add the pork and stir-fry for about 3 minutes. Add the cooked vegetables and stir-fry for 2 minutes. Garnish with the tree tips, shallot, herbs, and sesame seeds and serve.

ตับหวาน

Spicy Pork Liver Salad

Origin Northeast
Preparation time 15 minutes
Cooking time 2 minutes
Serves 2

⅓ cup (2½ fl oz/75 ml) chicken broth (stock)
5 oz/150 g pork liver, rinsed, drained, and cut into
  bite-size pieces
2 teaspoons dried chili flakes
1 tablespoon lime juice
1 tablespoon fish sauce
1 shallot, sliced lengthwise
3 scallions (spring onions), finely sliced
2 sawtooth cilantro (coriander) leaves, finely sliced
1 handful of mint leaves
1 tablespoon Ground Toasted Rice (see p. 64)

To serve
Glutinous Rice (see p. 378)
raw or steamed vegetables, such as Chinese greens
  (leaves), cucumber, and napa (Chinese) cabbage

Bring the broth (stock) to a boil in a pan over
medium heat, add the pork liver, and blanch
for 1–2 minutes until medium cooked. Remove
from the heat and add the chili flakes, lime
juice, fish sauce, shallot, scallions (spring
onions), sawtooth cilantro (coriander) leaves,
mint leaves, and ground rice and mix well.
Transfer to a serving plate and serve with rice
and raw or steamed vegetables.

ย่าหนัง

Spicy Dried Buffalo Skin Salad

Origin North
Preparation time 15 minutes, plus soaking time
Cooking time 25 minutes
Serves 3

7 oz/200 g dried buffalo skin, shredded
2 tablespoons vegetable oil
6 cloves garlic, chopped
10 cherry tomatoes, halved
2 tablespoons white sesame seeds
1 tablespoon chopped scallion (spring onion)
1 cilantro (coriander) sprig, to garnish

For the chili paste
5 dried red chiles, seeded
3 shallots, coarsely chopped
5 cloves garlic
½ teaspoon salt
1 teaspoon shrimp paste

Heat the boiler (grill) to medium. Put the
buffalo skin on the broiler (grill) rack and char
to remove the hairs. Soak the skin in a bowl of
water for 3 hours, then drain, transfer to a pan
of boiling water, and boil for 20 minutes or until
tender. Drain and set aside.

For the chili paste, soak the dried chiles in
a bowl of warm water for 15 minutes or until
rehydrated, then drain and chop.

Pound the chiles, shallot, garlic, and salt in
a mortar with a pestle until smooth. Add the
shrimp paste and mix until combined.

Heat the oil in a wok over medium heat, add
the garlic and 1½ teaspoons chili paste and
cook for 1 minute or until fragrant. Add the
tomatoes, buffalo skin, and 2 tablespoons
water and stir-fry for 1–2 minutes. Transfer
to a serving plate, sprinkle with the sesame
seeds, and scallion (spring onion) and garnish
with the cilantro (coriander) sprig. Serve.

ยำเนื้อ

Spicy Beef Salad

Origin Central
Preparation time 20 minutes, plus marinating time
Cooking time 10 minutes
Serves 4

11 oz/300 g thin beef sirloin, tenderloin, or rump steak
2 teaspoons soy sauce
1 cucumber, halved lengthwise and sliced into
  1-inch/½-cm-thick pieces
2 tomatoes, quartered
3 shallots, sliced
1 handful of sawtooth cilantro (coriander), coarsely
  chopped

For the dressing
3 tablespoons fish sauce
3 tablespoons lime juice
1 tablespoon granulated sugar
5 red bird's eye chiles, chopped

Before you begin cooking, check that your
charcoal is glowing white hot, or your gas
grill (barbecue) is preheated to 400°F/200°C.
Alternatively, preheat a conventional indoor
broiler (grill) to medium.

Put the beef in a shallow dish, add the soy
sauce, and turn until coated. Let marinate for
about 10 minutes.

Grill the marinated beef on the charcoal grill
or broiler (grill) rack for 4–5 minutes on each
side. Remove, slice into strips, and set aside.

For the dressing, put the fish sauce, lime juice,
sugar, and chiles in a small bowl and stir until
the sugar has dissolved.

Put the beef, cucumber, tomatoes, shallot, and
cilantro (coriander) in a large bowl and pour in
the dressing. Toss lightly and serve.

ยำถั่วฟู

Peanut Curd in Spicy Salad

Origin North
Preparation time 10 minutes, plus soaking and
cooling time
Cooking time 5 minutes
Serves 2

6⅔ cups (2¼ lb/1 kg) peanuts, peeled
3¼ cups (1 lb 2 oz/500 g) rice flour

For the spicy salad
2 tablespoons Chili Jam (see p. 35)
1 teaspoon salt
1 shallot, sliced
1 garlic bulb, cloves separated and finely sliced
1 cup (5 oz/150 g) shredded pork, fried
1 tablespoon lime juice
1½ teaspoons lemon juice
¼ cup (¼ oz/10 g) finely chopped cilantro (coriander)
6 tablespoons Fried Garlic (see p. 64)
6 tablespoons Fried Shallots (see p. 64)

Soak the peanuts in a bowl of water overnight,
then drain. Grind thoroughly in a mortar with
a pestle until fine.

Bring 8½ cups (3½ pints/2 liters) water and the
ground peanuts to a boil in a large pan over
medium heat. Stir in the rice flour then strain
through cheesecloth (muslin) into a large,
shallow rectangular container. Spread out the
curd mixture and let cool until solidified.

To make the salad, cut the peanut curd into
1-inch/2.5-cm pieces, about ⅛ inch/3–4 mm
thick, and put into a large bowl. Add the chili
jam, salt, shallot, garlic, and pork, and mix
together. Add the lime juice, lemon juice, and
cilantro (coriander) and mix well. Sprinkle with
the fried garlic and shallots and serve.

ย่าพักกาดจอ

Chinese Mustard Green Salad

Origin North
Preparation time 10 minutes
Cooking time 1 minute
Serves 2

1 cup (2¼ oz/60 g) chopped Chinese mustard greens
  (with yellow flowers)
1 tomato, sliced
2 tablespoons chili powder
1 cup (5 oz/150 g) peanuts, roasted
½ cup (2¾ oz/70 g) white and black sesame seeds,
  roasted
1 teaspoon turmeric
1 teaspoon salt
3 tablespoons Fried Garlic (see p. 64)
2 tablespoons Fried Shallots (see p. 64)

Blanch the mustard greens in a pan of boiling water for 1 minute, then drain and plunge into ice cold water.

Mix the remaining ingredients together in a large bowl. Drain the mustard greens, add to the bowl, and mix well. Sprinkle with the fried garlic and shallots. Serve.

ย่ามะเขือยาา

Spicy Eggplant Salad

Origin Central
Preparation time 5 minutes
Cooking time 15 minutes
Serves 2–3

2 x 7-oz/200-g green long eggplants (aubergines),
  cut in half lengthwise
3½ oz/100 g ground (minced) pork
2 tablespoons fish sauce
2 tablespoons lime juice
1 tablespoon granulated sugar
1 shallot, sliced
4 red bird's eye chiles, chopped
1 handful of cilantro (coriander), coarsely chopped

Preheat the broiler (grill) or a ridged grill (griddle) pan to medium-high. Put the eggplants (aubergines) on the broiler (grill) rack or grill pan and broil (grill) for about 10 minutes on both sides until soft and the skin starts to blister. Let cool slightly, then peel off and discard the skin and cut the eggplant halves in half again. Transfer to a serving plate and set aside.

Blanch the ground (minced) pork in a pan of boiling water for 2–3 minutes. Drain but reserve about 2 tablespoons of the leftover cooking water. Put the pork into a bowl with the reserved water, add the fish sauce, lime, sugar, shallot, and chiles and mix well. Pour the pork mixture over the eggplants and sprinkle with the cilantro (coriander). Serve.

ส้ามะเขือ

Spicy Round Eggplant and Pork Salad

Origin North
Preparation time 10 minutes
Cooking time 5–7 minutes
Serves 2

3½ oz/100 g pork loin
½ teaspoon salt
5–7 young round eggplants (aubergines), stems
  discarded
2 tablespoons vegetable oil
7 cloves garlic, chopped
1 tablespoon chopped cilantro (coriander)
1 tablespoon chopped scallion (spring onion)
1 tablespoon chopped peppermint leaves
1 tablespoon chopped Vietnamese cilantro (coriander)

For the chili paste
5 chopped dried red bird's eye chiles
2 shallots, chopped
4 cloves garlic, sliced
2 thin slices galangal
½ teaspoon salt
1 teaspoon shrimp paste

Boil the pork in a pan of boiling water for
3–4 minutes or until cooked. Drain and pat dry
with paper towels and then pound thoroughly
in a mortar with a pestle. Tear the pork into
small pieces and set aside.

Mix 2 cups (16 fl oz/475 ml) water and the salt
together in a bowl, stirring until the salt has
dissolved. Set aside.

Cut the round eggplants (aubergines) in
half lengthwise and then slice lengthwise
into ⅛-inch/3-mm-thick pieces. Soak in the
saltwater mixture for 5 minutes.

For the chili paste, soak the dried chiles in
a bowl of warm water for 15 minutes or until
rehydrated, then drain and chop.

Pound the chiles, shallot, garlic, galangal, and
salt in a mortar with a pestle until smooth. Add
the shrimp paste and mix until thoroughly
combined. Set aside.

Heat the oil in a wok over medium heat, add the
garlic and chili paste, and stir-fry for 1 minute
or until golden brown and fragrant. Add the
pork and 1 tablespoon water and stir-fry for
another 1–2 minutes. Remove from the heat
and set aside.

Drain the soaked eggplants and mix with
the stir-fried chili paste mixture. Sprinkle
with the cilantro (coriander), scallion (spring
onion), peppermint, and Vietnamese cilantro
(coriander) and serve.

ยำสามกรอบไข่แมงดา

Thai Spicy Salad with Giant Water Bug Eggs

Origin South
Preparation time 10 minutes
Cooking time 5 minutes
Serves 4

2 cups (16 fl oz/475 ml) vegetable oil, for deep-frying
¼ cup (1 oz/25 g) finely sliced dried squid
1 cup (2 oz/50 g) dried fish bladder
2 tablespoons fish sauce
2 tablespoons lime juice
1 tablespoon granulated sugar
¼ cup (1½ oz/40 g) cashew nuts, roasted
½ cup (1½ oz/40 g) sliced onions
½ small tomato, sliced
5–7 red and green bird's eye chiles, finely chopped
¼ cup (1 oz/30 g) sweet shrimp (optional)
2 scallions (spring onions), snipped into small lengths
1 cup (3½ oz/100 g) julienned carrots
1 cup (5¾ oz/165 g) julienned sour green mango
1 Chinese celery, chopped
2 tablespoons giant water bug eggs

Heat the oil for deep-frying in a wok or deep fryer to 350°F/180°C or until a cube of bread browns in 30 seconds. Deep-fry the squid and fish bladder for 5 minutes or until crispy, then remove with a slotted spoon and drain on paper towels.

Mix the fish sauce, lime juice, and sugar together in a large bowl. Add the crispy fish bladder and squid, the cashew nuts, then add the onions, tomatoes, chiles, sweet shrimp, scallions (spring onions), carrots, mango, celery, and giant water bug eggs and mix well. Serve.

ต่ำเมี่ยงย่ามดแดง

Spicy Red Ant Salad

Origin Northeast
Preparation time 10 minutes, plus chilling time
Cooking time 6–8 minutes
Serves 2

1 cup (3 oz/80 g) red ants
1 x 1½-inch/3.5-cm piece galangal, peeled and sliced
1 cup (2 oz/50 g) sliced lemongrass stalks
6 red and green bird's eye chiles, finely chopped
½ cup (2 oz/50 g) dried shrimp
½ cup (2¾ oz/75 g) roasted peanuts

For the dressing
1 tablespoon Tamarind Puree (see p. 63)
1 tablespoon jaggery, palm sugar, or soft light brown sugar
2 tablespoons boiled fermented fish sauce
1 teaspoon fish sauce
1 teaspoon shrimp paste
1 teaspoon lime juice
1 teaspoon salt

To serve
wild betel leaves, sliced
star gooseberry leaves, sliced
young jackfruit, peeled and seeded wearing gloves, and cut into chunks

Put the ants in an airtight container and chill in the refrigerator for 30 minutes, then remove and transfer to the freezer for 30 minutes.

Roast the ants in a wok over medium heat for 3–5 minutes until dry. Set aside.

For the dressing, mix the tamarind, sugar, fermented fish sauce, fish sauce, shrimp paste, lime juice, and salt together in a bowl, then transfer to a wok and warm over low heat for 2–3 minutes or until sugar has dissolved. Remove and let cool.

Add all the salad ingredients to the cooled dressing and stir well until combined. Serve with wild betel leaves, star gooseberry leaves, and young jackfruit chunks.

ยำหอยเปบ

Snail and Noodle Salad

Origin Northeast
Preparation time 30 minutes, plus soaking time
Cooking time 15 minutes
Serves 2

14 oz/400 g small freshwater snails
2 oz/60 g dried glass noodles
2 teaspoons white vinegar
1 small banana blossom
1 x 11-oz/300-g snakehead fish or catfish, cleaned
1 tablespoon chili flakes
3 shallots, sliced
1 tablespoon fish sauce
1 tablespoon fermented fish sauce
1 tablespoon granulated sugar
1½ teaspoons lime juice (optional)
1 tablespoon toasted sesame seeds
3 scallions (spring onions), finely sliced
1 handful young pink mempet leaves
  or tamarind leaves, sliced
1 handful chayote shoots or young spinach, sliced
1 handful of mint leaves

To garnish
4–5 spur chiles
2 tablespoons Fried Shallots (see p. 64)

Soak the snails in a bowl of tepid water for 1–2 hours, then drain and set aside.

Soak the noodles in a bowl of water for 10 minutes, then drain and blanch in a pan of boiling water for 1 minute or according to package directions, until cooked. Drain and set aside.

To clean and prepare the banana blossom, fill a large bowl with water and add the vinegar. Peel away and discard the outer red petals from the banana blossom and also the small white strips of banana flower. Cut off the tip and the end of the blossom, then split the blossom in half lengthwise, and cut the pieces in half again. Put the quarters into the bowl of water. Peel and clean each layer of the blossom, and discard the banana flowers inside. Finely slice into ¼-inch/5-mm-thick slices and return to the vinegar water. Repeat until all the leaves have been sliced. Set aside.

Bring 3 cups (1¼ pints/750 ml) water to a boil in a large pan. Add the snails, reduce the heat, and simmer for 5 minutes. Drain, discard the shells, and set aside.

Bring 1½ cups (12 fl oz/350 ml) water to a boil in another pan, add the fish, and cook for 7–10 minutes. Drain, discard the bones and skin, and tear the flesh into small pieces. Set aside.

Pound the chili flakes and shallots together in a mortar with a pestle until smooth. Transfer to a large bowl, add the snails and fish, and mix well. Drain the banana blossom, rinse under cold running water, and drain again. Add to the bowl with the remaining ingredients and mix until thoroughly combined. Garnish with the chiles and fried shallots and serve.

Photo p. 142

ลาบไข่มดแดง

Spicy Red Ant Egg Salad

Origin Northeast
Preparation time 10 minutes
Cooking time 5 minutes
Serves 8

3 cups (12 oz/350 g) red ant eggs
1 tablespoon chili powder
2 tablespoons Ground Toasted Rice (see p. 64)
1 tablespoon fermented fish sauce
1 teaspoon fish sauce
1½ teaspoons salt
2 shallots, sliced
6 scallions (spring onions), sliced
½ cup (1 oz/25 g) sliced cilantro (coriander)
½ cup (1 oz/25 g) peppermint leaves
½ cup (1 oz/25 g) sliced sawtooth cilantro (coriander)
Glutinous Rice (see p. 378), to serve
mixed leafy greens, to serve

Mix the ant eggs, chili powder, toasted rice, fermented fish sauce, fish sauce, salt, and shallots together in a bowl. Add the scallions (spring onions), cilantro (coriander), peppermint leaves, and sawtooth cilantro (coriander) and mix again. Serve with rice and mixed leafy greens.

ส้มผัก

Pickled Vegetable Salad

Origin Northeast
Preparation time 10 minutes
Serves 4

5 red bird's eye chiles
1 cup (4 oz/120 g) sliced pickled mustard greens
2 yellow round eggplants (aubergines), sliced
1 x 1½-inch/3.5-cm piece fresh ginger, peeled and sliced

Leave 3 chiles whole and finely chop the rest, then set aside.

Mix the pickled mustard greens, eggplant (aubergine), and ginger together in a large bowl. Sprinkle with the whole and finely chopped chiles. Serve.

Photo p. 145

ลาบเห็ดหอม

Spicy Shiitake Mushroom Salad

Origin Northeast
Preparation time 15 minutes
Cooking time 5 minutes
Serves 2

9 oz/250 g fresh shiitake mushrooms, stems discarded
1 tablespoon sliced cilantro (coriander)
2–3 small shallots, finely sliced lengthwise
3 kaffir lime leaves, finely sliced
2 scallions (spring onions), finely sliced
4 cloves garlic, thinly sliced
2 sawtooth cilantro (coriander) leaves, finely sliced
1 tablespoon Ground Toasted Rice (see p. 64)
1–2 teaspoons dried chili flakes
1 tablespoon lime juice
1 lemongrass, finely sliced
3–4 red and green bird's eye chiles, finely chopped
1½ tablespoons fish sauce
2 tablespoons chicken broth (stock)
1 tablespoon mint leaves, to garnish
raw vegetables, such as tomatoes, cucumber, lettuce, and cabbage, to serve

Blanch the sliced shiitake mushrooms in a pan of boiling water for 1 minute or until cooked, then drain and pat dry with paper towels. Slice into small ¼-inch/6-mm strips and put in a large bowl. Add the cilantro (coriander), shallot, kaffir lime leaves, scallion (spring onion), garlic, sawtooth cilantro (coriander), ground rice, chili flakes, lime juice, lemongrass, chiles, fish sauce, and chicken broth (stock) and mix well. Garnish with the mint leaves and serve with raw vegetables.

Photo p. 146

ยำเห็ด

Spicy Mushroom Salad

Origin Central
Preparation time 10 minutes
Cooking time 4–6 minutes
Serves 4

3½ oz/100 g ground (minced) pork
8–10 jumbo shrimp (king prawns), peeled and
  deveined
11 oz/300 g mixed mushrooms, such as straw,
  king oyster, and Shimeji mushrooms
3 tablespoons fish sauce
3 tablespoons lime juice
5–6 bird's eye chiles, finely chopped
1½ tablespoons jaggery, palm sugar, or soft light
  brown sugar
1 tablespoon finely chopped scallions (spring onions)
4–5 shallots, finely sliced
1 handful of cilantro (coriander), coarsely chopped,
  to garnish

Blanch the pork in a pan of boiling water
for about 2–3 minutes or until cooked. Drain
and set aside.

Blanch the shrimp (prawns) in another pan
of boiling water for 1–2 minutes, then drain
and set aside.

Blanch the mushrooms in another pan of
boiling water for about 30 seconds, then drain
and set aside.

For the dressing, stir the fish sauce, lime juice,
chiles, and sugar together in a bowl until the
sugar has dissolved. Set aside.

Put the pork, shrimp (prawns), mushrooms,
scallions (spring onions), shallots, and the
dressing in a large bowl and mix well. Transfer
to a serving plate, sprinkle with the cilantro
(coriander), and serve.

Photo p. 148

ลาบเห็ดเข็มทอง

Spicy Pork, Mushroom, and Seafood Salad

Origin Central
Preparation time 10 minutes
Cooking time 5 minutes
Serves 4

4–5 squid, sliced into rings
3½ oz/100 g ground (minced) pork
4–5 uncooked shrimp (prawns), peeled and deveined
3½ oz/100 g golden needle mushrooms
1 teaspoon granulated sugar
2 tablespoons fish sauce
1 tablespoon Ground Toasted Rice (see p. 64)
2 tablespoons lime juice
5 shallots, sliced
1 tablespoon dried chili flakes
½ cup (2 oz/50 g) chopped scallions (spring onions)
½ cup (1 oz/25 g) chopped sawtooth cilantro (coriander)
peppermint leaves, to garnish

Blanch the squid in a pan of boiling water
for 2–3 minutes, then drain and set aside.

Blanch the ground (minced) pork in another
pan of boiling water for 2–3 minutes, then drain
and set aside.

Blanch the shrimp (prawns) in another pan
of boiling water for 1–2 minutes, then drain
and set aside.

Blanch the mushrooms in another pan of
boiling water for 1 minute, then drain and
set aside.

Mix the pork, seafood, mushrooms, sugar, fish
sauce, toasted rice, lime juice, shallots, and
chili flakes together in a bowl until thoroughly
combined. Add the scallions (spring onions)
and sawtooth cilantro (coriander) and mix well.
Sprinkle with the peppermint leaves and serve.

ต่ากั่วผักยาว
Yard-Long Bean Salad

Origin Northeast
Preparation time 5 minutes
Serves 1

2 cloves garlic
5 red bird's eye chiles
1½ cups (5 oz/150 g) coarsely chopped yard-long beans
1½ teaspoons lime juice
1½ teaspoons jaggery, palm sugar, or soft light
  brown sugar
1 salted crab, carapace removed (optional)
1 tomato, quartered lengthwise
1 round eggplant (aubergine), sliced
1 tablespoon dried shrimp
1 tablespoon fermented fish sauce

Finely pound the garlic and chiles in a mortar with a pestle. Add the beans and pound coarsely, then add the lime juice, sugar, salted crab, tomato, eggplant (aubergine), dried shrimp, and fermented fish sauce. Coarsely pound and mix with the pestle until thoroughly combined. Serve.

ส้มตำแตงปลาร้า
Cucumber Salad

Origin Northeast
Preparation time 10 minutes
Serves 2

3–5 red bird's eye chiles
1 clove garlic
1 yard-long bean, cut into 1½-inch/4-cm lengths
2 tomatoes, cut into wedges
1 tablespoon jaggery, palm sugar, or soft light
  brown sugar
1 teaspoon lime juice
1½ teaspoons fish sauce
1½ tablespoons fermented fish sauce
1 small cucumber, shredded
1 salted crab, carapace removed (optional)

Coarsely pound the chiles, garlic, and yard-long bean in a mortar with a pestle. Add the tomatoes, sugar, lime juice, fish sauce, and fermented fish sauce and mix well until the sugar has dissolved. Add the cucumber and crabmeat, if using, and mix gently. Serve.

ต่าแหลก
Mixed Fruit and Vegetable Salad

Origin Northeast
Preparation time 25 minutes
Cooking time 5 minutes
Serves 5

2 teaspoons white vinegar
1 small banana blossom
1 cup (6 oz/175 g) julienned green papaya
1 cup (6 oz/175 g) julienned great morinda fruit
1 cup (5 oz/150 g) star gooseberries
6 scallions (spring onions), sliced
½ cup (1 oz/25 g) chopped cilantro (coriander)
½ cup (1 oz/25 g) chopped sawtooth cilantro (coriander)
2 shallots, sliced
2 tablespoons dried shrimp
2 tablespoons jaggery, palm sugar, or soft light
  brown sugar
1 tablespoon dried chili flakes
½ cup (4 fl oz/120 ml) fermented fish sauce, boiled
2 tablespoons fish sauce
3 tablespoons lead tree seeds
lettuce leaves, to serve

To clean and prepare the banana blossom, fill a large bowl with water and add the vinegar. Peel away and discard the outer red petals from the banana blossom and also the small white strips of banana flower. Cut off the tip and the end of the blossom, then split the blossom in half lengthwise, and cut the pieces in half again. Put the quarters into the bowl of water. Peel and clean each layer of the blossom, and discard the banana flowers inside. Finely slice into ¼-inch/5-mm-thick slices and return to the vinegar water. Repeat until all the leaves have been sliced, then drain, rinse under cold running water, and drain again.

Pound the drained banana blossom, the papaya, great morinda, star gooseberries, scallions (spring onions), cilantros (corianders), shallots, dried shrimp, sugar, chili flakes, fermented fish sauce, fish sauce, and lead tree seeds together in a mortar with a pestle. Serve on a bed of lettuce leaves.

ยำส้มโอ
Pomelo Salad

Origin Central
Preparation time 10 minutes
Serves 4

1⅓ cups (3½ oz/100 g) dry unsweetened (desiccated)
  coconut
⅓ cup (2 oz/50 g) peanuts
1 x 1 lb 2 oz/500 g pomelo
2½ cups (3½ oz/100 g) dried shrimp, rinsed
1 shallot, finely chopped
2 tablespoons fish sauce
3 tablespoons granulated sugar

Dry-fry the coconut and peanuts in a wok over
medium heat for 2–3 minutes or until golden
brown. Remove and set aside.

Peel the pomelo and cut the flesh into
segments. Remove and discard the pith and
membrane, then break the flesh into small
pieces and transfer to a large bowl. Add the
coconut, peanuts, dried shrimp, and shallot
and mix well. Add the fish sauce and sugar
and mix well. Serve.

ยำส้มโอสูตรโบราณ
Spicy Pomelo Salad

Origin Central
Preparation time 15 minutes
Cooking time 15 minutes
Serves 2

10 uncooked shrimp (prawns), peeled and deveined
3½ oz/100 g ground (minced) pork
⅔ cup (1½ oz/45 g) dry unsweetened (desiccated)
  coconut
1½ tablespoons jaggery, palm sugar, or soft light
  brown sugar
½ teaspoon salt
1 tablespoon dried chili flakes
7 tablespoons coconut milk
1 x 11-oz/300-g pomelo or passion fruit
1 cup (2 oz/50 g) dried shrimp, pounded
2 tablespoons peanuts, roasted and crushed
4 cloves garlic, thinly sliced
½ cup (2¾ oz/75 g) cashew nuts
3 tablespoons Fried Shallots (see p. 64)
1 handful of cilantro (coriander), chopped

Cook the shrimp (prawns) in a pan of boiling
water for 1–2 minutes or until pink, then drain
and set aside.

Cook the pork in another pan of boiling water
for 2–3 minutes, then drain and set aside.

Dry-fry the coconut in a skillet or frying pan
over medium heat, stirring frequently, for
1–2 minutes until light brown. Transfer to a
small bowl and set aside.

To make the dressing, put the sugar, salt, chili
flakes, and coconut milk in a bowl and mix until
the sugar has dissolved. Set aside.

Peel the pomelo and cut the flesh into
segments. Remove and discard the pith and
membrane, then break the flesh into small
pieces and transfer to a large bowl. Add
the dried shrimp, cooked shrimp (prawns),
coconut, peanuts, chili flakes, garlic, and the
dressing and gently toss until well mixed.
Transfer to a serving plate, sprinkle with the
cashew nuts, fried shallots, and chopped
cilantro (coriander), and serve.

ส้มตำปลาร้า

Papaya Salad

Origin Northeast
Preparation time 10 minutes
Serves 2

3–5 red bird's eye chiles, sliced
1 clove garlic, sliced
2 tomatoes, sliced
1 tablespoon lime juice
1 tablespoon fermented fish sauce
1½ teaspoons fish sauce
1 teaspoon jaggery, palm sugar, or soft light
 brown sugar
1 salted crab, carapace removed (optional)
1 yard-long bean, cut into 1½-inch/4-cm lengths
1½ cups (9 oz/250 g) shredded green papaya

To serve
Glutinous Rice (see p. 378)
Grilled Chicken (see p. 276)

Coarsely pound the chiles and garlic in a
mortar with a pestle. Add the tomatoes, lime
juice, fermented fish sauce, fish sauce, sugar,
crabmeat, and bean, then use a spoon and
the pestle to lightly pound and mix together
until the sugar has dissolved. Add the papaya
and pound to mix well. Serve with rice and
grilled chicken.

ตำซ่าหนองหาน

Papaya and Fish Salad

Origin Northeast
Preparation time 10 minutes
Cooking time 10 minutes
Serves 4

5 red bird's eye chiles
5 cloves garlic
generous 1 cup (7 oz/200 g) julienned green papaya
¼ cup (1 oz/25 g) bean sprouts
½ cup (2¾ oz/75 g) pickled cabbage, cut into
 small pieces
½ cup (4 fl oz/120 ml) boiled shellfish, cut into
 small pieces
½ cup (1 oz/25 g) dried shrimp
1 cup (5 oz/150 g) cooked fermented rice noodles
5 sawtooth cilantro (coriander) leaves, finely chopped
3 tomatoes, diced
½ cup (2¾ oz/75 g) roasted peanuts
3½ oz/100 g lead tree seed
¼ teaspoon salt
1 tablespoon boiled fermented fish sauce
1 teaspoon fish sauce
1 tablespoon lime juice

Finely pound finely the chiles and garlic in
a mortar with a pestle. Add the papaya, bean
sprouts, pickled cabbage, shellfish, dried
shrimp, fermented rice noodles, cilantro
(coriander), tomatoes, roasted peanuts, and
lead tree seed. Season with the salt, the fish
sauces, and lime juice and mix until thoroughly
combined. Serve.

ส้มตำผักหวาน

Senna Leaf and
Papaya Salad

Origin Northeast
Preparation time 10 minutes
Cooking time 5 minutes
Serves 3

1 cup (2 oz/50 g) senna sophera leaves
3–5 red and green bird's eye chiles
3 cloves garlic
1 tablespoon lime juice
1 teaspoon Tamarind Puree (see p. 63)
1 tablespoon jaggery, palm sugar, or soft light
  brown sugar
1 tablespoon fish sauce
2 tablespoons dried shrimp
1 cup (6 oz/175 g) julienned green papaya
½ cup (7 oz/50 g) julienned carrot
1 tomato, sliced
1 round eggplant (aubergine), sliced
3 tablespoons roasted peanuts
1 salted duck egg, cut into quarters, to garnish
lettuce leaves, to serve

Blanch the senna leaves in a pan of boiling
water for 1 minute, then drain and set aside.

Finely pound the chiles and garlic in a mortar
with a pestle, then season with lime juice,
tamarind, sugar, and fish sauce and adjust so
it's sour, salty, and sweet. Add the blanched
senna leaves, dried shrimp, papaya, carrot,
tomato, eggplant (aubergine), and peanuts and
mix well. Transfer to a serving plate lined with
lettuce leaves, garnish with the salted egg,
and serve.

ส้มตำไทย

Green Papaya Salad

Origin Northeast
Preparation time 10 minutes
Cooking time 5 minutes
Serves 2

3 bird's eye chiles
5 cloves garlic
1 yard-long bean, cut into 1½-inch/4-cm lengths
2 tomatoes, cut into small pieces
1 tablespoon jaggery, palm sugar, or soft light
  brown sugar
1 tablespoon roasted peanuts
1 tablespoon dried shrimp
1 tablespoon lime juice
2 limes, cut into wedges
1 tablespoon fish sauce
⅔ cup (4 oz/120 g) julienned green papaya
Grilled Chicken (see p. 276), to serve

Pound the chiles and garlic together in a mortar
with a pestle, then add the beans and lightly
crush. Add the tomato, sugar, roasted peanuts,
dried shrimp, lime juice, lime wedges, and fish
sauce to the mortar and gently mix together
until the sugar has dissolved. Add the papaya
and mix together. Serve either on its own or
with grilled chicken.

Photo p. 153

ส้มตำปูม้า

Spicy Blue Crab and Papaya Salad

Origin Central
Preparation time 20 minutes, plus freezing time
Cooking time 2 minutes
Serves 2

2 x 11-oz/300-g live blue crabs, cleaned
6–7 red bird's eye chiles
4–5 cloves garlic
2 cups (12 oz/350 g) julienned green papaya
2 small tomatoes, halved
1 yard-long bean, cut into 2–3-inch/5–7.5-cm pieces
1 tablespoon fish sauce
1½ teaspoons jaggery, palm sugar, or soft light
  brown sugar
1–2 tablespoons lime juice
¼ cup (1 oz/25g) cashew nuts, roasted
raw vegetables, such as yard-long beans, and napa
  (Chinese) cabbage, to serve

Put the crabs in the freezer for 20 minutes. Remove and put in a large bowl.

Take 1 crab and place on a cutting (chopping) board. Turn the crab onto its back with its legs facing upward. Raise the tail flap and push a small screwdriver or skewer through the hole underneath. Press firmly down on the screwdriver handle until it hits the other side of the shell. Remove the screwdriver and repeate with the remaining crab.

Remove the crab apron and carapace and rinse until clean. Cut the crabs in half vertically and then cut each piece horizontally again. Remove the crab claws, then crush the claws and set aside. Blanch the crab and crab claws in a pan of boiling water for 2–3 minutes or until cooked, then drain and set aside.

Finely pound the chiles and garlic in a mortar with a pestle. Add the papaya, tomatoes, and yard–long bean and pound again. Add the crabs and lightly pound and stir at the same time with the pestle and a spoon. Add the fish sauce, sugar, and lime juice and mix well. Transfer to a serving plate and sprinkle with the cashew nuts. Serve with raw vegetables.

ตำปลาย่างใส่มะม่วง

Mango Salad with Smoked Dried Fish

Origin Northeast
Preparation time 10 minutes
Serves 2

1 cup (5¾ oz/165 g) julienned sour green mango
2 tablespoons smoked dried fish, finely pounded
1½ teaspoons dried chili flakes
1 tablespoon fermented fish sauce
2 scallions (spring onions), cut into 1½-inch/4-cm
  lengths
½ cup (1 oz/25 g) cilantro (coriander), coarsely
  chopped, plus extra to garnish
2–3 shallots, sliced
1 teaspoon superfine (caster) sugar
1½ teaspoons Ground Toasted Rice (see p. 64)
10 kaffir lime leaves, finely sliced
½ cup (1 oz/25 g) peppermint leaves

To garnish
peppermint leaves, chopped
1 shallot, finely sliced

To serve
raw vegetables, such as pea eggplants (aubergines),
  lettuce leaves, and butterfly pea flowers
basil leaves

Lightly pound the mango, dried fish, chili flakes, fermented fish sauce, scallions (spring onions), cilantro (coriander), shallots, sugar, ground rice, kaffir lime leaves, and peppermint leaves in a mortar with a pestle until well mixed. Garnish with peppermint leaves and the shallot. Serve with raw or steamed vegetables and basil leaves.

Photo p. 155

ยำมะม่วง

Spicy Mango and Coconut Salad

Origin South
Preparation time 10 minutes
Cooking time 5 minutes
Serves 3

2 cups (3½ oz/100 g) dried shrimp
1⅓ cups (3½ oz/100 g) dry unsweetened (desiccated) coconut
½ cup (4 fl oz/120 ml) coconut milk
½ teaspoon salt
1½ tablespoons jaggery, palm sugar, or soft light brown sugar
2 tablespoons shrimp paste
11 oz/300 g sour green mango, peeled and finely sliced
3 shallots, thinly sliced
5–10 red bird's eye or spur chiles

Pound the dried shrimp to fine flakes in a mortar with a pestle. Set aside.

Dry-fry the coconut in a wok over low-medium heat, stirring frequently, for about 2 minutes until golden brown. Let cool.

Stir the coconut milk, salt, sugar, and shrimp paste together in a large bowl until the sugar has dissolved. Add the mango, dried shrimp, toasted coconut, shallots, and chiles and mix well. Transfer to a plate and serve.

ยำทุเรียน

Durian Salad

Origin Central
Preparation time 10 minutes
Cooking time 10 minutes
Serves 2

1 lb 2 oz/500 g young durian
11 oz/300 g ground (minced) pork, cooked
1 carrot, julienned
2 scallions (spring onions), sliced
3 celery stalks, cut into 1-inch/2.5-cm lengths

For the chili sauce
2 tablespoons lime juice
2 tablespoons fish sauce
1 tablespoon salt
2 tablespoons granulated sugar
2 tablespoons finely sliced red and green bird's eye chiles

Peel the durian, cut the flesh into 1½-inch/4-cm lengths, and then again into matchsticks.

For the chili sauce, mix the lime juice, fish sauce, salt, sugar, and chiles together in a bowl.

Put the durian, pork, carrot, scallions (spring onions), and celery in a large bowl, pour the chili sauce over the salad and mix well. Serve.

มะม่วงดิบพริกเกลือ

Mango Salad with Chili Dip

Origin Northeast
Preparation time 5 minutes
Serves 2

2 x 1 lb 2-oz/500-g sour green mango, peeled
1–2 teaspoons chili powder
2 tablespoons granulated sugar
1 teaspoon salt

Slice the mangoes lengthwise into ¼-inch/
5-mm-thick slices, then soak in a bowl of cold
water for 2–3 minutes or until firm and crunchy.

Mix the chili powder, sugar, and salt together
in another bowl. Serve as a dry dip with the
mango slices.

ยำสตรอเบอร์รี่

Spicy Strawberry Salad

Origin North
Preparation time 5 minutes
Serves 3–4

5 red bird's eye chiles
4 cloves garlic, finely chopped
½ cup (4 fl oz/120 ml) lime juice
1 teaspoon fish sauce
2 tablespoons jaggery, palm sugar, or soft light
  brown sugar
½ cup (1 oz/25 g) dried shrimp
20 strawberries, hulled and cut into quarters
1 tomato, finely sliced

Pound the chiles in a mortar with a pestle.

Mix the garlic, lime juice, fish sauce, sugar,
dried shrimp, and chiles together in a bowl.
Add the strawberries and tomatoes and mix
together. Serve.

ส้มตำผลไม้

Spicy Fruit Salad

Origin Central
Preparation time 15 minutes
Cooking time 5 minutes
Serves 3–4

3 red bird's eye chiles
¼ cup (2¼ oz/60 g) jaggery, palm sugar, or soft light
  brown sugar
1¾ tablespoons fish sauce
1½ teaspoons lime juice
1 rose apple, cut into 1¼-inch/3-cm dice
½ cup (2¾ oz/75 g) black grapes
½ green apple, cut into 1¼-inch/3-cm dice
½ cup (3 oz/80 g) pineapple chunks
½ cup (3 oz/80 g) bite-size guava pieces
½ tomato, cut into 1¼-inch/3-cm dice
2 tablespoons dried shrimp

Pound the chiles in a mortar with a pestle
until crushed. Add the sugar, fish sauce,
and lime juice and mix well until the sugar
has dissolved. Add the remaining ingredients
and use a spoon to gently mix the fruits and
the dressing together. Serve.

ยำสับปะรดภูเก็ต

Phuket Pineapple Salad

Origin South
Preparation time 10 minutes
Cooking time 10 minutes
Serves 2

1 pineapple
1 x 2 oz/50 g skinless and boneless chicken breast
8 uncooked shrimp (prawns), peeled and deveined,
 with tails intact
1½ tablespoons dry unsweetened (desiccated) coconut
2 tablespoons roasted peanuts, crushed
2 tablespoons dried shrimp, pounded
2 scallions (spring onions), finely chopped
1 tablespoon Fried Shallots (see p. 64)
lettuce leaves, to serve

For the dressing
1½ teaspoons Chili Jam (see p. 35)
1 tablespoon Tamarind Puree (see p. 63)
1 tablespoon jaggery, palm sugar, or soft light
 brown sugar
1½ teaspoons fish sauce
1½ teaspoons lime juice

To prepare the pineapple, cut off the stem,
then cut across the top, ¾–1¼ inches/2–3 cm
from the crown, and set aside. Use a long thin
knife to cut along the inside of the pineapple
to loosen the flesh, then scoop out the flesh to
leave a hollowed-out pineapple "bowl." Cut
5 oz/150 g of the pineapple flesh into ¾-inch/
2-cm cubes so you have 1 cup and set aside.

Cook the chicken breast in a pan of boiling
water for 2–3 minutes or until cooked. Remove
with a slotted spoon and let cool. Tear into
shreds and set aside.

Cook the shrimp (prawns) in another pan of
boiling water for 1–2 minutes or until pink, then
drain and set aside.

Dry-fry the coconut in a wok over medium heat
for 2–3 minutes or until light brown. Remove
and set aside.

For the dressing, put all the ingredients in
a large bowl and stir until the sugar has
dissolved. Add the pineapple, shrimp, chicken,
peanuts, dried shrimp, coconut, and scallions
(spring onions), and gently mix until combined.
Spoon into a pineapple shell, sprinkle with the
fried shallots, and serve with lettuce leaves.

ยำหัวปลี

Spicy Banana Blossom Salad

Origin Central
Preparation time 15 minutes
Cooking time 5 minutes
Serves 2

2 teaspoons white vinegar
1 banana blossom
10 uncooked shrimp (prawns), peeled and deveined,
 with tails still intact
1 tablespoon Chili Jam (see p. 35)
⅓ cup (2½ fl oz/75 ml) coconut milk
1½ tablespoons granulated sugar
2 tablespoons fish sauce
2 tablespoons lime juice
3–5 red and green bird's eye chiles, chopped
3 tablespoons unsalted roasted peanuts, crushed
1 shallot, sliced
4 tablespoons Fried Shallots (see p. 64), to garnish
1 hard-boiled egg, quartered, to serve

To clean and prepare the banana blossom, fill
a large bowl with water and add the vinegar.
Peel away and discard the outer red petals
from the banana blossom and also the small
white strips of banana flower. Cut off the tip and
the end of the blossom, then split the blossom
in half lengthwise and cut the pieces in half
again. Put the quarters into the bowl of water.
Peel and clean each layer of the blossom and
discard the banana flowers inside. Finely slice
into ¼-inch/5-mm-thick slices and return to
the vinegar water. Repeat until all the leaves
have been sliced, then drain, rinse under cold
running water, and drain again.

Transfer the banana blossom to a pan of boiling
water and blanch for 10–15 seconds. Drain,
rinse under cold running water, drain again,
and set aside.

Cook the shrimp (prawns) for 1–2 minutes in
a pan of boiling water, then drain and set aside.

Mix the chili jam and 3 tablespoons coconut
milk together in a large bowl. Add the sugar,
fish sauce, lime juice, chiles, peanuts, and
shallot and mix well. Add the banana blossom
and shrimp and mix well. Garnish with the
fried shallots and serve with the boiled egg.

ยำจิ๊นไก่ใส่ห้าปลี

Chicken and Banana Blossom Salad

Origin North
Preparation time 20 minutes
Cooking time 15 minutes
Serves 5

2 teaspoons white vinegar
1 banana blossom
2 tablespoons vegetable oil
3 cloves garlic, chopped
⅓ cup (2½ fl oz/75 ml) Larb Chili Paste (see p. 41)
5 shallots, chopped
2 skinless, boneless chicken breasts, chopped into
  bite-size pieces
3 tablespoons chopped sawtooth cilantro (coriander)
3 tablespoons chopped scallions (spring onions)
3 tablespoons chopped cilantro (coriander)
1 tablespoon chopped Vietnamese cilantro (coriander)
10 slices galangal
10 peppermint leaves, torn
10 kaffir lime leaves, torn, to garnish
3 lemongrass stalks, finely chopped, to garnish

To clean and prepare the banana blossom, fill
a large bowl with water and add the vinegar.
Peel away and discard the outer red petals
from the banana blossom and also the small
white strips of banana flower. Cut off the tip and
the end of the blossom, then split the blossom
in half lengthwise, and cut the pieces in half
again. Put the quarters into the bowl of water.
Peel and clean each layer of the blossom, and
discard the banana flowers inside. Finely slice
into ¼-inch/5-mm-thick slices and return to the
vinegar water. Repeat until all the leaves have
been sliced. Set aside.

Heat the oil in a wok over medium heat, add the
garlic and chili paste, and stir-fry for 1 minute
until fragrant. Add 3 cups (1¼ pints/750 ml)
water and bring to a boil. Add the shallots and
chicken, return to a boil, then reduce the heat
and simmer for 5 minutes.

Drain the banana blossom, rinse under cold
running water, and drain again. Add to the wok
and cook for 5 minutes. Add the remaining
ingredients and cook for another 3 minutes.
Sprinkle with the kaffir lime leaves and
lemongrass and serve.

Photo p. 159

ก้อยลิ้นฟ้า

Indian Trumpet Flower Pod Spicy Salad

Origin North
Preparation time 10 minutes
Cooking time 5 minutes
Serves 3

1 Indian trumpet flower pod
1 teaspoon salt
1 teaspoon lime juice
1 teaspoon fish sauce
1 teaspoon Ground Toasted Rice (see p. 64)
1 tablespoon sliced scallion (spring onion)
1 tablespoon chopped sawtooth cilantro (coriander)
1 teaspoon sliced kaffir lime leaves
1 teaspoon chili powder
peppermint leaves, to garnish

Dry-fry the flower pod in a wok over medium
heat for about 5 minutes until toasted. Let cool
slightly, then remove the outer layer of the pod
and rinse under cold running water. Slice into
¼-inch/5-mm pieces.

Put the sliced flower pod, the salt, lime juice,
fish sauce, ground rice, scallion (spring onion),
sawtooth cilantro (coriander), kaffir lime leaves,
and chili powder into a bowl and gently toss.
Sprinkle with the peppermint leaves and serve.

Photo p. 161

Soups

แกงจืดเต้าหู้หมูสับ

Egg Tofu and Ground Pork Soup

Origin Central
Preparation time 10 minutes
Cooking time 15 minutes
Serves 2–3

7 oz/200 g ground (minced) pork
1½ teaspoons Saam-Gler (see p. 41)
3 tablespoons soy sauce
2 cups (16 fl oz/475 ml) chicken or pork broth (stock)
1½ teaspoons salt
2 celery stalks, chopped
1 bunch of cilantro (coriander), leaves only, coarsely
  chopped, to garnish

For the egg tofu
1¼ cups (½ pint/300 ml) soy milk
¼ teaspoon salt
3 eggs

To make the egg tofu, put the soy milk and salt into a bowl, stir to combine, then add the eggs. Use a fork or whisk to beat the eggs and milk together very gently. Try to avoid creating bubbles. Pour the mixture into a shallow dish to a depth of 1½ inches/4 cm. Put the dish in a steamer and steam over very low heat for 12–15 minutes until cooked and firm. Remove and cut into 1¼ x 1¼ x ⅝-inch/3 x 3 x 1.5-cm-thick pieces. (This tofu can be stored in an airtight container in the refrigerator for 2–3 days.)

Put the pork and saam-gler in a large bowl and mix well. Add 1 tablespoon soy sauce and mix again. Shape the mixture into small balls, then place on a plate and set aside.

Bring the broth (stock) and 2 cups (16 fl oz/ 475 ml) water to a boil in a large pan over medium heat. Add the meatballs, reduce the heat slightly, and simmer for 2–3 minutes until the meatballs float to the surface. Add the salt and the remaining soy sauce, stir, and then add the egg tofu and celery. Increase the heat to medium and cook for another 2 minutes. Ladle into soup bowls, garnish with cilantro (coriander), and serve.

Photo p. 171

ต้มส้มปลากระบอก

Mullet Soup

Origin Central
Preparation time 10 minutes
Cooking time 12 minutes
Serves 4

1 x 2¾-inch/7-cm piece fresh ginger, peeled
  and sliced
3-inch/7.5-cm piece galangal, peeled and sliced
1½ lemongrass stalks, sliced
2 shallots, thinly sliced
1 x 1 lb 2 oz/500 g gray mullet or red snapper, cleaned,
  descaled, and cut into 2-inch/5-cm pieces
4–5 red bird's eye chiles, finely chopped
⅓ cup (2½ fl oz/75 ml) mangrove palm vinegar, white
  vinegar, or Tamarind Puree (see p. 63)
½ teaspoon salt

Bring 4 cups (1⅔ pints/950 ml) water to a
boil in a large pan. Add the ginger, galangal,
lemongrass, chiles, and shallots, return to
a boil, and cook for 5 minutes. Carefully add
the fish and cook for another 5 minutes.
Season with the vinegar and salt. Ladle into
soup bowls and serve.

ต้มปลาส้มขนุน

Fermented Fish and Jackfruit Soup

Origin Central
Preparation time 10 minutes
Cooking time 15 minutes
Serves 4

1 shallot, chopped
2 cloves garlic, chopped
¼ cup (1½ oz/40 g) chopped fingerroot
1 lemongrass stalk, chopped
1 broiled (grilled) sea bass, or sea bream, cut into
  bite-size pieces
4¼ cups (1¾ pints/1 liter) coconut milk
3½ oz/100 g fermented fish, bones removed
11 oz/300 g pork side (belly), diced
2¼ lb/1 kg young jackfruit, peeled and seeded
  wearing gloves, and cut into 1-inch/2.5-cm slices
1 teaspoon salt
3 tablespoons fish sauce
scant ½ cup (3½ oz/100 g) jaggery, palm sugar, or soft
  light brown sugar
4 teaspoons Tamarind Puree (see p. 63)
10 kaffir lime leaves

Pound the shallots, garlic, fingerroot, and
lemongrass thoroughly in a mortar with a
pestle until smooth. Add the broiled (grilled)
fish and pound until combined.

Bring the coconut milk to a boil in another pan
over medium heat, add the pounded fish paste
and the fermented fish, return to a boil, and add
the pork. Return to a boil and add the jackfruit,
then continue to boil for 5 minutes until cooked.
Add the salt, fish sauce, sugar, tamarind, and
kaffir lime leaves and stir. Ladle into soup
bowls and serve.

ปลาทูต้มเค็ม

Spicy-and-Sour Mackerel Soup

Origin Central
Preparation time 5 minutes
Cooking time 10 minutes
Serves 4

5 cups (2 pints/1.2 liters) chicken broth (stock)
¼ teaspoon salt
1 lemongrass stalk, crushed and sliced
3 cloves garlic, coarsely pounded
4 kaffir lime leaves, torn
3 tablespoons fish sauce
3 tablespoons lime juice
4 x 14 oz–1 lb 2 oz/400–500 g horse mackerel,
  cleaned and descaled
10 green and red bird's eye chiles, sliced
2 tablespoons chopped cilantro (coriander)

Bring the broth (stock) to a boil in a large
pan over medium heat. Add the salt,
lemongrass, garlic, and kaffir lime leaves
and boil for 2–3 minutes. Add the fish sauce
and lime juice, then stir and increase the
heat to high. Add the mackerel and return
to a boil without stirring, then reduce the
heat to medium-low and cook for another
2–3 minutes. Add the chiles and cilantro
(coriander) and stir. Ladle into soup bowls
and serve hot.

ต้มส้มปลาทู

Sweet-and-Sour Mackerel Soup

Origin Central
Preparation time 10 minutes
Cooking time 10 minutes
Serves 2–3

3 cilantro (coriander) roots, chopped
½ teaspoon salt
1 teaspoon shrimp paste
4 shallots, chopped
3½ cups (1¾ pints/800 ml) fish broth (stock) or water
4 tablespoons Tamarind Puree (see p. 63)
1 tablespoon granulated sugar
1 tablespoon fish sauce
5 small whole mackerels, cleaned and descaled
1 x 1-inch/2.5-cm piece fresh ginger, peeled
  and julienned
¼ cup (1 oz/25 g) chopped scallions (spring onions)
5 dried red chiles, seeded

Pound the cilantro (coriander) roots, salt,
shrimp paste, and shallots together in a mortar
with a pestle.

Bring the broth (stock) or water to a boil in a
large pan over medium heat. Add the pounded
mixture, stir, and return to a boil. Add the
tamarind, sugar, and fish sauce and return to
a boil. Add the mackerel and cook for about
10 minutes. Add the ginger and scallions
(spring onions) and stir. Ladle into soup bowls,
sprinkle with the dried chiles, and serve.

ปลากระพงต้มสมุนไพร

Sea Bass in Herb Soup

Origin South
Preparation time 10 minutes
Cooking time 6–8 minutes
Serves 2

2 tablespoons fish sauce
½ tablespoon shrimp paste
4 shallots, chopped
3 cloves garlic, chopped
2 tablespoons tamarind sauce
1 teaspoon jaggery, palm sugar, or soft light
  brown sugar
1 lb 2 oz/500 g sea bass fillets, cut into bite-size chunks
20 sweet basil leaves
20 star gooseberry leaves
20 hairy basil leaves

Bring 2 cups (16 fl oz/475 ml) water to a boil
in a large pan. Add the fish sauce, shrimp
paste, shallots, and garlic and return to a boil.
Add the tamarind sauce and sugar and return
to a boil, then add the sea bass and cook for
3–5 minutes. Remove from the heat and add the
sweet basil, star gooseberry, and hairy basil
leaves. Ladle into soup bowls and serve.

ปลากะพงต้มกระวาน

Sea Bass Soup with Cardamom Shoots

Origin Central
Preparation time 10 minutes
Cooking time 10 minutes
Serves 4

1 x 1 lb 2 oz/500 g sea bass fillet, cut into 1½-inch/
  4-cm pieces
7 oz/200 g Siam cardamom shoots, cut into ½-inch/
  4-cm lengths
7 oz/200 g salacca (snake fruit), peeled
2–3 kaffir lime leaves, torn
1 tablespoon fish sauce
1 teaspoon lime juice
3–5 green bird's eye chiles, chopped
1 small handful of cilantro (coriander), chopped

Bring a large pan of water to a boil and add
the sea bass, cardamom shoots, and salacca
(snake fruit). Return to a boil and add the kaffir
lime leaves, fish sauce, lime juice, chiles, and
cilantro (coriander) and cook for 3–4 minutes.
Ladle into soup bowls and serve.

บะหมี่ต้มยำ

Spicy-and-Sour Soup with Egg Noodles

Origin South
Preparation time 10 minutes
Cooking time 10 minutes
Serves 2

4 oz/120 g sea bass fillets, skinned
3½ oz/100 g egg noodles
6 slices galangal
4 kaffir lime leaves, torn
2 lemongrass stalk, chopped
2 shallots, halved
4 straw mushrooms, halved
2 tomatoes, quartered
1 x 3½ oz/100 g squid, halved and tentacles removed
4 uncooked shrimp (prawns), peeled and deveined,
    tails still intact
2 tablespoons Chili Jam (see p. 35)
½ teaspoon salt
2 tablespoons lime juice
2 tablespoons fish sauce
3 tablespoons milk
3 cups (1¼ pints/750 ml) chicken broth (stock)
2 sprigs cilantro (coriander)

Rinse the sea bass and pat dry with paper towels. Pour enough water into a large pan to cover the sea bass by about 1 inch/2.5 cm and bring to a boil. Put the fish into the water and reduce the heat to low. Simmer for 2–3 minutes until cooked. Drain.

Meanwhile, cook the noodles in a pan of boiling water for 1 minute or according to package directions, then drain, put into a serving bowl, and set aside.

Put the galangal, lime leaves, lemongrass, shallots, mushrooms, tomato, squid, shrimp (prawns), and fish into a large pan and mix well. Add the chili jam, salt, lime juice, fish sauce, and milk. Pour in the chicken broth (stock), bring to a simmer, and cook for about 3 minutes or until hot. Pour the soup over the noodles, garnish with cilantro (coriander), and serve.

ข้าวต้มปลากะพง

Sea Bass and Rice Soup

Origin Central
Preparation time 10 minutes, plus soaking time
Cooking time 10 minutes
Serves 3

5 dried shiitake mushrooms
2 cups (16 fl oz/475 ml) chicken broth (stock)
2 thin slices galangal, pounded
2 cloves garlic
1 teaspoon ground black pepper
1 x 11-oz/300-g sea bass, cleaned, filleted, and cut into
    1¼–1½-inch/3–4-cm slices and bones reserved
1 tablespoon soy sauce
1 teaspoon fish sauce
1½ cups (9¼ oz/260 g) cooked long-grain rice
¼ cup (1¼ oz/30 g) chopped Chinese celery

To garnish
3 tablespoons Fried Garlic (see p. 64)
2–3 scallions (spring onions), chopped
1 handful of cilantro (coriander), chopped
2-inch/5-cm piece fresh ginger, peeled and julienned

Soak the shiitake mushrooms in a bowl of warm water for 15 minutes, then squeeze to drain and cut into quarters. Set aside.

Bring the chicken broth (stock) and 1½ cups (12 fl oz/350 ml) water to a boil in a large pan over high heat. Add the galangal, garlic, black pepper, and the fish bones and boil for 4–5 minutes without stirring. Strain through a fine strainer (sieve) into a clean pan. Return to a boil over medium heat, then add the soy sauce, fish sauce, and shiitake mushrooms and stir. Return to a boil again, then add the sea bass. Cook for 2 minutes, without stirring, or until the fish is cooked. Add the rice and celery and boil for another 1–2 minutes. Ladle into soup bowls, garnish with the fried garlic, scallions (spring onions), cilantro (coriander), and ginger, and serve.

ต้มยำปลาช่อนใส่สายบัว

Spicy Snakehead Fish and Lotus Stem Soup

Origin Central
Preparation time 10 minutes
Cooking time 10 minutes
Serves 4

3 lemongrass stalks, cut into 1-inch/2.5-cm pieces
4–5 slices galangal
6 kaffir lime leaves
3–5 shallots, sliced
2 tablespoons Tamarind Puree (see p. 63)
1 teaspoon salt
1 x 1¾-lb/800-g snakehead fish or catfish, cleaned, descaled, and cut into 1-inch/2.5-cm pieces
2 cups (7 oz/200g) peeled and sliced lotus stem
2 tablespoons fish sauce
2 tablespoons lemon juice
4–5 dried red chiles, seeded and chopped
2 sawtooth cilantro (coriander) sprigs, chopped, to garnish

Bring 4 cups (1⅔ pints/950 ml) water to a boil in a large pan over medium heat. Add the lemongrass, galangal, kaffir lime leaves, shallots, tamarind, and salt and bring to a boil. Add the fish and lotus stem and cook for about 8 minutes, then remove from the heat and set aside. Add the fish sauce, lemon juice, and chiles. Ladle into soup bowls, garnish with the cilantro (coriander), and serve.

Photo p. 177

แกงผักเซียงดา

Spicy Vegetable Soup

Origin North
Preparation time 10 minutes, plus soaking time
Cooking time 7 minutes
Serves 2

1½ cups (12 fl oz/350 ml) vegetable broth (stock)
2 oz/50 g chopped dried snakehead fish
3½ oz/100 g chayote shoots or young spinach
5 cherry tomatoes

For the chili paste
5 dried red chiles
5 cloves garlic, sliced
5 shallots, chopped
1 teaspoon salt
1 teaspoon shrimp paste

For the chili paste, soak the dried chiles in a bowl of warm water for 15 minutes or until rehydrated, then drain and chop.

Pound the chiles, garlic, shallot, and salt in a mortar with a pestle until smooth. Add the shrimp paste and mix to combine. Set aside.

Bring the broth (stock) to a boil in a large pan over medium heat, add the chili paste, and stir until dissolved. Add the dried snakehead fish, then return to a boil. Reduce the heat and simmer for 5–7 minutes or until the fish has softened. Add the chayote shoots or young spinach and cherry tomatoes, and continue to simmer, stirring occasionally, for 3–4 minutes. Ladle into soup bowls and serve.

ต้มส้มปลาแซลมอน

Salmon Sour Soup

Origin South
Preparation time 10 minutes
Cooking time 5–7 minutes
Serves 2

generous 1 cup (9½ fl oz/275 ml) fish or chicken
  broth (stock)
4 shallots, crushed
2 x 1½ oz/40 g salmon fillets, cut into ½-inch/
  1-cm-thick slices
1 x 2-inch/5-cm piece fresh ginger, peeled
  and julienned
2 teaspoons Tamarind Puree (see p. 63)
1 tablespoon jaggery, palm sugar, or soft light
  brown sugar
2 tablespoons fish sauce
2 scallions (spring onions), cut into ¾-inch/
  2-cm-long pieces
4 dried red chiles, seeded, to garnish

For the paste
½ teaspoon black peppercorns
3 shallots, chopped
2 cilantro (coriander) roots, chopped
½ teaspoon shrimp paste

For the paste, pound the black pepper, shallots,
and cilantro (coriander) roots in a mortar with
a pestle until smooth. Add the shrimp paste
and mix until thoroughly combined. Set aside.

Bring the broth (stock) to a boil in a large
pan over medium heat. Add the paste and
crushed shallots and boil for 1–2 minutes. Add
the salmon and ginger, return to a boil, then
reduce the heat and simmer for 2–3 minutes.
Add tamarind, sugar, and fish sauce, then add
the scallions (spring onions). Ladle into a soup
bowl, garnish with the dried chiles, and serve.

แกงเหลืองปลาใส่ผัก

Very Spicy Papaya and Young Coconut Soup

Origin South
Preparation time 15 minutes, plus soaking time
Cooking time 10 minutes
Serves 6

juice of 2 limes, strained
1 lb 5 oz/600 g mixed fruit, such as young papaya,
  young coconut meat, ripe banana, pineapple, and
  pickled bamboo
2¼ lb/1 kg sea bass, mullet, or king mackerel fillets,
  cut into 1–2-inch/2.5–5-cm pieces
1 tablespoon salt
1 tablespoon jaggery, palm sugar, or soft light
  brown sugar

For the chili paste
2 oz/50 g dried red chiles, seeded
2 oz/50 g red bird's eye chiles, chopped
⅓ cup (1½ oz/40 g) chopped turmeric root
1 garlic bulb, cloves separated and chopped
3 shallots, chopped
1½ tablespoons shrimp paste

For the chili paste, soak the dried chiles in
a bowl of warm water for 15 minutes or until
rehydrated, then drain and chop.

Pound the dried and fresh chiles, the turmeric,
garlic, and shallots in a mortar with a pestle
until smooth. Add the shrimp paste and mix
until thoroughly combined.

Bring 8½ cups (3½ pints/2 liters) water to a boil
in a large pan. Add the chili paste and lime
juice, return to a boil, then add all the fruits.
Return to a boil again and add the fish. Cook for
5 minutes. Season with the salt and sugar, ladle
into soup bowls, and serve.

แกงเลียงสมุนไพร

Spicy Vegetable and Fish Soup

Origin Central
Preparation time 10 minutes
Cooking time 10 minutes
Serves 4

1 x 1¾-lb/800-g whole snakehead fish
5 cups (2 pints/1.2 liters) chicken broth (stock)
1 tablespoon fish sauce
1 cup (3½ oz/100 g) pumpkin slices (⅛ x 1-inch/
   1 x 2.5-cm slices)
½ cup (3 oz/80 g) baby corn
3½ oz/100 g straw mushrooms halved
1 x 7-oz/200 g angled gourd, peeled, halved, and
   chopped into ¾-inch/2-cm-thick pieces
10–15 young Ceylon spinach or ordinary spinach
1 handful of young ivy gourd leaves (optional)
2 handfuls of sweet basil leaves

For the chili paste
3 red bird's eye chiles
½ teaspoon salt
1 teaspoon white peppercorns
3 fingerroots
3 shallots chopped
2 teaspoons shrimp paste

Preheat the boiler (grill) to medium-high,
place the fish on the broiler (grill) rack, and
broil (grill) for about 10 minutes on each side.
Remove the meat and discard the skin and
bones. Set aside.

For the chili paste, pound the chiles, salt,
peppercorns, fingerroot, shallots, and shrimp
paste together thoroughly in a mortar with
a pestle. Add the fish and pound again until
smooth. Set aside.

Bring the chicken broth (stock) to a boil in
a pan over high heat. Add the chili paste and
fish sauce and return to a boil. Reduce the
heat to medium, add the pumpkin and baby
corn and return to a boil for 5 minutes. Add the
mushrooms, angled gourd, Ceylon spinach,
ivy gourd leaves, if using, and basil. Serve.

ต้มส้มปลานิล

Spicy-and-Sour Tilapia Soup

Origin Northeast
Preparation time 10 minutes
Cooking time 15 minutes
Serves 4

5 cups (2 pints/1.2 liters) chicken broth (stock)
1 teaspoon salt
7 thin slices galangal
2 lemongrass stalks, coarsely crushed and cut into
2-inch/5-cm lengths
5 kaffir lime leaves
4–5 shallots, roughly crushed
3 cloves garlic
3 tablespoons fish sauce
3 tablespoons lime juice
5 cherry tomatoes
1 x 1-lb 5-oz/600-g tilapia, cleaned, filleted, and cut
   into bite-size pieces
10–15 red and green bird's eye chiles, pounded
½ cup (1 oz/25 g) finely chopped cilantro (coriander)

Bring the broth (stock) and salt to a boil in a
pan over medium-high heat. Add the galangal,
lemongrass, kaffir lime, shallots, and garlic and
return to a boil for about 2 minutes. Add the fish
sauce, lime juice, and tomatoes and return to
a boil. Add the fish and cook for 3–4 minutes,
without stirring, until cooked. Stir in the chiles
and finely chopped cilantro (coriander), ladle
into soup bowls, and serve.

ต้มเปรตปลาไหล

Spicy Eel Soup

Origin Northeast
Preparation time 10–15 minutes
Cooking time 15 minutes
Serves 4

2 cups (16 fl oz/475 ml) fish or chicken broth (stock)
3 fingerroots, peeled and coarsely pounded
4 kaffir lime leaves, torn
5 thin slices galangal
3 lemongrass stalks, diagonally sliced into 1½-inch/
   4-cm-length pieces
4 cloves garlic, coarsely crushed
5 small shallots
2 teaspoons dried bird's eye chili powder
11 oz/300 g eel, cleaned, and cut into 2-inch/
   5-cm-length pieces
3 tablespoons fish sauce
2 tablespoons Tamarind Puree (see p. 63)
1 cup (2 oz/50 g) sweet basil leaves (optional)

Bring the broth (stock) and 2 cups (16 fl oz/
475 ml) water to a boil in a large pan. Add the
fingerroot, kaffir leaves, galangal, lemongrass,
garlic, shallots, and chili powder and return
to a boil. Add the eel and return to a boil again.
Add the fish sauce and tamarind puree and
boil for another 7–10 minutes or until the fish is
tender. Add the basil leaves (if using) and stir.
Ladle into soup bowls and serve.

ต้มยำกุ้ง

Spicy Shrimp Soup

Origin Central
Preparation time 10 minutes
Cooking time 7–10 minutes
Serves 4

2 cups (16 fl oz/475 ml) chicken broth (stock)
1 teaspoon salt
10 thin slices galangal
4 kaffir lime leaves, torn
5–7 lemongrass stalks, sliced diagonally into
   1¼-inch/3-cm lengths
½ onion, sliced
2 tomatoes, quartered
5 oz/150 g straw mushrooms, halved
12 uncooked jumbo shrimp (king prawns), peeled
   and deveined
3 tablespoons lime juice
5 green bird's eye chiles, crushed
¼ teaspoon granulated sugar
2 tablespoons fish sauce
3 small shallots, crushed

To garnish
1 handful of cilantro (coriander) chopped
3 scallions (spring onions), cut into 1½-inch/
   4-cm lengths

Pour the chicken broth (stock) and 2 cups
(16 fl oz/475 ml) water into a large pan, add
the salt, and bring to a boil over medium
heat. Add the galangal, kaffir lime leaves,
and lemongrass and return to a boil for
1–2 minutes. Add the onion and tomatoes,
bring to a boil again, and add the mushrooms
and shrimp (prawns). Boil for 1 minute or until
the shrimp are cooked. Add the lime juice,
chiles, sugar, fish sauce, and shallots and
stir. Ladel into soup bowls, garnish with the
cilantro (coriander) and scallions (spring
onions), and serve.

Photo p. 181

ต้มกะทิผักเหมียงกุ้งสด

Melinjo Leaf and Shrimp in Coconut Milk Soup

Origin South
Preparation time 5 minutes
Cooking time 5 minutes
Serves 2

2 cups (16 fl oz/475 ml) coconut milk
1 tablespoon shrimp paste
1 teaspoon granulated sugar
½ teaspoon salt
1 handful of melinjo leaves or young spinach
4–5 uncooked shrimp (prawns), peeled and deveined,
  tails still intact

Bring the coconut milk to a boil in a large pan.
Add the shrimp paste, sugar, and salt, then stir
and return to a boil. Add the melinjo leaves and
shrimp (prawns), bring to a boil, then reduce
the heat and simmer for 2 minutes or until the
shrimp are cooked. Ladle into soup bowls
and serve.

Photo p. 182

แกงเลียงสมุนไพรสดผักราม

Spicy Vegetable Soup with Shrimp

Origin Central
Preparation time 10 minutes, plus soaking time
Cooking time 7–10 minutes
Serves 4

1 tablespoon fish sauce
1 teaspoon salt
1 tablespoon granulated sugar
1⅔ cups (7 oz/200 g) uncooked shrimp (prawns),
  peeled and deveined, with tails intact
4 cups (1 lb 2 oz/500 g) diced Thai pumpkin
1 whole angled loofah (luffa), diced
2 young watermelons, diced
2 waxy corns (seeds only)
1 lb 2 oz/500 g bottle gourd, diced
5 cups (7 oz/200 g) dried shrimp
½ cup (1 oz/25 g) lemon basil leaves

For the chili paste
5 dried red chiles, seeded
2 tablespoons chopped fingerroot
1 tablespoon black peppercorns
7 shallots, chopped
1 tablespoon shrimp paste
2 tablespoons dried shrimp

For the chili paste, soak the dried chiles in
a bowl of warm water for 15 minutes or until
rehydrated, then drain and chop.

Pound the chiles, fingerroot, peppercorns, and
shallots in a mortar with a pestle until smooth.
Add the shrimp paste and mix until combined.

Bring 2 cups (16 fl oz/475 ml) water and the
chili paste to a simmer in a pan over low heat.
Add the fish sauce, salt, and sugar and stir well.
Add the pumpkin, angled loofah, watermelons,
corn, bottle gourd, and dried shrimp and stir
well. Cook for 7–10 minutes. Add the lemon
basil leaves and serve.

ต้มจืดปลาหมึกยัดไส้

Stuffed Squid Soup

Origin South
Preparation time 20 minutes, plus marinating time
Cooking time 10 minutes
Serves 2

10 cloves garlic, chopped
1 teaspoon white peppercorns
4 oz/120 g ground (minced) pork
1 tablespoon soy sauce, plus 1 teaspoon
7–9 oz/200–250 g small squid, cleaned, tentacles
  removed but kept
2 cups (16 fl oz/475 ml) pork or chicken broth (stock)
2 cilantro (coriander) roots, crushed
¼ teaspoon salt
⅓ cup (1½ oz/40 g) sliced Chinese celery

Pound the garlic and peppercorns in a
mortar with a pestle until smooth. Transfer to
a large bowl, add the pork and 1 teaspoon soy
sauce, and mix well. Cover with plastic wrap
(clingfilm) and let marinate in the refrigerator
for 10–15 minutes.

Insert the pork into the squid cavity, then lightly
score the squid 1–2 times.

Pour the broth (stock) and 1½ cups (12 fl oz/
350 ml) water into a large pan. Add the cilantro
(coriander) root and salt and bring to a boil
over medium heat. Add the squid and tentacles
and cook for 5–7 minutes or until cooked. Add
the remaining soy sauce and the celery, and
stir a couple times. Remove from the heat, ladle
into soup bowls, and serve.

แกงจืดปลาหมึกแห้งซี่โครงหมูหัวไชเท้า

Dried Squid, Pork Rib, and Radish Soup

Origin South
Preparation time 10 minutes, plus soaking time
Cooking time 35–40 minutes
Serves 4

2 x 2-oz/50-g dried squid, sliced crosswise
  into ¾-inch/2-cm-wide pieces
1 teaspoon salt
1 teaspoon black peppercorns
2 cilantro (coriander) roots, roughly crushed
14 oz/400 g soft-bone pork ribs cleaned and chopped
  into 1¼-inch/3-cm pieces
14 oz/400 g daikon (mooli) radish, peeled, halved
  lengthwise, and cut crosswise into ¾-inch/
  2-cm-thick pieces
1 tablespoon soy sauce
1 cilantro (coriander) sprig, coarsely chopped
3 scallions (spring onions), chopped into 1½-inch/
  4-cm lengths

Soak the dried squid in a bowl of water for
10 minutes, then drain and set aside.

Bring 4 cups (1⅔ pints/950 ml) water, the salt,
peppercorns, and cilantro (coriander) roots to
a boil in a pan over medium heat. Add the pork
and boil for 4–5 minutes, then add the daikon
(mooli) and boil for another 4–5 minutes. Add
the soy sauce and soaked squid, reduce the
heat to low, cover with a lid, and simmer for
another 25–30 minutes until the pork is tender.
Ladle into soup bowls, sprinkle with cilantro
(coriander) and scallions (spring onions),
and serve.

ก๋วยเตี๋ยวปลา
Fish Noodle Soup

Origin Central
Preparation time 15 minutes, plus soaking time
Cooking time 35 minutes
Serves 4

7–11 oz/200–300 g dried rice noodles
11 oz/300 g fish balls
2 cups (7 oz/200 g) bean sprouts
1 Chinese fish cake, sliced
½ cup (1 oz/25 g) finely chopped scallions
   (spring onions)
½ cup (1 oz/25 g) finely sliced cilantro (coriander)
2 tablespoons Fried Garlic (see p. 64)

For the soup
7 cups (2¾ pints/1.6 liters) chicken broth (stock)
3 cilantro (coriander) roots
2 cloves garlic, coarsely crushed
1 teaspoon black peppercorns
1 teaspoon salt
1 tablespoon soy sauce
1½ teaspoons rock sugar

Soak the noodles in a bowl of water for
10 minutes, then drain and blanch in a pan
of boiling water for 1 minute or prepare
according to package directions, until cooked.
Drain and set aside.

Blanch the fish balls in a pan of boiling water
for 2 minutes. Remove with a slotted spoon
and set aside.

For the soup, put the broth (stock) into a pan
over medium heat, add the cilantro (coriander)
roots, garlic, black pepper, salt, soy sauce,
and sugar. Bring to a boil, then reduce the
heat to low and simmer for 10 minutes or
until fully flavored.

Divide the noodles and bean sprouts among
serving bowls. Pour 1½ cups (12 fl oz/350 ml)
of the soup into each bowl and top with the
fish balls, fish cake, scallions (spring onions),
cilantro (coriander), and fried garlic. Serve.

แกงอ่อม
Spicy Buffalo Meat Soup

Origin North
Preparation time 10 minutes, plus soaking time
Cooking time 35 minutes
Serves 6

2¼ lb/1 kg buffalo meat or beef brisket, diced
1 lemongrass stalk, chopped
7 slices galangal
5 kaffir lime leaves, torn
1 tablespoon chopped cilantro (coriander)
1 tablespoon chopped scallions (spring onions)
2 tablespoons chopped sawtooth cilantro (coriander)

For the chili paste
9 dried red chiles
1 teaspoon Sichuan peppercorns
5 shallots, chopped
10 cloves garlic, sliced
2 lemongrass stalks, chopped
1 tablespoon finely chopped galangal
2 teaspoons coriander seeds
1½ teaspoons shrimp paste

For the chili paste, soak the dried chiles
in a bowl of warm water for 15 minutes or until
rehydrated, then drain and chop.

Pound the chiles, peppercorns, shallot, garlic,
lemongrass, galangal, and coriander seeds
in a mortar with a pestle until smooth. Add the
shrimp paste and pound again until combined.
Set aside.

Pour 3 cups (1¼ pints/750 ml) water into a
large pan, add the chili paste, and stir until
dissolved. Bring to a boil over medium heat,
add the buffalo or beef, then return to a boil.
Reduce the heat and simmer for 20 minutes.
Add the lemongrass, galangal, and kaffir lime
leaves and cook for another 10 minutes. Ladle
into soup bowls, sprinkle with the cilantro
(coriander), scallions (spring onions), and
sawtooth cilantro (coriander), and serve.

ซุปหางวัว

Oxtail Soup

Origin Central
Preparation time 15 minutes, plus soaking time
Cooking time 3–3½ hours
Serves 8–10

5 cardamom pods
2 bay leaves
3 cilantro (coriander) roots
4 cloves garlic, coarsely crushed
1 tablespoon white or black peppercorns
4½ lb/2 kg oxtail, cut into 1–2 inch/2.5–5-cm pieces
1 cinnamon stick
2 tablespoons vegetable oil
1 onion, sliced
1 x 2¾-inch/7-cm piece fresh ginger, peeled and sliced
5 cherry tomatoes
2 tablespoons fish sauce (optional)
3 tablespoons lime juice
salt

To garnish
1 tablespoon chopped green bird's eye chiles
6 tablespoons Fried Shallots (see p. 64)
½ cup (3½ oz/100 g) sliced celery
½ cup (1½ oz/40 g) chopped scallions (spring onions)
½ cup (1 oz/25 g) chopped cilantro (coriander)
lime wedges

Put the cardamom pods, bay leaves, cilantro (coriander) roots, garlic, and peppercorns into an herb infuser and set aside.

Bring 12⅔ cups (5¼ pints/3 liters) water to a boil in a large pan over high heat, add the oxtail, and boil for 20–30 minutes. Remove any scum with a slotted spoon. Add the herb infuser and cinnamon stick, reduce the heat to low, and simmer for 2 hours or until the oxtail is tender.

Remove the oxtail with a slotted spoon and set aside. Strain the soup through cheesecloth (muslin) into a clean pan and bring the soup to a boil over medium heat. Add more water if necessary.

Heat the oil in a wok over medium heat, add the onion and ginger, and stir-fry for 1–2 minutes until softened. Transfer to the soup, add the tomatoes, and cook for another 30 minutes.

Ladle the oxtail soup into serving bowls. Season with the fish sauce and lime juice. Garnish with the chiles, shallots, celery, chopped scallions (spring onions), cilantro (coriander), and lime wedges, and serve.

ก๋วยเตี๋ยวหมูตุ๋น

Pork and Anise Soup with Rice Noodles

Origin Central
Preparation time 30 minutes, plus soaking time
Cooking time 1½ hour
Serves 6

1 cinnamon sticks
3 star anise
5 cloves garlic, crushed
1 teaspoon white peppercorns
2–3 cilantro (coriander) roots, crushed
10½ cups (4⅓ pints/2½ liters) chicken or pork broth
3 pickled garlic bulbs
1 lb 8½ oz/700 g pork shoulder, cut into 1½-inch/
  3-cm cubes
1 teaspoon salt
3 tablespoons soy sauce
3 tablespoons oyster sauce
4 pieces rock sugar or ½ tablespoon granulated sugar
9 oz/250 g dried rice vermicelli
¼ cup (2 fl oz/60 ml) Fried Garlic oil (see p. 64)
3 cups (11 oz/300 g) bean sprouts

To garnish
4 tablespoons chopped salted pickled radish
½ cup (1½ oz/40 g) chopped scallions (spring onions)
  and cilantro (coriander)

To make the broth (stock), put the cinnamon stick, star anise, garlic, peppercorns and cilantro (coriander) roots into an herb infuser.

Bring the pork broth, herb infuser, and pickled garlic to a boil in a large pan over high heat. Add the pork, salt, soy sauce, oyster sauce, and sugar. Return to a boil, then reduce the heat to medium-low and simmer for 1½ hours or until the pork is tender.

Soak the vermicelli in a bowl of water for 10 minutes, then drain and blanch in a pan of boiling water for 1 minute or prepare according to package directions, until cooked. Drain.

Divide the vermicelli, fried garlic oil, cooked pork, and bean sprouts among serving bowls. Pour about 1½ cups (12 fl oz/350 ml) of the broth into each bowl and garnish with the radish, scallions (spring onions), and cilantro (coriander). Serve.

Photo p. 187

แกงจืดลูกเมาะ

Clear Soup with Pork Balls and Noodles

Origin Central
Preparation time 10 minutes, plus soaking
and marinating times
Cooking time 10 minutes
Serves 4

3½ oz/100 g dried glass noodles
11 oz/300 g ground (minced) pork
2 tablespoons granulated sugar
2 tablespoons soy sauce
3 cups (1¼ pints/750 ml) chicken broth (stock)
1½ teaspoons fish sauce
1 tablespoon cilantro (coriander) leaves

Soak the noodles in a bowl of water for 5 minutes or prepare according to package directions, then drain, cut into short lengths, and set aside.

Mix the pork, 1 tablespoon sugar, and the soy sauce together in a large bowl, then cover with plastic wrap (clingfilm) and let marinate in the refrigerator for 10–15 minutes. Add the noodles and mix together. Shape into small balls and set aside.

Bring the chicken broth (stock) to a boil in a large pan over medium heat. Add the fish sauce, and the remaining sugar, then add the pork balls. Reduce the heat and simmer for 4–5 minutes until the pork balls float to the surface. Ladle into soup bowls, sprinkle with the cilantro (coriander) leaves, and serve.

เส้นใหญ่เย็นตาโฟ

Red Sauce Noodle Soup

Origin Central
Preparation time 30 minutes
Cooking time 10 minutes
Serves 4

4¼ cups (1¾ pints/1 liter) pork stock
5 cilantro (coriander) roots
1 daikon (mooli) radish, cut diagonally into
  ½-inch/1-cm-thick slices
1 teaspoon salt

For the red sauce
3 cubes fermented red bean curd
1 clove garlic
1 cilantro (coriander) root, chopped
1–2 tablespoons white vinegar
3 tablespoons granulated sugar
½ teaspoon salt

For the pickled chiles
7 fresh red bird's eye chiles
5 cloves garlic
2 teaspoons salt
½ cup (4 fl oz/120 ml) vinegar

For the soup
2 cups (3½ oz/100 g) sliced water spinach (1-inch/
  2.5-cm slices)
14 oz/400 g large rice noodles
8 pieces cooked squid, cut into 1-inch/2.5-cm pieces
12 cubes pig's blood curd
8 fish balls
8 pieces deep-fried tofu (see p. 74)
4 fried wontons

Bring the broth (stock) to a boil in a large pan over medium heat. Add the cilantro (coriander) roots, daikon (mooli) radish, and salt, and return to a boil. Boil for 5 minutes, then reduce the heat to low and simmer for another 5 minutes.

To make the red sauce, put all the ingredients in a food processor with ⅓ cup (2½ fl oz/75 ml) water and process until smooth. Set aside.

To make the pickled chiles, process all the ingredients in a food processor until smooth. Set aside.

For the soup, blanch the water spinach with the rice noodles in a pan of boiling water for 1 minute or prepare the noodles according to package directions, then drain.

Divide the water spinach and noodles, sliced squid, pig's blood curd, fish balls, tofu, red sauce, and pickled chiles among serving bowls. Pour 1 cup (9 fl oz/250 ml) pork broth into to each bowl. Place the fried wontons on top and serve.

ก๋วยเตี๋ยวเกี๊ยวหมูแดง

Noodle Soup with Roasted Pork and Wontons

Origin Central
Preparation time 30 minutes, plus marinating time
Cooking time 1½ hours
Serves 6

14 oz/400 g dried rice noodles
5 oz/150 g ground (minced) pork
6 tablespoons Fried Garlic (see p. 64)
2 Chinese fish cakes, sliced into ¾-inch/2-cm
  thick pieces
⅓ cup (2 oz/50 g) roasted peanuts, ground
2 tablespoons chopped salted dried cabbage leaves
4 tablespoons chopped salted radish
fish sauce, to taste
granulated sugar, to taste
1 cup (2 oz/50 g) finely chopped scallions (spring
  onions) and cilantro (coriander), to garnish

For the roasted pork
14 oz/400 g grilled (barbecued) pork tenderloin (fillet)
1 tablespoon Saam-Gler (see p. 41)
1 tablespoon oyster sauce
1½ teaspoons soy sauce
1½ teaspoons granulated sugar
¼ teaspoon five spice powder
½ teaspoon red food coloring

For the wontons
7 oz/200 g ground (minced) pork
1 tablespoon Saam-Gler (see p. 41)
1½ teaspoons oyster sauce
1½ tablespoons soy sauce
½ teaspoon sugar
3½ oz/100 g wonton wrappers
vegetable oil, for drizzling

For the soup
10½ cups (4⅓ pints/2.5 liters) chicken or pork
  broth (stock)
3 cilantro (coriander) roots
2 cloves garlic, crushed
1 teaspoon black peppercorns
1½ teaspoons salt
1 tablespoon soy sauce
7 oz/200 g daikon (mooli), peeled and quartered
  crosswise

For the roasted pork, put the pork tenderloin (fillet), saam-gler, oyster sauce, soy sauce, sugar, five spice powder, and food coloring in a large bowl and mix well. Let marinate in the refrigerator overnight or for at least 2 hours.

Preheat the oven over 325°F/160°C/Gas Mark 3. Put the marinated pork in a roasting pan and roast for 45–55 minutes or until cooked. Remove, let cool slightly, then slice and set aside.

For the wontons, put the ground (minced) pork in a large bowl, add the saam-gler, oyster sauce, soy sauce, and sugar, and mix well.

Lay a wonton wrapper on a work surface and put about 1 teaspoon of the pork mixture in the middle of the wrapper. Fold over the wrapper to to make a triangle shape. Repeat until all the pork mixture has been used.

Bring a large pan of water to a boil over medium heat, add the wontons, and cook for 2–3 minutes or until they float to the surface. Remove with a slotted spoon, drizzle with a little oil, and set aside.

For the soup, bring the broth (stock) to a boil in a large pan over high heat, and add the cilantro (coriander) root, garlic, black peppercorns, salt, soy sauce, and radish. Return to a boil, then reduce the heat to medium-low and simmer for 15–20 minutes or until the radish has softened.

Meanwhile, soak the noodles in a bowl of water for 10 minutes, then drain and blanch in a pan of boiling water for 1 minute or prepare according to package directions, until cooked. Drain and set aside.

Blanch the ground (minced) pork in a pan of boiling water for 2–3 minutes or until cooked. Drain, transfer to a small bowl, and set aside.

Divide the noodles, wontons, roasted pork, fried garlic, fish cake slices, peanuts, salted dried cabbage and radish, and ground pork among serving bowls. Pour about 1 cup (8 fl oz/250 ml) of the soup into each bowl. Season to taste with fish sauce and sugar and garnish with the scallions (spring onions) and cilantro (coriander). Serve.

Photo p. 191

ก๋วยเตี๋ยวยาสุโขทัย

Pork Noodle Soup

Origin Central
Preparation time 15 minutes, plus soaking
Cooking time 15–20 minutes
Serves 5

11 oz/300 g dried rice noodles
7 oz/200 g pork loin
3½ oz/100 g pork liver, thinly sliced
3½ oz/100 g ground (minced) pork
1 cup (7 oz/200 g) jaggery, palm sugar, or soft light
  brown sugar
1½ cups (5 oz/140 g) diagonally sliced yard-long beans
  (¾-inch/2-cm lengths)

For the soup
2 cilantro (coriander) roots, crushed
2 cloves garlic, coarsely crushed
1½ teaspoons black peppercorns
7 cups (3 pints/1.7 liters) chicken or pork broth (stock)

For the sauce
⅓ cup (2½ fl oz/75 ml) fish sauce
⅓ cup (2½ fl oz/75 ml) lime juice
⅓ cup (2 oz/50 g) roasted peanuts, finely pounded
2 tablespoons chili flakes

To serve
3 tablespoons Fried Garlic oil (see p. 64)
3 hard-boiled eggs, halved
2 lettuce leaves, coarsely chopped
⅓ cup (1 oz/25 g) cilantro (coriander), finely chopped
1 scallion (spring onion), finely sliced
1½ teaspoons ground black pepper

Soak the dried noodles in a bowl of water for 10 minutes or according to package directions until soft, then drain and set aside.

Bring a medium pan of water to a boil over medium heat, add the pork loin, reduce the heat to a simmer, and cook for 8–10 minutes until cooked. Remove the pork from the pan with a slotted spoon, then drain in a colander and let cool.

Meanwhile, return the pan of boiling water to the heat, add the pork liver, and cook for about 2 minutes until cooked. Drain, let cool, and thinly slice, then cover with plastic wrap (clingfilm).

Bring ⅓ cup (2½ fl oz/75 ml) water to a boil in a small pan over medium heat. Add the ground (minced) pork and stir for 1–2 minutes or until cooked. Drain and set aside. Reserve the cooking water.

Heat the sugar and ½ cup (4 fl oz/120 ml) water in another small pan over medium heat, and stir until the sugar has dissolved and become syrupy. Set aside.

Blanch the yard-long beans in a pan of boiling water for 1 minute, then drain and set aside.

For the soup, put the cilantro (coriander) root, garlic, and black peppercorns in a cheesecloth (muslin) herb bag. Pour the broth (stock) into a large pan, add the cheesecloth bag, and bring to a boil, then reduce the heat and simmer for 2–3 minutes.

To make the sauce, put the fish sauce, lime juice, peanuts, chili flakes, 1½ tablespoons sugar syrup, 1½ tablespoons ground pork, and the reserved cooking water in a bowl and mix well. Set aside.

Cook the noodles in a pan of boiling water for 1 minute or prepare according to package directions, until soft. Drain and divide the noodles among serving bowls. Drizzle over the fried garlic oil and stir to combine. Pour a little of the sauce and 1½ cups (12 fl oz/350 ml) of the soup into each bowl. Add the pork liver, sliced pork, eggs, yard-long beans, lettuce, scallion (spring onion), and cilantro (coriander). Serve.

แกงยาหมูใบมะดัน

Spicy Pork and Madan Leaf Soup

Origin Central
Preparation time 5 minutes
Cooking time 15 minutes
Serves 6

1 tablespoon vegetable oil
2¼ lb/1 kg boneless pork leg, cut into bite-size pieces
½ cup (4 fl oz/120 ml) fish sauce
½ cup (4 oz/120 g) jaggery, palm sugar, or soft light brown sugar
1 cup (8 fl oz/250 ml) coconut milk
7 oz/ 200 g young madan leaves

For the chili paste
¾-inch(1.5-cm) piece galangal, peeled and chopped
2 shallots, sliced
1 garlic bulb, cloves separated and chopped
2 lemongrass stalks, sliced
1 teaspoon cilantro (coriander) root, chopped
15 dried red chiles
1 teaspoon salt
1 teaspoon Roasted Shrimp Paste (see p. 36)

To make the chili paste, dry-fry the galangal, shallots, garlic, lemongrass, and cilantro (coriander root) in a wok over medium heat for 1 minute or until fragrant. Transfer to a mortar and pound with the dried chiles, salt, and shrimp paste.

Heat the oil in a wok over medium heat, add the chili paste, and sauté for 1 minute. Add the pork, fish sauce, and sugar and mix well. Transfer to a pan, add the coconut milk, and bring to a boil. Reduce the heat and simmer for about 10 minutes or until the pork softens. Add the madan leaves and return to a boil. Ladle into soup bowls and serve.

ต้มแซ่บกระดูกแก้ว

Spicy Pork Soup with Straw Mushrooms

Origin Central
Preparation time 10 minutes
Cooking time 50 minutes
Serves 6

1 lb 2 oz/500 g pork short ribs, cut into bite-size pieces
5 cups (2 pints/1.2 liters) vegetable or chicken broth (stock)
2 lemongrass stalks, sliced
3½ oz/100 g straw mushrooms, halved
15 red and green bird's eye chiles, pounded
2 tablespoons fish sauce
3 tablespoons lime juice
1 tablespoon granulated sugar
1 sawtooth cilantro (coriander) sprig, chopped
3 tablespoons Fried Shallots (see p. 64)
½ tablespoon dried chili flakes

Bring 5 cups (2 pints/1.2 liters) water and the pork ribs to a boil in a large pan over medium heat, then reduce the heat and simmer for 40 minutes. Remove any scum with a slotted spoon. Drain and set aside.

Heat the broth (stock) in a pan over medium heat. Add the lemongrass, mushrooms, boiled meat, chiles, fish sauce, lime juice, sugar, and cilantro (coriander). Ladle into soup bowls, sprinkle with the fried shallots and chili flakes, and serve.

นะหมี่เป็ดย่าง
Roasted Duck
Noodle Soup

Origin Central
Preparation time 30–40 minutes, plus standing time
Cooking time 2 hours
Serves 4

For the roasted duck
1 x 2¼-lb/1-kg whole duck, cleaned without giblets
¼ cup (2¾ oz/70 g) salt flakes
5 slices fresh ginger
4 cloves garlic, chopped
3–4 cilantro (coriander) roots, chopped
1 teaspoon five spice powder
1½ tablespoon black salted soybeans, finely pounded
1 teaspoon salt
1 tablespoon 55 proof liquor or brandy
1 tablespoon sugar
2 tablespoons honey
1 tablespoon thick soy sauce

For the soup
7½ cups (3 pints/1.75 liters) chicken broth (stock)
2 star anise
1 small cinnamon stick, broken into small pieces
2 cloves garlic, coarsely crushed
2 cilantro (coriander) roots, coarsely crushed
½ teaspoon ground black pepper
2 tablespoons soy sauce
1 teaspoon salt
1½ teaspoons granulated sugar
1 teaspoon dark soy sauce

To serve
11 oz/300 g fresh green egg noodles
1 cups (3⅛ oz/100 g) bean sprouts
¼ cup (¾ oz/20 g) finely sliced scallions (spring onions)
4 tablespoons Fried Garlic (see p. 64)
¼ cup (2 fl oz/60 ml) white vinegar (optional)
¼ cup (2 fl oz/60 ml) soy sauce (optional)
¼ cup (2 oz/50 g) superfine (caster) sugar (optional)
2 tablespoons dried chili flakes (optional)

Preheat the oven to 300°F/150°C/Gas Mark 2.

Rinse the duck thoroughly in cold water and pat dry with paper towels. Rub the whole duck with the salt flakes and let stand for 30 minutes. Rinse off the salt and pat dry with paper towels, then set aside.

Pound the ginger, garlic, and cilantro (coriander) roots in a mortar with a pestle until smooth, then transfer to a bowl and add the five spice powder, salted soybeans, salt, liquor or brandy, and sugar and mix until combined. Put the mixture inside the duck, then place the duck on a roasting tray and set aside.

To make the honey sauce, mix the honey, thick soy sauce, and ⅓ cup (2½ fl oz/75 ml) water in a bowl. Brush the duck all over 2–3 times with this mixture, then roast the duck in the oven for about 1½ hours or until cooked. During roasting, brush the duck with some of the honey sauce every 30 minutes. When cooked, remove the duck from the oven, cover with kitchen foil, and let rest for at least 15 minutes. Remove the duck drumsticks and set aside, then carve the meat, slice into strips, and set aside.

To make the soup, heat the broth (stock) in a pan over medium heat. Put the star anise, cinnamon, garlic, cilantro (coriander) roots, and black pepper into a spice bag and add to the pan. Let the broth boil for 5 minutes. Season with the soy sauce, salt, sugar, and dark soy sauce, then reduce the heat and simmer for 2–3 minutes.

Divide the noodles, bean sprouts, scallion (spring onion), fried garlic, and sliced duck among serving bowls. Pour about 1 cup (8 fl oz/250 ml) of the soup into each bowl. Season to taste with the vinegar, soy sauce, sugar, and chili flakes, if using, and serve.

Photo p. 194

ตัมยำไก่ด่าใส่มะพร้าวอ่อน
Chicken and Coconut Soup

Origin Central
Preparation time 10 minutes
Cooking time 10–15 minutes
Serves 2

3½ cups (1¾ pints/800 ml) chicken broth (stock)
½ teaspoon salt
1 cilantro (coriander) root
1 shallot, halved
2 lemongrass stalk, diagonally sliced
6 thin slices galangal
4 kaffir lime leaves, torn
11 oz/300 g black-skinned chicken breast or
  boneless chicken thigh, sliced into 1¼ x 1½-inch/
  3 x 4-cm pieces
½ cup (3½ oz/100 g) young coconut flesh (scooped
  out from the inside of a young coconut)
1½ tablespoons fish sauce
2½ teaspoons lime juice
½ teaspoon granulated sugar
scant 1 cup (7 fl oz/200 ml) coconut milk
1–2 red bird's eye chiles, chopped
¼ cup (¼ oz/10 g) chopped cilantro (coriander)
1 teaspoon Chili Jam oil (see p. 35)
2 whole young coconuts, cut open at the top and
  drained (keep the top as a lid)
4 dried red bird's eye chiles, seeded, to garnish

Bring the chicken broth (stock) and salt to
a boil in a large pan over medium heat.

Pound the cilantro (coriander) root, shallot,
lemongrass, galangal, and kaffir leaves in
a mortar with a pestle, then add to the pan
and boil for 1–2 minutes. Add the chicken
and boil for 3–4 minutes or until the chicken
is cooked. Add the young coconut flesh, fish
sauce, lime juice, sugar, and coconut milk, stir,
and cook for another 2 minutes. Add the chiles
and cilantro (coriander), then ladle into the
whole young coconuts, garnish with the chili
jam oil and dried chiles, and serve.

Photo p. 197

แกงฮ้าเผือกใส่ไก่
Spicy Chicken and Taro Soup

Origin North
Preparation time 10 minutes, plus soaking time
Cooking time 15 minutes
Serves 3

3 tablespoons vegetable oil
11 oz/300 g chicken (either half a whole chicken or
  boneless chicken thighs), cut into bite-size pieces
2 cups (16 fl oz/475 ml) chicken broth (stock)
7 oz/200 g taro, peeled and cut into 1¼-inch/3-cm dice
¼ teaspoon salt
¼ cup (¾ oz/20 g) chopped scallions (spring onions),
  to garnish
¼ cup (¼ oz/10 g) chopped cilantro (coriander),
  to garnish

For the chili paste
5 dried red bird's eye chiles, chopped
½ teaspoon Sichuan peppercorns
5 cloves garlic, chopped
2 small shallots, chopped
1 lemongrass stalk, finely sliced
1 teaspoon shrimp paste

For the chili paste, soak the dried chiles in
a bowl of warm water for 15 minutes or until
rehydrated, then drain and chop.

Pound the chiles, peppercorns, garlic, shallots,
and lemongrass in a mortar with a pestle until
smooth. Add the shrimp paste and mix until
combined. Set aside.

Heat the oil in a wok over medium heat, add
the chili paste and cook for 1 minute or until
fragrant. Add the chicken and stir-fry for
3–4 minutes. Pour in the broth (stock) and bring
to a boil. Add the taro and salt, reduce the heat
to medium-low, and simmer for 4–5 minutes or
until the taro is tender. Remove from the heat.
Ladel into soup bowls and garnish with the
chopped scallions (spring onions) and cilantro
(coriander). Serve.

ต้มฟักไก่ตุ๋นมะนาวดอง

Winter Melon Soup with Chicken and Pickled Lime

Origin Central
Preparation time 10 minutes, plus soaking time
Cooking time 50 minutes
Serves 4

10 dried shiitake mushrooms
2 cups (16 fl oz/475 ml) chicken broth (stock)
14 oz/400 g chicken thighs or drumsticks
2 teaspoons cilantro (coriander) root, finely pounded
1¼ teaspoons salt
2 tablespoons pickled lime juice
2 pickled limes
½ winter melon, peeled, seeded, and cut into
  2¾ x 1¼-inch/7 x 3-cm pieces
1 tablespoon soy sauce
1 teaspoon ground white pepper

Soak the shiitake mushrooms in a bowl of hot water for 15 minutes, then squeeze to drain, slice into bite-size pieces, and set aside.

Bring the broth (stock) and 3 cups (1¼ pints/750 ml) water to a boil in a large pan over medium-high heat. Add the chicken, cilantro (coriander) root, and salt and return to a boil. Remove any scum with a slotted spoon. Reduce the heat to low and simmer for 15 minutes. Add the pickled lime juice, pickled limes, and shiitake mushrooms, then simmer again for 10 minutes. Add the winter melon and soy sauce and continue to simmer for another 20 minutes or until the chicken and winter melon are tender. Stir gently. Ladle into soup bowls, sprinkle with white pepper, and serve.

ต้มไก่บ้านใบมะขามอ่อน

Sour-and-spicy Chicken Soup with Tamarind Leaves

Origin Northeast
Preparation time 10 minutes
Cooking time 25 minutes
Serves 4

4 cups (1⅗ pints/950 ml) chicken broth (stock)
½ teaspoon salt
5 thin slices galangal
2 lemongrass stalks, cut into 1½-inch/4-cm
  diagonal slices
3 small shallots, coarsely crushed
½ x 14-oz/400-g chicken, chopped (with the bone)
  into small pieces
2 tablespoons fish sauce
4 kaffir lime leaves, torn
1 handful of young tamarind leaves
2 tomatoes, cut into wedges
5 red bird's eye chiles, lightly pounded

Bring the broth (stock) and salt to a boil over high heat in a large pan. Add the galangal, lemongrass, and shallots and boil for 1 minute. Add the chicken and return to a boil. Remove any scum with a slotted spoon. Reduce the heat and simmer for 15–20 minutes until cooked and tender. Add the fish sauce, kaffir lime leaves, young tamarind leaves, tomatoes, and chiles. Ladle into soup bowls and serve.

ต้มเย่อไผ่เห็ดหอม

Shiitake and Stinkhorn Mushroom Soup

Origin Central
Preparation time 10 minutes, plus soaking time
Cooking time 25–30 minutes
Serves 2–3

1 lb 2 oz/500 g pork short ribs, chopped
1 oz/25 g dried shiitake mushrooms, rinsed
2 oz/50 g dried stinkhorn mushrooms, sliced
2 tablespoons vegetable oil
¼ cup (2 fl oz/60 ml) soy sauce
1 tablespoon goji berries
1 tablespoon red dates, chopped
1 teaspoon salt
2 teaspoons ground black pepper

Bring 4¼ cups (1¾ pints/1 liter) water to a boil in a large pan over medium heat, add the pork ribs, and return to a boil. Remove any scum with a slotted spoon. Reduce the heat and simmer for 20–25 minutes or until tender.

Meanwhile, in separate bowls, soak the shiitake and stinkhorn mushrooms in hot water for about 15 minutes. When the shiitake mushrooms have softened, squeeze to drain and slice into bite-size pieces. Rinse the stinkhorns to remove the dirt, squeeze to drain, and cut into bite-size pieces.

Heat the oil in a wok over medium heat, add the mushrooms, and sauté for 1–2 minutes or until dry. Season with the soy sauce, then remove from the heat and set aside.

When the pork-rib broth is clear, add the goji berries, red dates, salt, black pepper, and remaining soy sauce. When the ribs have softened, add the mushrooms. Ladle into soup bowls and serve.

ต้มดอกไม้จีนเห็ดหอม

Daylily and Shiitake Mushroom Soup

Origin Central
Preparation time 15 minutes, plus soaking time
Cooking time 20–25 minutes
Serves 2–3

9 oz/250 g pork short ribs, cut into bite-size pieces
1 teaspoon ground white pepper
6–7 cloves garlic, pounded
3 cilantro (coriander) roots
2 oz/50 g dried daylily
8 shiitake mushrooms, rinsed
2 tablespoons goji berries
salt

Bring 5 cups (2 pints/1.2 liters) water to a boil in a large pan over medium heat. Add the pork ribs, white pepper, garlic, and cilantro (coriander) roots and return to a boil. Remove any scum with a slotted spoon. Reduce the heat and simmer for 20–25 minutes or until tender.

Meanwhile, soak the dried daylily in a bowl of water for 15–20 minutes. Rinse well 4–5 times under cold running water and squeeze to drain. Cut off and discard the coarse stems and tie each daylily into a knot. Add the daylily, shiitake mushrooms, and goji berries to the pan and simmer for about 10 minutes until the daylily has softened. Season to taste, ladle into soup bowls, and serve.

ต้มมะระซี่โครงหมู

Bitter Gourd and
Pork Rib Soup

Origin Central
Preparation time 10 minutes, plus soaking time
Cooking time 1 hour 20 minutes
Serves 4

12 oz/350 g bitter gourd
1 tablespoon plus 1 teaspoon salt
3 cloves garlic
2 cilantro (coriander) roots, crushed
½ teaspoon white peppercorns
14 oz/400 g pork short ribs, rinsed
1½ tablespoons soy sauce
1 teaspoon chopped cilantro (coriander), to garnish

Trim the bottom and the top off the bitter gourd. Halve lengthwise and scrape out the seeds and white fiber (until you see the green flesh). Halve each piece lengthwise again and cut crosswise into 2-inch/5-cm-length pieces.

Mix 1 tablespoon salt and 2 cups (16 fl oz/ 475 ml) water and in large bowl, and stir until the salt has dissolved. Add the bitter gourd and let soak for 15–30 minutes. Drain, rinse, and set aside.

Pour 4 cups (1⅔ pints/950 ml) water, into a large pan, add the garlic, cilantro (coriander) roots, peppercorns, and 1 teaspoon salt, and bring to a boil over high heat. Add the pork ribs and soy sauce and boil for 4–5 minutes, then add the bitter gourd and boil for another 10 minutes, without stirring. Remove any scum with a slotted spoon. Reduce the heat to low, cover with a lid, and cook for another 50–60 minutes or until the pork is tender. Ladle into soup bowls, garnish with chopped cilantro (coriander), and serve.

น้ำซุป

Pork and Bottle
Gourd Soup

Origin North
Preparation time 8 minutes
Cooking time 30 minutes
Serves 5

14 oz/400 g pork tenderloin or short ribs, sliced
1 cup (4 oz/115 g) cubed mature bottle gourd
1 tablespoon granulated sugar
1½ teaspoons salt
3 scallions (spring onions), chopped
4 cilantro (coriander) stalks, chopped

Bring 8½ cups (3½ pints/2 liters) water to a boil in a large pan over medium heat. Add the pork, bottle gourd, sugar, and salt and cook for about 30 minutes. Ladle into soup bowls, sprinkle with the scallion (spring onion) and cilantro (coriander) and serve.

ผักกาดจอ

Chinese Cabbage Soup

Origin North
Preparation time 10 minutes
Cooking time 30–40 minutes
Serves 4

2 shallots, coarsely chopped
2 cloves garlic
1¼ teaspoons shrimp paste
1 fermented soybean sheet (see p. 34)
11 oz/300 g pork side (belly), cut into ¾-inch/
   2-cm-thick slices
1 teaspoon salt
1 tablespoon Tamarind Puree (see p. 63)
1½ teaspoons fish sauce
1½ teaspoons granulated sugar
9 oz/250 g choy sum (Chinese flowering cabbage),
   cut into 2½-inch/6-cm strips

To garnish
2 teaspoons Fried Garlic (see p. 64)
5 dried red bird's eye chiles, roasted

Preheat the broiler (grill) to medium.

Pound the shallots, garlic, and shrimp paste
together in a mortar with a pestle to a fine
paste and set aside.

Place the soybean sheet on the broiler (grill)
pan and broil (grill) for about 2 minutes until
fragrant and dark brown. Let cool, then
add to the mortar and pound with the pestle
until ground.

Bring 6 cups (2½ pints/1.4 liters) water to a boil
in a pan over medium heat. Add the pork and
salt and boil for 20–30 minutes until softened,
Remove any scum with a slotted spoon. Add
the paste and ground soybean sheet, the
tamarind, fish sauce, sugar, and cabbage
and continue to boil for 4–5 minutes until the
cabbage is soft. Ladle into soup bowls, sprinkle
with the fried garlic and chiles, and serve.

แกงจอผักกาดกะเหรี่ยง

Spicy Soup with Chinese Mustard Greens

Origin North
Preparation time 5 minutes
Cooking time 10 minutes
Serves 2

10 green bird's eye chiles, chopped
3 shallots, chopped
5 cloves garlic, sliced
½ teaspoon salt
1 fermented soybean sheet (see p. 34)
7 oz/200 g Chinese mustard greens
scallions (spring onions), chopped, to garnish

Pound the chiles, shallots, garlic, and salt
together in a mortar with a pestle.

Place the soybean sheet on the broiler (grill)
pan and broil (grill) for about 2 minutes until
fragrant and dark brown. Let cool, then
add to the mortar and pound with the pestle
until ground.

Bring 2 cups (16 fl oz/475 ml) water to a boil
in a pan over medium heat, add the Chinese
mustard greens, and cook for 3–4 minutes.
Add the chile and shallot mixture, stir, and
simmer for 2–3 minutes. Ladle into in soup
bowls, sprinkle with the scallions (spring
onions), and serve.

Curries

แกงปลาดุกบานู

Spicy Catfish and Snake Gourd Curry

Origin Northeast
Preparation time 10 minutes, plus soaking time
Cooking time 10 minutes
Serves 4

2 cups (16 fl oz/475 ml) chicken broth (stock)
1 x 11-oz/300-g catfish, cleaned, head removed,
   and cut into 1-inch/2.5-cm-thick pieces
1 tablespoon Ground Toasted Rice (see p. 64)
1 tablespoon fermented fish sauce
1 tablespoon fish sauce
2 cups (9 oz/250 g) sliced snake gourd or zucchini
   (courgette), cut into 1-inch/2.5-cm-thick slices
½ cup (2½ oz/65 g) pea eggplants (aubergines)
4 round eggplants (aubergines), cut into wedges
a handful of wild bitter gourd leaves or other bitter
   green leaves
2 scallions (spring onions), sliced
a handful of sweet basil leaves

For the chili paste
5 dried red chiles
3 small shallots, chopped
1 lemongrass stalk, chopped
¼ teaspoon salt

To serve
Steamed Jasmine Rice (see p. 378) or Glutinous Rice
   (see p. 378)

For the chili paste, soak the chiles in a bowl of warm water for 15 minutes or until rehydrated, then drain and chop.

Pound the chiles, shallots, lemongrass, and salt in a mortar with a pestle until smooth. Set aside.

Bring the broth (stock) to a boil in a pan over medium heat. Add the chili paste and boil for 1 minute. Add the fish and ground rice and return to a boil, then season with the fermented fish sauce and fish sauce. Stir and add the snake gourd or zucchini (courgette), both eggplants (aubergines), the wild bitter gourd leaves, and scallions (spring onions). Gently stir and boil for 3–5 minutes or until the vegetables soften. Add the basil leaves, stir again, and remove from the heat. Serve with rice.

Photo p. 211

แกงปลาขนุนใส่ปลาแห้ง

Spicy Catfish and Jackfruit Curry

Origin North
Preparation time 10 minutes
Cooking time 10 minutes
Serves 4

11 oz/300 g young jackfruit, peeled and seeded
   wearing gloves, and cut into 1-inch/2.5-cm slices
3½ oz/100 g dried catfish fillets, diced
8 cherry tomatoes
3½ tablespoons Tamarind Puree (see p. 63)
1 tablespoon fermented fish sauce
2 teaspoons granulated sugar
1 cup (2 oz/50 g) chopped cilantro (coriander)
2 scallions (spring onions), chopped

For the chili paste
6 dried red chiles, chopped
5 cloves garlic, chopped
3 shallots, chopped
3 slices galangal
2 tablespoons chopped lemongrass

For the chili paste, soak the dried chiles in a bowl of warm water for 15 minutes or until rehydrated, then drain and chop.

Pound the chiles and the remaining chili paste ingredients in a mortar with a pestle until smooth. Set aside.

Bring 2 cups (16 fl oz/475 ml) water to a boil in a large pan, add the chili paste and jackfruit, and cook for 3–4 minutes or until the jackfruit has softened. Add the catfish and cook for another 3–4 minutes, then add the tomatoes, tamarind, fermented fish sauce, and sugar and stir gently. Remove from the heat and sprinkle with the chopped cilantro (coriander) and scallions (spring onions). Serve.

ปลาดุกทะเลแกงคั่วใบยี่หร่า

Spicy Catfish and Tree Basil Curry

Origin South
Preparation time 10 minutes
Cooking time 10 minutes
Serves 3–4

2 tablespoons vegetable oil
2 tablespoons Southern Chili Paste (see p. 38)
1⅔ cups (14 fl oz/400 ml) coconut milk
1 x 1 lb 2-oz/500-g catfish, head removed and cut
   into ¾-inch/2-cm-thick pieces
1 green spur chile, diagonally sliced
1 red spur chile, diagonally sliced
1½ teaspoons fish sauce
½ teaspoon granulated sugar
2 handfuls of tree basil or holy basil leaves, chopped
salt

Heat the oil in a wok over medium heat, add the chili paste, and cook for 1–2 minutes or until fragrant. Add the coconut milk and bring to a boil. Add the fish, cook for 4 minutes, then add the chiles, fish sauce, sugar, and a pinch of salt. Stir and cook for another 1–2 minutes or until the fish is fully flavored. Add the tree basil, stir a couple times, then serve.

Photo p. 212

Spicy Catfish and Bamboo Shoot Curry

Origin North
Preparation time 10 minutes
Cooking time 10 minutes
Serves 2

2 cups (16 fl oz/475 ml) chicken broth (stock)
2 cups (7 oz/200 g) sour and salty pickled bamboo
  shoots, rinsed and coarsely chopped
1½ tablespoons fish sauce
1 x 11-oz/300-g catfish, cleaned and chopped
  into ¾-inch/2-cm-thick pieces
3 cilantro (coriander) sprigs, chopped
3 scallions (spring onions), chopped

For the chili paste
5 red and green bird's eye chiles, chopped
5 cloves garlic, chopped
1 lemongrass stalk, finely sliced
2 small shallots, chopped
½ teaspoon ground turmeric
½ teaspoon salt
½ tablespoon fermented fish

For the paste, pound the chiles, garlic, lemongrass, shallots, turmeric, and salt thoroughly in a mortar with a pestle. Add the fermented fish and pound until thoroughly combined. Set aside.

Bring the broth (stock) and 2 cups (16 fl oz/ 475 ml) water to a boil in a pan over high heat. Add the bamboo shoots and boil for 4–5 minutes to allow the pickled bamboo to flavor the stock. Add the fish sauce and fish and cook for another 4–5 minutes. Transfer to a serving bowl and sprinkle with the cilantro (coriander) and scallions (spring onions). Serve.

Fried Sheatfish Curry

Origin Central
Preparation time 15 minutes, plus soaking time
Cooking time 15–20 minutes
Serves 2

2 cups (16 fl oz/475 ml) vegetable oil, for deep-frying
1 x 11-oz/300-g small white sheatfish, cleaned, gutted,
  and halved crosswise
1 cup (9 fl oz/250 ml) coconut milk
1 tablespoon fish sauce
2 tablespoons jaggery, palm sugar, or soft light
  brown sugar
2 tablespoons evaporated milk (optional)
1½ tablespoons Red Curry Paste (see p. 38)
2–3 orange spur chiles, finely sliced diagonally
1 handful of sweet basil leaves

Heat the oil for deep-frying in a wok or deep fryer to 350°F/180°C or until a cube of bread browns in 30 seconds. Deep-fry the fish for 8–10 minutes until golden brown and crispy. Remove with a slotted spoon and drain on paper towels. Set aside.

Bring the coconut milk to boil in a clean wok over medium heat and add the chili paste. Stir for 2 minutes or until thoroughly combined and the coconut milk has thickened. Season with the fish sauce, sugar, and evaporated milk, if using. Stir until the sugar has dissolved. Add the fish and cook for 1–2 minutes or until full-flavored. Add the chiles and most of the basil leaves. Stir 3–4 times and remove from the heat. Garnish with the remaining basil leaves and serve.

แกงส้มปลากระพง

Sour-and-Spicy Sea Bass Curry

Origin South
Preparation time 10 minutes, plus soaking time
Cooking time 15 minutes
Serves 2–3

3½ cups (1¾ pints/800 ml) chicken or fish broth (stock)
1 x 11-oz/300-g sea bass, cleaned, descaled, and cut
  into ¾-inch/2-cm-thick pieces
5 slices dried asam gelugor, washed, or
  2–3 tablespoons lime juice
2 tablespoons fish sauce
1 tablespoons Tamarind Puree (see p. 63)
7 oz/200 g heart of palm, cut into 2-inch/5-cm strips,
  or cauliflower florets

For the chili paste
20 dried red chiles
1 teaspoon salt
10 cloves garlic
2-inch/5-cm piece long turmeric root
1½ teaspoons shrimp paste

For the chili paste, soak the dried chiles in
a bowl of warm water for 15 minutes or until
rehydrated, then drain and chop.

Pound the chiles, salt, garlic, turmeric, and
shrimp paste in a mortar with a pestle until
smooth. Add about 2 tablespoons water and
pound with a pestle until smooth. Set aside.

Bring the broth (stock) to a boil in a pan over
medium heat. Add the chili paste and boil for
another 2 minutes. Add the sea bass, increase
the heat to high, and return to a boil without
stirring. Reduce the heat to medium and boil
for another 2 minutes. Gently remove the fish
from the pan and set aside.

Add the asam geluger, fish sauce, and tamarind
to the pan. Reduce the heat to low-medium and
simmer for 5–7 minutes until the som khaek
fully releases its sourness. Increase the heat
back to medium, add the heart of palm or
cauliflower, and boil for 2 minutes for the heart
of palm or 3 minutes for the cauliflower until
softened. Return the fish to the pan and boil
for another 1 minute. Serve.

ปลากะพงต้มส้มระกำ

Sour Sea Bass and Salacca Curry

Origin Central
Preparation time 10 minutes
Cooking time 10 minutes
Serves 6

5 shallots, halved
3 garlic bulbs, cloves separated and halved
1 lb 2 oz/500 g salacca (snake fruit), skin removed
1 teaspoon shrimp paste
1 x 2¼-lb/1-kg sea bass, cleaned, filleted, and cut into
  2-inch/5-cm pieces
½ cup (2 oz/50 g) red and green bird's eye chiles,
  coarsely chopped
½ cup (1 oz/25 g) mint leaves
1 tablespoon fish sauce

Bring 4¼ cups (1¾ pints/1 liter) water to a
boil in a large pan over medium heat. Add
the shallots, garlic, salacca (snake fruit), and
shrimp paste, return to a boil, then add the fish
and cook for about 3 minutes. Remove from the
heat, add the chiles and mint, and stir. Season
with fish sauce and serve.

แกงป่า

Jungle Fish Curry

Origin Central
Preparation time 10 minutes, plus soaking time
Cooking time 20–30 minutes
Serves 4

2 cups (16 fl oz/475 ml) chicken broth (stock)
4 round eggplants (aubergines), quartered
½ cup (2½ oz/65 g) pea eggplants (aubergines)
1 cup (3¼ oz/90 g) sliced yard-long beans or green
  beans, cut into 1¼-inch/3-cm lengths
8–10 baby corn, diagonally sliced
1½ tablespoons fish sauce
1 teaspoon granulated sugar
4 sticks fingerroot, sliced lengthwise
2 red finger chiles, diagonally sliced
1 x 11-oz/300-g sea bass or sea bream fillet, cut into
  2-inch/5-cm-thick slices
1 handful of sweet basil leaves, plus extra to garnish

For the chili paste
6 dried red bird's eye chiles
3 dried red spur chiles
½ teaspoon salt
2 lemongrass stalks, finely sliced
1-inch/2.5-cm piece fresh galangal, peeled and
  finely chopped
1 teaspoon finely chopped kaffir lime zest
½ teaspoon black peppercorns
4 cloves garlic
1 shallot, chopped
1 cilantro (coriander) root
1½ teaspoons shrimp paste

For the chili paste, soak the chiles in a bowl of warm water for 15 minutes or until rehydrated, then drain and chop.

Pound the chiles and salt in a mortar with a pestle until the chiles are fine flakes. Add the lemongrass and pound until smooth. Add the galangal and kaffir lime zest and pound thoroughly. Add the black peppercorns, garlic, and shallot and pound again, then add the cilantro (coriander) root and pound until smooth. Add the shrimp paste and pound until thoroughly combined and a smooth paste. Set aside.

Bring 1 cup (9 fl oz/250 ml) water and the chicken broth (stock) to a boil in a pan over high heat. Add 3 tablespoons of the chili paste, stir, and boil for 2–3 minutes. Add both eggplants (aubergines), the beans and baby corn, then reduce the heat to medium and boil for 3–4 minutes. Add the fish sauce, sugar, fingerroots, and finger chiles and stir a couple times. Gently add the fish and cook for 2–3 minutes, without stirring, until the fish is cooked. Add the basil and stir. Serve garnished with a few basil leaves.

ลาบปลาตอง

Fish Curry in Banana leaf

Origin Northeast
Preparation time 20 minutes
Cooking time 20 minutes
Serves 5

½ cup (4 fl oz/120 ml) fermented fish sauce
⅓ cup (2 oz/50 g) sliced shallot
11 oz/300 g Asian knifefish, bronze featherback,
  or sea bass fillet
3 tablespoons Ground Toasted Rice (see p. 64)
3 tablespoons chili powder
1⅔ cups (2 oz/50 g) kaffir lime leaves, finely sliced
1 cup (2 oz/50 g) finely chopped cilantro (coriander)
⅔ cup (1½ oz/40 g) sliced scallions (spring onions)
banana leaves, for wrapping

To serve
Steamed Jasmine Rice (see p. 378), to serve
raw or steamed vegetables, such as cucumber,
  Chinese leaves, carrots, and yard-long beans

Before you begin cooking, check that your charcoal is glowing white hot, or your gas grill (barbecue) is preheated to 300°F/150°C.

Bring 2 cups (16 fl oz/475 ml) water to a boil in a large pan over high heat. Add the fermented fish sauce, stir, then set aside and keep warm.

Pound half the shallot slices in a mortar with a pestle. Add the fish and pound until smooth. Gradually pour in the warm fermented fish water and stir continuously. Gradually add the ground rice and chili powder and mix well. Add the kaffir lime leaves, cilantro (coriander), scallions (spring onions), and remaining sliced shallot, and stir until thoroughly combined.

Lay the banana leaves on a work surface. Place the fish curry in the center of the banana leaf and flatten the curry slightly to make it easy to wrap. Cover the curry with the sides of the leaf, fold over the ends, and secure with toothpicks.

Grill the banana leaf package over low heat for 10–15 minutes or until cooked. Unwrap the package and serve with rice and raw or steamed vegetables.

ฉู่ฉี่ปลาเนื้ออ่อน

Dry Fish Curry

Origin Central
Preparation time 10 minutes, plus soaking time
Cooking time 15 minutes
Serves 10

2¼ lb/1 kg whisker sheatfish, red snapper, or red
　mullet, cleaned and tails removed
4 cups (1⅔ pints/950 ml) vegetable oil, for deep-frying,
　plus ¼ cup (2 fl oz/60 ml)
2 tablespoons fish sauce
1 tablespoon granulated sugar
1 teaspoon ground white pepper
zest of ½ kaffir lime

For the chili paste
¾ oz/20 g dried red chiles, chopped
1 shallot, chopped
1 large clove garlic, chopped
1 teaspoon peeled and chopped galangal
1 tablespoon chopped fingerroot
1 tablespoon chopped lemongrass stalk
1 tablespoon shrimp paste
1 teaspoon salt

For the chili paste, soak the dried chiles in
a bowl of warm water for 15 minutes or until
rehydrated, then drain and chop.

Pound the chiles, shallot, garlic, galangal,
fingerroot, and lemongrass in a mortar with
a pestle until smooth. Add the shrimp paste
and salt and pound again until thoroughly
combined. Set aside.

Cut each fish into 3 pieces crosswise.

Heat the oil for deep-frying in a wok or deep
fryer to 340°F/170°C or until a cube of bread
browns in 30 seconds. Deep-fry the fish for
about 7 minutes or until golden brown and
crispy. Remove with a slotted spoon and drain
on paper towels.

Heat the ¼ cup (2 fl oz/60 ml) oil in a pan over
medium heat, add the chili paste, and stir-fry
for about 3 minutes until fragrant. Carefully
pour in ½ cup (4 fl oz/120 ml) water, then
season with the fish sauce, sugar, and white
pepper. Add the deep-fried fish, stir, and
cook for another 3–4 minutes. Garnish with the
kaffir lime zest and serve.

Photo p. 219

แกงผักกาดหน้อยใส่ปลาแห้ง

Spicy Dried Fish and Vegetable Curry

Origin North
Preparation time 10 minutes, plus soaking time
Cooking time 15 minutes
Serves 2

3 cups (1¼ pints/750 ml) chicken broth (stock)
¼ teaspoon salt
2 oz/50 g dried smoked snakefish fillet, broken
　into small pieces
1 cup (3½ oz/100 g) chopped yard-long beans
7 oz/200 g choy sum (Chinese flowering cabbage),
　chopped into 2-inch/5-cm pieces
2 tablespoons fermented fish sauce
1 handful of fresh dill, coarsely chopped

For the chili paste
7 dried red chiles, chopped
3 cloves garlic, sliced
¼ teaspoon salt
2 shallots, chopped

For the chili paste, soak the dried chiles in
a bowl of warm water for 15 minutes or until
rehydrated, then drain and chop.

Pound the chiles, garlic, salt, and shallots in
a mortar with a pestle until smooth. Set aside.

Bring the broth (stock) and salt to a boil in
a pan over high heat. Add the chili paste and
boil for 1–2 minutes. Add the dried fish and
boil for another 3 minutes or until the fish has
softened. Add the yard-long beans, choy sum,
and fermented fish sauce and boil for another
4–5 minutes or until the vegetables have
softened. Add the dill and stir. Serve.

ขนมจีนน้ำยา

Spicy Fish Ball Curry with Rice Vermicelli

Origin South
Preparation time 10 minutes, plus soaking time
Cooking time 10 minutes
Serves 5

1 cup (5 oz/150 g) boiled fish meat
2 cups (16 fl oz/475 ml) coconut milk
5 oz/150 g fish balls
¼ cup (2 fl oz/60 ml) fish sauce
2 tablespoons jaggery, palm sugar, or soft light
  brown sugar
2 dried garcinia or 1 tablespoon Tamarind Puree
  (see p. 63)
½ cup (4 fl oz/120 ml) coconut cream
1¾ lb/800 g cooked rice vermicelli
hard-boiled eggs, to garnish
peppermint leaves, to garnish
raw or steamed vegetables, such as yard-long
  beans, bean sprouts, shredded lettuce, and
  cucumbers, to serve

For the chili paste
2 tablespoons dried bird's eye chiles, soaked
5–8 dried red chiles, seeded and soaked
1 teaspoon salt
1½ teaspoons chopped lemongrass
2 teaspoons chopped galangal
2 shallots, chopped
3 cloves garlic, coarsely chopped
1½ teaspoons finely chopped turmeric root
2 tablespoons shrimp paste

For the chili paste, soak the dried chiles in a bowl of warm water for 15 minutes or until rehydrated, then drain and chop.

Pound the chiles, salt, lemongrass, galangal, shallots, garlic, and turmeric together in a mortar with a pestle until smooth. Add the shrimp paste and boiled fish meat and pound to a paste.

Heat the coconut milk in a pan over medium-low heat. Add the pounded fish mixture, stir, and bring to a boil. Boil for 3–4 minutes, then add the fish balls and season with the fish sauce, sugar, and dried garcinia or tamarind. Reduce the heat to low, then add the coconut cream and simmer for 3 minutes. Remove from the heat and transfer the curry to a large serving bowl.

Place the rice vermicelli on a serving plate and garnish with hard-boiled eggs. Serve with the spicy curry and raw or steamed vegetables.

Photo p. 221

แกงปูใบชะพลู

Crab Curry with Betel Leaves

Origin South
Preparation time 10 minutes, plus soaking time
Cooking time 15–20 minutes
Serves 2

14 oz/400 g dried rice vermicelli
2 tablespoons vegetable oil
2 cups (16 fl oz/475 ml) coconut milk
1½ teaspoons jaggery, palm sugar, or soft light
  brown sugar
1½ teaspoons fish sauce
2 kaffir lime leaves
3½ oz/100 g betel leaves, thinly sliced
9 oz/250 g crabmeat
10 betal leaves
10 cilantro (coriander) leaves
1 red spur chile, seeded and finely sliced lengthwise

For the red curry paste
7 large dried red chiles
10 dried bird's eye chiles
1 cilantro (coriander) root
1½ tablespoons thinly sliced lemongrass
1½ tablespoons thinly sliced galangal
4 shallots, chopped
5 cloves garlic
1½ teaspoons thinly sliced kaffir lime zest
½ teaspoon salt
¼ teaspoon ground white pepper
1½ tablespoons roasted ground black pepper
1 teaspoon roasted cumin seeds
1 teaspoon roasted coriander seeds
1¼-inch/3-cm piece fresh turmeric, peeled
  and chopped
½ teaspoon shrimp paste

Soak the vermicelli in a bowl of water for
5 minutes or according to package directions.
Drain and set aside.

For the red curry paste, soak the dried chiles
in a bowl of warm water for 15 minutes or until
rehydrated, then drain and chop.

Pound the chiles and the remaining curry
paste ingredients in a mortar with a pestle
until smooth. Set aside.

Fill a pan halfway with water and bring to a
boil over medium heat. Add the vermicelli and
cook for 1–2 minutes. Drain and rinse under
cold water, then let stand in a strainer (sieve)
to drain completely. Use your hand or a fork
to roll the vermicelli into small rolls. Place
on a serving plate.

Heat the oil in a pan over medium heat, add
3 tablespoons of the curry paste, and stir-fry
for 1–2 minutes or until fragant. Gradually pour
in the coconut milk and bring to a boil. Season
with the fish sauce, sugar, and lime leaves,
then add the sliced betel leaves and cook for
1–2 minutes. Add the crabmeat and gently stir
for 1 minute.

To serve, ladle the curry into serving bowls
and place each vermicelli roll on a betal leaf
and top with a cilantro (coriander) leaf and
2 strips of chile.

Photo p. 222

ผัดเส้นจันทร์

Fish Curry with Fermented Rice Noodles

Origin South
Preparation time 30 minutes
Cooking time 10 minutes
Serves 4

1 x 1 lb 8½-oz/700-g snakehead fish, catfish,
  or sea bass fillet
3 tablespoon Southern Chili Paste (see p. 38)
4¼ cups (1¾ pints/1 liter) coconut milk
3½ tablespoons fish sauce
4 kaffir lime leaves, torn
½ teaspoon granulated sugar

To serve
2¼ lb/1 kg cooked fermented rice noodles
1 cup (3½ oz/100 g) bean sprouts
3 cups (11 oz/300 g) finely sliced yard-long beans
1 lemongrass stalk, finely sliced
1 cucumber, sliced

Put the fish in a steamer and steam for
5–7 minutes or until cooked. Remove from
the steamer and remove and discard the skin.
Pound the fish and chili paste in a mortar with
a pestle until combined. Set aside.

Bring the coconut milk to boil in a large pan
over medium heat, add the chili paste mixture,
and stir until thoroughly combined. Return to
a boil, then reduce the heat to low and simmer
for about 2 minutes. Season with the fish sauce,
add the kaffir leaves, and simmer for another
5 minutes or until full-flavored. Remove from
the heat and set aside.

Divide the noodles among serving bowls
and pour ¾ cup (6 fl oz/175 ml) of the curry
into each bowl. Top with the bean sprouts,
yard-long beans, lemongrass, and cucumber
and serve.

ห่อหมกขนมครก

Spicy Fish Curry Bites

Origin South
Preparation time 10 minutes
Cooking time 3–5 minutes
Serves 2

1 cup (9 oz/250 g) pounded white fish meat
2 tablespoons Red Curry Paste (see p. 38)
1½ teaspoons fish sauce
1 egg, beaten
1 cup (9 fl oz/250 ml) coconut milk
1 tablespoon finely sliced kaffir lime leaves
1 red spur chile, cut into rings

Put the fish meat, curry paste, fish sauce, and
beaten egg in a large bowl and mix well, then
while stirring, slowly pour in the coconut milk
and stir until smooth.

Pour the mixture into a *khanom krok* pan or
pancake puff pan, sprinkle with the kaffir lime
leaves and chiles, then cover with the lids,
and put the pan over medium heat. Cook for
3–5 minutes. Serve.

แกงคั่วหอยทานสับปะรด

Red Curry with Clams and Pineapple

Origin Central
Preparation time 10 minutes, plus soaking time
Cooking time 20 minutes
Serves 2

1 lb 2 oz/500 g live Atlantic surf clams, cleaned, or 11 oz/300 g clam meat
1⅔ cups (14 fl oz/400 ml) coconut milk
2 pineapples, peeled, cored, and chopped into ¾-inch/2-cm pieces
1 tablespoon fish sauce
2 tablespoons finely shredded kaffir lime leaves
1 tablespoon jaggery, palm sugar, or soft light brown sugar

For the chili paste
5 dried red bird's eye chiles, seeded
4 dried red spur chiles, seeded
¼ teaspoon salt
3 thin slices galangal, chopped
2 lemongrass stalks, finely chopped
2 small shallots, chopped
2–3 cloves garlic
1 teaspoon shrimp paste

For the chili paste, soak the dried chiles in a bowl of warm water for 15 minutes or until rehydrated, then drain and chop.

Pound the chiles and salt in a mortar with a pestle until fine flakes. Gradually add the galangal, lemongrass, shallots, and garlic and pound until smooth. Add the shrimp paste and pound again until smooth and thoroughly combined. Set aside.

Put the clams in a wok or pan, cover with a lid, then steam over medium heat for 2 minutes or until the clam shells have opened and the clams begin to cook. Discard any clams that are still closed. Let cool, then open the clams and remove the meat and set aside. Discard the shells.

Bring half the coconut milk to a boil in a pan over medium heat. Add 2 tablespoons of the chili paste, stir, and mix until the chili paste has dissolved and combined with the coconut milk. Boil for 3–4 minutes, stirring occasionally, until fragrant and the oil from the coconut milk has separated. Pour in the remaining coconut milk and return to a boil. Add the pineapple and cook for 5–7 minutes or until the pineapple has softened. Add the clam meat, fish sauce, kaffir lime leaves, and sugar, then gently stir and cook for another 2 minutes or until the sugar has dissolved. Serve.

ผัดปูม้า

Stir-Fried Blue Crab Curry

Origin South
Preparation time 20 minutes, plus freezing time
Cooking time 8 minutes
Serves 2

2 x 11-oz/300-g live blue crabs, cleaned
3 tablespoons vegetable oil
5 cloves garlic, finely pounded
1 egg, beaten
1 tablespoon soy sauce
1 teaspoon fish sauce
1½ teaspoons granulated sugar
1½ teaspoons curry powder
3 tablespoons chicken broth (stock) or water
6 scallions (spring onions), diagonally sliced into
   1½-inch/4-cm lengths
1 cup (3½ oz/100 g) Chinese celery, cut into 1½-inch/
   4-cm lengths

Put the crabs in the freezer for 20 minutes. Remove and put into a large bowl.

Take 1 crab and place on a cutting (chopping) board. Turn the crab onto its back with its legs facing upward. Raise the tail flap and push a small screwdriver or skewer through the hole underneath. Press firmly down on the screwdriver handle until it hits the other side of the shell. Remove the screwdriver and repeat with the remaining crab.

Remove the crab apron and carapace and rinse until clean. Cut the crabs in half vertically and then cut each piece horizontally again. Remove the crab claws, then crush the claws and set aside. Blanch the crab and crab claws in a pan of boiling water for 2 minutes or until cooked, then drain and set aside.

Heat the oil in a wok over medium heat, add the garlic, and quickly stir-fry for 1 minute or until fragrant. Add the crab, increase the heat to medium-high, and stir-fry for another 1 minute. Add the egg and stir-fry for about 10 seconds or until the egg is cooked. Season with the soy sauce, fish sauce, sugar, curry powder, and add the broth (stock) or water, scallions (spring onions), and celery. Stir-fry for another 1–2 minutes or until well mixed. Serve.

Photo p. 227

แกงกะทิปูม้า

Blue Crab and Coconut Milk Curry

Origin South
Preparation time 20 minutes, plus freezing time
Cooking time 15 minutes
Serves 2

2 x 11-oz/300-g live blue crabs, cleaned
1⅔ cups (14 fl oz/400 ml) coconut milk
2 tablespoons Southern Chili Paste (see p. 38)
½ cup (4 fl oz/120 ml) chicken or fish broth (stock)
1½ tablespoons fish sauce
1½ teaspoons jaggery, palm sugar, or soft light
   brown sugar

To serve
Steamed Jasmine Rice (see p.378)
raw and steamed vegetables, such as sliced cucumber
   and round eggplants (aubergines)

Put the crabs in the freezer for 20 minutes. Remove and put into a large bowl.

Take 1 crab and place on a cutting (chopping) board. Turn the crab onto its back with its legs facing upward. Raise the tail flap and push a small screwdriver or skewer through the hole underneath. Press firmly down on the screwdriver handle until it hits the other side of the shell. Remove the screwdriver and repeat with the remaining crab.

Remove the crab apron and carapace and rinse until clean. Cut the crabs in half vertically and then cut each piece horizontally again. Remove the crab claws, then crush the claws and set aside.

Bring half the coconut milk to a boil in a pan over medium heat. Add the chili paste and stir continuously for 2–3 minutes or until fragrant. Add the crab and crab claws and broth (stock), then bring to a boil and boil for 2 minutes. Add the fish sauce, sugar, and the rest of the coconut milk, then reduce the heat slightly and let it lightly boil for another 2–3 minutes or until the crab is cooked and full flavored. Serve with rice and vegetables.

Spicy Coconut Milk Curry (Made from Field Crab)

น้ำแกงกะทิ [น้ำแกงปู]

Origin Central
Preparation time 15 minutes
Cooking time 10 minutes
Serves 6

15–20 field crabs
4¼ cups (1¾ pints/1 liter) coconut milk
2 tablespoons Tamarind Puree (see p. 63)
⅓ cup (2½ oz/75 g) jaggery, palm sugar, or soft light brown sugar
4–5 kaffir lime leaves
salt
2¼ lb/1 kg cooked rice noodles, to serve

For the chili paste
10 dried red bird's eye chiles, chopped
1 teaspoon black pepper
1 garlic bulb, cloves separated and chopped
5 shallots, chopped
1 tablespoon finely sliced turmeric root
4–5 thin slices galangal
2 lemongrass stalks, chopped
1 teaspoon shrimp paste

For the chili paste, soak the dried chiles in a bowl of warm water for 15 minutes or until rehydrated, then drain and chop.

Pound the chiles, black pepper, garlic, shallots, turmeric, galangal, and lemongrass in a mortar with a pestle until smooth. Add the shrimp paste and pound again until smooth. Remove from the mortar and set aside.

Pound the field crabs in the mortar with the pestle to release the juices, then strain through a colander or strainer (sieve) into a bowl and reserve the juice.

Bring the coconut milk to a boil in a large pan. Add the chili paste and return to a boil. Add the crab juice, tamarind, sugar, and kaffir lime leaves, then season to taste with salt. Serve with rice noodles.

Shrimp and Vegetable Yellow Curry

แกงกะหรี่กุ้ง

Origin South
Preparation time 15 minutes
Cooking time 15 minutes
Serves 2

2 cups (16 fl oz/475 ml) coconut milk
1½ tablespoons Yellow Curry Paste (see p. 42)
2 tablespoons fish sauce
4 tablespoons jaggery, palm sugar, or soft light brown sugar
2 teaspoons Tamarind Puree (see p. 63)
12 cherry tomatoes
1½ onions, sliced
8 uncooked jumbo shrimp (king prawns)
20 snow peas (mangetout)
2 tablespoons Fried Shallots (see p. 64), to garnish
Steamed Jasmine Rice (see p. 378), to serve

Bring scant 1½ cup (12 fl oz/350 ml) coconut milk to a boil in a wok over medium heat. Add the curry paste, stir, and cook for 3–4 minutes or until fragrant and the texture has thickened. Add the fish sauce, sugar, tamarind, tomatoes, onion, 2 tablespoons water and the remaining coconut milk, and and return to a boil. Reduce the heat slightly and cook for 2–3 minutes or until the tomatoes and onion have softened. Add the shrimp (prawns) and cook for another 3–4 minutes or until the shrimp are cooked. Add the snow peas (mangetout) and cook for 1 minute. Sprinkle with the fried shallots and serve with rice.

Spicy-and-Sour Curry with Shrimp and Acacia Leaf Omelet

Origin Central
Preparation time 10 minutes
Cooking time 15–20 minutes
Serves 4

3 cups (1¼ pints/750 ml) chicken broth (stock)
4 tablespoons Kaeng Som Chili Paste (see p. 36)
3 tablespoons fish sauce
3 tablespoons Tamarind Puree (see p. 63)
1½ teaspoons lime juice (optional)
12 uncooked jumbo shrimp (king prawns), peeled
   and deveined, with tails still intact
Steamed Jasmine Rice (see p. 378), to serve

For the deep-fried acacia leaf omelet
1 bunch acacia leaves
3 eggs, beaten
½ cup (4 fl oz/120 ml) vegetable oil, for deep-frying

For the deep-fried acacia leaf omelet, rinse the acacia twigs and pick only the leaves and young stems.

Put the beaten eggs and acacia leaves and stems in a bowl and mix well with a fork.

Heat the oil for deep-frying in a large wok over medium heat. When fully heated, carefully pour in the acacia leaf mixture and cook for about 3 minutes on both sides or until golden brown and crispy. Remove with a slotted spoon and drain on paper towels. Cut into 1-inch/2.5-cm-square pieces and set aside.

Bring the broth (stock) to a boil in a large pan over medium heat. Add the chili paste, and stir until the paste has dissolved. Return to a boil for 2–3 minutes, then season with the fish sauce, tamarind, sugar, and lime juice, if using. Return to a boil then add the acacia leaf omelet and shrimp (prawns). Cook for another 2–3 mintues or until the shrimp are cooked. Remove from the heat and ladle into serving bowls. Serve with rice.

น้ายาน้ำพริก

Spicy-and-Sweet Curry

Origin South
Preparation time 10 minutes, plus soaking time
Cooking time 40–45 minutes
Serves 4

½ cup (3½ oz/100 g) split mung beans
1⅔ cups (14 fl oz/400 ml) coconut milk
1⅔ cups (7 oz/200 g) uncooked shrimp (prawns),
  peeled deveined, and ground (minced)
½ cup (2¾ oz/75 g) unsalted roasted peanuts, pounded
1½ cups (12 fl oz/350 ml) chicken broth (stock)
1 tablespoon fish sauce
1½ teaspoons jaggery, palm sugar, or soft light
  brown sugar
2 teaspoons Tamarind Puree (see p. 63)
2 tablespoons vegetable oil
8 green and red bird's eye chiles
rice vermicelli, to serve

For the chili paste
5 dried red spur chiles
2 tablespoons vegetable oil
5 cloves garlic, chopped
5 shallots, chopped
½ teaspoon salt

For the chili paste, soak the chiles in a bowl of warm water for 15 minutes or until rehydrated, then drain and chop. Set aside.

Toast the mung beans in a wok over medium heat for 5–6 minutes or until they begin to brown and become fragrant. Transfer to a food processor and process into fine flakes. Set aside.

To make the chili paste, heat the oil in a wok over medium heat, add the chiles, and sauté for 30 seconds or until fragrant and they begin to brown. Drain and set aside. Dry-fry the garlic and shallots in a wok or pan over medium heat for 5–6 minutes or until they turn brown and become fragrant. Set aside.

Pound the chiles and salt together in a mortar with a pestle until smooth, then add the toasted garlic and shallots and pound again until smooth. Set aside.

Bring 2 cups (16 fl oz/475 ml) coconut milk to a boil in a wok or pan over medium heat. Add the chili paste and sauté for 5–6 minutes or until the oil from the coconut milk has separated. Add the shrimp (prawns) and stir-fry for 1–2 minutes or until the shrimp are cooked. Add the peanuts, mung beans, chicken broth (stock), and the remaining coconut milk, and stir until combined. Season with the fish sauce, sugar, and tamarind. Reduce the heat to low and simmer for 10–15 minutes, stirring occasionally, until the mung beans and peanuts are cooked and fully flavored.

Meanwhile, heat the oil in a skillet or frying pan over medium heat, add the whole chiles, and sauté for 1–2 minutes or until they have darkened in color. Set aiside.

Serve the curry with rice vermicelli and topped with the fried chiles.

แกงส้มกุ้ง

Spicy-and-Sour Curry with Shrimp

Origin Central
Preparation time 15 minutes, plus soaking time
Cooking time 15 minutes
Serves 4

2 cups (16 fl oz/475 ml) chicken or vegetable
  broth (stock)
3½ oz/100 g zucchini (courgette) flowers
1⅔ cups (7 oz/200 g) sliced young watermelon
  or round zucchini (courgettes), cut into ¾-inch/
  2-cm-thick pieces
1 cup (3½ oz/100 g) sliced yard-long beans, sliced
  into 1-inch/2.5-cm pieces
3 tablespoons fish sauce
2 tablespoons granulated sugar
½ cup (4 fl oz/120 ml) Tamarind Puree (see p. 63)
3⅓ cups (14 oz/400 g) uncooked shrimp (prawns),
  peeled and deveined, with tails still intact

For the kaeng som paste
4 dried red spur chilies, seeded
½ teaspoon salt
3 cloves garlic
3 shallots, chopped
1 teaspoon shrimp paste

To serve
Steamed Jasmine Rice (see p. 378)

For the paste, soak the dried chiles in a bowl of warm water for 15 minutes or until rehydrated, then drain, put in a mortar with the salt, and pound together until smooth. Add the garlic and shallots and pound again until smooth. Add the shrimp paste and pound until thoroughly combined. Set aside.

Bring the broth (stock), 2 cups (16 fl oz/475 ml) water, and the paste to a boil in a large pan over medium heat. Add the vegetables and boil for 3 minutes. Season with the fish sauce, sugar, and tamarind and gently stir. Add the shrimp (prawns) and boil for 1–2 minutes or until the shrimp are just cooked. Adjust the taste, if necessary, with fish sauce, tamarind, and sugar. The taste should be sweet, sour, and salty. Serve with rice.

มัสมั่นเนื้อ

Beef Massaman Curry

Origin South
Preparation time 15 minutes
Cooking time 2 hours 20 minutes
Serves 4–6

3½ cups (1¾ pints/800 ml) coconut milk
1 lb 2 oz/500 g brisket or chuck beef cut into 1¼-inch/
  3-cm cubes
2 tablespoons vegetable oil
½ cup (4 oz/120 ml) Massaman Curry Paste (see p. 40)
10 onions, quartered
⅔ cup (3½ oz/100 g) unsalted peanuts, roasted
3 bay leaves
2 tablespoons fish sauce
½ cup (3½ oz/100 g) soft light brown sugar
1½ teaspoons Tamarind Puree (see p. 63)
1 small cinnamon stick
5 cardamom pods
4 potatoes, peeled and cut into 1½-inch/4-cm pieces
1 small sweet potato, peeled and cut into 1½-inch/
  4-cm pieces

To serve
Steamed Jasmine Rice (see p. 378) or roti
Cucumber Relish (see p. 35)

Bring half the coconut milk and scant ½ cup (3½ fl oz/100 ml) water to a boil in a large pan over medium-high heat. Add the beef and return to a boil. Reduce the heat, cover with a lid, and simmer for 50–60 minutes.

Meanwhile, heat the oil in a wok over medium heat, add the curry paste, and stir for 1–2 minutes or until sizzling and fragrant. Gradually add ⅔ cup (¼ pint/150 ml) coconut milk and stir for 2 minutes. Remove from the heat and set aside

After the beef has finished simmering, add the paste, onions, peanuts, bay leaves, fish sauce, sugar, tamarind, cinnamon, cardamom pods, and the rest of the coconut milk and put over low-medium heat for 40 minutes. Add the potatoes and sweet potato, then reduce the heat to low, partly cover, and simmer for another 30–40 minutes or until the beef is tender. Serve with rice or roti.

Photo p. 232

พะแนงเนื้อโพนยาง

Dry Beef Curry

Origin Central
Preparation time 25 minutes, plus soaking time
Cooking time 15 minutes
Serves 4

2 tablespoons vegetable oil
scant 1 cup (7 fl oz/200 ml) coconut milk
14 oz/400 g beef shank or rump, cut into bite-size
  pieces
1 tablespoon granulated sugar
1 tablespoon fish sauce
½ teaspoon ground roasted cumin and coriander seeds
Steamed Jasmine Rice (see p. 378), to serve

For the dry curry paste
5 dried red spur chiles, seeded
½ teaspoon salt
1 tablespoon sliced lemongrass
1 teaspoon sliced galangal
1½ teaspoons kaffir lime zest
4–5 small shallots
6 cloves garlic
1 teaspoon sliced cilantro (coriander) root
½ teaspoon black peppercorns
½ teaspoon ground coriander
1 teaspoon ground cumin seeds
½ teaspoon ground cardamom
1 teaspoon shrimp paste

To garnish
coconut cream
1 red spur chile, thinly sliced diagonally
2 kaffir lime leaves, finely chopped
a handful of sweet basil leaves

For the curry paste, soak the dried chiles in a bowl of warm water for 15 minutes or until rehydrated, then drain and chop.

Pound the chiles and salt in a mortar with the pestle until fine flakes form. Add the lemongrass, galangal, kaffir zest, shallots, garlic, cilantro (coriander) root, peppercorns, ground coriander, ground cumin, ground cardamom, and pound again until smooth. Add the shrimp paste and pound until combined. Set aside.

Heat the oil in a wok over medium heat, add 1½ tablespoons curry paste and sauté for 1 minute or until fragrant. Add half the coconut milk, stir, and cook for 1–2 minutes or until the coconut milk thickens. Add the beef and cook for 4–5 minutes or until the beef is cooked. Add the sugar, fish sauce, ground cumin and coriander seeds, and the rest of the coconut milk and stir until combined. Reduce the heat to low and simmer for another 4–5 minutes or until fully flavored. Add a swirl of coconut cream, garnish with the chile, kaffir lime leaves, and basil and serve with rice.

แกงอ่อมเนื้อ

Spicy Beef and Vegetable Curry

Origin North
Preparation time 10 minutes
Cooking time 35 minutes
Serves 2–3

2 tablespoons vegetable oil
11 oz/300 g chuck beef, sliced into thin bite-size pieces
5 thin slices young galangal
1 lemongrass stalk, thinly diagonally sliced
2 cilantro (coriander) roots, coarsely crushed
4 cups (1⅝ pints/950 ml) chicken broth (stock)
1 tablespoon fermented fish sauce
1 tablespoon fish sauce
5 kaffir lime leaves, torn
1 handful of dill, coarsely chopped
3 skunk-vine tips (optional)
7 red bird's eye chiles
3 scallions (spring onions), chopped into 1½-inch/
    4-cm lengths

For the chili paste
5–7 dried red bird's eye chiles, chopped
½ teaspoon salt
2 small shallots, chopped
5 cloves garlic, chopped
1 lemongrass stalk, finely sliced
2 thin slices galangal, chopped
1 long pepper
½ teaspoon Sichuan peppercorns
¼ teaspoon coriander seeds
¼ teaspoon dill seed

For the chili paste, pound the chiles, salt, shallots, garlic, lemongrass, galangal, long pepper, peppercorns, coriander seeds, and dill seeds together in a mortar with a pestle until smooth. Set aside.

Heat the oil in a large pan over medium heat, add the chili paste, and sauté for 1 minute or until fragrant. Add the beef, galangal, lemongrass, and cilantro (coriander) roots and stir-fry for 2 minutes or until the beef starts to cook. Add the broth (stock), fermented fish sauce, and fish sauce and simmer for 30 minutes or until the beef is tender. Add the kaffir lime leaves, dill, skunk-vine tips, chiles, and scallions (spring onions), and cook for another 1–2 minutes. Serve.

ขนมจีนแกงเขียวหวานเนื้อ

Beef and Coconut Milk Curry

Origin Central
Preparation time 10 minutes
Cooking time 30–35 minutes
Serves 4

3 tablespoons vegetable oil
3½ tablespoons Green Curry Paste (see p. 37)
2½ cups (1 pint/600 ml) coconut milk
1 lb 2 oz/500 g beef brisket, thinly sliced
2½ tablespoons fish sauce
2 tablespoons granulated sugar
10–12 round eggplants (aubergines), quartered
5 red spur chiles, sliced lengthwise diagonally
2 handfuls of sweet basil

To serve
1 lb 2 oz/500 g cooked rice vermicelli
2½ cups (9 oz/250 g) bean sprouts
11 oz/300 g water spinach, finely sliced and blanched
3–4 hard-boiled eggs, halved

Heat the oil in a wok over medium heat, add the green curry paste, and sauté for 1–2 minutes until fragrant. Add 1 cup (9 fl oz/250 ml) coconut milk and cook for 2–3 minutes until the mixture thickens and the oil from the coconut milk separates and comes to the surface. Add the beef and stir for about 4 minutes, then add 2 cups (16 fl oz/475 ml) water and bring to a boil over high heat. Reduce the heat to low, cover, and simmer for about 20 minutes, stirring occasionally.

Season with the fish sauce and sugar and cook for another 5 minutes. Add the eggplants (aubergine) and chiles, then bring to a boil and cook for 5 minutes. Add the basil leaves, stir, and remove from the heat.

Serve the beef curry with the cooked vermicelli, bean sprouts, water spinach, and hard-boiled eggs.

Photo p. 234

ก๋วยเตี๋ยวแกง

Beef Curry with Noodles

Origin Central
Preparation time 15 minutes, plus soaking time
Cooking time 55 minutes
Serves 4

12 oz/350 g dried rice vermicelli
1–2 tablespoons vegetable oil
3 cups (1¼ pints/750 ml) coconut milk
1 lb 2 oz/500 g beef brisket, sliced
1½ cups (12 fl oz/350 ml) beef broth (stock)
1 teaspoon salt
2 tablespoons jaggery, palm sugar, or soft light
  brown sugar
½ cup (2½ oz/65 g) chopped salted turnips
2 cups (7 oz/200 g) bean sprouts
½ cup (2¾ oz/75 g) peanuts, roasted and coarsely
  pounded
3½ oz/100 g extra-firm tofu, cut into small cubes
2 tablespoons Fried Shallots (see p. 64)
2–3 hard-boiled eggs, halved

For the yellow curry paste
7 dried red spur chiles
5 cloves garlic
⅝-inch/1½-cm piece fresh ginger, peeled
  and sliced
1 teaspoon salt
1 tablespoon sliced lemongrass
3 thin slices galangal
3 shallots, sliced
2 teaspoons ground coriander
1⅛ teaspoons curry powder
½ teaspoon ground turmeric
½ teaspoon ground cumin
1 teaspoon shrimp paste

To garnish
½ cup (1 oz/25 g) chopped cilantro (coriander)
½ cup (1½ oz/40 g) chopped scallions (spring onions)

Soak the rice vermicelli in a bowl of water for 10 minutes or according to package directions, then drain and set aside.

Meanwhile, for the curry paste, soak the dried chiles in a bowl of warm water for 15 minutes or until rehydrated, then drain and chop.

Dry-fry the garlic and ginger in a wok over medium heat for 5 minutes or until fragrant and brown. Set aside.

Pound the drained chiles and salt in a mortar with a pestle until smooth. Add the lemongrass and galangal and continue to pound until thoroughly combined. Add the roasted garlic and ginger and pound until mixed well. Add the shallots and continue to pound, then add the spices and shrimp paste and pound to a smooth paste.

Heat the oil in a pan over medium heat, add the curry paste, and sauté for 2–3 minutes until fragrant. Remove from the heat and set aside.

Bring 4 cups (1⅔ pints/950 ml) water and half the coconut milk to a boil in a large pan over medium heat. Add the beef and return to a boil. Reduce the heat and simmer for 40 minutes.

Add the remaining coconut milk and the broth (stock), and return to a boil. Add the fried chili paste, and season with the salt and sugar. Boil for about 5 minutes, then remove from the heat.

Cook the vermicelli in a pan of boiling water for 2 minutes or until soft. Drain and divide among serving bowls. Add 1½ cups (12 fl oz/350 ml) of the curried soup and 3–4 slices of beef to each serving bowl. Top with the salted turnips, bean sprouts, peanuts, tofu, fried shallots, and egg. Garnish with the cilantro (coriander) and scallions (spring onions) and serve.

Photo p. 237

แกงโฮะ

Leftover Curry
with Noodles

Origin North
Preparation time 1 hour, plus soaking time
Cooking time 5 minutes
Serves 4

3 tablespoons vegetable oil
1½ cups (9 oz/250 g) Hunglei Curry (see p. 239)
½ cup (2½ oz/65 g) pea eggplants (aubergines)
1 cup (3¼ oz/90 g) sliced yard-long beans, cut into
  1¼-inch/3-cm lengths
1 cup (3½ oz/100 g) sour pickled bamboo shoots
5 oz/150 g glass noodles, soaked and cut into 2-inch/
  5-cm-long pieces
1–2 teaspoons fish sauce
1 cup (2 oz/50 g) ivy gourd leaves
5 kaffir lime leaves, torn
½ cup (1 oz/25 g) chopped sawtooth cilantro (coriander)
½ cup (1 oz/25 g) chopped holy basil
1 teaspoon granulated sugar

For the chili paste
5 dried red spur chiles
½ teaspoon salt
2 tablespoons chopped lemongrass
2 cloves garlic, chopped
2 thin slices galangal
1 shallot, chopped

For the chili paste, soak the dried chiles in
a bowl of warm water for 15 minutes or until
rehydrated, then drain and chop.

Pound the chiles and salt in a mortar with a
pestle. Add the lemongrass, garlic, galangal,
and shallot and pound until smooth, then
set aside.

Heat the oil in a wok over medium heat, add
the chili paste, and sauté for 1 minute or until
sizzling and fragrant. Add the curry and cook
for another 1 minute before adding the pea
eggplants (aubergines) and yard-long beans.
Stir-fry for 1 minute, then add the bamboo
shoots and stir for 30 seconds. Add the noodles
and fish sauce and stir-fry for 1 minute before
adding the ivy gourd leaves, lime leaves,
cilantro (coriander), basil, and sugar. Continue
stirring for another minute until thoroughly
combined. Serve.

แกงเห็ดซี่โครงอ่อน

Spicy Pork Rib and
Mushroom Curry

Origin North
Preparation time 10 minutes
Cooking time 40 minutes
Serves 2

2 cups (16 fl oz/475 ml) pork or chicken broth (stock)
¼ teaspoon salt
11 oz/300 g soft bone pork spareribs
1½ teaspoons vegetable oil
1 tablespoon fish sauce
1 tablespoon oyster sauce
2 teaspoons superfine (caster) sugar
2 oz/50 g young acacia leaves
10 betel leaves coarsely sliced
5 cloud ear fungus
3 oz/80 g enoki mushrooms
5 straw mushrooms, halved
3 sawtooth cilantro (coriander) leaves

For the red curry paste
3 dried red spur chiles
3 dried red bird's eye chiles
2 shallots, chopped
5 cloves garlic, sliced
1 teaspoon shrimp paste

For the curry paste, soak the dried chiles in
a bowl of warm water for 15 minutes or until
rehydrated, then drain and chop.

Pound the chiles, shallots, garlic, and shrimp
paste in a mortar with a pestle until smooth.
Set aside.

Bring the broth (stock), 2 cups (16 fl oz/475 ml)
water, and the salt to a boil in a large pan over
high heat. Add the ribs and return to a boil.
Remove any scum on the surface. Reduce the
heat to low, cover the pan, and simmer for
30 minutes or until the ribs are tender.

Heat the oil in a pan over medium heat, add
the curry paste, and sauté for 1 minute or
until fragrant. Add the paste to the broth, then
season with the fish sauce, oyster sauce, and
sugar and cook for another 3–4 minutes. Add
the acacia leaves, betel leaves, and mushrooms
and simmer for 1 minute or until softened.
Add the cilantro (coriander), stir, and serve.

แกงฮังเล

Hunglei Curry

Origin North
Preparation time 15 minutes, plus soaking
and marinating time
Cooking time 50 minutes
Serves 4

11 oz/300 g pork shoulder, cut into 1¼-inch/3-cm pieces
9 oz/250 g pork side (belly), cut into ¾-inch/
  2-cm pieces
1 cup (5½ oz/165 g) pineapple chunks
3 tablespoons vegetable oil
1 tablespoon fish sauce
1½ teaspoons Tamarind Puree (see p. 63)
⅓ cup (2¾ oz/75 g) jaggery, palm sugar, or soft light
  brown sugar
1 cup (5 oz/150 g) unsalted roasted peanuts
1½-inch/4-cm piece fresh ginger, peeled and finely
  julienned
½ cup (3¼ oz/90 g) finely diced tomatoes
1 large clove garlic
Steamed Jasmine Rice (see p. 378) or Glutinous Rice
  (see p. 378), to serve

For the chili paste
5 dried red spur chiles, chopped
1 teaspoon salt
1 teaspoon sliced galangal
2 lemongrass stalks, finely sliced
3 cloves garlic, chopped
2 shallots, chopped
2 teaspoons shrimp paste
1½ teaspoons Hunglei or ordinary curry powder

For the chili paste, soak the dried chiles in a bowl of warm water for 15 minutes or until rehydrated, then drain and chop.

Pound the chiles and salt in a mortar with a pestle. Add the galangal and lemongrass and pound again thoroughly. Add the garlic and shallots, pound to a paste, then add the shrimp paste and curry powder and pound until thoroughly combined.

Put both cuts of pork, the chili paste, and pineapple into a large bowl and mix well. Cover with plastic wrap (clingfilm) and let marinate in the refrigerator for at least an hour.

Heat the oil in a pan or casserole over medium heat, add the marinated pork, and sauté for 3–4 minutes or until the pork is fragrant. Carefully pour in 2½ cups (1 pint/600 ml) water and stir well. Increase the heat to high and let boil for 10 minutes, then add the fish sauce, tamarind, sugar, peanuts, ginger, tomatoes, and garlic. Partly cover the pan with a lid, reduce the heat to medium-low, and simmer gently for another 30–35 minutes or until the pork is tender and the liquid has reduced by half. Serve with rice.

แกงหมูชะมวง

Pork and Cow Leaf Curry

Origin Northeast
Preparation time 10 minutes, plus marinating time
Cooking time 35–40 minutes
Serves 6

2¼ lb/1 kg pork shoulder joint with fat, cut into
  bite-size pieces
1 cup (8 oz/225 g) jaggery, palm sugar, or soft
  light brown sugar
3 teaspoons salt
1 tablespoon dark soy sauce
3–4 tablespoons vegetable oil
3 cups (1¼ pints/750 ml) chicken broth (stock)
1 lb 2 oz/500 g cow tree leaves or tamarind leaves
4 tablespoons Tamarind Puree (see p. 63)
1 tablespoon fish sauce

For the chili paste
2 oz/50 g dried red chiles, chopped
1 x 2¾-inch/7-cm piece galangal, peeled and chopped
5 shallots, chopped
1 garlic bulb, cloves separated and chopped
1½ cups (3½ oz/100 g) chopped lemongrass stalks
1 tablespoon shrimp paste

Mix the pork, sugar, salt, and soy sauce
together in a large bowl. Cover with plastic
wrap (clingfilm) and let marinate in the
refrigerator for 15 minutes.

For the chili paste, pound all the ingredients
together thoroughly in a mortar with a pestle
until smooth.

Heat the oil in a large wok over medium heat,
add the chili paste, and stir-fry for 1–2 minutes
or until fragrant. Add the pork and stir-fry for
about 5 minutes, stirring continuously. Pour in
the broth (stock), bring to a boil, and boil for
10 minutes. Reduce the heat to low, add the
cow tree leaves, tamarind, and fish sauce and
simmer for 20–30 minutes or until the pork
is tender. Serve.

แกงปลาร้าหน่อไม้

Fermented Fish and Bamboo Shoot Curry

Origin Central
Preparation time 15 minutes
Cooking time 15 minutes
Serves 2

1 lemongrass stalk, finely sliced
3 thin slices galangal
2 small shallots, chopped
2 fingerroots, chopped
1 clove garlic, sliced
1 teaspoon shrimp paste
1¼ cups (½ pint/300 ml) coconut milk
5 oz/150 g ground (minced) pork side (belly) cut
  into bite-size pieces
½ cup (2 oz/50 g) crumbled dried fish
7 oz/200 g canned bamboo shoots, diced into
  ¾-inch/2-cm pieces
1½ tablespoons fermented fish sauce
1½ teaspoons jaggery, palm sugar, or soft light
  brown sugar
¾ teaspoon salt
4 kaffir lime leaves, torn
1 red spur chile, chopped

Pound the lemongrass, galangal, shallots,
fingerroots, garlic, and shrimp paste together
in a mortar with a pestle until smooth. Set aside.

Bring the coconut milk to a boil in a large pan
over medium heat. Add the paste and boil for
3–4 minutes or until fragrant. Add the pork side
(belly), dried fish, and bamboo shoots, then
boil for 5 minutes or until the pork is cooked
through. Season with the fermented fish sauce,
sugar, and salt and cook for another 2 minutes,
or until the bamboo shoots are fully flavored.
Add the kaffir lime leaves and chopped chile
and stir, then serve.

แกงคั่วกลิ้ง

Spicy Dry Pork Curry

Origin South
Preparation time 20 minutes, plus soaking time
Cooking time 15 minutes
Serves 4

3 tablespoons vegetable oil
1 x 2¼-lb/1-kg pork loin, thinly sliced
1½ teaspoons fish sauce
1½ teaspoons jaggery, palm sugar, or soft light
   brown sugar
10 kaffir lime leaves, chopped
1½ oz/40 g young green peppercorns

For the chili paste
2 oz/50 g dried red bird's eye chiles
3½ oz/100 g fresh red chiles, chopped
1 tablespoon black peppercorns
5–7 lemongrass stalks, chopped
1½-inch/4-cm piece galangal, peeled and chopped
3 tablespoons turmeric
1 garlic bulb, cloves separated and chopped
2 shallots, chopped
zest of 1 kaffir lime
1–2 teaspoons salt
1 tablespoon shrimp paste

For the chili paste, soak the dried chiles in
a bowl of warm water for 15 minutes or until
rehydrated, then drain and chop.

Pound the rehydrated and fresh chiles, the
peppercorns, lemongrass, galangal, turmeric,
garlic, shallots, kaffir lime zest, and salt in a
mortar with a pestle until smooth. Add the
shrimp paste and pound again until thoroughly
combined. Set aside.

Heat the oil in a wok over medium heat. Add
the chili paste and stir-fry for 1–2 minutes or
until fragrant. Add the pork and stir-fry for
about 10 minutes or until dry. Season with the
fish sauce and sugar, stir, and add the kaffir
lime leaves and green peppercorns. Stir-fry
for 1–2 minutes. Serve.

แกงหมูหน่อกระวาน

Pork Curry with Siam Cardamom Shoots

Origin South
Preparation time 10 minutes, plus soaking time
Cooking time 15 minutes
Serves 2

2 cups (5 oz/150 g) thinly sliced Siam cardamom
   shoots or fresh ginger
1⅔ cups (14 fl oz/400 ml) coconut milk
3 tablespoons Southern Chili Paste (see p. 38)
1 x 11-oz/300-g pork tenderloin or loin steak, thinly
   sliced
1½ teaspoons fish sauce
½ teaspoon salt
½ teaspoon granulated sugar
5 kaffir lime leaves, torn
Steamed Jasmine Rice (see p. 378), to serve

Soak the cardamom shoots in a bowl of water
for 1–2 minutes, then drain and set aside.

Bring half the coconut milk to a boil in a pan
over medium heat. Add the chili paste and
stir for 4–5 minutes or until fragrant and the
coconut milk has thickened. Add the pork
and cardamon shoots or ginger and cook for
about 5 minutes or until the pork is cooked.
Add the remaining coconut milk and season
with the fish sauce, salt, sugar, and kaffir lime
leaves. Return to a boil for 3–4 minutes, then
serve with rice.

แกงเผ็ดเป็ดย่างลิ้นจี่

Roasted Duck Curry with Lychee

Origin Central
Preparation time 15 minutes, plus marinating time
Cooking time 20 minutes
Serves 4

1 x 14-oz/400-g duck breast
1 tablespoon soy sauce
3 tablespoons vegetable oil
2½ tablespoons Red Curry Paste (see p. 38)
1⅔ cups (14 fl oz/400 ml) coconut milk
scant ½ cup (3½ fl oz/100 ml) chicken broth (stock)
2½ tablespoons fish sauce
2½ tablespoons jaggery, palm sugar, or soft light
  brown sugar
2–3 round eggplants (aubergines), quartered
scant 1 cup (3½ oz/100 g) pea eggplants (aubergines)
⅔ cup (3½ oz/100 g) cubed pineapple, cut into
1¼-inch/3-cm cubes
5–6 kaffir lime leaves, torn
10 lychees or rambutans, peeled and pitted
sweet basil leaves, to garnish
1 red spur chile, finely sliced, to garnish
Steamed Jasmine Rice (see p. 378), to serve

Put the duck breast in a shallow dish and rub the soy sauce all over the meat, then let marinate for 5–10 minutes.

Preheat the broiler (grill) to high. Place the duck breast on the broiler (grill) rack and broil (grill) for about 7–8 minutes on each side until the skin is brown. Remove and slice the duck into ⅝-inch/1½-cm thick pieces. Set aside.

Heat the oil in a wok over medium heat, add the curry paste, and sauté for 1–2 minutes until sizzling and fragrant. Pour in the coconut milk, bring to a boil, and boil for 2–3 minutes. Add the duck and broth (stock) and boil for another 3–4 minutes, then add the fish sauce, sugar, round and pea eggplants (aubergines), pineapple, kaffir lime leaves, and lychees or rambutans. Boil for another 4–5 minutes, then garnish with basil leaves and the red chile and serve with rice.

Photo p. 242

แกงเผ็ดเป็ดย่าง

Roasted Duck Curry

Origin South
Preparation time 10 minutes
Cooking time 10 minutes
Serves 5

2 cloves garlic
1 cilantro (coriander) root
1½ tablespoon Red Curry Paste (see p. 38)
1 tablespoon vegetable oil
1 cup (9 fl oz/250 ml) coconut milk
⅓ cup (1½ oz/40 g) diced pineapple
2 cherry tomatoes, halved
½ cup (2¼ oz/60 g) sliced roasted duck fillet
6 red seedless grapes
¼ teaspoon ground roasted cumin seeds
¼ teaspoon ground roasted coriander seeds
1 kaffir lime leaf, torn
1 red spur chile, diagonally sliced
1½ tablespoons fish sauce
1 teaspoon granulated sugar
15 sweet basil leaves

To garnish
1 red spur chile, diagonally sliced
1 tablespoon coconut cream

Pound the garlic and cilantro (coriander) root in a mortar with a pestle until smooth. Add the curry paste, pound again until thoroughly combined, and set aside.

Heat the oil in a pan over medium heat, add the paste, and stir-fry for 1–2 minutes or until fragrant. Gradually add ⅔ cup (¼ pint/150 ml) coconut milk and bring to a boil. Add the pineapple, tomatoes, duck, grapes, and remaining coconut milk and stir. Add both ground seeds, the kaffir lime leaf, and red chile, reduce the heat, and simmer for about 3 minutes. Season with the fish sauce and sugar, add the basil leaves, and stir. Garnish with the sliced red chile and a swirl of coconut cream. Serve.

แกงเขียวหวานไก่

Green Chicken Curry

Origin Central
Preparation time 15 minutes
Cooking time 15 minutes
Serves 4

3 tablespoons vegetable oil
2 tablespoons Green Curry Paste (see p. 37)
14 oz/400 g boneless chicken thighs, cut into
  1¼-inch/3-cm cubes
1⅔ cups (14 fl oz/400 ml) coconut milk
1 tablespoon fish sauce
1 tablespoon jaggery, palm sugar, or soft light
  brown sugar
scant 1 cup (3½ oz/100 g) pea eggplants (aubergines)
3½ oz/100 g round eggplants (aubergines), cut
  into quarters
1 cup (2 oz/50 g) sweet basil leaves
1 red spur chile, diagonally sliced
Steamed Jasmine Rice (see p. 378), to serve

To garnish
sweet basil leaves
1 red spur chile, diagonally sliced

Heat the oil in a wok over low-medium heat,
add the curry paste, and stir-fry for about
2 minutes until sizzling and fragrant. Add the
chicken and cook for 1–2 minutes. Pour in half
the coconut milk, stir well, then increase the
heat to medium and cook for 2–3 minutes. Add
the remaining coconut milk, the fish sauce,
and sugar and stir again. Add both eggplants
(aubergines), then cover the wok and let
boil for 4–5 minutes until the eggplants are
cooked. Add the basil leaves and chile, stir for
30 seconds, then transfer to a serving bowl.
Garnish with basil leaves and sliced chiles
and serve with rice.

แกงคั่วไพรไก่บ้าน

Chicken Curry with Herbs

Origin Central
Preparation time 10 minutes
Cooking time 20 minutes
Serves 6

3 tablespoons vegetable oil
3 tablespoons Red Curry Paste (see p. 38)
1½ lb/700 g) boneless chicken thigh, cut into
  small pieces
1 teaspoon salt
1 cup (3 oz/80 g) chopped Siamese cardamom shoots
½ cup (2½ oz/65 g) pea eggplants (aubergines)
½ tablespoon chopped kaffir lime leaves
1 green spur chile
1 red spur chile
Steamed Jasmine Rice (see p. 378), to serve

Heat the oil in a wok over medium heat,
add the curry paste, and sauté for 1 minute
until fragrant. Add the chicken and stir-fry for
4–5 minutes. Carefully pour in ½ cup (4 fl oz/
120 ml) water and cook for another 10 minutes
until the chicken is cooked. Season with salt.
Add the cardamom shoots and eggplants
(aubergines) and cook for 2 minutes, then
add the kaffir lime leaves and chiles and
cook for 2 minutes.

Fill a small bowl to the rim with the rice and
turn upside down in the middle of a serving
plate. Serve with the curry.

Photo p. 245

Spicy Chicken Curry

Origin South
Preparation time 10 minutes
Cooking time 15–20 minutes
Serves 6

2 cups (16 fl oz/475 ml) chicken broth (stock)
3 tablespoons Southern Chili Paste (see p. 38)
1 lb 2 oz/500 g chicken thighs, boned and cut into
  small pieces
1½-inch/4-cm piece galangal, peeled and sliced
1½ teaspoons fish sauce
1 teaspoon granulated sugar
½ teaspoon salt
7 kaffir lime leaves, torn
2 cups (2½ oz/65 g) pennywort or watercress (optional)
Steamed Jasmine Rice (see p. 378), to serve

Bring the broth (stock) to a boil in a large
pan. Add the chili paste and return to a boil
for 2–3 minutes. Add the chicken and boil for
another 4–5 minutes. Add the galangal, fish
sauce, sugar, and salt and return to a boil for
5–6 minutes until the chicken is cooked and
fully flavored. Add the kaffir lime leaves and
pennywort or watercress and cook for another
1 minute. Serve with rice.

Spicy Chicken Curry and Young Banana

Origin Central
Preparation time 10 minutes
Cooking time 15 minutes
Serves 4

2 teaspoons salt
6 young small bananas
1 cup (9 fl oz/250 ml) coconut cream
1 lb 2 oz/500 g chicken meat, sliced
3 cups (1¼ pints/750 ml) coconut milk
1 tablespoon fish sauce
1 tablespoon granulated sugar
Steamed Jasmine Rice (see p. 378), to serve

For the chili paste
20 red and green bird's eye chiles, chopped
1 teaspoon white peppercorns
1 shallot, sliced
6 cloves garlic, chopped
1 tablespoon chopped galangal
3 lemongrass stalks, sliced
2 teaspoons salt
2 tablespoons shrimp paste

To garnish
1 red finger chile
1 handful of sweet basil leaves

For the chili paste, pound all the ingredients
together in a mortar with a pestle until smooth.
Set aside.

Dissolve the salt in 2 cups (16 fl oz/475 ml)
water, then wash the peeled bananas in the
saltwater before slicing them about 1¼ inches/
3 cm thick.

Heat the coconut cream in a wok over medium
heat, add the chili paste, chicken meat, and the
coconut milk and simmer for about 10 minutes
until the banana is cooked. Season with the fish
sauce and sugar, garnish with the chile and
basil, and serve with rice.

Photo p. 247

ผัดเผ็ดไก่หน่อไม้

Spicy Chicken Curry with Bamboo Shoots

Origin Central
Preparation time 10 minutes
Cooking time 12 minutes
Serves 2

4–5 orange and red spur chiles, chopped
4–5 cloves garlic, chopped
2 tablespoons vegetable oil
7 oz/200 g boneless, skinless chicken breast,
  cut into bite-size pieces
2¼ cups (11 oz/300 g) sliced bamboo shoot strips
2 tablespoons fish sauce
1 teaspoon granulated sugar
4–5 kaffir lime leaves, torn
1 handful of holy basil leaves
1 red spur chile, diagonally sliced, to garnish
Steamed Jasmine Rice (see p. 378), to serve

Pound the chiles and garlic together in a mortar with a pestle until smooth.

Heat the oil in a wok over medium heat, add the chile-garlic mixture, and sauté for 1 minute or until fragrant. Add the chicken and stir-fry for 3–4 minutes or until the chicken is cooked. Add the bamboo shoots and stir-fry for another 1 minute. Season with the fish sauce, sugar, and kaffir lime leaves and stir-fry for 3–4 minutes until thoroughly combined. Garnish with the basil leaves and sliced red chile, and serve with rice.

Photo p. 248

ก๋วยเตี๋ยวไก่ตุ๋นมะระ

Chicken and Bitter Gourd Curry Soup with Noodles

Origin Central
Preparation time 15 minutes, plus soaking time
Cooking time 45–50 minutes
Serves 2

3½ oz/100 g dried rice noodles
1 x 3½-oz/100-g boneless, skinless chicken breast
1 cup (3½ oz/100 g) bean sprouts
6 slices pork blood curd
2 tablespoons chopped cilantro (coriander)
2 tablespoons chopped scallions (spring onions)

For the curry soup
4¼ cups (1¾ pints/1 liter) chicken broth (stock)
2 star anise
2 cinnamon sticks
¼ cup (2 fl oz/60 ml) soy sauce
2 teaspoons salt
scant ¼ cup (1½ oz/40 g) superfine (caster) sugar
1 tablespoon coriander seeds
1 tablespoon dark soy sauce
2 tablespoons soy sauce
½ cup (2½ oz/65 g) diced bitter gourd

Soak the dried noodles in a bowl of water for 10 minutes or prepare according to package directions. Drain and set aside.

Cook the chicken in a pan of boiling water over medium heat for 4–5 minutes or until cooked. Remove with a slotted spoon and shred into bite-size pieces with a fork. Set aside.

For the curry soup, bring the broth (stock) to a boil in a large pan over medium heat and add the remaining ingredients except for the bitter gourd and boil for about 5 minutes. Add the bitter gourd, return to a boil, and cook for another 5 minutes. Reduce the heat to low and let simmer for 30 minutes.

Blanch the bean sprouts in a pan of boiling water for 1–2 minutes, then drain, add to the noodles, and divide among serving bowls. Add the shredded chicken, pork blood curd, cilantro (coriander), and scallions (spring onions), then pour the soup into the bowls and serve.

ข้าวเหลืองจิ๊นไก่

Chicken Curry with Yellow Glutinous Rice

Origin North
Preparation time 15–30 minutes, plus soaking and marinating time
Cooking time 1 hour
Serves 6

1 cup (7 oz/200 g) glutinous (sticky) rice
1 teaspoon ground turmeric
1 x 1 lb 2-oz/500 g boneless chicken thigh, cut into
    4 x 1½-inch/4-cm pieces
3 tablespoons vegetable oil
10 cherry tomatoes
¼ teaspoon salt
3 tablespoons Fried Shallots (see p. 64), to garnish

For the chili paste
5 red dried spur chiles, seeded
1 fermented soybean sheet (see p. 34)
1 teaspoon salt
1 lemongrass stalk, finely sliced
2 shallots, chopped
5 cloves garlic, chopped
½ teaspoon shrimp paste

Soak the glutinous (sticky) rice in a bowl of water with the ground turmeric overnight, then drain.Wrap the rice in cheesecloth (muslin) and steam for 30–35 minutes, stirring the rice every 10 minutes until cooked through. The rice will look transparent when cooked. Keep covered until ready to serve.

For the chili paste, soak the dried chiles in a bowl of warm water for 15 minutes or until rehydrated, then drain, chop, and set aside.

Preheat the broiler (grill) to medium. Place the soybean sheet on the broiler (grill) pan and broil (grill) for 1–2 minutes until fragrant and dark brown. Let cool and set aside.

Pound the chiles and salt together thoroughly in a mortar with a pestle. Add the soybean sheet, lemongrass, shallots, garlic, and shrimp paste and pound until smooth. Mix the chicken with the chili paste, cover with plastic wrap (clingfilm), and let marinate in the refrigerator for 15–30 minutes.

Heat the oil in a wok over medium heat, add the marinated chicken, and cook for 6–7 minutes or until the chicken starts to brown. Carefully pour in about 2 cups (16 fl oz/475 ml) water, add the tomatoes and salt, and bring to a boil. Reduce the heat and simmer for 40–50 minutes or until the chicken is tender and the liquid has reduced by a third.

Pour the fried shallot oil over the yellow glutinous rice, sprinkle with the fried shallots, and serve with the curry.

Green Curry with Silkworm Pupae

Origin Northeast
Preparation time 10 minutes, plus marinating time
Cooking time 10 minutes
Serves 4

2¼ lb/1 kg silkworm pupae, cleaned
2 tablespoons fish sauce
4 cups (1⅔ pints/950 ml) coconut milk
3 tablspoons Green Curry Paste (see p. 37)
2 long eggplants (aubergines), sliced into 1-inch/
   2.5-cm pieces
7 dried red spur chiles, sliced
½ cup (1 oz/25 g) sweet basil leaves
¼ cup (½ oz/15 g) kaffir lime leaves, torn

Blanch the silkworm pupae in a pan of boiling water for 1 minute, then drain and transfer to a heatproof bowl. Add the fish sauce and let marinate for 10 minutes.

Bring the coconut milk to a boil in a pan over medium heat, add the curry paste, and return to a boil. Reduce the heat and simmer for about 2 minutes until fragrant. Add the pupae and eggplants (aubergines) and return to a boil. Cook for 5–7 minutes. Add the chiles, basil, and kaffir lime leaves, stir, and serve.

Sour Horse Mango Curry

Origin South
Preparation time 7 minutes, plus soaking time
Cooking time 8–10 minutes
Serves 2

1 teaspoon salt
2 horse mangoes, peeled and sliced
2 x 7-oz/200-g mackerels, sliced into bite-size pieces
1 tablespoon jaggery, palm sugar, or soft light
   brown sugar

For the chili paste
10 dried red chiles
1 teaspoon salt
4 shallots, chopped
1 tablespoon shrimp paste

For the chili paste, soak the dried chiles in a bowl of warm water for 15 minutes or until rehydrated, then drain and chop.

Pound the dried chiles, salt, shallots, and the shrimp paste in a mortar with a pestle until smooth, then set aside.

Dissolve the salt in 2 cups (16 fl oz/475 ml) water. Soak the horse mangoes in the salt water for 5 minutes, then drain.

Bring 3 cups (1¼ pints/750 ml) water to a boil in a pan over medium heat. Add the paste, stir, and return to a boil. Add the mackerel and horse mango and cook for 6–8 minutes. Add the sugar and stir until dissolved. Serve.

หมกเห็ดยอนซาา

Steamed Mushroom Curry in Banana Leaves

Origin Northeast
Preparation time 15 minutes
Cooking time 15 minutes
Serves 2

5 oz/150 g mushrooms, such as white beach, cleaned
  and stems removed
2 tablespoons beaten egg
1 lemongrass stalk, finely sliced
1 handful of sweet basil leaves
2–3 red bird's eye chiles
1 shallot, sliced
1½ teaspoons fermented fish sauce
1 teaspoon fish sauce
2 banana leaf sheets, about 8 x 9 inches/20 x 23 cm

Mix the mushrooms, egg, lemongrass, basil leaves, chiles, and shallot together in a bowl. Add the fish sauce and fermented fish sauce and mix again.

Place the 2 banana leaf sheets back to back on a work surface with the shiny surface face outward on both sides. Put the mushroom mixture in the center of the banana leaf sheets and flatten the mixture slightly to make it easy to wrap. Cover the curry with the sides of the sheets, fold over the ends, and secure with a toothpick.

Steam the banana-leaf package in a steamer over medium heat for 15 minutes or until cooked. Unwrap and serve.

Photo p. 253

งบข้าาไพด

Corn Curry in Banana Leaves

Origin South
Preparation time 10 minutes
Cooking time 20 minutes
Serves 2

2¼-inch/7-cm fingerroot, chopped
2 teaspoons Red Curry Paste (see p. 38)
1 cup (6 oz/175 g) corn kernels
½ cup (1½ oz/40 g) grated coconut, or dry unsweetened
  (desiccated) coconut
a pinch of salt
2 banana leaf sheets, about 8 x 9 inches/20 x 23 cm

Before you begin cooking, check that your charcoal is glowing white hot, or your gas grill (barbecue) is preheated to 400°F/200°C.

Pound the fingerroot thoroughly in a mortar with a pestle, then add the chili paste, and pound again until smooth. Add the corn kernels, coconut, and salt and pound until the mixture becomes sticky.

Place the 2 banana leaf sheets back to back on a work surface with the shiny surface face outward on both sides. Put the curry mixture in the center of the banana leaf sheets and flatten the mixture slightly to make it easy to wrap. Cover the curry with the sides of the sheets, fold over the ends, and secure with a toothpick.

Grill the banana-leaf package over low heat for 8 minutes on each side or until the curry is cooked. Unwrap and serve.

ต้มกะทิฟักใส่วุ้นเส้น

Coconut Curry with Wax Gourd and Noodles

Origin South
Preparation time 10 minutes, plus soaking time
Cooking time 15–20 minutes
Serves 4

2¼ oz/60 g glass noodles
3 small shallots, sliced
1 teaspoon white peppercorns
½ teaspoon salt
2 teaspoons shrimp paste
1⅔ cups (14 fl oz/400 ml) coconut milk
11 oz/300 g wax gourd, peeled and cut into ¾-inch/
  2-cm cubes
1 tablespoon jaggery, palm sugar, or soft light
  brown sugar

Soak the noodles in a bowl of water for
10 minutes or prepare according to package
directions, then drain and set aside.

Pound the shallots, peppercorns, salt, and
shrimp paste in a mortar with a pestle until
smooth, then set aside.

Bring the coconut milk to a boil in a pan over
medium heat. Add the paste and boil for about
2 minutes or until fragrant. Add the wax gourd
and sugar and cook for 12 minutes or until the
wax gourd has softened and become fully
flavored. Add the drained vermicelli and cook
for another 1–2 minutes or until the noodles
are soft and cooked. Serve.

แกงส้มทุเรียนกุ้ง

Spicy-and-Sour Curry with Durian and Shrimp

Origin South
Preparation time 10 minutes, plus soaking time
Cooking time 10 minutes
Serves 4

2 tablespoons jaggery, palm sugar, or soft light
  brown sugar
2 tablespoons fish sauce
⅓ cup (2½ fl oz/75 ml) Tamarind Puree (see p. 63)
2 tablespoons lime juice
11 oz/300 g durian flesh, cut to bite-size pieces
7 oz/200 g uncooked shrimp (prawns), peeled and
  deveined, with tails intact

For the curry paste
10 dried spur chiles
10 fresh red and green bird's eye chiles
5 shallots, sliced
1 tablespoon finely sliced turmeric root
2 teaspoons shrimp paste
1 teaspoon salt

For the curry paste, soak the dried chiles in
a bowl of warm water for 15 minutes or until
rehydrated, then drain and chop.

Pound the rehydrated and fresh chiles, the
shallots, and turmeric in a mortar with a pestle
until smooth. Add the shrimp paste and pound
again until combined. Set aside.

Bring 2½ cups (1 pint/600 ml) water to a boil in
a pan over medium-high heat, add the curry
paste, sugar, fish sauce, tamarind, lime juice,
durian, and shrimp (prawns), and bring to a
boil. Cook for 10 minutes. Serve.

Durian Massaman Curry

แกงมัสมั่นทุเรียน

Origin Central
Preparation time 20 minutes, plus soaking time
Cooking time 30 minutes
Serves 4

2 tablespoons peanuts
1 tablespoon ground coriander
1 teaspoon ground tree basil
½ teaspoon ground cloves
5 cardamom pods
1 cinnamon stick
4 cups (½ pints/950 ml) coconut milk
1 x 1 lb 2-oz/500-g boneless chicken, cut into 2-inch/
  5-cm pieces
1 tablespoon fish sauce
3 bay leaves
4 tablespoons Tamarind Puree (see p. 63)
3 tablespoons jaggery, palm sugar, or soft light
  brown sugar
11 oz/300 g young durian

For the massaman chili paste
3 large red dried chiles
1 teaspoon salt
1 teaspoon chopped roasted galangal
1 tablespoon chopped roasted lemongrass
6 shallots, roasted and chopped
2 cloves garlic, roasted and chopped
6 white peppercorns
1 teaspoon shrimp paste

To serve
pickled ginger
pickled cucumber
salad greens (leaves)

For the chili paste, soak the dried chiles in a bowl of warm water for 15 minutes or until rehydrated, then drain and chop. Pound the chiles and remaining chili paste ingredients in a mortar with a pestle until smooth. Set aside.

Dry-fry the peanuts, ground coriander, tree basil, cloves, cardamom, and cinnamon in a wok for 1 minute or until fragrant. Set aside.

Bring the coconut milk to a simmer in a clean wok over low heat, stirring continuously, until grainy. Add the chili paste and stir for 1–2 minutes or until fragrant. Add the chicken, roasted spices, fish sauce, bay, tamarind, and sugar and cook for 20–25 minutes. Add the durian and cook for 5 minutes. Serve with pickled ginger, cucumber, and salad greens.

Spicy Taro Stem Curry

แกงบอน

Origin Central
Preparation time 15 minutes
Cooking time 15 minutes
Serves 4

1 x 1¾-lb/800-g snakehead fish, cleaned and descaled
2¼ lb/1 kg fresh taro stems, washed and cut into
  2-inch/5-cm pieces
2 cups (16 fl oz/475 ml) coconut milk
2 tablespoons boneless fermented fish
11 oz/300 g pork side (belly), cut into 1-inch/
  2.5-cm pieces
1 tablespoon fish sauce
2 tablespoons jaggery, palm sugar, or soft light
  brown sugar
1½ tablespoons Tamarind Puree (see p. 63)
⅓ cup (¼ oz/10 g) kaffir lime leaves

For the chili paste
1 oz/25 g dried red chiles, ground
1¼-inch/4-cm piece galangal, peeled and chopped
1 garlic bulb, cloves separated and chopped
1 shallot, chopped
¼ cup (1½ oz/40 g) chopped fingerroot
¼ cup (¾ oz/20 g) chopped lemongrass stalk

Preheat the boiler (grill) to medium-high, place the fish on the broiler (grill) rack, and broil (grill) for 10–12 minutes on each side. Remove the meat and discard the skin and bones. Set aside.

For the chili paste, soak the dried chiles in a bowl of warm water for 15 minutes or until rehydrated, then drain and chop.

Pound the chiles, galangal, garlic, shallot, fingerroot, and lemongrass in a mortar with a pestle until smooth. Add the grilled fish meat and pound again, then set aside.

Bring a large pan of water to a boil over medium heat. Add the taro stems and boil for 5–7 minutes or until softened. Drain, squeeze to remove any excess liquid, and set aside.

Bring the coconut milk, chili paste, and fermented fish to a boil in a pan over medium heat. Add the pork and return to a boil. Add the taro stems, reduce the heat, and simmer for 5 minutes or until cooked. Add the fish sauce, sugar, tamarind, and kaffir lime leaves and serve.

แกงบอนหวาน

Sweet Taro Stem Curry

Origin Northeast
Preparation time 10 minutes
Cooking time 30 minutes
Serves 2

11 oz/300 g pork loin
3 taro stems, washed, peeled, and cut into
  large pieces
1 cup (9 fl oz/250 ml) coconut milk
½ cup (3½ oz/100 g) chili paste
1 teaspoon granulated sugar
1 teaspoon Tamarind Puree (see p. 63)
1 teaspoon fish sauce
2 teaspoons fermented fish sauce
3–5 acacia leaves (optional)

Before you begin cooking, check that your
charcoal is glowing white hot, or your gas grill
(barbecue) is preheated to 400°F/200°C. Grill
the pork over medium heat for 7–8 minutes on
each side or until cooked. Alternatively, use
a conventional indoor broiler (grill) preheated
to medium. Put the broiler (grill) rack about
4 inches/10 cm away from the heat source, then
place the pork on the broiler (grill) rack and
broil (grill) for 7–8 minutes on each side until
cooked. Remove, slice into bite-size pieces
and set aside.

Bring a large pan of water to a boil over
medium heat. Add the taro stems and boil for
5–7 minutes or until softened. Drain, squeeze
to remove any excess liquid, and set aside.

Bring the coconut milk to a boil in a wok over
medium heat. Add the chili paste and stir-fry
for 1–2 minutes or until fragrant. Add the pork
and season with the sugar, tamarind, fish
sauce, and fermented fish sauce and return
to a boil. Add the taro stems and acacia leaves,
if using, then return to a boil and cook for about
5 minutes. Serve.

แกงปาปลีกล้วย

Spicy Banana Blossom Curry

Origin South
Preparation time 10 minutes, plus soaking time
Cooking time 10 minutes
Serves 4

1 teaspoon salt
1 banana blossom
2 x 14-oz/400-g mackerel, cleaned, filleted, and sliced
  into bite-size pieces
1 cup (2 oz/50 g) sweet basil leaves

For the chili paste
1 tablespoon sliced galangal
2 tablespoons sliced lemongrass
2 tablespoons sliced shallot
3 cloves garlic, sliced
1 teaspoon salt
10 dried red chiles
1½ teaspoons sliced fingerroot
1 teaspoon white peppercorns
1 tablespoon shrimp paste

For the chilli paste, pound all the ingredients
together in a mortar with a pestle until smooth.
Set aside.

To clean and prepare banana blossom, pour
2 cups (16 fl oz/475 ml) water into a large bowl,
add the salt, and stir until dissolved. Peel away
and discard the outer red petals from the
banana blossom and also the small white strips
of banana flower. Cut off the tip and the end of
the blossom, then cut the blossom crosswise
into thin slices. Put the slices into the bowl of
water and let soak for 10 minutes, then drain
and set aside.

Bring a large pan of water to a boil over
medium heat, add the chili paste and banana
blossom, stir, and return to a boil. Add the
mackerel, then return to a boil and cook for
about 3 minutes. Add the sweet basil leaves
and stir. Serve.

Photo p. 256

Grilled, Boiled & Fried

ปลาหมึกย่าง
Grilled Squid

Origin Central
Preparation time 10 minutes
Cooking time 6–7 minutes
Serves 2

1 x 14-oz/400-g squid, cleaned
Seafood Dipping Sauce (see p. 58), to serve

Before you begin cooking, check that your charcoal is glowing white hot, or your gas grill (barbecue) is preheated to 400°F/200°C. Alternatively, use a conventional indoor broiler (grill) preheated to high.

Score 3–4 cuts across the body of the squid, making sure that you don't cut all the way through the flesh. Grill the squid over high heat for 6–7 minutes on each side until cooked. If using an indoor broiler, put the broiler (grill) rack about 4 inches/10 cm away from the heat source, then place the squid on the rack and broil (grill) for 6–7 minutes on each side or until cooked. Remove and slice into small rings. Serve with Seafood Sauce.

Photo p. 267

เนื้อย่างเสือร้องไห้
Grilled Marinated Beef

Origin Northeast
Preparation time 8 minutes, plus marinating time
Cooking time 10 minutes
Serves 6

2¼ lb/1 kg beef brisket, sliced lengthwise
1 tablespoon jaggery, palm sugar, or soft light brown sugar
3 tablespoons oyster sauce
3 tablespoons soy sauce
1 egg, beaten

To serve
Glutinous Rice (see p. 378)
Barbecue Sauce (see p. 63)

Mix all the ingredients together in a large bowl, cover with plastic wrap (clingfilm), and let marinate in the refrigerator for 1 hour.

Before you begin cooking, check that your charcoal is glowing white hot, or your gas grill (barbecue) is preheated to 400°F/200°C. Grill the beef over medium heat for 5 minutes on each side or until cooked. Serve with rice and barbecue sauce.

ปลากะมงเผา

Grilled Trevally Fish

Origin South
Preparation time 5 minutes
Cooking time 16 minutes
Serves 2

1 x 1 lb 7-oz/650-g trevally fish or kingfish
  or sea bream, cleaned and descaled
1 banana leaf, for wrapping

For the dipping sauce
⅓ cup (4 fl oz/120 ml) Tamarind Puree (see p. 63)
2½ tablespoons jaggery, palm sugar, or soft light
  brown sugar
3 red and green bird's eye chiles, chopped
2 shallots, chopped
1 teaspoon salt

Before you begin cooking, check that your
charcoal is glowing white hot, or your gas
grill (barbecue) is preheated to 350°F/180°C.
Alternatively, use a conventional indoor broiler
(grill) preheated to medium.

For the dipping sauce, bring the tamarind and
sugar to a boil in a pan over medium heat and
stir until the sugar has dissolved. Let cool, then
add the chiles, shallots, and salt and mix well.
Set aside.

Rub the fish with the salt and place in the center
of the banana leaf. Cover the fish with the sides
of the leaf, fold over the ends, and secure with
toothpicks.

Grill the fish over medium heat for 7–8 minutes
on each side until cooked. If using an indoor
broiler, put the broiler (grill) rack about
4 inches/10 cm away from the heat source,
then place the fish on the rack and broil
(grill) for 7–8 minutes on each side, turning
occasionally, until cooked.

Unwrap the fish and serve with the dipping
sauce on the side.

กุ้งนางย่าง

Grilled Giant Freshwater Shrimp

Origin Central
Preparation time 5 minutes
Cooking time 5 minutes
Serves 4

2¼ lb/1 kg uncooked giant freshwater shrimp (prawns),
  halved lengthwise
Seafood Dipping Sauce (see p. 58)

Before you begin cooking, check that your
charcoal is glowing white hot, or your gas grill
(barbecue) is preheated to 400°F/200°C. Grill
the giant freshwater shrimp (prawns) over a
low heat for 3–4 minutes on each side or until
they turn pink and are cooked. Serve with the
seafood dipping sauce.

Photo p. 269

เมี่ยงปลาเผา

Grilled Tilapia with Spicy Dips

Origin Northeast
Preparation time 15 minutes
Cooking time 45 minutes
Serves 3

2–3 lemongrass stalks, chopped and lightly pounded
1 x 1¾-lb/800-g tilapia, cleaned
½ cup (4½ oz/130 g) salt flakes
raw vegetables, such as cabbage, lettuce, galangal,
  ginger, garlic, and round eggplant, to serve
fresh herbs, such as dill and cilantro (coriander),
  to serve

For the spicy fermented fish dip
5 shallots, unpeeled
2 large cloves garlic, unpeeled
1½-inch/4-cm piece galangal, unpeeled
2–3 lemongrass stalks
¼ cup (¾ oz/20 g) dried chili flakes
3½ oz/100 g fermented fish, chopped

For the spicy seafood dip
3½ oz/100 g bird's eye chiles
2 garlic bulbs, cloves separated and peeled
1½ teaspoons salt
2–3 tablespoons lime juice
3 tablespoons fish sauce
2 teaspoons superfine (caster) sugar

For the spicy tamarind dip
10 bird's eye chiles
8 cloves garlic, peeled
1½ teaspoons salt
2 tablespoons Tamarind Puree (see p. 63)
1 tablespoon granulated sugar

To make the fermented fish dip, dry-fry the shallots, garlic, galangal, and lemongrass in a wok for 2–3 minutes or until fragrant. Let cool slightly, then peel. Transfer to a mortar, add the chili flakes, and finely pound with a pestle. Add the fermented fish, then pound thoroughly until combined. Set aside.

For the spicy seafood dip, finely pound the chiles, garlic, and salt together in a mortar with a pestle. Add the fish sauce and sugar and stir. Set aside.

For the spicy tamarind dip, finely pound the chiles, garlic, and salt together in a mortar with a pestle. Add the tamarind and sugar and stir. Set aside.

Before you begin cooking, check that your charcoal is glowing white hot, or your gas grill (barbecue) is preheated to 400°F/200°C. Alternatively, use a conventional indoor broiler (grill) preheated to medium.

Stuff the lemongrass into the fish cavity and rub both sides of the fish with the salt.

Grill the fish over medium heat for about 10 minutes on each side or until cooked. If using an indoor broiler, put the broiler (grill) rack about 4 inches/10 cm away from the heat source, then place the fish on the rack and broil (grill) for about 10 minutes on each side or until cooked.

Serve with the spicy dips, vegetables, and fresh herbs.

ปลาช่อนเผาในกระบอก

Grilled Snakehead Fish in Bamboo

Origin North
Preparation time 10 minutes, plus soaking time
Cooking time 30 minutes
Serves 3

10 dried red chiles
2½-inch/4-cm piece turmeric root, peeled
  and chopped
¾-inch/2-cm piece galangal, peeled
  and chopped
5 shallots, chopped
2 lemongrass stalks, finely chopped
1 tablespoon salt
1 x 1 lb 2-oz/500-g snakehead fish, cleaned
  and descaled
2 handfuls of sweet basil, chopped
16-inch/40-cm-long bamboo, 4 inches/10 cm
  in diameter

To serve
Tomato Chili Sauce (see p. 64), Barbecue Sauce (see
  p. 63), or Seafood Dipping Sauce (see p. 58)
raw or steamed vegetables, such as cucumber, napa
  (Chinese) cabbage, and small bitter gourd

Before you begin cooking, check that your
charcoal is glowing white hot, or your gas
grill (barbecue) is preheated to 400°F/200°C.
Alternatively, preheat the oven to 325°F/160°C/
Gas Mark 3.

Soak the dried chiles in a bowl of warm water
for 15 minutes, then drain and chop.

Pound the chiles, turmeric, galangal, shallots,
lemongrass, and salt together in a mortar with
a pestle until smooth. Rub the paste over the
whole fish.

Push the basil inside the bamboo, followed
by the fish. Roast on the grill or in the oven
for about 30 minutes, rotating the bamboo
regularly. Remove from the grill, break open
the bamboo, and serve with a sauce and raw
or steamed vegetables.

ปลาช่อนเผาเกลือ

Grilled Snakehead Fish

Origin Northeast
Preparation time 5 minutes
Cooking time 30 minutes
Serves 4

⅔ cup (7 oz/200 g) salt flakes
1 tablespoon all-purpose (plain) flour
1 x 1¾-lb/800-g snakehead fish, cleaned
3 lemongrass stalks, coarsely pounded

To serve
Seafood Dipping Sauce (see p. 58)
raw or steamed vegetables, such as cucumber, napa
  (Chinese) cabbage, and yard-long beans

Before you begin cooking, check that your
charcoal is glowing white hot, or your gas
grill (barbecue) is preheated to 400°F/200°C.
Alternatively, use a conventional indoor broiler
(grill) preheated to medium.

Mix the salt and flour together in a bowl and
set aside.

Stuff the lemongrass into the fish's mouth, then
rub the fish all over with the salt mixture.

Cook the fish over medium heat for 15 minutes
on each side or until the fish is cooked. If using
an indoor broiler, place the fish on a broiler
(grill) rack and broil (grill) over medium heat
for 15 minutes on each side. Transfer to a
serving plate and serve with seafood dipping
sauce and raw or steamed vegetables.

น้ำปลาหวานสะเดา

Catfish and Neem with Sweet Sauce

Origin Central
Preparation time 10 minutes
Cooking time 20–25 minutes
Serves 2

1 x 1 lb 5-oz/600-g catfish, cleaned
2 lemongrass stalks, finely sliced and pounded
¼ teaspoon ground black pepper
2 cilantro (coriander) roots, pounded
1 tablespoon soy sauce
9 oz/250 g young neem (sadao)
10–15 dried red chiles, fried, to serve
Steamed Jasmine Rice (see p. 378), to serve

For the sweet sauce
4½ tablespoons jaggery, palm sugar, or soft light
  brown sugar
3 tablespoons Tamarind Puree (see p. 63)
1½ tablespoons fish sauce
pinch of salt
3 tablespoons Fried Shallots (see p. 64)

Place the fish on a cutting (chopping) board, and using a sharp knife, score the fish 2–3 times on both sides.

Mix the lemongrass, black pepper, cilantro (coriander) roots, and soy sauce together in a bowl. Rub the mixture all over the fish and just inside the fish cavity. Set aside.

Before you begin cooking, check that your charcoal is glowing white hot, or your gas grill (barbecue) is preheated to 400°F/200°C. Cook the fish over medium heat for 10–15 minutes on each side. Alternatively, use a conventional indoor broiler (grill) preheated to medium-high, place the fish about 2¾ inches/7 cm away from the broiler (grill), and broil (grill) for 13–15 minutes on each side or until the fish is cooked and the skin is dry and brown. Set aside.

To make the sauce, mix the sugar, tamarind, fish sauce, salt, and 1–2 tablespoons water together in a wok over medium heat, stirring for 4–5 minutes or until thickened. Add the fried shallots and set aside.

Blanch the neem (sadao) in hot water 2–3 times. Remove, drain, and refresh in cold water.

To serve, take a little neem leaf, fish, chile, and sauce together and eat whole with rice.

Grilled Beef with Peppermint Leaves

เนื้อหมักเครื่องน้ำตกย่าง

Origin Central
Preparation time 10 minutes, plus marinating time
Cooking time 15 minutes
Serves 2

5 oz/150 g tenderloin steak (beef fillet)
1 shallot, chopped
2 kaffir lime leaves
¼ cup (¼ oz/10 g) sawtooth cilantro (coriander)
1 teaspoon red chile flakes
1 teaspoon Ground Toasted Rice (see p. 64)
2 tablespoons lime juice
2 tablespoons fish sauce
vegetable oil, for brushing
peppermint leaves, to garnish

Put the tenderloin steak (beef fillet) and all the remaining ingredients, except the oil and peppermint leaves, in a large bowl and mix well. Cover with plastic wrap (clingfilm) and let marinate for in the refrigerator for 15 minutes.

Brush a grill pan (griddle) with oil and put over medium heat. Add the marinated beef and grill for 4–5 minutes on each side. Let rest for about 2 minutes, then slice into bite-size pieces. Garnish with peppermint leaves and serve.

Grilled Pork with Black Pepper

หมูย่างพริกไทยดำ

Origin Central
Preparation time 10 minutes, plus marinating time
Cooking time 15 minutes
Serves 4

5 cloves garlic
1½ tablespoons black peppercorns
1 tablespoon chopped cilantro (coriander) root
1 lb 2 oz/500 g pork shoulder, cut into ½-inch/1-cm pieces
1 tablespoon soy sauce
1 tablespoon oyster sauce
1½ teaspoons fish sauce

To serve
Steamed Jasmine Rice (see p. 378)
Barbecue Sauce (see p. 63) or Seafood Dipping Sauce (see p. 58)

Pound the garlic, peppercorns, and cilantro (coriander) root together in a mortar with a pestle. Transfer to a bowl, add the remaining ingredients, and mix well. Cover with plastic wrap (clingfilm) and let marinate in the refrigerator for 2 hours.

Before you begin cooking, check that your charcoal is glowing white hot, or your gas grill (barbecue) is preheated to 350°F/180°C. Cook the marinated pork over medium heat for 6–7 minutes on each side or until cooked. Alternatively, use a conventional indoor broiler (grill) preheated to medium. Put the broiler (grill) rack about 4 inches/10 cm away from the heat source, then place the pork on the rack, with a tray underneath, and broil (grill) for 6–7 minutes on each side or until cooked. Serve with rice and a sauce on the side.

ไส้อั่ว

Spicy Thai-Style Sausage

Origin North
Preparation time 15 minutes, plus soaking time
Cooking time 40 minutes
Serves 4

2 x 2-foot/0.6-meter pork casings, cleaned
1 lb 2 oz/500 g ground (minced) pork
½ cup (1 oz/25 g) chopped cilantro (coriander)
2 sawtooth cilantro (coriander) leaves, chopped
6 scallions (spring onions), chopped
6 kaffir lime leaves, finely sliced
salt
Glutinous Rice (see p. 378), to serve

For the chili paste
5 dried red spur chiles, seeded
½ teaspoon salt
2 lemongrass stalks, chopped
1½ teaspoons chopped turmeric root
3 cloves garlic, chopped
1 shallot, chopped
½ teaspoon shrimp paste

For the chili paste, soak the dried chiles in a bowl of warm water for 15 minutes or until rehydrated, then drain and chop.

Pound the chiles and salt together thoroughly in a mortar with a pestle. Add the lemongrass, turmeric, garlic, and shallot and pound until smooth. Add the shrimp paste and pound until thoroughly combined. Set aside.

Turn the pork casings inside out and soak in a bowl of salted water made from 1½ tablespoons salt and 2 cups (16 fl oz/475 ml) water for about 10 minutes. Remove from the water and turn the casings the right way around. Set aside.

Mix the pork and the chili paste together in a large bowl. Add the chopped cilantros (corianders), scallions (spring onions), kaffir lime leaves, and 1 teaspoon salt and mix well.

Before you begin cooking, check that your charcoal is glowing white hot, or your gas grill (barbecue) is preheated to 400°F/200°C. Alternatively, use a conventional indoor broiler (grill) preheated to medium-high.

Fill the pork casings with the pork mixture by using a sausage funnel (or you can use the cut off top of a small plastic beverage bottle). When filled, tie both ends, then prick the sausages with a toothpick to prevent them from bursting.

Grill each sausage over medium heat for 15–18 minutes on each side or until brown and cooked. If using an indoor boiler, put the broiler (grill) rack about 4 inches/10 cm away from the heat source, then place the sausage on the rack, with a tray underneath, and broil (grill) for 15 minutes on each side or until brown and cooked. Slice diagonally and serve with rice.

คอหมูย่างจิ้มแจ่ว

Grilled Pork with Spicy Fish Sauce

Origin Northeast
Preparation time 10 minutes, plus marinating time
Cooking time 15 minutes
Serves 4

1 lb 2 oz/500 g pork shoulder, sliced
1 tablespoon soy sauce
1 tablespoon vegetable oil
2 tablespoons oyster sauce

For the spicy fish sauce
2 tablespoons Tamarind Puree (see p. 63)
½ teaspoon jaggery, palm sugar, or soft light
  brown sugar
1–2 tablespoons fish sauce
1–2 tablespoons Ground Toasted Rice (see p. 64)
1 teaspoon dried chili flakes
1 teaspoon chopped sawtooth cilantro (coriander)
1 teaspoon chopped cilantro (coriander)

For the spicy fish sauce, bring the tamarind, sugar, fish sauce, toasted rice, and chili flakes to a boil in a pan over medium heat. Sprinkle with the cilantros (corianders) and transfer to a sauceboat.

Put the sliced pork in a large bowl, add the soy sauce, oil, and oyster sauce, mix, and let marinate in the refrigerator.

Before you begin cooking, check that your charcoal is glowing white hot, or your gas grill (barbecue) is preheated to 400°F/200°C. Grill the pork over medium heat for 4–5 minutes on each side or until cooked. Serve with the spicy fish sauce.

แอ๊บอ่องออ

Spicy Grilled Pork Brain

Origin North
Preparation time 10 minutes, plus soaking time
Cooking time 30–40 minutes
Serves 5

11 oz/300 g pork brains
2 sawtooth cilantro (coriander) leaves, chopped
2 scallions (spring onions), chopped
2 banana leaves, about 8 x 9 inches/20 x 23 cm

For the chili paste
15 dried red bird's eye chiles, chopped
5 shallots, chopped
10 cloves garlic, sliced
2 lemongrass stalks, chopped
1 tablespoon chopped galangal
1 tablespoon chopped turmeric root
½ teaspoon salt
½ teaspoon shrimp paste

For the chili paste, soak the chiles in a bowl of warm water for 15 minutes or until rehydrated, then drain and chop.

Pound the chiles, shallots, garlic, lemongrass, galangal, tumeric, and salt in a mortar with a pestle until smooth. Add the shrimp paste and pound until combined.

Put the chili paste and pork brains in a large bowl and mix until thoroughly combined. Add the sawtooth cilantro (coriander) and scallions (spring onions) and mix again. Set aside.

Lay the 2 banana leaves on a work surface. Spoon about ½ cup (3½ oz/100 g) of the pork mixture into the center of each leaf, wrap into a square shape, and secure with a bamboo pin or toothpick.

Before you begin cooking, check that your charcoal is glowing white hot, or your gas grill (barbecue) is preheated to 325°F/160°C. Grill the package over low heat for 30–40 minutes, turning occasionally to prevent it from burning. Unwrap and serve.

หมูย่างน้ำตก

Spicy Grilled Pork Salad

Origin Central
Preparation time 10 minutes
Cooking time 10 minutes
Serves 2

14 oz/400 g pork loin, about ½ inch/1 cm thick
2 tablespoons fish sauce
2 tablespoons lime juice
1½ teaspoons dried chili flakes
1 tablespoon Ground Toasted Rice (see p. 64)
1 shallot, chopped
3 scallions (spring onions), chopped
2 sawtooth cilantro (coriander) leaves, chopped

Before you begin cooking, check that your charcoal is glowing white hot, or your gas grill (barbecue) is preheated to 400°F/200°C. Grill the pork over medium heat for 7–8 minutes on each side or until cooked. Alternatively, use a conventional indoor broiler (grill) preheated to medium. Put the broiler (grill) rack about 4 inches/10 cm away from the heat source, then place the pork on the broiler (grill) rack and broil (grill) for 7–8 minutes on each side until cooked. Remove and slice into bite-size pieces. Transfer the sliced pork to a serving plate and set aside.

Put the fish sauce, lime juice, dried chili flakes, and ground rice in a bowl and mix well. Add the shallot, scallions (spring onions), and sawtooth cilantro (coriander) and mix again until thoroughly combined. Sprinkle the dressing over the pork and serve.

ไก่ย่าง

Grilled Chicken

Origin Northeast
Preparation time 2 hours, plus marinating and standing time
Cooking time 40 minutes
Serves 2

6 cloves garlic, crushed
1 teaspoon salt
1 teaspoon ground black pepper
1 tablespoon jaggery, palm sugar, or soft light brown sugar
1 tablespoon soy sauce
1 chicken, butterflied
Glutinous Rice (see p. 378), to serve

Put the garlic, salt, black pepper, sugar, and soy sauce in a large bowl and mix well until thoroughly combined. Add the chicken and massage with the seasoning mixture. Cover with plastic wrap (clingfilm) and let marinate in the refrigerator for 2 hours or for at least 30 minutes.

Bring the chicken to room temperature for 30 minutes before cooking.

Before you begin cooking, check that your charcoal is glowing white hot, or your gas grill (barbecue) is preheated to 300°F/150°C. Grill the chicken over low-medium heat for about 20 minutes on each side until cooked. Alternatively, use a conventional indoor broiler (grill) preheated to low-medium. Put the broiler (grill) rack about 4 inches/10 cm away from the heat source, then place the chicken on the rack with a tray underneath, and broil (grill) for about 20 minutes on each side or until cooked. Serve with rice.

Photo p. 277

เป็ดซอสมะขาม

Duck with Tamarind Sauce

Origin Central
Preparation time 20 minutes, plus marinating time
Cooking time 25 minutes
Serves 4

2 cups (16 fl oz/475 ml) vegetable oil
1 cup (2¾ oz/70 g) finely sliced kale leaves
2 x 14-oz/400-g lean duck breast
1½ teaspoons soy sauce
¼ teaspoon ground white pepper
1 teaspoon five-spice powder

For the tamarind sauce
3 tablespoons jaggery, palm sugar, or soft light
  brown sugar
1½ tablespoons Tamarind Puree (see p. 63)
1 tablespoon soy sauce

To garnish
2 tablespoons Fried Garlic (see p. 64)
2 tablespoons Fried Shallots (see p. 64)
3 large dried red chile, roasted
1 cilantro (coriander) sprig

Heat the oil in a wok over medium heat, add
the kale leaves, and fry for 1 minute or until the
kale starts to become crispy. Remove with a
slotted spoon and drain on paper towels.

Put the duck, soy sauce, white pepper, and
five-spice powder in a bowl and mix well.
Cover with plastic wrap (clingfilm) and let
marinate in the refrigerator for 20 minutes.

Preheat a grill pan (griddle) over high heat.
Place the duck, skin side down, in the pan,
then reduce the heat to low and grill for
7 minutes or until brown and crispy. Turn over
and grill for 10 minutes. Remove and set aside.

For the sauce, heat the sugar, tamarind,
soy sauce, and 1 tablespoon water together
in a pan over medium-low heat. Cook for
5–6 minutes or until thickened. Set aside.

Carve the duck breast into ½-inch/1-cm-thick
pieces and place on a serving plate with the
pieces overlapping in a fan shape. Put the
crispy kale to one side of the duck and pour
over the sauce. Sprinkle with the fried garlic,
fried shallots, roasted chile, and cilantro
(coriander) leaves and serve.

เสลิ้มจิ้นย่าง

Grilled Pork Salad

Origin North
Preparation time 10 minutes, plus marinating time
Cooking time 30–40 minutes
Serves 4

1 tablespoon soy sauce
1 x 14-oz/400-g skinless pork neck, fillet, or shoulder
5 cloves garlic, finely chopped
4 shallots, finely sliced
2 lemongrass stalks, finely sliced
10 dried red chiles, seeded and chopped
3 tablespoons lemon juice
2 tablespoons fish sauce

To serve
Glutinous Rice (see p. 378)
raw vegetables such as carrots, cucumbers,
  and Chinese greens (leaves)

Before you begin cooking, check that your
charcoal is glowing white hot, or your gas
grill (barbecue) is preheated to 325°F/160°C.
Alternatively, use a conventional indoor broiler
(grill) preheated to medium-low.

Put the soy sauce in a bowl, add the pork, and
rub the soy sauce over the pork until coated.
Cover with plastic wrap (clingfilm) and let
marinate for 15 minutes.

Cook the marinated pork over medium-low
heat for 15–20 minutes on each side until brown
and cooked. If using an indoor broiler, put the
broiler (grill) rack about 4 inches/10 cm away
from the heat source, then place the pork on the
rack and leave the broiler/oven door slightly
open. Broil (grill) for 15–20 minutes on each
side until the pork is cooked. Remove and
shred the pork with a fork.

Pound the shredded pork in a mortar with a
pestle. Transfer to a large bowl, add the garlic,
shallots, lemongrass, chiles, lemon juice, and
fish sauce in a large bowl and mix well. Serve
with rice and raw vegetables.

Photo p. 278

หมูฮ้อง

Stewed Pork Side

Origin South
Preparation time 15 minutes
Cooking time 1 hour 35 minutes
Serves 4

3 tablespoons vegetable oil
4 tablespoons Saam-Gler (see p. 41)
1 lb 2 oz/500 g pork side (belly), cut into 2-inch/
  5-cm cubes
½ cup (4 oz/120 g) jaggery, palm sugar, or soft light
  brown sugar
3 tablespoons soy sauce
1 tablespoon dark soy sauce
½ tablespoon five-spice powder
½ teaspoon ground black pepper
4 hard-boiled eggs
Steamed Jasmine Rice (see p. 378), to serve

Heat the oil in a pan or casserole over medium
heat, add the saam-gler, and sauté for 1 minute
or until fragrant. Add the pork and cook for
about 4 minutes or until golden brown. Add
2 cups (16 fl oz/475 ml) water, the sugar, soy
sauces, five-spice powder, and black pepper,
mix well, and return to a boil. Reduce the heat
and simmer for 30 minutes.

Add the eggs and partly cover with a lid.
Simmer for 1 hour or until the pork is tender,
stirring occasionally, and topping off with
water, if needed, to prevent the meat from
drying out. Serve with rice.

หมูหอง

Stewed Pork with Peanuts and Dried Bamboo Shoots

Origin Central
Preparation time 20 minutes, plus soaking time
Cooking time 10 minutes
Serves 6

7 oz/200 g dried bamboo shoots
1⅓ cups (7 oz/200 g) raw peanuts
3 tablespoons vegetable oil
2¼ lb/1 kg pork side (belly), diced (with fat)
scant 1 cup (7 oz/200 g) jaggery, palm sugar, or soft
  light brown sugar
2 tablespoons fish sauce

For the chili paste
7 shallots, chopped
1 medium garlic bulb, cloves separated and chopped
5-inch/12.5-cm piece galangal, peeled and chopped
4 lemongrass stalks, chopped
1 teaspoon shrimp paste

Soak the dried bamboo shoots in a bowl
of water for 15 minutes, then drain. Cut into
3-inch/7.5-cm-long segments and set aside.

Cook the peanuts in a pan of boiling water
for about 5 minutes or until soft. Drain and
set aside.

For the chili paste, pound all the ingredients
together in a mortar with a pestle until smooth.

Heat the oil in a wok over medium heat, add
the chili paste, and stir-fry for 1 minute or
until fragrant. Add the pork, peanuts, bamboo
shoots, sugar, and fish sauce and stir-fry for
5–6 minutes or until cooked. Serve.

ปลานึ่งมะนาว

Steamed Sea Bass with Spicy Lime Sauce

Origin North
Preparation time 20 minutes
Cooking time 10–15 minutes
Serves 4

1 x 1¾-lb/800-g whole sea bass, cleaned and filleted
3 thin slices galangal
3 lemongrass stalks, crushed
4 kaffir lime leaves
1 handful of Chinese celery

For the sauce
3–4 red and green bird's eye chiles, chopped
4 cloves garlic, chopped
1½ teaspoons chopped cilantro (coriander) root
¼ cup (2 fl oz/60 ml) chicken broth (stock)
3 tablespoons fish sauce
2 tablespoons lime juice
1 tablespoon granulated sugar

To garnish
4 lime slices
1 small handul of cilantro (coriander) sprigs
3 red bird's eye chiles, sliced

For the sauce, pound the chiles, garlic, and cilantro (coriander) root in a mortar with a pestle until smooth. Transfer to a bowl. Add the chicken broth (stock), fish sauce, lime juice, sugar, and ¼ cup (2 fl oz/60 ml) water and stir until thoroughly combined.

Place one of the fillets, skin side down, in a deep plate. Cover with the galangal and half the lemongrass, then put the remaining fillet on top, skin side up. Arrange the kaffir lime leaves and the remaining lemongrass around the fillets. Steam in a steamer for 5–7 minutes, then pour over the sauce and steam for another 5 minutes or until the fish is cooked through. Transfer to a shallow serving bowl. Garnish with sliced lime, cilantro (coriander) sprigs, and chile and serve.

ปลานึ่งแจ่วมะเขือเทศ

Steamed Tilapia with Spicy Tomato Dip

Origin Northeast
Preparation time 15 minutes
Cooking time 35 minutes
Serves 4

1 x 1¾-lb/800-g tilapia, cleaned
2–3 lemongrass stalks, chopped and lightly pounded
1 piece galangal, lightly pounded
10 kaffir lime leaves, plus a few extra
2 tablespoons coarse sea salt
raw vegetables, such as cabbage, snake gourd,
    and napa (Chinese) cabbage
flowers of vegetable humming bird (white) and
    Chinese mustard greens (yellow), coarsely chopped

For the spicy tomato dip
1 tomato
2 red and green bird's eye chiles
5 shallots
1 teaspoon salt
3 tablespoons Tamarind Puree (see p. 63)
½ cup (1 oz/25 g) chopped cilantro (coriander)

For the tomato dip, roast the tomato, chiles, and shallots in a skillet or frying pan over low heat for 2–3 minutes or until fragrant. Lightly pound the chiles and shallots together in a mortar with a pestle. Add the tomato to the mortar and pound again. Add the salt and tamarind and mix until thoroughly combined. Sprinkle with the cilantro (coriander).

Place the fish on a cutting (chopping) board, and using a sharp knife, score the fish 2–3 times on both sides.

Stuff the lemongrass, galangal, and kaffir lime leaves into the fish cavity and generously season both sides of the fish with the sea salt and stuff a few extra kaffir lime leaves into the incisions.

Place the fish on a plate and steam in a steamer for about 20 minutes. In a separate steamer, steam all the vegetables and flowers for about 10 minutes. Serve the fish, vegetables, and flowers with the spicy tomato dip.

ปลานึ่ง

Steamed Fish with Pumpkin and Herbs

Origin Northeast
Preparation time 10 minutes
Cooking time 15 minutes
Serves 4

1 x 14-oz/400-g tilapia, cleaned and descaled
½ teaspoon salt
2 shallots, chopped
2 cloves garlic, chopped
1 teaspoon black peppercorns
3 cilantro (coriander) roots, chopped
1 tablespoon soy sauce
2 lemongrass stalks, halved crosswise and crushed
8 thin slices galangal
7 oz/200 g pumpkin wedge, cut into 3–4 pieces
1 handful of basil or Greek basil, to garnish

To serve
Spicy Tomato Dip (see p. 54) or Seafood Dipping Sauce
  (see p. 58)
Glutinous Rice (see p. 378)

Rinse the fish in cold water, pat dry with paper towels, then rub the whole fish with the salt and set aside.

Coarsely pound the shallots, garlic, black peppercorns, and cilantro (coriander) root together in a mortar with a pestle. Add the soy sauce and stuff the mixture inside the fish cavity.

Put the lemongrass and galangal in the center of a large heatproof plate, then place the fish on the top. Arrange the pumpkin around the fish and steam in a steamer for about 15 minutes or until the fish is cooked. Garnish with the basil and serve with rice and spicy tomato dip or seafood sauce.

Photo p. 283

ห่อหมกปลาช่อน

Steamed Catfish in Banana Leaf

Origin Central
Preparation time 15 minutes
Cooking time 20 minutes
Makes 6–7

banana leaves, cut into circles about 8 inches/
  20 cm in diameter
1 cup (9 fl oz/250 ml) coconut cream
3–4 tablespoons Red Curry Paste (see p. 38)
2 eggs, beaten
1 tablespoon oyster sauce
1½ teaspoons fish sauce
1 tablespoon superfine (caster) sugar
1 x 9-oz/250-g snakehead fish fillet, sliced into
  1-inch/2.5-cm-cube pieces
¼ cup (½ oz/15 g) finely sliced kaffir lime leaves
1½ cups (3 oz/75 g) finely sliced great morinda leaves
  or sweet basil leaves
1 red spur chile, finely sliced lengthwise, to garnish

Prepare the banana cups. For each cup, place 2 banana leaf circles back to back with the shiny surface facing outward on both sides. From the outside of the circle, fold up about 2 inches/5 cm of banana leaf and then fold in on itself to create a corner. Secure with a toothpick. Repeat until there are 4 corners. Set aside.

Put the coconut cream and chili paste in a large mixing bowl and whisk until the curry paste has dissolved. Add the eggs, oyster sauce, fish sauce, and sugar and whisk until thoroughly combined. Add the fish, kaffiir lime leaves, and morinda leaves or basil leaves and gently mix.

Fill each banana cup with the coconut mixture so that each cup contains at least 4–5 pieces of fish. Repeat until all the mixture is used.

Place the cups in a steamer and steam over medium-high heat for 20–25 minutes until the mixture has solidified and is cooked. It should be firm to the touch.

Garnish each cup with 2 slices of red chile and serve.

Photo p. 284

ไข่ตุ๋น

Steamed Egg with Shrimp and Mushrooms

Origin Central
Preparation time 10 minutes, plus soaking time
Cooking time 20–25 minutes
Serves 4

4 dried shiitake mushrooms
½ cup (4 fl oz/120 ml) chicken broth (stock) or water
4–5 eggs, beaten
6–8 shrimp (prawns), peeled, deveined, and chopped
½ teaspoon fish sauce
2 teaspoons soy sauce
1 small carrot, finely shredded
1 onion, finely chopped
1 tablespoon sliced scallion (spring onion)

Soak the mushrooms in a bowl of boiling water for 15 minutes, then drain, slice, and set aside.

Pour the broth (stock) or water into a large bowl, add the eggs, mushrooms, shrimp, fish sauce, and soy sauce, and beat until thoroughly combined. Let sit for about 2 minutes to let the air bubbles dissipate.

Pour the mixture into a small heatproof bowl and steam in a steamer over medium heat for 15–20 minutes or until cooked. To see if the eggs are cooked, push a skewer through the center—only clear water should come out. Serve sprinkled with the carrot, onion, and scallion (spring onion).

ไข่ตุ๋นเคยเค็ม

Steamed Egg with Shrimp and Coconut Milk

Origin South
Preparation time 5 minutes
Cooking time 10 minutes
Serves 2

2 eggs, beaten
1 cup (9 fl oz/250 ml) coconut milk
1 tablespoon salted tiny freshwater shrimp
  or 1½ teaspoons shrimp paste mixed with
  1 tablespoon water
1 shallot, sliced
red and green bird's eye chiles, sliced, to garnish

Beat the eggs and coconut milk in a large bowl, then add the shrimp and shallot and beat again until thoroughly combined. Let sit for about 2 minutes to let the air bubbles dissipate.

Pour the mixture into small heatproof cups and steam in a steamer over medium heat for 15–20 minutes or until cooked. To see if the eggs are cooked, push a skewer through the center—only clear water should come out. Sprinkle with the chiles and serve.

Stuffed Squid with Garlic and Pepper

ปลาหมึกยัดผัดกระเทียมพริกไทย

Origin Central
Preparation time 20 minutes
Cooking time 20 minutes
Serves 4

9 oz/250 g ground (minced) pork
1½ tablespoons soy sauce
¼ teaspoon salt
1 teaspoon granulated sugar
2 tablespoons Saam-Gler (see p. 41)
14-oz/400-g small squid, cleaned, with tentacles intact
½ cup (4 fl oz/120 ml) vegetable oil
1 handful of cilantro (coriander), coarsely chopped

Mix the ground (minced) pork with
1 tablespoon soy sauce, the salt, sugar, and
1½ teaspoons saam-gler in a large bowl until
thoroughly combined. Stuff the squid with
the pork mixture until three-quarters full.
Thread the sides of the squid together, using a
toothpick or skewer. Steam the stuffed squid in
a steamer over medium heat for 10–12 minutes
or until cooked. Remove and set aside.

Heat the oil in a wok over medium heat, add the
remaining saam-gler, and stir-fry for 1 minute
or until fragrant. Add the steamed squid and
remaining soy sauce, then stir-fry for another
1–2 minutes or until the squid is well coated
with the saam-gler. Serve sprinkled with the
cilantro (coriander).

Stuffed Mangrove Trumpet Tree Flowers

อั่วปลาดอกแคปา

Origin Northeast
Preparation time 20 minutes, plus soaking time
Cooking time 30 minutes
Makes 20

½ cup (3½ oz/100 g) uncooked glutinous (sticky) rice
4 lemongrass stalks, sliced
½ cup (2 oz/50 g) bird's eye chiles
1 teaspoon salt
1 lb 2 oz/500 g clown featherback or flounder fillet, finely chopped
7 oz/200 g ground (minced) pork
2 tablespoons fermented fish sauce
1⅔ cups (3 oz/80 g) chopped dill
1 cup (1¼ oz/30 g) kaffir lime leaves, finely sliced, plus whole ones to garnish
20 mangrove trumpet tree flowers or zucchini (courgette) flowers

Put the glutinous (sticky) rice in a large bowl,
add ½ cup (4 fl oz/120 ml) water, and let soak
for 20 minutes, stirring occasionally. Drain
and reserve the rice water.

Pound the lemongrass, chiles, salt, and
glutinous rice water in a mortar with a pestle.
Add the fish, pork, and fermented fish sauce
and pound thoroughly. Add the dill and kaffir
lime leaves, then pound again until smooth.
Spoon the paste into the flowers and place on
cheesecloth (muslin) in a steamer. Steam for
about 30 minutes. Serve garnished with kaffir
lime leaves.

Photo p. 287

หมูอบไข่เค็ม

Steamed Pork Patties with Salted Egg

Origin Central
Preparation time 1 hour
Cooking time 20 minutes
Makes 10 patties

1 tablespoon finely sliced cilantro (coriander) root
10 cloves garlic
2 teaspoons white peppercorns
1 lb 2 oz/500 g ground (minced) pork
10 salted eggs, separated
2 tablespoons soy sauce
1 tablespoon sesame oil

Finely pound the cilantro (coriander) root, garlic, and white peppercorns together in a mortar with a pestle.

Put the ground (minced) pork, salted egg whites, soy sauce, sesame oil, and the cilantro root paste in a large bowl and mix well. Mold the pork mixture into flat round patties, about 4 inches/10 cm in diameter. Lightly press a piece of salted egg yolk into the center of each patty.

Arrange the patties in a shallow dish and steam in a steamer for 15–20 minutes over medium heat until cooked. Serve.

ปลาทูต้มหวาน

Sweet Boiled Mackerel

Origin Central
Preparation time 5 minutes
Cooking time 20 minutes
Serves 3

5 small mackerels, cleaned and descaled
5 cloves garlic, pounded
2–3-inch/5–7.5-cm piece fresh ginger, peeled and pounded
2 tablespoons jaggery, palm sugar, or soft light brown sugar
1 tablespoon Tamarind Puree (see p. 63)
1 teaspoon salt

Bring a large pan of water to a boil, then add all the ingredients, reduce the heat to low, and simmer for 20 minutes. Serve hot or cold.

ปลาทูต้มหวาน

Slow-Cooked Mackerel

Origin Northeast
Preparation time 10 minutes
Cooking time 3½–4 hours
Serves 6

1-inch/2.5-cm piece galangal, peeled and chopped
3 lemongrass stalks, finely chopped
4-inch/10-cm piece sugar cane, quartered lengthways
11 oz/300 g pork side (belly), cut into ½-inch/1-cm dice
2¼ lb/1 kg horse mackerel, cleaned and heads
  removed
1 shallot, chopped
3 cloves garlic, chopped
½ teaspoon salt
½ cup (4 oz/120 g) soft light brown sugar
2 tablespoon fish sauce
2 tablespoons dark soy sauce
Steamed Jasmine Rice (see p. 378), to serve

Put the galangal, lemongrass, and half of the
sugar cane in a large, deep pan, then place the
pork side (belly) and the mackerel on top. Fill
the pan with enough water to cover the fish.
Do not stir the mixture from this point.

Pound the shallot, garlic, and salt in a mortar
with a pestle and add to the pan with the sugar,
fish sauce, and soy sauce.

Place the remaining sugar cane on top of the
fish and bring to boil over medium heat. Cook
for 30 minutes. Remove any scum with a slotted
spoon. Reduce the heat to low, cover, and
simmer for 3–4 hours or until the fish is cooked
through and fish bone has softened. Add more
water if the liquid dries out, and only gently stir
if necessary. Serve with rice.

กุ้งต้มหวาน

Sweet Boiled Shrimp

Origin Central
Preparation time 5 minutes
Cooking time 7–8 minutes
Serves 2

1 lb 2 oz/500 g uncooked shrimp (prawns)
¾ cup (5 oz/150 g) superfine (caster) sugar
1 teaspoon salt
Steamed Jasmine Rice (see p. 378), to serve

Bring ½ cup (4 fl oz/120 ml) water to a boil in
a large pan, add the shrimp (prawns), sugar,
and salt, and mix well. Reduce the heat and
simmer for 7–8 minutes or until the water has
evaporated. Let cool, then serve with the rice.

กะปิหวานตะลิงปลิง

Bilimbi with Dipping Sauce

Origin Central
Preparation time 5 minutes, plus cooling time
Cooking time 3–4 minutes
Serves 4

30 bilimbi, sliced

For the dipping sauce
¼ cup (2 oz/50 g) shrimp paste
⅓ cup (3 oz/80 g) jaggery, palm sugar, or soft light
  brown sugar
5 red bird's eye chiles, chopped
2 shallots, sliced

For the dipping sauce, put the shrimp paste,
sugar, and ½ cup (4 fl oz/120 ml) water in
a pan over medium heat, stir, and cook for
3–4 minutes. Remove from heat and let cool.
Add the chiles and shallots, stir well, then
transfer to a small serving bowl.

Arrange the sliced bilimbi on a serving plate
and serve with the dipping sauce on the side.

ปลาหมึกนึ่งมะนาว

Squid with Lime

Origin Central
Preparation time 10 minutes
Cooking time 10 minutes
Serves 2

10 cloves garlic, chopped
10–15 red and green bird's eye chiles, chopped
2 tablespoons fish sauce
2 tablespoons lime juice
2 squid, about 5 inches/12.5 cm, cleaned and cut into
  ¼-inch/5-mm rings
5 celery leaves
2 cilantro (coriander) sprigs

Pound the garlic and chiles together in a mortar
with a pestle. Add the fish sauce and lime juice
and mix until combined.

Bring 1 cup (9 fl oz/250 ml) water to a boil in
a pan, add the squid, and cook for 5 minutes.
Add the garlic paste, celery leaves, and cilantro
(coriander) and cook for another 2 minutes,
then serve.

หอยซักตีนลาก

Sea Snails with Dipping Sauce

Origin South
Preparation time 15 minutes, plus soaking time
Cooking time 2–3 minutes
Serves 4

1 tablespoon white vinegar
5 red bird's eye chiles, pounded
2¼ lb/1 kg dog conch or wing shell sea snails with
  shells intact, cleaned
Seafood Dipping Sauce (see p. 58)

Pour 4¼ cups (1¾ pints/1 liter) water in a large
bowl, add the vinegar and chiles and mix well.
Add the snails, let soak for about 15 minutes,
and drain.

Bring a large pan of water to a boil over
medium heat, add the snails, and boil for about
2 minutes until cooked. Drain and serve with
the seafood dipping sauce.

หมูลุ

Pork and Herb Meatballs

Origin Central
Preparation time 10 minutes
Cooking time 6–7 minutes
Serves 4

1 lb 2 oz/500 g ground (minced) pork
3 tomatoes, diced
3–4 shallots, chopped
½ cup (1 oz/25 g) chopped cilantro (coriander)
5 sawtooth cilantro (coriander) leaves, chopped
6 cloves garlic
¾-inch/2-cm piece fresh ginger, peeled and finely
  chopped
2–3 lemongrass stalks, finely chopped
6 scallions (spring onions), finely chopped
1 tablespoon ground turmeric
1 teaspoon salt
Glutinous Rice (see p. 378), to serve

Put the pork, tomatoes, shallots, cilantro
(coriander), sawtooth cilantro (coriander),
garlic, ginger, lemongrass, scallions (spring
onions), turmeric, and salt in a large bowl and
mix until thoroughly combined.

Using dampened hands, roll the pork mixture
into 2-inch/5-cm-diameter balls and set aside.

Heat the oil in a large skillet or frying pan over
medium heat. Add the meatballs, in batches
and sauté for 6–7 minutes until well browned
all over. Transfer to a serving plate and serve
with rice.

ไก่บาดาล

Boiled Chicken with Herbs

Origin Northeast
Preparation time 10 minutes
Cooking time 1 hour
Serves 4

1 x 2¾-lb/1.3-kg chicken, chopped into pieces
3 tablespoons chopped cilantro (coriander) leaves
3 tablespoons sweet basil leaves

For the paste
3 slices galangal
2 lemongrass stalks, chopped
5 shallots, sliced
2¾-inch/7-cm piece fresh ginger, peeled and chopped
3 cilantro (coriander) roots chopped
5 cloves garlic, sliced
5 kaffir lime leaves, sliced
1 teaspoon salt
1 tablespoon black pepper
1 tablespoon soy sauce

For the pastry, pound the galangal, lemongrass, shallots, ginger, cilantro (coriander), garlic, kaffir lime leaves, salt, black pepper, and soy sauce together in a mortar with a pestle until smooth.

Coat the chicken all over with the paste, then put the chicken in a large pan or in the top of a double boiler.

Pour in 8½–12½ cups (3½–5¼ pints/2–3 liters) water into another pan, slightly larger than the first or in the bottom of the double boiler. Bring to a boil and carefully place the first pan (with the chicken) on top. Cover with a lid and cook for 1 hour or until the chicken is cooked.

Transfer to a serving plate, sprinkle with the cilantro (coriander) and sweet basil, and serve.

แกงเลียมตำลึงใส่ไข่

Spiced Ivy Gourd and Egg

Origin Central
Preparation time 5 minutes, plus soaking time
Cooking time 8 minutes
Serves 2

4 dried red chiles, seeded
2 shallots, chopped
2 teaspoons shrimp paste
7 oz/200 g ivy gourd leaves or Chinese kale
2 eggs
2 teaspoons fish sauce

Soak the dried chiles in a bowl of warm water for 15 minutes or until rehydrated, then drain and chop.

Pound the chiles, shallots, and shrimp paste in a mortar with a pestle until smooth.

Bring 1 cup (9 fl oz/250 ml) water to a boil in a pan over medium heat, add the chili paste, and return to a boil. Add the ivy gourd leaves, reduce the heat, and simmer for 1–2 minutes. Break the eggs into the mixture and beat with a fork. Bring to a boil, then reduce the heat. Season with the fish sauce and serve.

Pumpkin in Coconut Milk

Origin Central
Preparation time 10 minutes
Cooking time 10 minutes
Serves 4

2¼ lb/1 kg Thai pumpkin, peeled and seeded
6 cups (2½ pints/1.4 liters) coconut milk
1 cup (8 oz/225 g) jaggery, palm sugar, or soft light
  brown sugar
¼ cup (2 oz/50 g) granulated sugar
1 teaspoon salt
1¼ cups (½ pint/300 ml) coconut cream

Cut the pumpkin into ½ x 1-inch/1 x 2.5-cm
sticks, rinse under cold running water, and
set aside.

Bring the coconut milk and pumpkin sticks
to a boil in a pan over medium heat. Reduce
the heat to medium-low and simmer for about
10 minutes or until the pumpkin has softened.
Add the sugars and salt, bring to a boil, then
add the coconut cream. Return to a boil,
remove from the heat, and serve.

Photo p. 293

Water Spinach with Shrimp and Tofu

Origin South
Preparation time 20 minutes
Cooking time 10 minutes
Serves 2

2 tablespoons vegetable oil
5 oz/150 g extra firm tofu, cut into cubes
8 uncooked freshwater shrimp (prawns), heads and
  tails still on
2 cups (7 oz/200 g) water spinach
1 small cucumber, julienned
2 tablespoons white sesame seeds, roasted
2 tablespoons peanuts, roasted
2 tablespoons Fried Garlic (see p. 64)

For the sauce
3–5 dried red chiles, finely pounded
2 cloves garlic, finely pounded
3 tablespoons white vinegar
3 tablespoons granulated sugar
1 teaspoon salt
3 tablespoons fish sauce

Heat the oil in a wok over medium heat, add
the tofu, and stir-fry for 5–7 minutes or until
golden brown. Remove with a slotted spoon,
and set aside.

Add the shrimp (prawns) to the wok and stir-fry
for about 2 minutes or until they turn pink, then
remove and set aside.

Put all the ingredients for the sauce in a pan
over medium heat and simmer until thick.

Blanch the water spinach in a separate pan
of boiling water for 1 minute, then drain.

Place the cucumber on a serving plate and
then cover with the water spinach. Drizzle with
the sauce, then sprinkle with the sesame seeds,
peanuts, and fried garlic. Top with the tofu and
shrimp and serve.

ยำปลาสลิดทอด

Spicy Gourami Salad

Origin Central
Preparation time 5 minutes
Cooking time 10 minutes
Serves 3

3 cups (1¼ pints/750 ml) vegetable oil, for deep-frying
3 gourami, filleted and each cut into 3 pieces
5 red and green bird's eye chiles, chopped
1 tablespoon fish sauce
1 tablespoon lime juice
1 tablespoon granulated sugar
5 shallots, sliced
2 cilantro (coriander) sprigs, leaves only, to garnish

Heat the oil for deep-frying in a wok or deep fryer to 350°F/180°C or until a cube of bread browns in 30 seconds. Deep-fry the fish for 8–10 minutes or until golden and crispy. Remove with a slotted spoon and drain on paper towels.

Mix the fish sauce, lime juice, sugar, chiles, and shallots together in a bowl until the sugar has dissolved. Add the deep-fried fish and mix well. Serve garnished with the cilantro (coriander).

น้ำพริกปลาทู

Fried Mackerel with Spicy Shrimp Dip

Origin Central
Preparation time 5 minutes
Cooking time 10 minutes
Serves 2

1 cup (9 fl oz/250 ml) vegetable oil
1 x 9¾-oz/275-g smoked mackerel
lettuce, wilted spinach, bok choy (pak choi), or other leafy greens, to serve

For the spicy shrimp dip
5–8 green bird's eye chiles
6 cloves garlic
2 tablespoons jaggery, palm sugar, or soft light brown sugar
1½ tablespoons shrimp paste
1½ tablespoons fish sauce
1 tablespoon dried shrimp, finely ground (minced)
2 tablespoons lime juice

To garnish
red bird's eye chiles, seeded
4–5 pea eggplants (aubergines), broiled (grilled) whole

To make the spicy dip, pound the chiles and garlic in a mortar with a pestle until smooth. Add the sugar, shrimp paste, and fish sauce and pound until combined. Add the dried shrimp and lime juice and mix well. Transfer to a small serving bowl, garnish with the red chiles and eggplants (aubergines), and set aside.

Heat the oil in a wok over medium heat, add the mackerel, and fry for 1–2 minutes on each side or until browned and the skin is crispy. Drain and transfer to a serving plate and serve with the spicy shrimp dip and leafy greens.

ปลากะพงทอดราดน้ำปลา

Fried Sea Bass

Origin Central
Preparation time 10 minutes
Cooking time 20 minutes
Serves 4

½ cup (3 oz/80 g) green (sour) mango, peeled
  and julienned
1 carrot, julienned
5 shallots, chopped
3 tablespoons fish sauce
2 tablespoons lime juice
1½ tablespoons superfine (caster) sugar
1 x 1 lb 2-oz/500-g sea bass or red snapper, cleaned
  and descaled
3 cups (1¼ pints/750 ml) vegetable oil, for deep-frying
4–5 red and green bird's eye chiles, chopped

For the topping
1 tablespoon fish sauce
1 tablespoon jaggery, palm sugar, or soft light
  brown sugar

Put the mango, carrot, shallots, fish sauce, lime juice, and superfine (caster) sugar in a large bowl and mix well. Set aside.

Butterfly the fish by cutting the fish lengthwise down the middle to the backbone, without cutting all the way through, then open out to create a butterfly fillet, leaving the head and bones intact. Pat dry with paper towels.

Heat the oil for deep-frying in a wok or deep fryer to 350°F/180°C or until a cube of bread browns in 30 seconds. Deep-fry the sea bass for 15 minutes, or until golden brown and crispy. Remove with a slotted spoon and drain on paper towels. Set aside 1 tablespoon of the oil.

For the fish topping, put the fish sauce and sugar in a small bowl and mix until the sugar has dissolved.

Heat the reserved oil in a wok over medium heat, add the fish sauce and palm sugar mixture, and heat for 1 minute or until it starts sizzling. Pour the sizzling mixture over the fish and top with the mango and carrot. Serve.

Photo p. 297

ปลากะพงราดพริก

Spicy Fried Sea Bass

Origin Central
Preparation time 10 minutes
Cooking time 20–25 minutes
Serves 4

1 x 1 lb 5-oz/600-g sea bass, cleaned and descaled
4¼ cups (1¾ pints/1 liter) vegetable oil, for deep-frying,
  plus 2 tablespoons vegetable oil
6 cloves garlic, chopped
2 red spur chiles, chopped
2 tablespoons granulated sugar
2 tablespoons fish sauce

Place the fish on a cutting (chopping) board, and using a sharp knife, score the fish 2–3 times on both sides. Set aside.

Heat the oil for deep-frying in a large wok or deep fryer that's big enough for your whole fish to 350°F/180°C or until a cube of bread browns in 30 seconds. Deep-fry the sea bass for 10–12 minutes on each side until golden brown, then remove with a slotted spoon and drain on paper towels. Set aside.

In the same wok, heat the 2 tablespoons oil over medium heat, then add the garlic, chiles, sugar, fish sauce, and 1 tablespoon water and stir-fry for 1 minute until the sugar has dissolved. Spoon into a bowl and serve with the sea bass.

Photo p. 295

ปลากะพงเคี่ยวเมี่ยง

Deep-Fried Sea Bass on Betel Leaves

Origin Central
Preparation time 10 minutes
Cooking time 20 minutes
Serves 4

1 x 14-oz/400-g whole sea bass, cleaned and filleted,
  with skin still on and the whole fish bone kept
½ cup (2¼ oz/60 g) all-purpose (plain) flour
3 cups (1¼ pints/750 ml) vegetable oil, for deep-frying
1 tablespoon fish sauce
3 tablespoons jaggery, palm sugar, or soft light
  brown sugar
¼ cup (1½ oz/40 g) peanuts
1½-inch/4-cm piece fresh ginger, peeled and cut
  into ½-inch/1-cm dice
1–2 limes, cut into ½-inch/1-cm dice
1 shallot, cut into ½-inch/1-cm dice
8 bird's eye chiles, chopped
3 lemongrass stalks, finely sliced
4 tablespoons Fried Shallots (see p. 64)
20 betel leaves, to serve

Cut the sea bass fillets into ¾-inch/2-cm cubes. Put the flour in a mixing bowl, add the fish cubes, and toss until well coated. Remove the coated fish from the bowl and set aside, then sprinkle the remaining flour over the fish bone and set aside.

Heat the oil for deep-frying in a wok or deep fryer to 350°F/180°C or until a cube of bread browns in 30 seconds. Deep-fry the fish for 3–4 minutes or until golden brown. Remove with a slotted spoon and drain on paper towels.

In the same wok, add the fish bone and fry on each side for 3 minutes or until golden brown and crispy. Remove with a slotted spoon and drain on paper towels.

For the sauce, mix the fish sauce and sugar together in a small pan, then put over low-medium heat and stir for 2–3 minutes or until the sugar dissolves. Let cool.

Mix the peanuts, ginger, lime, shallot, chiles, lemongrass, and the sauce together in a large bowl until thoroughly combined. Set aside.

Place the deep-fried fish bone on a serving plate and arrange the fish cubes on top. Pour over the peanut mixture and sprinkle with the fried shallots. To serve, wrap bite-size portions of the fish mixture in a betel leaf and eat whole.

Photo p. 298

ปลาน้ำเงินทอดกระเทียมพริกไทย

Fried Sheatfish with Garlic and Peppercorns

Origin Northeast
Preparation time 5 minutes
Cooking time 8 minutes
Serves 4

10 cloves garlic, unpeeled
1 tablespoon black peppercorns
1½ teaspoons salt
1 x 1 lb 2-oz/500-g sheatfish, cleaned, head removed, and cut into slices about ½ inch/1 cm thick
2–3 cups (16 fl oz–1¼ pints/475–750 ml) vegetable oil, for deep-frying

Pound the unpeeled garlic in a mortar with a pestle, then set aside.

Put the peppercorns, salt, and fish slices in a bowl, mix well, and set aside.

Heat the oil for deep-frying in a large wok or deep fryer to 350°F/180°C or until a cube of bread browns in 30 seconds. Deep-fry the fish for 8–10 minutes, then remove with a slotted spoon and drain on paper towels.

Deep-fry the pounded garlic in the wok for 1 minute or until golden, then remove with a slotted spoon and drain on paper towels.

To serve, crumble the deep-fried garlic over the fish.

ปลาทอดสามรส

Fried Sea Bass with Three-Flavored Sauce

Origin Central
Preparation time 15 minutes
Cooking time 25–30 minutes
Serves 4

1 x 1¾-lb/800-g sea bass or sea bream, cleaned and descaled
¼ cup (1 oz/30 g) all-purpose (plain) flour
3 cups (1½ pints/700 ml) vegetable oil, for deep-frying
3 cloves garlic, finely chopped
3 red spur chiles, seeded and finely pounded
½ cup (4 fl oz/120 ml) chicken broth (stock)
¼ cup (2 oz/50 g) jaggery, palm sugar, or soft light brown sugar
1 tablespoon Tamarind Puree (see p. 63)
1 tablespoon fish sauce
¼ teaspoon salt
1 handful of sweet basil leaves
3 bell peppers, 1 each red, green, and orange, cut in half, seeded and diced, to garnish
1 red chile, sliced in oval shapes, to garnish

Place the fish on a cutting (chopping) board, and using a sharp knife, score the fish 2–3 times on both sides. Sprinkle with the flour on both sides and set aside.

Heat the oil for deep-frying in a large wok or deep fryer that's big enough for your whole fish to 350°F/180°C or until a cube of bread browns in 30 seconds. Deep-fry the fish for 10–12 minutes on each side until golden brown, then remove with a slotted spoon and drain on paper towels. Set aside.

Take 2 tablespoons of oil from the wok and place in a small pan over medium heat. Add the garlic and pounded chiles and sauté for about 30 seconds or until fragrant. Stir in the chicken broth (stock) and bring to a boil. Reduce the heat, add the sugar, tamarind, fish sauce, and salt and simmer for 3–4 minutes until the liquid is reduced and begins to caramelize. Just before ready to serve, add the basil leaves.

Place the fish on a serving plate, pour over the sauce, and garnish with the diced bell peppers and sliced chile. Serve.

Photo p. 300

ปลากะพงราดพริกสด

Deep-Fried Sea Bass with Chili Sauce

Origin Central
Preparation time 20 minutes, plus chilling time
Cooking time 15 minutes
Serves 2

1 x 1 lb 5-oz/600-g sea bass, cleaned and descaled
1 tablespoon ground black pepper
2 cups (16 fl oz/475 ml) vegetable oil, for deep-frying
¼ cup (2 fl oz/60 ml) pork broth (stock)
2 tablespoons jaggery, palm sugar, or soft light
  brown sugar
½ teaspoon salt
10 red bird's eye chiles, chopped
2 cloves garlic, chopped
1½ tablespoons lime juice
2 cilantro (coriander) sprigs, coarsely chopped

Place the fish on a cutting (chopping) board, and using a sharp knife, score the fish 2–3 times on both sides. Season with the black pepper and chill in the refrigerator for 30 minutes.

Heat the oil for deep-frying in a wok or deep fryer to 350°F/180°C or until a cube of bread browns in 30 seconds. Deep-fry the fish for 10–12 minutes or until golden brown and crispy. Remove with a slotted spoon and drain on paper towels.

Bring the broth (stock) to a boil in a pan. Add the sugar and salt, and stir. Add the chiles and garlic and stir for 3 minutes. Season with the lime juice.

Place the fish on a serving plate, pour over the sauce, garnish with the cilantro (coriander), and serve.

ปลาเนื้ออ่อนทอดกระเทียมพริกไทย

Fried Whisker Sheatfish in Garlic and Pepper

Origin Central
Preparation time 10 minutes
Cooking time 8–10 minutes
Serves 4

4 whisker sheatfish, cleaned and tails removed
2 tablespoons soy sauce
3 tablespoons ground black pepper
1 garlic bulb, cloves separated and coarsely pounded
4 cups (1⅔ pints/950 ml) vegetable oil, for deep-frying

To serve
Steamed Jasmine Rice (see p. 378)
Seafood Dipping Sauce (see p. 58)

Place the fish on a cutting (chopping) board, and using a sharp knife, score each fish 2–3 times on both sides.

Put the soy sauce and black pepper into a shallow dish, add the fish, and coat in the mixture.

Heat the oil for deep-frying in a wok or deep fryer to 350°F/180°C or until a cube of bread browns in 30 seconds. Deep-fry the coated fish for 8–10 minutes or until golden brown, then remove with a slotted spoon and drain on paper towels.

Deep-fry the garlic for 1 minute or until golden brown and crispy, then remove with a slotted spoon and drain on paper towels.

Place the fish on a serving plate, sprinkle with the deef-fried garlic, and serve.

ปลาช่อนและปลาสลิดทอดเกลือ

Fried Snakehead Fish

Origin Central
Preparation time 20 minutes, plus marinating and
drying time
Cooking time 10–15 minutes
Serves 4

2 x 1 lb 2-oz/600-g snakehead fish, cleaned
2 tablespoons salt flakes
3 cups (1¼ pints/750 ml) vegetable oil, for deep-frying

To serve
Glutinous Rice (see p. 378)
Tomato Chili Sauce (see p. 64)

Butterfly the fish by cutting it lengthwise down
the middle to the backbone, without cutting
all the way through, then open out to create
a butterfly fillet, leaving the head and bones
intact. Pat dry with paper towels.

Rub the fish with the salt, place on a large plate,
cover with plastic wrap (clingfilm), and let
marinate in the refrigerator for 2–3 hours.

Remove from the refrigerator, rinse thoroughly,
then drain, wrap in cheesecloth (muslin), and
sun-dry for 1–2 hours. Alternatively, preheat
the oven to 140°F/60°C and heat the fish for
1½–2 hours until dry.

Heat the oil for deep-frying in a deep, heavy
pan or deep fryer to 350°F/180°C or until a
cube of bread browns in 30 seconds. Cut the
fish into pieces and deep-fry for 10–15 minutes
or until golden. Remove with a slotted spoon
and drain on paper towels. Serve with rice
and tomato chili sauce.

ปลานิลภูกามยา

Deep-Fried Tilapia with Vegetables

Origin North
Preparation time 10 minutes
Cooking time 12–15 minutes
Serves 2

1 x 1 lb 5-oz/600-g tilapia, cleaned and descaled
2 cups (16 fl oz/475 ml) vegetable oil, for deep-frying
2 tablespoons Tamarind Puree (see p. 63)
1 tablespoon jaggery, palm sugar, or soft light
  brown sugar
5–7 red bird's eye chiles, chopped
⅓ cup (3½ oz/100 g) Chili Jam (see p. 35)
2 tablespoons fish sauce
½ green (sour) mango, diced
scant ½ cup (2 oz/50 g) diced carrot
1 tablespoon fresh green peppercorns
1 tablespoon finely sliced kaffir lime leaves
2 tablespoons finely sliced lemongrass
2 oz/50 g finely sliced betel leaf
3 shallots, finely sliced
1 tablespoon black and white sesame seeds
⅓ cup (3 oz/80 g) roasted chili paste (Nam Prik Pao)

Place the fish on a cutting (chopping) board,
and using a sharp knife, score the fish
2–3 times on both sides.

Heat the oil for deep-frying in a wok or deep
fryer to 350°F/180°C or until a cube of bread
browns in 30 seconds. Deep-fry the fish for
12–15 minutes on each side until golden brown
and crispy, then remove with a slotted spoon
and drain on paper towels.

For the sauce, mix the tamarind, sugar, chiles,
chili jam, and fish sauce together in a large
bowl. Add all the remaining ingredients and
mix together until combined.

Place the fish on a serving plate and pour over
the sauce. Serve.

ทอดมันปลา

Fish Cakes

Origin Central
Preparation time 10 minutes, plus chilling time
Cooking time 30 minutes
Makes 20–25

1 x 1 lb 2-oz/500-g skinless spotted featherback,
 cod, or salmon fillets, ground (minced)
½ tablespoon Red Curry Paste (see p. 38)
1 egg, beaten
1½ tablespoons granulated sugar
1½ tablespoons fish sauce
½ tablespoon cornstarch (cornflour)
¼ teaspoon salt
¾ cup (3 oz/80 g) finely chopped yard-long beans
1 tablespoon thinly sliced kaffir lime leaves
3 cups (1¼ pints/750 ml) vegetable oil, for deep-frying
Cucumber Relish, to serve (see p. 35)

Using your hands, mix the fish and curry paste
together in a bowl until thoroughly combined.
Add the egg, sugar, fish sauce, cornstarch
(cornflour), and salt and mix well. Add the
beans and kaffir lime leaves and continue
to mix until the mixture is firm and sticky.
Cover with plastic wrap (clingfilm) and chill
in the refrigerator for at least 1 hour.

Dampen your hands and mold the mixture
into 20–25 round cakes, about 2 inches/5 cm
in diameter and ⅜ inch/7–8 mm thick.

Heat the oil for deep-frying in a wok or deep
fryer to 350°F/180°C or until a cube of bread
browns in 30 seconds. Deep-fry the fish cakes
in batches, for 3–4 minutes or until golden
brown. Remove with a slotted spoon and drain
on paper towels. Serve with cucumber relish.

ปลาเจี๋ยนตะไคร้

Fish with Lemongrass-Tamarind Sauce

Origin South
Preparation time 10 minutes
Cooking time 20 minutes
Serves 2

½ cup (2¼ oz/60 g) all-purpose (plain) flour
14-oz/400-g cobia fish or any white fish such as tilapia,
 halved crosswise
3–4 cups (1¼–1⅔ pints/750–950 ml) vegetable oil,
 plus 3 tablespoons
6 cloves garlic, finely chopped
1 shallot, finely sliced
4 lemongrass stalks, finely sliced
1½ teaspoons Tamarind Puree (see p. 63)
¼ cup (2 fl oz/60 ml) chicken or vegetable broth (stock)
1 tablespoon soy sauce
2 tablespoons granulated sugar
1 red spur chile, diagonally sliced
2 scallions (spring onions), chopped into 2-inch/
 5-cm lengths

Spread the flour out on a plate and coat both
sides of the fish fillets in the flour.

Heat the oil for deep-frying in a wok or deep
fryer to 350°F/180°C or until a cube of bread
browns in 30 seconds. Deep-fry the fish for
6–8 minutes or until golden brown. Remove
with a slotted spoon and drain on paper towels,
then transfer to a serving plate and set aside.

Heat the 3 tablespoons of oil in a clean wok,
skillet, or frying pan over medium heat. Add
the garlic, shallot, and lemongrass and sauté
for 2–3 minutes until the shallots have softened
and the lemongrass is lightly browned. Add the
tamarind, broth (stock), soy sauce, and sugar
and stir well for 4–5 minutes until the sugar has
dissolved and the mixture has thickened. Add
the chile and scallions (spring onions) and cook
for another 1 minute. Pour the mixture over the
fish and serve.

เมี่ยงปลาทับทิม

Sea Bass Wrapped in Kale Leaves

Origin Central
Preparation time 15 minutes
Cooking time 10 minutes
Serves 2

1 lb 5 oz/600 g sea bass fillets, cut into 1-inch/
 2.5-cm dice
2 cups (16 fl oz/475 ml) vegetable oil, for deep-frying
10 Chinese kale leaves
4-inch/10-cm piece fresh ginger, peeled and diced
2 limes, diced
10 red and green bird's eye chiles, finely chopped
1 shallot, chopped
½ cup (2¾ oz/75 g) roasted peanuts

For the sauce
2 tablespoons jaggery, palm sugar, or soft light
 brown sugar
2 tablespoons fish sauce
3 tablespoons lime juice
1 tablespoon pickled plum juice

For the sauce, heat a wok over medium heat, add the sugar and fish sauce, and stir for 4–5 minutes until thick. Remove from the heat, add the lime juice and pickled plum juice, and stir until thoroughly combined. Transfer to a small serving bowl and set aside.

Heat the oil for deep-frying in a clean wok or deep fryer to 350°F/180°C or until a cube of bread browns in 30 seconds. Deep-fry the fish dice for 6–7 minutes or until golden brown, then remove with a slotted spoon and drain on paper towels.

Lay the kale leaves on a large serving plate and place a couple of fish dice in the center of each leaf. Top with the ginger, limes, chiles, shallot, and peanuts. Serve with the sauce on the side.

ปูจ๋า

Deep-Fried Pork and Crabmeat in Shells

Origin Central
Preparation time 10 minutes
Cooking time 20 minutes
Serves 5

1 lb 2 oz/500 g ground (minced) pork
8–10 water chestnuts, peeled and diced
1 lb 2 oz/500 g crabmeat
2 onions, finely chopped
3 cilantro (coriander) roots, finely crushed
2 tablespoons soy sauce
2 duck eggs
3 tablespoons all-purpose (plain) flour
10 crab or scallop shells
2 cups (16 fl oz/475 ml) vegetable oil, for deep-frying
red, green, and orange bell peppers, seeded and
 sliced, to garnish

To serve
Sweet Chili Dipping Sauce (see p. 60)
lettuce leaves

Put the ground (minced) pork, water chestnuts, crabmeat, and onions in a large bowl and mix well. Add the cilantro (coriander) root and soy sauce and mix well.

Spoon the seasoned pork and crabmeat mixture into the crab or scallop shells, then steam in a steamer for 10–15 minutes.

Beat the eggs with the flour in a bowl until thoroughly combined and set aside.

Heat the oil for deep-frying in a large wok or deep fryer to 350°F/180°C or until a cube of bread browns in 30 seconds. Dip the steamed filled shells into the beaten egg mixture until coated, and then carefully drop into the hot oil and deep-fry for 4–6 minutes until golden brown and crispy. Remove with a slotted spoon and drain on paper towels. Repeat with the remaining shells.

Place the crab on a bed of lettuce leaves, sprinkle with the pepper flowers, and serve with sweet chili dipping sauce on the side.

Photo p. 305

ปูนิ่มทอดกระเทียมพริกไทย

Deep-Fried Soft Shell Crab with Garlic

Origin Central
Preparation time 10 minutes
Cooking time 13 minutes
Serves 2

4 cups (1⅔ pints/950 ml) vegetable oil
10 cloves garlic, unpeeled and chopped
1 tablespoon Saam-Gler (see p. 41)
3 tablespoons oyster sauce
1 tablespoon superfine (caster) sugar
4 x 3½-oz/100-g soft shell crabs, cleaned
  and cut into quarters

To serve
lettuce leaves
Thai chili sauce

Heat ⅓ cup (2½ fl oz/75 ml) of the oil in a wok over low-medium heat, add the garlic, and fry for 1 minute or until brown and crispy. Remove with a slotted spoon and drain on paper towels.

Put the saam-gler, oyster sauce, and sugar in a large bowl and mix well until combined. Add the crabs and gently mix.

Heat the remaining oil in a clean wok or deep fryer to 350°F/180°C or until a cube of bread browns in 30 seconds. Deep-fry the crabs for 8–10 minutes or until golden brown and crispy. Remove with a slotted spoon and drain on paper towels.

Place the crab on a bed of lettuce leaves, sprinkle with the crispy garlic, and serve with Thai chili sauce.

Photo p. 307

กุ้งชุบแป้งทอด

Deep-Fried Shrimp

Origin Central
Preparation time 5 minutes
Cooking time 10 minutes
Serves 2

½ cup (2¼ oz/60 g) all-purpose (plain) flour
¼ cup (3 oz/80 g) rice flour
½ cup (2¼ oz/60 g) tapioca flour
¼ teaspoon baking powder
¼ teaspoon salt
1 cup (2 oz/50 g) fresh breadcrumbs
3 cups (1¼ pints/750 ml) vegetable oil, for deep-frying
9 oz/250 g shrimp (prawns), peeled and deveined, with
  tails still intact
Sweet Chili Dipping Sauce (see p. 60), to serve

Put the all-purpose (plain) flour, rice flour, tapioca flour, baking powder, salt, and ⅓ cup (2½ fl oz/75 ml) water in a large bowl and mix well until the flours have dissolved. Set aside.

Spread the bread crumbs out on a plate. Dip the shrimp (prawns) into the flour mixture, then coat in the breadcrumbs.

Heat the oil for deep-frying in a wok or deep fryer to 350°F/180°C or until a cube of bread browns in 30 seconds. Deep-fry the shrimp in batches for 4–5 minutes or until golden brown. Remove with a slotted spoon and drain on paper towels. Serve with the sweet chili dipping sauce.

Photo p. 309

กุ้งผัดซอสมะขาม

Deep-Fried Shrimp in Tamarind Sauce

Origin Central
Preparation time 10 minutes
Cooking time 10 minutes
Serves 2

3 cups (1¼ pints/750 ml) vegetable oil, for deep-frying
12 jumbo shrimp (king prawns), peeled and deveined
1½ teaspoons Sriracha sauce or other chili sauce (optional)
3 tablespoons superfine (caster) sugar
3 tablespoons Tamarind Puree (see p. 63)
5 red and green spur chiles, chopped
1½ teaspoons fish sauce
1 teaspoon oyster sauce
2 tablespoons Fried Garlic (see p. 64)
10 dried red chiles, roasted

Heat the oil for deep-frying in a wok or deep fryer to 350°F/180°C or until a cube of bread browns in 30 seconds. Deep-fry the shrimp (prawns) for 1–2 minutes or until cooked. Remove with a slotted spoon and drain on paper towels.

In a clean wok, mix the Sriracha sauce, if using, sugar, tamarind, chiles, fish sauce, oyster sauce, and 2 tablespoons water together. Put over medium heat and stir for 3–4 minutes or until the mixture starts to become sticky. Add the shrimp and mix well. Sprinkle with the fried garlic and dried chiles and serve.

กุ้งลายเสือต้มยำแห้ง

Fried Shrimp in Spicy Sauce

Origin South
Preparation time 5 minutes
Cooking time 6 minutes
Serves 2

3 tablespoons vegetable oil
4 slices galangal
2 lemongrass stalks, finely sliced
2 cloves garlic, chopped
2 shallots, finely sliced
3 tablespoons Tamarind Puree (see p. 63)
1 tablespoon Chili Jam (see p. 35)
2 teaspoons oyster sauce
1½ teaspoons granulated sugar
6 jumbo shrimp (king prawns), peeled and deveined
6 kaffir lime leaves, torn
2 scallions (spring onions), finely sliced

Heat the oil in a wok over medium heat, add the galangal, lemongrass, garlic, and shallots, and stir-fry for 1–2 minutes until fragrant. Add the tamarind, chili jam, oyster sauce, sugar, and ½ cup (4 fl oz/120 ml) water and mix well. Add the shrimp (prawns) and fry for 3–4 minutes or until cooked. Sprinkle with the kaffir lime leaves and scallions (spring onions) and serve.

หมึกแดดเดียว

Deep-Fried Sundried Squid

Origin Central
Preparation time 10 minutes, plus drying time
Cooking time 3 minutes
Serves 4

1 lb 2 oz/500 g squid, cleaned and cut into ¼-inch/
  5-mm-thick rings
1½ tablespoons fish sauce
2 tablespoons granulated sugar
2 cups (16 fl oz/475 ml) vegetable oil, for deep-frying

Mix the squid, fish sauce, and sugar together in a large bowl until thoroughly combined.

Place the squid on a wire rack, cover with insect proof mesh, and sundry for 3–4 hours or until the squid has dried. Alternatively, let dry at room temperature for 24 hours.

Heat the oil for deep-frying in a wok or deep fryer to 375°F/190°C or until a cube of bread browns in 30 seconds. Deep-fry the squid for 2–3 minutes or until cooked and brown. Remove with a slotted spoon and drain on paper towels, then serve.

หมูทอดกระเทียมพริกไทย

Deep-Fried Pork with Garlic and Pepper

Origin Central
Preparation time 10 minutes, plus marinating time
Cooking time 15 minutes
Serves 4

1 x 1 lb 2-oz/500-g shoulder pork, cut into 3 x 2-inch/
  7.5 x 5-cm pieces, ¼ inch/5 mm thick
2 tablespoons Saam-Gler (see p. 41)
1 teaspoon salt
1 tablespoon soy sauce (optional)
2 cups (16 fl oz/475 ml) vegetable oil, for deep-frying

To serve
Glutinous Rice (see p. 378)
raw vegetables, such as cucumber and lettuce

Put the pork, saam-gler, salt, and soy sauce, if using, in a large bowl and mix well. Cover with plastic wrap (clingfilm) and let marinate in the refrigerator for 1–2 hours.

Heat the oil for deep-frying in a wok or deep fryer to 350°F/180°C or until a cube of bread browns in 30 seconds. Deep-fry the pork for 10–15 minutes until golden. Remove with a slotted spoon and drain on paper towels. Serve with rice and raw vegetables.

ไข่เจียวหมูสับ

Pork Omelet

Origin Central
Preparation time 5 minutes
Cooking time 4 minutes
Serves 2

3 eggs, beaten
1 scallion (spring onion), chopped
2¼ oz/60 g ground (minced) pork
2 teaspoons soy sauce
⅓ cup (2½ fl oz/75 ml) vegetable oil
Steamed Jasmine Rice (see p. 378), to serve

Put the eggs, scallion (spring onion), pork, and soy sauce in a bowl and whisk until thoroughly combined.

Heat the oil in a nonstick skillet or frying pan over medium heat. Pour the egg mixture into the skillet or pan and cook for about 1½ minutes or until golden brown. Carefully flip over the omelet and cook for another 1½ minutes to color the other side. Transfer to a serving plate and serve with rice.

หมูแดดเดียว

Sundried Pork

Origin Central
Preparation time 10 minutes, plus drying time
Cooking time 12 minutes
Serves 4

1 lb 2 oz/500 g thin shoulder pork cutlet or pork loin
    steak, cut into ⅝-inch/1.5cm-wide strips
1½ tablespoons Saam-Gler (see p. 41)
1½ tablespoons soy sauce
1 tablespoon jaggery, palm sugar, or soft light
    brown sugar
1 tablespoon oyster sauce
1 tablespoon white sesame seeds
¼ teaspoon salt
3 cups (1¼ pints/750 ml) vegetable oil, for deep-frying
Thai chili sauce, to serve

Mix the pork strips and saam-gler together in a large bowl. Add the soy sauce, sugar, oyster sauce, sesame seeds, and salt and mix well. Place the strips of pork onto a wire rack or tray, cover with an insect-proof mesh, and dry in the sun for 5–6 hours. Alternatively, dry indoors for 24 hours.

Heat the oil for deep-frying in a wok or deep fryer to 350°F/180°C or until a cube of bread browns in 30 seconds. Deep-fry the pork for 9–10 minutes or until brown and crispy. Remove with a slotted spoon and drain on paper towels. Serve with chili sauce.

Photo p. 313

ข้าวหมูกรอบ

Crispy Pork Side with Rice

Origin Central
Preparation time 10 minutes, plus resting time
Cooking time 2 hours
Serves 6

1 x 1¾-lb/800-g boneless pork side (belly)
1½ tablespoons sea salt flakes
1½ tablespoons white vinegar
2 cups (16 fl oz/475 ml) vegetable oil

For the sauce
1½ cups (12 fl oz/350 ml) chicken or pork broth (stock)
1 cilantro (coriander) root, crushed
2 tablespoons soy sauce
3 tablespoons jaggery, palm sugar, or soft light brown sugar
½ teaspoon five-spice powder
1 tablespoon oyster sauce
1 tablespoon salted soybeans
1 teaspoon dark soy sauce
1 teaspoon sesame oil
2 tablespoons ketchup
2 tablespoons cornstarch (cornflour)

To serve
6 cups (2¼ lb/1 kg) Steamed Jasmine Rice (see p. 378)
3 hard-boiled eggs, peeled and halved
sliced cucumber

Bring a large pan of water to a boil over high heat. Carefully place the pork side (belly), skin side down, in the pan and return to a boil. Add half the salt, then reduce the heat to medium, and simmer for 30 minutes. Transfer to a wire rack, let rest for 5–10 minutes, then pierce the skin all over with a fork. Rub with the vinegar, then the remaining salt. Score the skin in a ½-inch/1-cm crisscross pattern and set aside.

Preheat the oven to 375°F/190°C/Gas Mark 5. Transfer the seasoned pork to a large roasting pan, skin side up, and roast for about 1½ hours. Remove and set aside.

Meanwhile, make the sauce. Bring 1 cup (9 fl oz/250 ml) water, the broth (stock), and cilantro (coriander) root to a boil in a pan over medium heat. Add the remaining ingredients except the cornstarch (cornflour) and boil for 5 minutes or until the mixture has slightly reduced and is thoroughly combined.

Dissolve the cornstarch in 4 tablespoons water and add to the pan, stirring well. Let the sauce boil for another 2 minutes or until thickened.

Heat the oil in a skillet or frying pan over medium heat. Sauté the pork, skin side down, for 2–3 minutes or until the skin is puffed up and crisped, then turn and sauté the other side for another 1–2 minutes. Remove, drain, and let cool.

Slice the cooled pork into bite-size pieces and place on top of the rice. Pour over the sauce and serve with the egg and cucumber.

ซี่โครงหมูทอดกระเทียมพริกไทย

Deep-Fried Baby Ribs with Garlic and Peppercorns

Origin Central
Preparation time 10 minutes, plus marinating time
Cooking time 20 minutes
Serves 4

2 teaspoons white peppercorns
10 cloves garlic, coarsely pounded
3 cilantro (coriander) roots
2 tablespoons soy sauce
2 tablespoons oyster sauce
2 cups (16 fl oz/475 ml) vegetable oil
1¾ lb/800 g boneless baby back ribs, chopped into
   1½-inch/4-cm pieces
Steamed Jasmine Rice (see p. 378), to serve
sliced cucumber, to serve

To garnish
15 cloves garlic
½ teaspoon soy sauce

Pound the white peppercorns, 10 garlic cloves, and cilantro (coriander) root in a mortar with a pestle until fine, then add to the bowl with the ribs. Add the soy sauce and oyster sauce, cover with plastic wrap (clingfilm), and let marinate in the refrigerator for at least 15–30 minutes.

Meanwhile, for the garnish, coarsely pound the 15 garlic cloves with the ½ teaspoon soy sauce in a mortar with a pestle. Set aside.

Heat the oil for deep-frying in a wok or deep fryer to 350°F/180°C or until a cube of bread browns in 30 seconds. Deep-fry the ribs for 8–10 minutes until brown. Remove with a slotted spoon and drain on paper towels.

Remove half the oil from the wok or deep fryer, reduce the heat to low, and add the pounded garlic mixture. Deep-fry for 1–2 minutes until brown. Remove with a slotted spoon and drain on paper towels. Let cool.

Place the ribs on a serving plate, sprinkle with the crispy garlic, and serve with steamed rice and sliced cucumber.

ไก่ตะไคร้

Crispy Chicken and Lemongrass

Origin Central
Preparation time 10 minutes
Cooking time 20 minutes
Serves 4

5 lemongrass stalks, diagonally sliced into 1½-inch/
   4-cm lengths
5–6 kaffir lime leaves, torn
1 tablespoon tempura batter mix
1½ tablespoons soy sauce
1 x 1 lb 2-oz/500-g boneless chicken thighs, each cut
   into 4 pieces about 1½-inch/4-cm thick
5 cups (2 pints/1.2 liters) vegetable oil, for deep-frying
Sweet Chili Dipping Sauce (see p. 60), to serve

Coarsely pound the lemongrass in a mortar with a pestle until shredded, then use your hand to crumble until finely shredded. Transfer to a small bowl, add the kaffir lime leaves, batter mix, and ½ tablespoon soy sauce, and mix well. Set aside.

Put the chicken and the remaining 1 tablespoon soy sauce in another bowl and mix until the chicken is well coated. Set aside.

Heat the oil for deep-frying in a wok or deep fryer to 350°F/180°C or until a cube of bread browns in 30 seconds. Deep-fry the chicken for 13–15 minutes or until golden brown and crispy. Increase the heat for 1 minute, then remove the chicken with a slotted spoon and drain on paper towels. Set aside.

Reduce the temperature to 325°F/160°C or until a cube of bread browns in 45 seconds. Deep-fry the lemongrass mixture for about 2 minutes or until golden brown and crispy. Quickly remove with a slotted spoon and drain on paper towels.

Place the chicken on a serving plate, top with the crispy lemongrass, and serve with the sweet chili dipping sauce on the side.

ไก่เมืองคั่วเกลือ

Deep-Fried Salted Chicken

Origin North
Preparation time 50 minutes, plus marinating time
Cooking time 15 minutes
Serves 2

14 oz/400 g boneless chicken thighs, cut into
    1-inch/2.5-cm cubes
5 cloves garlic, crushed
1 tablespoon soy sauce
1½ teaspoons salt
1 teaspoon granulated sugar
pinch of white pepper
2 cups (16 fl oz/475 ml) vegetable oil, for deep-frying
2 red spur chiles, diagonally sliced, to garnish

For the roasted chili dip
10 dried red bird's eye chiles, seeded
3 cloves garlic, halved
1 shallot, quartered
1 slice galangal, chopped
1 teaspoon shrimp paste
1½ tablespoons fish sauce
1 tablespoon lime juice
1½ teaspoons granulated sugar

Put the chicken, garlic, soy sauce, salt, and
sugar in a bowl, mix well, then cover with
plastic wrap (clingfilm) and let marinate in
the refrigerator for 10–15 minutes.

For the chili dip, heat a wok over medium heat,
add the dried chiles, and toast for 2–3 minutes
or until fragrant and dark in color. Remove from
the wok with a slotted spoon and set aside.

Add the garlic and shallot to the wok and toast
for 2–3 minutes or until soft and lightly burned.
Transfer to a mortar. Add the chiles, galangal,
and shrimp paste and pound with a pestle until
smooth. Add the fish sauce, lime juice, sugar,
and 2 tablespoons water and stir well. Transfer
to a small serving bowl and set aside.

Heat the oil for deep-frying in a wok or deep
fryer to 350°F/180°C or until a cube of bread
browns in 30 seconds. Deep-fry the chicken
for 8–10 minutes or until golden and crispy.
Remove with a slotted spoon and drain on
paper towels. Garnish with the red chiles,
and serve with the roasted chili dip.

น้ำเต้าทอด

Deep-Fried Bottle Gourd

Origin North
Preparation time 20 minutes, plus soaking time
Cooking time 10 minutes
Serves 4

½ cup (2¼ oz/60 g) tempura batter mix
1 x 14-oz/400-g young bottle gourd, cut into
    ½ x 3-inch/1 x 7-cm sticks
3 cups (1¼ pints/750 ml) vegetable oil, for deep-frying
½ teaspoon salt

For the dipping sauce
7 dried red chiles, seeded
2 cloves garlic, chopped
2 tablespoons Tamarind Puree (see p. 63)
½ teaspoon salt
1 teaspoon granulated sugar
2 tablespoons chopped cilantro (coriander)

For the dipping sauce, soak the dried chiles
in a bowl of warm water for 15 minutes or until
rehydrated, then drain and chop.

Pound the chiles, garlic, and tamarind in a
mortar with a pestle. Add the salt, sugar, and
1 tablespoon water, then add the cilantro
(coriander) and mix together until the salt
ans sugar have dissolved. Transfer to a small
serving bowl and set aside.

Spread the tempura batter mix out on a plate
and dip the gourd sticks into the batter mix
until well coated.

Heat the oil for deep-frying in a wok or deep
fryer to 350°F/180°C or until a cube of bread
browns in 30 seconds. Deep-fry the coated
gourd in batches for 4–5 minutes until golden
brown. Remove with a slotted spoon and drain
on paper towels. Transfer the gourd sticks to
a serving plate, season with the salt, and serve
with the dipping sauce.

ยำผักบุ้งกรอบ

Spicy Water Spinach and Shrimp Salad

Origin Central
Preparation time 5 minutes
Cooking time 10 minutes
Serves 2

5 cups (5 oz/150 g) water spinach, sliced
1 cup (9 fl oz/250 ml) vegetable oil, for deep-frying
4 uncooked jumbo shrimp (king prawns), peeled and deveined, with tails still intact
3 red finger chiles, sliced into fine strips
3 tablespoons Fried Shallots (see p. 64)

For the batter
1 cup (4 oz/120 g) wheat flour
pinch of salt
pinch of ground black pepper

For the sauce
¼ cup (2 fl oz/60 ml) coconut milk
2 tablespoons fish sauce
1 tablespoon jaggery, palm sugar, or soft light brown sugar
1 tablespoon Chili Jam (see p. 35)
2 tablespoons lime juice

To make the batter, put the flour, salt, and black pepper into a bowl and stir to combine. Add ¾ cup (6 fl oz/175 ml) water and stir until a batter forms.

Coat the water spinach in the batter.

Heat the oil for deep-frying in a wok or deep fryer to 350°F/180°C or until a cube of bread browns in 30 seconds. Gradually add the coated water spinach to the hot oil, and deep-fry for 4–5 minutes or until cooked. Remove with a slotted spoon and drain on paper towels.

Deep-fry the shrimp (prawns) for 2–3 minutes or until cooked. Remove with a slotted spoon and drain on paper towels. Set aside.

For the sauce, bring the coconut milk and fish sauce to a boil in a separate wok over medium heat. Add the sugar, chili jam, and lime juice, stir, and return to a boil. Remove from the heat.

To serve, place the deep-fried water spinach and shrimp on a serving plate and pour over the sauce. Sprinkle with the chiles and fried shallots and serve.

ปูนิ่มแช่น้ำปลา

Raw Soft-Shell Crab in Fish Sauce

Origin Central
Preparation time 10 minutes, plus marinating time
Serves 3

3 live soft-shell crabs
⅓ cup (2½ fl oz/75 ml) fish sauce
15 cloves garlic, chopped
10–15 red and green bird's eye chiles, chopped
1 tablespoon lime juice
1 tablespoon granulated sugar

To serve
1 bitter gourd, peeled and thinly sliced
2–3 mint sprigs
3 cloves garlic, peeled and left whole

Rince the crabs under cold running water. Using a pair of sharp scissors, cut off the front part of the crab behind the eyes, then open the top shell and remove and discard the gills. Turn the crab over and remove the apron. Repeat with the remaining crabs.

Place the crabs on a plate with 3 tablespoons fish sauce. Cover with plastic wrap (clingfilm) and let marinate in the refrigerator for 2 hours.

Pound the garlic and the chiles together in a mortar with a pestle. Add the lime juice, sugar, and the remaining fish sauce and stir until thoroughly combined.

Place the marinated crabs on a serving plate and drizzle with the sauce. Arrange the bitter gourd around the crabs and sprinkle with the mint and the whole garlic cloves. Serve.

กุ้งแช่น้ำปลา

Spicy Raw Shrimp in Fish Sauce

Origin Central
Preparation time 10 minutes, plus chilling time
Serves 2

15 uncooked shrimp (prawns), peeled and deveined,
  with tails intact
1½ teaspoons fish sauce
¼ cup (2 fl oz/60 ml) Seafood Dipping Sauce (see p. 58)

To garnish
5 red and green bird's eye chiles
½ cup (3½ oz/100 g) sliced bitter gourd
5 cloves garlic, thinly sliced lengthwise
15 mint leaves

Arrange the uncooked shrimp (prawns) on
a serving plate.

Mix the fish sauce with 1½ tablespoons water
in a bowl, then pour over the shrimp. Cover
the plate with plastic wrap (clingfilm) and chill
in the refrigerator for 30–50 minutes or until
the shrimp have absorbed the sauce.

To serve, pour the seafood sauce over the
shrimp and garnish with the chiles, bitter
gourd, garlic, and mint leaves.

เมี่ยงหมูหยอง

Pork Floss Wrapped in Kale Leaves

Origin Central
Preparation time 10 minutes
Cooking time 5 minutes
Makes 20

2-inch/5-cm piece fresh ginger, peeled and cut into
  ½-inch/1-cm dice
10–15 red and green bird's eye chiles, finely chopped
4 shallots, chopped to ⅜-inch/8-mm pieces
4 lemongrass stalks, finely sliced
⅓ cup (1½ oz/40 g) roasted peanuts
2 limes, cut into ½-inch/1-cm dice
3½ oz/100 g pork floss
20 young Chinese kale leaves

For the sweet-and-sour dressing
2½ tablespoons jaggery, palm sugar, or soft light
  brown sugar
1 tablespoon fish sauce
1 tablespoon lime juice
1½ teaspoons pickled plum juice (optional)

For the dressing, mix the sugar, fish sauce,
lime juice, and pickled plum juice, if using,
together in a pan and put over medium heat.
Stir for about 2 minutes or until the sugar has
dissolved and starts to caramelize. Let cool.

Mix the ginger, chiles, shallots, lemongrass,
roasted peanuts, limes, pork floss, and the
dressing together in a large bowl.

To serve, place the kale leaves on a serving
plate and put a teaspoon of the pork mixture
into the center of each leaf.

Photo p. 319

Stir Fries

ผัดบวบใส่ไข่
Stir-Fried Angled Gourd with Egg

Origin Central
Preparation time 5 minutes
Cooking time 4–5 minutes
Serves 2

2 tablespoons vegetable oil
3 cloves garlic, crushed
1–2 x 14-oz/400-g angled gourds, peeled and sliced
2 eggs
1 tablespoon oyster sauce
1 teaspoon soy sauce
1 teaspoon fish sauce
½ teaspoon granulated sugar

Heat the oil in a wok over high heat, add the garlic, and stir-fry for 30 seconds or until fragrant. Add the gourds and stir-fry for 1–2 minutes. Add the eggs and stir-fry for another minute or until the eggs are cooked. Add the oyster sauce, soy sauce, fish sauce, and sugar and mix well. Serve.

เต้าหู้ผัดถั่วงอก
Stir-Fried Tofu with Bean Sprouts

Origin Central
Preparation time 5 minutes
Cooking time 8–10 minutes
Serves 2

1 cup (9 fl oz/250 ml) vegetable oil
3½-oz/100-g extra firm tofu, cut into ¾-inch/2-cm cubes
5 cloves garlic, finely chopped
3 cups (11 oz/300 g) bean sprouts
3 red spur chiles, diagonally sliced
2 scallions (spring onions), sliced into 1¼-inch/ 3-cm lengths
2 tablespoons oyster sauce
1 teaspoon soy sauce

Heat the oil in a wok over medium heat, add the tofu, and stir-fry for 4–5 minutes or until golden. Remove with a slotted spoon and set aside. Reserve 2 tablespoons of the oil, then drain the rest from the wok. Increase the heat to medium-high and heat the reserved oil. Add the garlic and bean sprouts and stir-fry for 1–2 minutes. Add the chiles, scallions (spring onions), oyster sauce, soy sauce, and tofu and stir-fry for another 1 minute. Serve.

Photo p. 329

ปลาผัดฉ่า

Stir-Fried Fried Fish with Vegetables

Origin North
Preparation time 10 minutes
Cooking time 5 minutes
Serves 4

3 cloves garlic, chopped
¼ shallot
1 red bird's eye chile
3 tablespoons vegetable oil
11 oz/300 g white fish fillet, cut into ½-inch/1-cm slices
⅔ cup (3½ oz/100 g) peeled and chopped fingerroots
5 fresh young green pepeprcorns (on their stalks)
3 round eggplants (aubergines), cut into quarters
3 baby corn
2 yard-long beans, cut into 2-inch/5-cm long lengths
7 kaffir lime leaves, shredded
2 tablespoons fish sauce
2 tablespoons oyster sauce
1 tablespoon superfine (caster) sugar
3 sweet basil sprigs
2 red spur chiles, sliced lengthwise

Pound the garlic, shallot, and bird's eye chile thoroughly in a mortar with a pestle, then set aside.

Heat the oil in a wok over medium heat, add the fish, and cook for 2–3 minutes until cooked. Transfer the fish to a plate.

Add the pounded mixture to the wok and stir-fry for 1 minute or until fragrant. Add the fish, fingerroot, peppercorns, eggplant (aubergine), baby corn, yard-long beans, and kaffir lime leaves and stir-fry for 1 minute. Season with the fish sauce, oyster sauce, and sugar and mix well. Add the basil and red spur chiles, then serve.

ปลาดุกทะเลผัดฉ่า

Spicy Stir-Fried Basa Fish

Origin Central
Preparation time 15 minutes
Cooking time 10 minutes
Serves 3

1 x 14-oz/400-g whole basa fish or river cobbler, cleaned
3 tablespoons vegetable oil
4–5 kaffir lime leaves, ripped
3 sweet basil sprigs, leaves only
½ cup (4 oz/120 g) finely sliced heart of palm
3 round eggplants (aubergines), quartered
7 fresh young green peppercorns (on their stalks)
1 teaspoon granulated sugar
2 tablespoons soy sauce

For the chili paste
5 red and green bird's eye chiles
7 orange finger chiles, pounded
3–4 red finger chiles, sliced
⅓ cup (2 oz/50 g) peeled and sliced fingerroots
5 cloves garlic

Cut through the basa fish belly and remove the innards, then cut the fish into slices and rinse under cold running water. Drain and set aside.

Roughly pound all the chiles, sliced fingerroot, and garlic together in a mortar with a pestle.

Heat the oil in a wok over medium heat. Add the chile mixture and stir-fry for 1 minute or until fragrant. Add the sliced fish and stir-fry for 6 minutes. Add the remaining ingredients and stir-fry for 2 minutes. Serve.

ผัดเผ็ดปลากราย

Spicy Stir-Fried Fish with Mixed Vegetables

Origin Central
Preparation time 10 minutes
Cooking time 7 minutes
Serves 6

1 tablespoon vegetable oil
1 lb 2 oz/500 g clown featherback fish or cod fillet,
  cut into bite-size pieces
1 cup (2 oz/50 g) sweet basil leaves
3 red and green finger chiles, chopped
3 fingerroots, peeled and chopped
5 round eggplants (aubergines), sliced
3 yard-long beans, chopped
1 tablespoon fish sauce
1 tablespoon jaggery, palm sugar, or soft light
  brown sugar
4 fresh young green peppercorns (on their stalks),
  to garnish

For the chili paste
9 dried red chiles, seeded
6 cloves garlic, chopped
6 shallots, chopped
1 kaffir lime leaf, torn
zest of 1 kaffir lime
1 tablespoon salt

For the chili paste, soak the dried chiles in a bowl of warm water for 15 minutes or until rehydrated, then drain and chop. Transfer to a mortar with the remaining chili paste ingredients and pound with a pestle until smooth. Set aside.

Heat the oil in a wok over medium heat, add the chili paste, and stir-fry for 1 minute or until fragrant. Add the fish, basil, chiles, fingerroot, eggplant (aubergine), yard-long beans, fish sauce, and sugar and stir-fry for 3 minutes or until cooked. Garnish with the green peppercorns and serve.

ปลาอินทรีย์ผัดขึ้นฉ่าย

Stir-Fried Spanish Mackerel with Celery

Origin Central
Preparation time 10 minutes
Cooking time 15 minutes
Serves 2

½ cup (2¼ oz/60 g) all-purpose (plain) flour
11 oz/300 g Spanish mackerel fillet, sliced into
  1¼–1½-inch/3–4-cm pieces
3 cups (1¼ pints/750 ml) vegetable oil, for deep-frying
5 cloves garlic, finely chopped
2 tablespoons oyster sauce
½ teaspoon soy sauce
¼ teaspoon granulated sugar
1 teaspoon salted soybeans
¼ cup (2 fl oz/60 ml) chicken broth (stock)
2 red spur chiles, diagonally sliced
1 cup (5 oz/150 g) chopped Chinese celery (2 inches/
  5 cm long)
Steamed Jasmine Rice (see p. 378), to serve

Spread the flour out on a plate and coat the fish pieces in the flour, then set aside.

Heat the oil for deep-frying in a wok or deep-fryer to 350°F/180°C or until a cube of bread browns in 30 seconds. Deep-fry the mackerel for 5–7 minutes or until golden brown. Remove with a slotted spoon and drain on paper towels.

Drain all but 2 tablespoons of oil from the wok and heat over medium heat. Add the garlic and stir-fry for 1 minute or until fragrant. Reduce the heat to low, add the oyster sauce, soy sauce, sugar, soybeans, and broth (stock), and stir. Add the deep-fried fish, the chiles, and celery and stir-fry for 20 seconds or until the mixture is thoroughly combined. Serve with rice.

ผัดปลากะพงกระวาน

Stir-Fried Sea Bass with Cardamom Shoots

Origin Central
Preparation time 5 minutes
Cooking time 10 minutes
Serves 2

3–5 orange finger chiles, chopped
5–10 cloves garlic, chopped
3 tablespoons vegetable oil
11 oz/300 g sea bass fillet, cut into ½-inch/1-cm pieces
1½ tablespoons fish sauce
1 cup (4 oz/120 g) chopped cardamom shoots
1 cup (2 oz/50 g) sweet basil leaves, plus extra to serve

Pound the chiles and garlic together in a mortar with a pestle until smooth.

Heat the oil in a wok over medium heat, add the paste, and stir-fry for 1 minute or until fragrant. Add the sea bass and fish sauce and cook for 3–5 minutes. Add the cardamom shoots and basil and cook for another 2 minutes. Serve with extra cardamom shoots, sweet basil, and garlic cloves.

Photo p. 332

ปลากะพงผัดเต้าเจี้ยว

Stir-Fried Snakehead Fish with Salted Soybeans

Origin Central
Preparation time 10 minutes, plus soaking time
Cooking time 10 minutes
Serves 4

4–5 dried cloud ear mushrooms
3 tablespoons vegetable oil
5 cloves garlic, finely chopped
11 oz/300 g snakehead, catfish, or tilapia fish fillet, cut into bite-size pieces
⅓ cup (2¾ oz/70 g) salted soybeans
1 tablespoon sesame oil
2 tablespoons oyster sauce
½ teaspoon soy sauce
1 teaspoon granulated sugar
½ teaspoon ground black pepper
4-inch/10-cm piece fresh ginger, peeled and finely julienned
5 green finger chiles, cut into strips
1 cup (5 oz/150 g) chopped Chinese celery (2 inches/ 5-cm long)

Soak the dried mushrooms in a bowl of boiling water for 10 minutes or until softened. Drain and set aside.

Heat the vegetable oil in a wok over medium heat, add the garlic, and stir-fry for 1 minute or until fragrant. Add the fish and gently stir-fry for 3 minutes or until cooked. Add the soybeans, sesame oil, oyster sauce, soy sauce, sugar, pepper, and 2 tablespoons water and stir-fry for 3 minutes until thoroughly combined. Add the ginger and cloud ear mushroom and stir-fry for 1–2 minutes until the mushroom is cooked. Add the green chiles and Chinese celery and stir 2–3 times until well mixed. Serve.

คะน้าปลาเค็ม

Stir-Fried Kale with Salted Fish

Origin Central
Preparation time 10 minutes
Cooking time 5 minutes
Serves 2

2 tablespoons vegetable oil
2 tablespoons Fried Garlic (see p. 64)
2 red bird's eye chiles, chopped and pounded
3½ oz/100 g sun-dried salted fish (Spanish mackerel),
  rinsed, dried, and cut into bite-size pieces
5–7 Chinese kale stems, chopped
1 teaspoon oyster sauce
½ teaspoon superfine (caster) sugar

Heat the oil in a wok over medium heat and add the Fried Garlic, chiles, and fish. Then add the kale and stir-fry for about 4 minutes until cooked. Add the oyster sauce and sugar and serve.

Photo p. 335

ผัดหอยกะพง

Stir-Fried Small Horse Mussels

Origin Northeast
Preparation time 10 minutes
Cooking time 5 minutes
Serves 2

1 lb 2 oz/500 g small horse mussels, cleaned
3 tablespoons vegetable oil
3 cloves garlic, roughly pounded
1 tablespoon soy sauce
1 teaspoon granulated sugar
1 cup (2 oz/50 g) sweet basil leaves

Sort through the mussels and discard any with open shells. Scrub the mussels with a scourer to remove any barnacles and then pull away the beards.

Put the mussels in a wok or pan, cover, and steam over medium heat for 2 minutes, stirring occasionally, until the shells open and the mussels start to cook. Immediately remove from the heat. When cool enough to handle, remove the mussel flesh from the shells, and set aside. Discard the shells.

Heat the oil in a clean wok over medium heat, add the garlic, and stir-fry for 1 minute or until fragrant. Increase the heat a little, add the mussel meat, soy sauce, and sugar, and stir-fry for 1 minute or until the mussels are cooked. Add the basil leaves and stir-fry for another 1 minute. Serve.

Stir-Fried Broccoli with Salted Fish

Origin Central
Preparation time 5 minutes
Cooking time 4 minutes
Serves 2

14 oz/400 g Chinese broccoli
2 tablespoons vegetable oil
3 cloves garlic, chopped
3½ oz/100 g dry salted fish (Spanish mackerel), rinsed, dried, and cut into bite-size pieces
1 tablespoon oyster sauce
1 teaspoon granulated sugar

Rinse the Chinese broccoli, then trim the ends of the stems and discard. Cut the stems from the leaves, then slice the stems and leaves diagonally into 1½-inch/4-cm pieces. Set aside.

Heat the oil in a wok over medium-high heat, add the garlic, and sauté for 30 seconds. Add the fish and sauté for 1 minute or until cooked. Add the broccoli, oyster sauce, and sugar and stir-fry for another 2 minutes. Serve.

Spicy Stir-Fried Shrimp with Rice

Origin Central
Preparation time 10 minutes
Cooking time 5 minutes
Serves 1

1 tablespoon vegetable oil
5 cloves garlic, roughly chopped
5 uncooked shrimp (prawns), peeled and deveined, then coarsely chopped
5 red and green bird's eye chiles, pounded
1 tablespoon fish sauce
1 tablespoon oyster sauce
¼ teaspoon ground white pepper
½ teaspoon granulated sugar
¼ cup (2 fl oz/60 ml) pork broth (stock) or water
1 cup (6 oz/175 g) Steamed Jasmine Rice (see p. 378)
cilantro (coriander) sprigs, to garnish

Heat the oil in a wok over medium heat, add the garlic, and stir-fry for 1 minute or until fragrant. Add the shrimp (prawns), chiles, fish sauce, oyster sauce, white pepper, sugar, and broth (stock) and stir-fry for 2–3 minutes or until cooked.

Place the rice on a serving plate, add the shrimp mixture, garnish with cilantro (coriander), and serve.

กุ้งจ่อมกระทะเหล็ก

Spicy Stir-Fried Pickled Shrimp

Origin Central
Preparation time 5 minutes
Cooking time 4 minutes
Serves 2

2 tablespoons vegetable oil
2 tablespoons pickled shrimp
2 eggs, beaten
5–7 red bird's eye chiles
2 shallots, finely sliced
dried red chiles, seeded, to garnish (optional)
Steamed Jasmine Rice (see p. 378), to serve

Heat the oil in a wok over medium heat, add the pickled shrimp, eggs, bird's eye chiles, and shallot and mix well. Stir-fry for 3 minutes. Transfer to a serving dish, sprinkle with dried red chiles, if using, and serve with rice.

ผัดผักเหมียงกุ้งเสียบ

Stir-Fried Melinjo Leaves and Dried Shrimp

Origin South
Preparation time 10 minutes
Cooking time 10 minutes
Serves 2

3 tablespoons vegetable oil
1 small shallot, chopped
3 cloves garlic, chopped
3 cups (3½ oz/100 g) melinjo leaves or young spinach
2 eggs, beaten
1 tablespoon oyster sauce
1 teaspoon soy sauce
2 teaspoons granulated sugar
1 teaspoon salt
½ cup (¾ oz/20 g) dried shrimp

Heat the oil in a wok over medium heat, add the shallot and garlic, and stir-fry for 1 minute or until fragrant. Add the melinjo leaves, eggs, oyster sauce, soy sauce, sugar, and salt and stir-fry for 3 minutes. Add the dried shrimp and stir-fry until thoroughly cooked. Serve.

ต้มยำทะเลแห้ง

Spicy Stir-Fried Seafood

Origin Central
Preparation time 10 minutes
Cooking time 7 minutes
Serves 4

1 tablespoon vegetable oil
1 lemongrass stalk, diagonally sliced
5 thin slices galangal
1½ tablespoons Chili Jam (see p. 35)
5–7 straw mushrooms, quartered lengthwise
¼ cup (2 fl oz/60 ml) fish or chicken broth (stock), plus extra if needed
5 oz/150 g uncooked shrimp (prawns), peeled and deveined, with tails still intact
5 oz/150 g squid, cleaned and cut into ½-inch/ 1-cm-thick rings
1 tablespoon fish sauce
1 tablespoon lime juice
2 teaspoons granulated sugar
3–5 red bird's eye chiles, halved
3–4 kaffir lime leaves, torn
1 sawtooth cilantro (coriander) sprig, chopped
Steamed Jasmine Rice (see p. 378), to serve

Heat the oil in a wok over medium heat, add the lemongrass and galangal, and sauté for 1 minute or until fragrant. Add the chili jam and fry for another 1 minute or until fragrant, then add the mushrooms and stir-fry for another 1 minute. Add the broth (stock), shrimp (prawns), and squid and stir-fry for 3 minutes. Season with the fish sauce, lime juice, sugar, chiles, and kaffir lime leaves. Stir-fry for another 1 minute, then add the sawtooth cilantro (coriander) and stir until thoroughly combined. Transfer to a serving plate or shallow bowl and add a little more broth. Serve with rice.

ปูนิ่มผัดผงกะหรี่

Stir-Fried Blue Crab with Curry Powder

Origin Central
Preparation time 20 minutes, plus freezing time
Cooking time 10 minutes
Serves 2

2 x 11-oz/300-g live blue crab
3 tablespoons vegetable oil
3 cloves garlic, chopped
1 onion, sliced lengthwise
2 red spur chiles, diagonally sliced
2 Chinese celery stalks, cut into 1¼-inch/3-cm pieces
3 scallions (spring onions), cut into 1¼-inch/3-cm slices

For the sauce
1½ cups (12 fl oz/350 ml) whole milk
1 egg
1 tablespoon Chili Jam (see p. 35)
2 teaspoons curry powder
2 tablespoons oyster sauce
¼ teaspoon ground white pepper
1 teaspoon granulated sugar
1 teaspoon soy sauce

Put the crabs in the freezer for 20 minutes. Remove and put in a large bowl. Take 1 crab and place on a cutting (chopping) board. Turn the crab onto its back with its legs facing upward. Raise the tail flap and push a small screwdriver or skewer through the hole underneath. Press firmly down on the screwdriver handle until it hits the other side of the shell. Repeate with the remaining crab.

Cook the crabs in a pan of boiling water for 2–3 minutes, then transfer to a bowl of cold water and let cool. Remove and discard the crab apron and carapace and rinse until clean. Chop the crab into quarters. Set aside.

Put all the sauce ingredients in a bowl and whisk until combined. Set aside.

Heat the oil in a wok over medium heat, add the garlic and onion, and sauté for 1 minute. Add the chile and sauté for about 10 seconds, then add the crabs and cook for 1–2 minutes. Pour in the sauce and cook for another 2 minutes. Add the celery and scallions (spring onions) and cook for another 1 minute. Serve.

Photo p. 339

ไข่เจียวสมุนไพรซาวัง

Stir-Fried Shrimp with Garlic Sauce

Origin Central
Preparation time 5 minutes, plus marinating time
Cooking time 6 minutes
Serves 2

11 oz/300 g uncooked shrimp (prawns), peeled and deveined
¼ teaspoon salt
½ cup (4 fl oz/120 ml) vegetable oil
10 cloves garlic, coarsely chopped
1 tablespoon butter
1 tablespoon white peppercorns, crushed
1 teaspoon soy sauce
1½ tablespoons oyster sauce
2 cilantro (coriander) sprigs, to garnish

Put the shrimp (prawns) and salt in a bowl, mix well, and let marinate for 5 minutes.

Heat the oil in a wok over high heat, add the shrimp, and stir-fry for 2–3 minutes until golden brown. Transfer to a serving plate and set aside.

Remove all but 3 tablespoons of the oil from the wok. Add the garlic and sauté for 1 minute or until golden, then add the butter, peppercorns, soy sauce, and oyster sauce, and sauté for about 30 seconds. Add 2 tablespoons water, mix for another 20 seconds, then pour the garlic sauce over the shrimp. Garnish with the cilantro (coriander) sprigs and serve.

ผัดเห็ดโคน ข้าวโพดอ่อนกุ้ง

Stir-Fried Mushrooms, Baby Corn, and Shrimp

Origin Central
Preparation time 10 minutes
Cooking time 5–7 minutes
Serves 2

2 tablespoons vegetable oil
2–3 cloves garlic, chopped
8–10 shrimp (prawns), peeled and deveined,
  with tails still intact
14 baby corn, sliced diagonally into 1½-inch/
  4-cm lengths
3½ oz/100 g termite mushrooms, sliced
1 teaspoon soy sauce
2 tablespoons oyster sauce
½ teaspoon superfine (caster) sugar
1 scallion (spring onion), sliced into 1¼-inch/
  3-cm lengths

Heat the oil in a wok over medium-high heat,
add the garlic, and stir-fry for 30 seconds or
until fragrant. Add the shrimp (prawns) and
stir-fry for 1 minute or until cooked. Remove
and set aside.

Add the baby corn to the wok and stir-fry
for 2–3 minutes until softened. While stir-
frying add ¼ cup (2 fl oz/60 ml) water. Add
the mushrooms, stir-fry for another 1 minute,
then return the shrimp to the wok. Add the soy
sauce, oyster sauce, sugar, and scallion (spring
onion) and stir-fry for 30 seconds. Serve.

Photo p. 340

ผัดปลาหมึกสะตอ

Stir-Fried Squid with Sator Beans

Origin South
Preparation time 15 minutes
Cooking time 5–7 minutes
Serves 4

1 tablespoon vegetable oil
2 tablespoons Chili Jam (see p. 35)
7-oz/200-g squid, cleaned and cut into small pieces
½ teaspoon salt
1 tablespoon jaggery, palm sugar, or soft light
  brown sugar
2 cups (7 oz/200 g) sator or chopped green beans
10 red finger chiles

Heat the oil in a wok over medium heat; add
the chili jam, and stir-fry for 1 minute or until
fragrant. Add the squid, salt, and sugar and
stir-fry for 2–3 minutes or until cooked. Add
the sator or grean beans and chiles and stir-fry
for 2–3 minutes or until cooked. Serve.

ปลาหมึกผัดกะปิ

Stir-Fried Squid

Origin South
Preparation time 10 minutes
Cooking time 6–7 minutes
Serves 4

5 cloves garlic
2 shallots, chopped
5 teaspoons shrimp paste
¼ teaspoon ground white pepper
3 tablespoons vegetable oil
1 x 14-oz/400-g squid, cleaned and sliced into
  ½-inch/1-cm thick rings, tentacles reserved
5 scallions (spring onions), white part only, sliced
1½ tablespoons oyster sauce
1 tablespoon fish sauce
1 teaspoon granulated sugar
1 tablespoon small pickled garlic cloves
lettuce leaves, to serve

Pound the garlic, shallot, shrimp paste, and
white pepper in a mortar with a pestle until
a smooth paste.

Heat the oil in a wok over medium heat, add
the paste, and stir-fry for 1 minute or until
fragrant. Increase the heat to medium-high,
add the squid rings and tentacles, and stir-fry
for another 5 minutes. Add the scallions (spring
onions), oyster sauce, fish sauce, and sugar
and mix well. Add the pickled garlic and
stir-fry for another 30 seconds, then serve on
a bed of lettuce.

Photo p. 343

ผัดผักกูดปลาหมึกแห้ง

Stir-Fried Fiddlehead Ferns and Dried Squid

Origin South
Preparation time 5 minutes, plus soaking time
Cooking time 5 minutes
Serves 3

1 large dried squid
2 cups (14 oz/400 g) fiddlehead ferns, washed
2 tablespoons vegetable oil
7 cloves garlic, chopped
1 tablespoon soy sauce
1 tablespoon oyster sauce

Soak the dried squid in a bowl of warm water
for 30 minutes until soft. Drain, then cut into
½-inch/1-cm slices and set aside.

Blanch the fern leaves in a pan of boiling water
for 1 minute. Drain and plunge immediately
into cold water. Drain and set aside.

Heat the oil in a wok over medium heat, add
the garlic, and stir-fry for 1 minute or until
fragrant and golden. Add the squid, soy sauce,
oyster sauce, and ferns and stir-fry for about
3 minutes until cooked. Serve.

คะน้าเนื้อผัดน้ำมันหอย

Stir-Fried Beef with Broccoli in Oyster Sauce

Origin Central
Preparation time 10 minutes
Cooking time 5 minutes
Serves 4

2 tablespoons vegetable oil
3 cloves garlic, finely chopped
5 oz/150 g sirloin or tenderloin beef, cut into
  ¼-inch/5-mm thick slices
2½ tablespoons oyster sauce
1 tablespoon soy sauce
14 oz/400 g Chinese broccoli, cut into 2-inch/
  5-cm lengths

Heat the oil in a wok over medium heat, add the garlic, and stir-fry for 1 minute or until fragrant. Add the beef and stir-fry for 1 minute, then season with the oyster sauce and soy sauce, and stir-fry for 30 seconds. Add the broccoli and 2 tablespoons water and stir-fry for another 2 minutes or until the broccoli has softened slightly. Serve.

Photo p. 345

เนื้อผัดพริกอ่อน

Spicy Stir-Fried Beef with Peppers

Origin Central
Preparation time 10 minutes
Cooking time 5 minutes
Serves 2

2 tablespoons vegetable oil
5 oz/150 g sliced beef tenderloin or fillet
¼ green bell pepper, seeded and sliced
1 green finger chile, sliced
1 red finger chile, sliced
¼ onion, sliced
3 oz/80 g Jew's ear mushrooms sliced
1 teaspoon fish sauce
1 teaspoon soy sauce
1 teaspoon oyster sauce
½ teaspoon granulated sugar
¼ cup (2 fl oz/60 ml) vegetable broth (stock)

Heat the oil in a wok over medium heat, add the beef, and stir-fry for 1–2 minutes until cooked. Add the remaining ingredients and stir-fry for another 2–3 minutes. Serve.

หมูหวาน

Sweet Stir-Fried Pork

Origin Central
Preparation time 10 minutes
Cooking time 10–15 minutes
Serves 4

3 tablespoons vegetable oil
5 cloves garlic, finely chopped
1 lb 2 oz/500 g pork side (belly), cut into ½-inch/
  1-cm thick slices
2 tablespoons light soy sauce
2 tablespoons oyster sauce
2½ tablepoons dark soy sauce
⅓ cup (2¾ oz/75 g) jaggery, palm sugar, or soft light
  brown sugar
2 teaspoons ground black pepper
Steamed Jasmine Rice (see p. 378) or Shrimp Paste
  Fried Rice (see p. 383), to serve

Heat the oil in a wok over medium heat,
add the garlic, and stir-fry for 1 minute or
until fragrant and golden. Add the pork and
stir-fry for 6–7 minutes until cooked. Add the
soy sauce, oyster sauce, dark soy sauce, sugar,
and black pepper and stir. Reduce the heat a
little and let it evaporate for 5 minutes until the
liquid caramelizes. Serve with steamed rice
or shrimp paste fried rice.

ผักกาดเต้าหู้หมู

Stir-Fried Cabbage, Pork, and Tofu

Origin Central
Preparation time 10 minutes
Cooking time 10 minutes
Serves 2

¼ cup (1¼ oz/30 g) all-purpose (plain) flour
½ quantity (4½ oz/125 g) egg tofu (see p. 170), cut
  into ¾-inch/2-cm-thick slices
2 cups (16 fl oz/475 ml) vegetable oil, plus
  3 tablespoons
1 tablespoon oyster sauce
2½ teaspoons soy sauce
3 cloves garlic, finely chopped
5 oz/150 g ground (minced) pork
1 lb 2 oz/500 g bok choy (pak choi), cut to
  2½–2¾-inch/6–7-cm lengths
3 tablespoons vegetable broth (stock)
½ teaspoon ground black pepper
a pinch of granulated sugar
½ cup (2¾ oz/70 g) chopped Chinese celery,
  (1¼-inch/3-cm lengths)
Steamed Jasmine Rice (see p. 378), to serve

Spread the flour out on a plate and dredge the
tofu in the flour until well coated. Set aside.

Heat the 2 cups (16 fl oz/475 ml) oil for
deep-frying in a wok or deep fryer to
350°F/180°C or until a cube of bread browns
in 30 seconds. Reduce the heat to medium,
carefully add the tofu, and deep-fry for 4–5
minutes or until golden brown. Remove with
a slotted spoon and drain on paper towels.

Combine the oyster and soy sauces in a small
bowl and set aside.

Heat the 3 tablespoons oil in a clean wok over
medium-high heat. Add the garlic and stir-fry
for 30 seconds or until fragrant. Add the pork
and stir-fry for about 1 minute or until the pork
begins to brown. Add the bok choy (pak choi)
and stir-fry for 2 minutes, then add the soy
sauce mixture, the broth (stock), black pepper,
sugar, and celery. Stir well, then add the tofu.
Gently stir for another 40–50 seconds or until
well mixed. Serve with rice.

เคยเค็มหมูกรอบ

Stir-Fried Crispy Pork with Salted Shrimp

Origin South
Preparation time 2¼ hours
Cooking time 3 minutes
Serves 2

2 tablespoons vegetable oil
2 cloves garlic, chopped
2–3 red and green bird's eye chiles, chopped
2 tablespoons salted freshwater shrimp
2 tablespoons granulated sugar
¼ quantity (9 oz/250 g) Crispy Pork Side (see p. 314),
 cut into bite-size pieces

Heat the oil in a wok over medium heat, add the garlic and chiles, and stir-fry for 1 minute or until fragrant. Add the shrimp and sugar, mix well, then add the pork and stir-fry for 2 minutes. Serve.

หมูกรอบผัดพริกแกง

Stir-Fried Crispy Pork with Red Chili Paste

Origin Central
Preparation time 2¼ hours
Cooking time 8 minutes
Serves 2

2 tablespoons vegetable oil
1½ tablespoons Red Curry Paste (see p. 38)
¼ quantity (9 oz/250 g) Crispy Pork Side (see p. 314),
 cut into bite-size pieces
½ cup (1½ oz/45 g) sliced yard-long beans (cut into
 1¼-inch/3-cm length pieces)
1½ tablespoons oyster sauce
½ teaspoon fish sauce
1 teaspoon granulated sugar
1 handful of sweet basil leaves
Steamed Jasmine Rice (see p. 378), to serve

Heat the oil in a wok over medium heat, add the curry paste, and stir-fry for 1 minute or until fragrant. Add the pork, yard-long beans, oyster sauce, fish sauce, 1–2 tablespoons water, and the sugar, then stir-fry for 2 minutes or until the beans are cooked. Add the basil leaves and stir 3–4 times or until well mixed. Serve with rice.

ข้าวผัดกระเพราหมูไข่ดาว

Stir-Fried Pork with Basil, Rice, and Fried Egg

Origin Central
Preparation time 5 minutes
Cooking time 5 minutes
Serves 2

5–7 red bird's eye chiles
3 cloves garlic, chopped
1 tablespoon vegetable oil
3½ oz/100 g pork loin or shoulder, sliced into
 bite-size pieces
1 yard-long bean, sliced into ¾-inch/2-cm lengths
1 teaspoon light soy sauce
1 teaspoon granulated sugar
1 tablespoon oyster sauce
1 cup (2 oz/50 g) sweet basil leaves

To serve
Steamed Jasmine Rice (see p. 378)
2 eggs, fried

Pound the chiles and garlic together in a mortar with a pestle, then set aside.

Heat the oil in a wok over medium heat, add the pounded chile mixture, and stir-fry for 1 minute or until fragrant. Add the pork and stir-fry for 3 minutes. Add the yard-long bean, soy sauce, sugar, and oyster sauce and stir-fry for about 1 minute. Add the basil leaves, stir-fry briefly, and remove from the heat.

To serve, arrange the steamed rice on a serving plate, place the pork on top of the rice, and put the fried eggs on top of the pork.

ผัดไทยไร้เส้น

Phat Thai without Noodles

Origin Central
Preparation time 15 minutes
Cooking time 15–20 minutes
Serves 2

1 cup (9 fl oz/250 ml) vegetable oil, for deep-frying
3½ oz/100 g extra firm white or yellow tofu, cut into
 ½-inch/1-cm cubes
1 shallot, finely chopped
3½ oz/100 g shoulder or pork loin, thinly sliced
2 tablespoons pickled radish, chopped
10 uncooked shrimp (prawns), peeled and deveined,
 with tails still intact
2 eggs, beaten
2 tablespoons dried shrimp
4 teaspoons granulated sugar
1½ teaspoons lime juice
1 tablespoon fish sauce
2–3 tablespoons roasted peanuts, finely pounded,
 plus extra to garnish
3 red chiles, finely chopped
½ teaspoon chili flakes
1 cup (3½ oz/100 g) bean sprouts
2 Chinese chives, cut into 1½-inch/4-cm-long pieces
cilantro (coriander) sprigs, to garnish

To serve
raw vegetables, such as Chinese chives, bean sprouts,
 and banana blossom
lime wedges

Heat the oil for deep-frying in a wok or deep
fryer to 350°F/180°C or until a cube of bread
browns in 30 seconds. Deep-fry the tofu for
4–5 minutes or until golden brown. Remove
with a slotted spoon and drain on paper towels.

Drain all but 3 tablespoons of the oil from
the wok, then put over medium heat, add the
shallot, and stir-fry for 1 minute. Add the pork
and stir-fry for 2–3 minutes or until cooked.
Add the pickled radish and shrimp (prawns)
and stir-fry for another 2–3 minutes or until the
shrimp are cooked.

Add the eggs and cook for 10 seconds. Add the
dried shrimp and tofu and stir-fry for another
1 minute. Increase the heat a little, add the
sugar, lime juice, fish sauce, roasted peanuts,
chile, and the chili flakes and quickly stir-fry
for 1 minute. Add the bean sprouts and chives
and stir 2–3 times. Transfer to a serving dish,
sprinkle with the reserved peanuts and the
cilantro (coriander) sprigs, and serve with raw
vegetables and lime wedges.

Photo p. 349

ผัดพริกยัง

Spicy Stir-Fried
Pork Side

Origin Central
Preparation time 10 minutes
Cooking time 10 minutes
Serves 4

2 tablespoons vegetable oil
14 oz/400 g pork side (belly) cut into ½-inch/
  1-cm thick pieces
2 tablespoons Red Curry Paste (see p. 38)
1 tablespoon jaggery, palm sugar, or soft light
  brown sugar
1 tablespoon fish sauce
5 kaffir lime leaves, finely sliced
Steamed Jasmine Rice (see p. 378), to serve

Heat the oil in a wok over high heat, add the
pork, and stir-fry for 6–7 minutes or until the
pork is cooked and starts to brown. Remove
the pork with a slotted spoon, reduce the heat
to medium, and add the chili paste to the wok.
Stir-fry for about 1 minute or until fragrant.
Return the pork to the wok and stir-fry for
1–2 minutes or until fully coated with the paste.
Add the sugar and fish sauce and stir until the
sugar has dissolved. Add the kaffir lime leaves
and stir-fry for 30 seconds. Serve with rice.

Photo p. 351

ผัดพริกหมู

Spicy Stir-Fried Pork
Tenderloin

Origin North
Preparation time 5 minutes
Cooking time 5 minutes
Serves 3

1½ tablespoons vegetable oil
3 cloves garlic, finely chopped
12 oz/350 g pork tenderloin, thinly sliced
1 tablespoon soy sauce
1 teaspoon granulated sugar
5 red or green finger chiles, diagonally sliced

Heat the oil in a wok over medium heat, add the
garlic, and stir-fry for 1 minute or until fragrant.
Add the pork and soy sauce and stir-fry for
3–4 minutes or until cooked. Add the sugar and
chiles and stir-fry for another 1 minute. Serve.

ผัดกระเพราหมูสับ

Spicy Stir-Fried Pork
with Basil

Origin North
Preparation time 5 minutes
Cooking time 5 minutes
Serves 2

10 red and green bird's eye chiles
5 cloves garlic
1½ tablespoons vegetable oil
7 oz/200 g ground (minced) pork
½ teaspoon light soy sauce
½ teaspoon granulated sugar
1 cup (2 oz/50 g) sweet basil leaves

Coarsely pound the chiles and garlic together
in a mortar with a pestle, then set aside.

Heat the oil in a wok over medium heat, add
the pounded chile mixture, and stir-fry for
1 minute or until fragrant. Add the pork, soy
sauce, and sugar and stir-fry for 3–4 minutes
or until cooked. Add the basil leaves, mix well,
and serve.

หมูน้ำมันหอย
Stir-Fried Pork in Oyster Sauce

Origin Central
Preparation time 15 minutes, plus marinating time
Cooking time 5 minutes
Serves 4

14 oz/400 g shoulder pork, cut into ¹⁄₁₆-inch/
  2-mm-thick slices
1 egg, beaten
2 teaspoons tapioca flour
3½ tablespoons oyster sauce
1½ teaspoons soy sauce
½ teaspoon granulated sugar
1½ teaspoons brandy or whiskey
3 tablespoons vegetable oil
6 cloves garlic, finely chopped
3 scallions (spring onions), cut into 1½-inch/4-cm
  lengths

Mix the pork, egg, tapioca flour, oyster sauce, soy sauce, sugar, and brandy or whiskey together in a large bowl, then cover with plastic wrap (clingfilm) and let marinate for 10 minutes.

Heat the oil in a wok over medium heat, add the garlic, and stir-fry for 1 minute until fragrant. Add the marinated pork and stir-fry for 1 minute, then add ¼ cup (2 fl oz/60 ml) water and stir-fry for another 3–4 minutes or until the pork is cooked. Add the scallions (spring onions) and stir for 30 seconds. Serve.

ไก่ผัดกระาาน
Stir-Fried Chicken with Siam Cardamom Shoots

Origin Central
Preparation time 10 minutes
Cooking time 15 minutes
Serves 6

2 tablespoons vegetable oil
3–4 tablespoons Red Curry Paste (see p. 38)
7 oz/200 g African basil leaves and flowers, pounded
2¼ lb/1 kg chicken, cut into small pieces
1 lb 2 oz/500 g pea eggplants (aubergines)
7 oz/200 g orange finger chiles, sliced into long strips
3½ oz/100 g kaffir lime leaves, chopped
1 lb 2 oz/500 g Siam cardamom shoots
2 tablespoons fish sauce

Heat the oil a wok over medium heat, add the curry paste, basil leaves, and chicken, and stir-fry for about 10 minutes. Add the pea eggplants (aubergines), finger chiles, kaffir lime leaves, cardamom shoots, fish sauce, and about 3 tablespoons water and cook for another 3 minutes. Serve.

แกงไก่กะลามะพร้าว

Spicy Stir-Fried Chicken and Coconut

Origin Central
Preparation time 10 minutes, plus soaking time
Cooking time 15 minutes
Serves 4

5 young coconuts
3 tablespoons vegetable oil
2 tablespoons Red Curry Paste (see p. 38)
11 oz/300 g boneless chicken breast, cut into
  bite-size pieces
3 tablespoons fish sauce
1 teaspoon jaggery, palm sugar, or soft light
  brown sugar
1 cup (2 oz/50 g) sweet basil leaves
Steamed Jasmine Rice (see p. 378), to serve

Break open the coconuts and use a spoon to scoop out the coconut meat. Cut the meat into bite-size pieces and let soak in a bowl of water.

Heat the oil in a wok over medium heat, add the curry paste, and stir-fry for 1 minute or until fragrant. Carefully add 3–4 tablespoons water and the chicken and stir-fry for 5 minutes or until cooked. Add the coconut meat and ¼ cup (2 fl oz/60 ml) water, mix, and cook for about 4 minutes. Add the fish sauce and sugar, then stir and cook for 4 minutes until the chicken has softened. Add the basil leaves and mix well. Serve with rice.

ผัดไก่บ้านมะเขือเหลือง

Stir-Fried Chicken with Eggplant

Origin Central
Preparation time 10 minutes
Cooking time 12 minutes
Serves 2

1½ tablespoons Red Curry Paste (see p. 38)
9 oz/250 g chicken thighs (bone-in), chopped
  into bite-size pieces
4 yellow round eggplants (aubergines), quartered
  with stems discarded
4 green round eggplants (aubergines), quartered
  with stems discarded
1½ tablespoons fish sauce
pinch of granulated sugar
pinch of salt
3 green spur chiles, diagonally sliced
1 cup (2 oz/50 g) sweet basil leaves
Steamed Jasmine Rice (see p. 378), to serve

Heat a wok over medium heat, add the curry paste, and stir-fry for 1–2 minutes or until fragrant. Add the chicken and stir-fry for 3–4 minutes. Add the eggplants (aubergines), fish sauce, sugar, salt, and 2–3 tablespoons water and stir-fry for about 3 minutes or until the eggplants have softened. Add the chiles and stir-fry for 1 minute. Serve with rice.

ไก่ผัดกาหยู

Stir-Fried Chicken with Cashew Nuts

Origin Central
Preparation time 5 minutes
Cooking time 15 minutes
Serves 4

1 cup (9 fl oz/250 ml) vegetable oil
½ cup (2¾ oz/75 g) raw cashew nuts
3 dried red spur chiles, seeded and sliced into
  1½-inch/4-cm long pieces
14 oz/400 g skinless boneless chicken thigh or breast,
  cut into bite-size pieces
½ small onion, sliced
2 tablespoons oyster sauce
1 teaspoon granulated sugar
4 scallions (spring onions), cut into 1½-inch/
  4-cm lengths

Heat the oil in a wok over low-medium heat, add the cashew nuts, and fry for 5–6 minutes or until golden brown. Remove with a slotted spoon and drain on paper towels.

Add the dried chiles to the wok and fry for 20–30 seconds or until fragrant and the color turns darker. Remove with a slotted spoon and drain on paper towels.

Add the chicken to the wok and fry for about 5 minutes or until cooked and golden brown. Remove with a slotted spoon and drain on paper towels.

Drain all but 1 tablespoon of oil from the wok, then heat the oil over medium heat. Add the onion and stir-fry for 1 minute. Add the oyster sauce and sugar, mix well, then add the chicken, cashew nuts, and scallions (spring onions) and stir for 1 minute. Remove from the heat, sprinkle with the fried dried chiles, and serve.

ไก่ผัดขิง

Stir-Fried Ginger Chicken

Origin Central
Preparation time 15 minutes
Cooking time 10 minutes
Serves 2–3

3 tablespoons vegetable oil
3 cloves garlic, chopped
11 oz /300 g skinless boneless chicken breast,
  cut into ¼-inch/7 mm-thick slices
1 teaspoon soy sauce
2 tablespoons oyster sauce
1 teaspoon granulated sugar
3½ oz/100 g Jew's ear mushrooms, chopped
1 x 2¾-inch/7-cm piece fresh ginger, peeled
  and julienned
½ teaspoon ground black pepper
1 scallion (spring onion), sliced into 1-inch/
  2.5-cm pieces
2 red spur chiles, sliced

Heat the oil in a wok over medium heat, add the garlic, and stir-fry for 1 minute or until fragrant. Add the chicken and stir-fry for 4–5 minutes until almost cooked. Add the soy sauce, oyster sauce, sugar, and mushrooms, and stir-fry for 2–3 minutes until the chicken is cooked. Adding 2 tablespoons water if the sauce dries out. Add the ginger, black pepper, scallion (spring onion), and chiles and stir-fry for 30 seconds. Serve.

Photo p. 355

Stir-Fried Silkworm Pupae

ผัดเปรี้ยวหวานดักแด้ไหม

Origin Northeast
Preparation time 10 minutes, plus soaking time
Cooking time 5 minutes
Serves 5

10 dried cloud ear mushrooms, halved
2 tablespoons vegetable oil
10 cloves garlic, sliced
7 oz/200 g uncooked shrimp (prawns), peeled and deveined, with tails still intact
11 oz/300 g silkworm pupae, washed
10 baby cucumbers, quartered
5 bell peppers, seeded and cut into large dice
1 teaspoon fish sauce
1 teaspoon white vinegar
2 tablespoons superfine (caster) sugar
2 tablespoons ketchup (optional)
1 tablespoon cornstarch (cornflour)
2 tomatoes, quartered
1 onion, chopped
5 scallions (spring onions), chopped
15–20 mulberries
2 red spur chiles, thinly sliced
5 cilantro (coriander) sprigs
1 teaspoon ground white pepper

Soak the mushrooms in a bowl of water for 30 minutes, then drain and rinse. Set aside.

Heat the oil in a wok over medium heat, add the garlic, shrimp (prawns), and silkworm pupae and stir-fry for 1–2 minutes. Add the cucumbers, soaked mushrooms, bell peppers, fish sauce, vinegar, sugar, and ketchup and stir well.

Combine the cornstarch (cornflour) and 3 tablespoons of water and add to the wok along with the tomatoes, onion, and scallions (spring onions). Stir-fry for 1 minute, then add the mulberries and stir again. Sprinkle with the red chiles, cilantro (coriander), and white pepper and serve.

Spicy Stir-Fried Straw Mushroom Salad

ต้มยำเห็ดฟาง

Origin North
Preparation time 10 minutes
Cooking time 5 minutes
Serves 3

1 tablespoon Larb Chili Paste (see p. 41)
½ teaspoon shrimp paste
¼ teaspoon salt
1 tablespoon vegetable oil
3 cloves garlic, chopped
¾ cup (6 fl oz/175 ml) chicken broth (stock)
1 lb 2 oz/500 g straw mushrooms, halved
¼ teaspoon granulated sugar
1 shallot, halved and finely sliced
1 sawtooth cilantro (coriander) sprig, chopped
1 cilantro (coriander) sprigs chopped
3 scallions (spring onions), chopped
mint leaves, chopped

To serve
Glutinous Rice (see p. 378)
raw or steamed vegetables, such as cucumber, Chinese greens (leaves), yard-long beans, and lettuce

Pound the chili paste, shrimp paste, and salt in a mortar with a pestle until smooth. Set aside.

Heat the oil in a wok over medium heat, add the garlic, and quickly stir-fry for 30 seconds or until fragrant. Add the chili paste and sauté for 3 minutes or until fragrant. Add the chicken broth (stock), bring to a boil, then add the mushrooms and sugar and cook for 5 minutes. Transfer the mixture to a serving bowl and sprinkle with the shallot, both cilantros (corianders), the scallions (spring onions), and mint. Serve with rice and raw or steamed vegetables.

Photo p. 356

ยอดมะระเห็ดหอม

Stir-Fried Chayote Leaves and Shiitake Mushrooms

Origin North
Preparation time 10 minutes
Cooking time 3 minutes
Serves 2

8 shiitake mushrooms
2 tablespoons vegetable oil
7 oz/200 g chayote stems and leaves, chopped
1½ tablespoons oyster sauce
pinch of ground white pepper
½ tablespoon Fried Garlic (see p. 64)
1 tablespoon soy sauce
¼ cup (2 fl oz/60 ml) chicken broth (stock)

Make a cross on the top of the mushrooms. Heat the oil in a wok over high heat, add the chayote leaves and mushrooms, and stir-fry for about 1 minute. Add the oyster sauce, white pepper, fried garlic, soy sauce, and chicken broth (stock) and stir-fry for about 1 minute until well mixed and the chayote leaves have softened. Serve.

ผัดเห็ดออรินจิ

Fried King Oyster Mushrooms

Origin Central
Preparation time 7 minutes
Cooking time 5 minutes
Serves 2

2 tablespoons vegetable oil
7 cloves garlic, chopped
7 oz/200 g king oyster mushrooms, rinsed and sliced
1 tablespoon oyster sauce
3 tablespoons chicken broth (stock)
1½ teaspoons soy sauce
1 teaspoon granulated sugar
5 uncooked shrimp (prawns), peeled and deveined, with tails still intact
4 scallions (spring onions), cut into 1-inch/ 2.5-cm lengths

Heat the oil in a wok over medium heat, add the garlic, and stir-fry for 1 minute or until fragrant. Add the mushrooms, oyster sauce, and broth (stock) and stir-fry for 1 minute. Add the soy sauce, sugar, and shrimp (prawns) and stir-fry for another 2–3 minutes or until the shrimp are cooked. Add the scallions (spring onions), stir well, then serve.

ผัดกระเพราเห็ดภูฐาน

Spicy Stir-Fried Mushrooms with Basil

Origin South
Preparation time 7 minutes
Cooking time 5 minutes
Serves 2

10 cloves garlic
15 red bird's eye chiles
3 teaspoons vegetable oil
11 oz/300 g abalone mushrooms, rinsed and chopped
1 tablespoon oyster sauce
1 teaspoon light soy sauce
1 cup (2 oz/50 g) sweet basil leaves
1 teaspoon granulated sugar

Finely pound the garlic and chiles in a mortar with a pestle and set aside.

Heat the oil in a wok over medium heat, add the pounded mixture, and stir-fry for 1 minute or until fragrant. Add the remaining ingredients. Stir-fry for about 3 minutes until thoroughly combined, then serve.

ผัดเห็ดหอมน้ำมันหอย

Stir-Fried Shiitake Mushrooms

Origin Central
Preparation time 10 minutes
Cooking time 5 minutes
Serves 2

2–3 tablespoons vegetable oil
3 cloves garlic, finely chopped
9 oz/250 g fresh shiitake mushrooms, stems trimmed and mushrooms halved
2½ tablespoons oyster sauce
1 teaspoon soy sauce
¼ cup (2 fl oz/60 ml) chicken broth (stock)
3 scallions (spring onions), chopped into 1½-inch/ 4-cm lengths

Heat the oil in a wok over medium heat, add the garlic, and stir-fry for 1 minute or until fragrant. Add the mushrooms and stir-fry for 2 minutes or until cooked. Add the remaining ingredients and stir-fry for another 1 minute. Serve.

Photo p. 361

ผัดเห็ดฟางน้ำมันหอย

Stir-Fried Straw Mushrooms with Pork

Origin Central
Preparation time 5 minutes, plus marinating time
Cooking time 5 minutes
Serves 4

12 oz/350 g pork tenderloin, finely sliced
6 cloves garlic, finely chopped
2 tablespoons soy sauce
1 tablespoon vegetable oil
3½ oz/100 g fresh straw mushrooms, halved
1 red finger chile, quartered
5 scallions (spring onions), cut into 1–2-inch/ 2.5–5-cm lengths
3 tablespoons oyster sauce

Put the pork, garlic, and soy sauce into a large bowl and mix well. Cover with plastic wrap (clingfilm) and let marinate in the refrigerator for 30 minutes.

Heat the oil in a wok over medium heat, add the marinated pork, and stir-fry for 2 minutes until half cooked. Add the mushrooms, chile, scallions (spring onions), and oyster sauce and stir-fry for 2 minutes, or until cooked. Serve.

ผัดมะเขือยาว

Stir-Fried Eggplant with Ground Pork

Origin Central
Preparation time 5 minutes
Cooking time 7–10 minutes
Serves 2

2 tablespoons vegetable oil
1 clove garlic, chopped
3½ oz/100 g ground (minced) pork
2 x 11-oz/300-g long green eggplants (aubergines),
   cut crosswise into 2-inch/5-cm long pieces, and
   then quartered lengthwise
¼ teaspoon granulated sugar
1 teaspoon soy sauce
1 tablespoon oyster sauce
1½ teaspoons salted soybeans
1 red spur chile, diagonally sliced
1 green spur chile, diagonally sliced
1 cup (2 oz/50 g) sweet basil leaves
Steamed Jasmine Rice (see p. 378), to serve

Heat the oil in a wok over medium heat, add
the garlic, and stir-fry for 1 minute or until
fragrant. Add the pork and stir-fry for 1 minute.
Add the eggplants (aubergine) and stir-fry
for 4–5 minutes. While stir-frying, add
2–3 tablespoons of water, then add the sugar,
soy sauce, oyster sauce, and soybeans. Stir
2–3 times or until thoroughly combined.
Cover the wok with a lid and cook for another
2 minutes. Add the chiles and basil leaves
and stir 2–3 times. Serve with rice.

ผัดมันแกว

Stir-Fried Jicama

Origin South
Preparation time 8 minutes
Cooking time 10 minutes
Serves 4–5

3 tablespoons vegetable oil
7–10 cloves garlic, chopped
7 oz/200 g uncooked shrimp (prawns), peeled and
   deveined, with tails still intact
7 oz/200 g squid, cleaned and sliced, with tentacles
   removed
11 oz/300 g jicama or white radish (daikon or mooli),
   peeled and finely julienned
1 tablespoon granulated sugar
1 tablespoon oyster sauce
1 tablespoon fish sauce
½ teaspoon salt
2–3 scallions (spring onions), cut into 1-inch/
   2.5-cm pieces
1½ cups (6 oz/175 g) julienned carrot

Heat the oil in a wok over medium heat, add the
garlic, and stir-fry for 1 minute or until fragrant
and golden. Add the shrimp and squid and
stir-fry for 2–3 minutes until cooked. Add the
jicama or white radish (daikon or mooli) and
stir-fry for another 3 minutes, then season with
the sugar, oyster sauce, fish sauce, and salt.
Add the scallions (spring onions) and carrots
and stir until thoroughly mixed. Serve.

สายบัวผัดกุ้ง

Stir-Fried Lotus Stems with Shrimp

Origin Central
Preparation time 5 minutes
Cooking time 5 minutes
Serves 2

2 tablespoons vegetable oil
3 cloves garlic, chopped
8 uncooked shrimp (prawns), peeled and deveined,
  with tails still intact
2 cups (9 oz/250 g) peeled and cut young lotus stems
  (1½-inch/4-cm lengths)
1 tablespoon fish sauce
1½ tablespoons oyster sauce
1 tablespoon granulated sugar
1 tablespoon salted soybeans
Steamed Jasmine Rice (see p. 378), to serve

Heat the oil in a wok over medium heat, add the
garlic, and stir-fry for 1 minute or until fragrant.
Add the shrimp (prawns) and lotus stems,
increase the heat, and cook for 1–2 minutes
until cooked. Add the fish sauce, oyster sauce,
sugar, and soybeans, stir, and serve with rice.

Photo p. 362

มะระผัดไข่

Stir-Fried Bitter Gourd and Egg

Origin Central
Preparation time 5 minutes, plus standing time
Cooking time 5 minutes
Serves 2

2 tablespoons salt
7 oz/200 g bitter gourd, peeled, cut lengthwise,
  and then cut into ¹⁄₁₆-inch/2-mm slices
1 tablespoon vegetable oil
3 cloves garlic, crushed
2 eggs, beaten
1 tablespoon soy sauce
1 teaspoon granulated sugar
Steamed Jasmine Rice (see p. 378), to serve

Mix the salt and bitter gourd together in a large
bowl. Set aside for 15 minutes, then rinse twice
with water and drain.

Heat the oil in a wok over medium heat, add
the garlic, and stir-fry for 30 seconds or until
fragrant. Increase to the heat to high, add the
bitter gourd, and stir-fry for 2–3 minutes until
softened. Add the eggs and stir-fry for about
1 minute or until cooked. Season with the
soy sauce and sugar and stir-fry for another
1–2 minutes. Serve with rice.

ต้ายนุน

Spicy Stir-Fried Jackfruit

Origin North
Preparation time 10 minutes, plus soaking time
Cooking time 35 minutes
Serves 3

14 oz/400 g young jackfruit, peeled and seeded
 wearing gloves, and cut into 1¼-inch/3-cm slices
1 tablespoon vegetable oil
7 garlic cloves, chopped
10 cherry tomatoes, chopped
5 kaffir lime leaves, chopped, to garnish

For the chili paste
15 dried red chiles, seeded
½ teaspoon salt
5 shallots, chopped
10 garlic cloves, sliced
1 teaspoon shrimp paste

For the chili paste, soak the dried chiles in
a bowl of warm water for 15 minutes or until
rehydrated, then drain and chop.

Pound the chiles, salt, shallot, and garlic in
a mortar with a pestle until smooth. Add the
shrimp paste and mix to combine. Set aside.

Bring a large pan of water to a boil over
medium heat. Add the jackfruit slices, reduce
the heat to medium-low, and cook for 30
minutes or until tender. Drain, cut the flesh from
the rind, and chop into small pieces. Set aside.

Heat the oil in a wok over medium heat, add
the chopped garlic, and stir-fry for 30 seconds.
Add the chili paste, cherry tomatoes, and
jackfruit and stir-fry for 3–4 minutes until
everything is thoroughly combined. Garnish
with kaffir lime leaves and serve.

ผัดตำลึงหมูสับ

Stir-Fried Ivy Gourd with Pork

Origin South
Preparation time 7 minutes
Cooking time 5 minutes
Serves 2

2 tablespoons vegetable oil
3 cloves garlic, chopped
4 oz/120 g ground (minced) pork side (belly)
1 tablespoon oyster sauce
1 teaspoon granulated sugar
4 handfuls ivy gourd or spinach leaves

Heat the oil in a wok over medium heat, add
the garlic, and stir-fry for 1 minute or until
fragrant. Add the pork, oyster sauce, sugar,
and ivy gourd or spinach leaves and stir-fry
for 1–2 minutes or until cooked. Serve.

ผัดดอกหอม

Stir-Fried Scallion Flowers with Pork Liver

Origin North
Preparation time 5 minutes
Cooking time 5 minutes
Serves 3

1 tablespoon vegetable oil
3 cloves garlic, finely chopped
3½ oz/100 g pork liver, finely sliced
2–3 bunches scallions (spring onions) with
 flowers, cut into ¾–1¼-inch/2–3-cm lengths
2 teaspoons soy sauce

Heat the oil in a wok over medium heat, add
the garlic and pork liver, and stir-fry for 2–3
minutes or until the poork is cooked. Add the
scallions (spring onions) and soy sauce and
mix well. Serve.

ผัดพริกถั่วฝักยาว

Spicy Stir-Fried Yard-Long Beans with Pork

Origin North
Preparation time 5 minutes, plus soaking time
Cooking time 7 minutes
Serves 4

1 tablespoon vegetable oil
14 oz/400 g pork side (belly), sliced into thin strips
2 cups (6 oz/175 g) sliced yard-long beans
  (1–2 inches/2.5–5 cm lengths)
1 tablespoon soy sauce
1 teaspoon sugar
1 tablespoon chopped kaffir lime leaves

For the chili paste
3 dried red chiles, seeded and chopped
2 shallots, chopped
7 garlic cloves, sliced
1 tablespoon chopped lemongrass
1 teaspoon finely chopped galangal
1 teaspoon shrimp paste

For the chili paste, soak the dried chiles in a bowl of warm water for 15 minutes or until rehydrated, then drain and chop.

Pound the chiles, shallot, garlic, lemongrass, and galangal in a mortar with a pestle until smooth. Add the shrimp paste and mix to combine. Set aside.

Heat the oil in a wok over medium heat, add the chili paste, and stir-fry for 1 minute or until fragrant. Add the pork and stir-fry for 2–3 minutes or until cooked. Add the yard-long beans, soy sauce, and sugar and stir-fry for another 4 minutes. Sprinkle with the chopped kaffir lime leaves, then serve.

ผักกาดขาวผัดปลาหมึกแห้ง

Stir-Fried Cabbage with Dried Squid

Origin Central
Preparation time 5 minutes
Cooking time 5 minutes
Serves 4

1 tablespoon vegetable oil
6 cloves garlic, finely chopped
½ cup (2 oz/50 g) finely sliced dried squid
3 cups (11 oz/300 g) shredded napa (Chinese) cabbage
  (1-inch/2.5-cm pieces)
1 tablespoon soy sauce

Heat the oil in a wok over medium heat, add the garlic, and stir-fry for 1 minute or until fragrant. Add the dried squid and stir-fry for 1 minute or until cooked. Add the cabbage, soy sauce, and 1 tablespoon water and stir-fry for another 2 minutes. Serve.

ผัดกะหล่ำปลีน้ำปลา

Stir-Fried Cabbage

Origin Central
Preparation time 5 minutes
Cooking time 3 minutes
Serves 4

1 x 11-oz/300-g head Thai cabbage leaves (pointed spring cabbage), chopped into 2½-inch/6-cm chunks
1 tablespoon fish sauce
5 cloves garlic, finely chopped
2 tablespoons vegetable oil

Put the cabbage, fish sauce, garlic, and 2 tablespoons water into a bowl and mix well. Set aside.

Heat the oil in a wok over high heat. Add the cabbage mixture and stir-fry for 2–3 minutes or until cooked. Serve.

ผัดผัก

Stir-Fried Vegetables

Origin Central
Preparation time 10 minutes
Cooking time 4 minutes
Serves 3

2 tablespoons vegetable oil
2 tablespoons Fried Garlic (see p. 64)
3 stems Chinese kale, chopped
5 amaranth leaves or spinach, chopped
¼ napa (Chinese) white cabbage, chopped
3½ oz/100 g enoki mushrooms
2 tablespoons oyster sauce
1 tablespoon fish sauce
1½ teaspoons granulated sugar

Heat the oil in a wok over medium heat, add
the fried garlic, kale, amaranth, cabbage, and
mushrooms, and stir-fry for 4 minutes. Add the
oyster sauce, fish sauce, and sugar and serve.

ผักปวยเล้งน้ำมันหอย

Fried Spinach with Oyster Sauce

Origin Central
Preparation time 5 minutes
Cooking time 5 minutes
Serves 2–3

1 lb 2 oz/500 g Chinese spinach
3 tablespoons vegetable oil
5 cloves garlic, finely chopped
2 tablespoons oyster sauce
½ teaspoon soy sauce

Clean the spinach, shake off the excess water,
and remove the bottom 2 inches/5 cm of
the stems. Slice the remaining spinach into
1½-inch/4-cm lengths.

Heat the oil in a wok over medium heat, add
the garlic, and stir-fry for 1 minute or until
fragrant. Increase the heat to medium-high
and add the spinach, oyster sauce, and soy
sauce. Stir-fry for 2–3 minutes until the spinach
is cooked. Serve.

Photo p. 367

ไกย [สาหร่ายน้ำลึกแม่น้ำโขง]

Stir-Fried Mekong River Seaweed

Origin North
Preparation time 20 minutes
Cooking time 10 minutes
Serves 5

1 Mekong River seaweed sheet
1 Fermented Soybean Sheet (see p. 34)
⅔ cup (5 fl oz/150 ml) vegetable oil
4 oz/120 g pork skin with fat, diced
½ garlic bulb, cloves separated and chopped
½ tablespoon dried chili flakes
½ tablespoon salt
1 tablespoon white sesame seeds

Heat the broiler (grill) to low and broil (grill)
the seaweed sheet until it is golden, then chop.
Set aside.

Place the soybean sheet on the broiler pan and
broil for about 2 minutes until fragrant and dark
brown. Let cool, then grind in a mortar with a
pestle until ground. Set aside.

Heat ½ cup (4 fl oz/120 ml) of the oil in a wok
over medium-high heat, add the pork skin,
and fry for 5 minutes until golden, then add the
garlic and stir for 1 minute. Transfer to a plate
and set aside.

Heat the remaining oil in the wok, add the chili
flakes and ground soybean sheet, and stir-fry
for 1 minute. Add the chopped seaweed sheet
and the pork skin and garlic and stir-fry for
another 1–2 minutes until the pork is cooked.
Season with the salt and sprinkle with the
sesame seeds, then serve.

Spicy Stir-Fried Water Spinach

Origin Central
Preparation time 5 minutes
Cooking time 4 minutes
Serves 1–2

¼ cup (2 fl oz/60 ml) chicken broth (stock)
11 oz/300 g water spinach, chopped into 4-inch/
  10-cm lengths
4 cloves garlic, finely chopped
3 red bird's eye chiles, diagonally sliced
1½ tablespoons oyster sauce
1 tablespoon salted soybeans
1½ teaspoons soy sauce
2 tablespoons vegetable oil

Put the chicken broth (stock), water spinach, garlic, chiles, oyster sauce, soybeans, and soy sauce in a bowl. Toss and set aside.

Heat the oil in a wok over high heat. Carefully add the water spinach mixture and stir-fry for 1–2 minutes or until cooked. Serve.

Photo p. 369

Stir-Fried Amaranth with Tofu and Garlic

Origin North
Preparation time 10 minutes
Cooking time 3 minutes
Serves 2

2 tablespoons vegetable oil
5 cups (7 oz/200 g) amaranth or spinach
2 tablespoons diced firm tofu
1½ teaspoons Fried Garlic (see p. 64)
1 tablespoon oyster sauce
1 tablespoon soy sauce
¼ cup (2 fl oz/60 ml) chicken broth (stock)
pinch of ground white pepper

Heat the oil in a wok over medium-high heat. Add all the ingredients and stir-fry for 30–60 seconds or until the amaranth has softened. Serve.

Stir-fried Amaranth with Oyster Sauce

Origin Central
Preparation time 5 minutes
Cooking time 4 minutes
Serves 3

2 tablespoons vegetable oil
2 tablespoons Fried Garlic (see p. 64)
10 cups (14 oz/400 g) amaranth leaves or
  spinach, chopped
3 tablespoons oyster sauce
1½ teaspoons granulated sugar

Heat the oil in a wok over medium heat, add the fried garlic and amaranth leaves, and stir-fry for 4 minutes. Add the oyster sauce and sugar and serve.

Rice & Noodles

ข้าวผัดพริกขี้หนูกุ้งสด
Glutinous Rice

Origin North
Preparation time 5 minutes, plus soaking time
Cooking time 30–35 minutes
Serves 4

1½ cups (11 oz/300 g) uncooked glutinous
  (sticky) rice

Soak the rice in a large bowl of cold water
overnight or for at least 3 hours. Wash and
drain. Wrap the rice in cheesecloth (muslin)
and steam for 30–35 minutes, stirring the rice
every 10 minutes until cooked through. The
rice will look transparent when cooked. Keep
covered until ready to serve.

ข้าวหอมมะลิ
Steamed Jasmine Rice

Origin Central
Preparation time 5 minutes
Cooking time 20–25 minutes
Serves 4

2 cups (14 oz/400 g) uncooked jasmine rice

Wash the rice and drain through a strainer
(sieve). Transfer to a large pan, pour in enough
water to cover, and bring to a boil over medium
heat. Reduce the heat to low, cover the pan
with a lid, and cook for 20–25 minutes, stirring
occasionally, until the rice is soft. Serve.

ข้าวผัดปู

Crab Fried Rice

Origin South
Preparation time 10 minutes
Cooking time 5 minutes
Serves 2

3–4 tablespoons vegetable oil
5 cloves garlic, finely chopped
1 egg, beaten
1 cup (6 oz/175 g) Steamed Jasmine Rice (see p. 378)
3½ oz/100 g crabmeat
½ onion, diced
4 tablespoons diced carrot
½ tomato, sliced
2 scallions (spring onions), chopped
1 tablespoon soy sauce
1 tablespoon oyster sauce
1 tablespoon granulated sugar
2 tablespoons fish sauce, plus extra to serve
2 cilantro (coriander) stalks, chopped
juice of 1 lime

To serve
1 cucumber, peeled and sliced
2 scallions (spring onions)
lime wedges

Heat the oil in a wok over medium heat, add the garlic, and sauté for 30 seconds. Add the egg and stir until half-cooked. Increase the heat to medium-high, add the rice, crabmeat, onion, carrot, tomato, and scallions (spring onions), and stir-fry for 2 minutes until cooked. Add the soy sauce, oyster sauce, and sugar and stir-fry for another 2 minutes. Transfer to a serving plate and sprinkle with cilantro (coriander). Season with lime juice and serve with cucumber, scallions (spring onions), and lime wedges.

Photo p. 381

ข้าวคลุกปลาทู

Mackerel Fried Rice

Origin Central
Preparation time 10 minutes
Cooking time 8 minutes
Serves 2

¼ cup (2 fl oz/60 ml) vegetable oil, plus 2 tablespoons
5 oz/150 g salted horse mackerel or smoked mackerel fillet
2 shallots, sliced
3 cups (18½ oz/525 g) Steamed Jasmine Rice (see p. 378)
1 tablespoon soy sauce
4 red and green bird's eye chiles, chopped, plus extra, finely chopped to garnish

To serve
1 small cucumber, peeled and sliced
2 lime wedges

Heat the ¼ cup (2 fl oz/60 ml) oil in a pan over medium heat. Add the mackerel and cook for 3 minutes on each side or until the fish starts to brown. Remove from the wok and let cool, then break the mackerel into smaller pieces.

Heat the 2 tablespoons oil in a wok over medium heat. Add half the shallots and sauté for 1 minute or until softened and fragrant. Add the steamed rice and stir-fry for about 1 minute, then add the mackerel and soy sauce, and stir-fry for another 1 minute. Add the rest of the shallots and the chiles and stir until thoroughly combined. Transfer to a serving plate, garnish with finely chopped chiles, and serve with the sliced cucumber and lime wedges.

ข้าวคลุกกะปิ

Shrimp Paste Fried Rice with Sweet Pork

Origin Central
Preparation time 40 minutes
Cooking time 10 minutes
Serves 2–3

1½ tablespoons Roasted Shrimp Paste (see p. 36)
1 banana leaf
2½ cups (1 lb/450 g) Steamed Jasmine Rice (see p. 378)
4 tablespoons vegetable oil
¾ cup (1¼ oz/30 g) dried shrimp
1 small Chinese pork sausage, diagonally sliced
1 duck egg, beaten
2 shallots, sliced
5 red bird's eye chiles, sliced
2 tablespoons sliced green mango
2 yard-long beans, sliced into ¼-inch/5-mm pieces
5 dried red chiles, roasted
½ lime, to serve

For the sweet pork
4 oz/120 g pork, cut into small pieces
1 tablespoon fish sauce
3 tablespoons jaggery, palm sugar, or soft light
  brown sugar
2 teaspoons dark soy sauce
2 teaspoons sliced shallot

Put the roasted shrimp paste in a bowl and add 1 tablespoon boiled water. Stir until the shrimp paste becomes liquid, then add the steamed rice and stir until thoroughly combined.

Heat 2 tablespoons oil in a wok over medium heat, add the rice, and stir-fry for 2–3 minutes, then remove from the heat and let cool.

Heat 1 tablespoon oil in a wok over low heat, add the dried shrimp, and sauté for 2 minutes until crispy. Remove the shrimp with a slotted spoon and set aside. Add the sliced Chinese sausage to the wok and stir-fry for 2–3 minutes, until cooked, then remove from the heat.

Heat 1 tablespoon oil in a clean wok over low heat. Roll the oil around the wok so it coats the whole surface of the wok, then pour in the beaten egg and roll around the wok to create a thin omelet. Remove, let cool, then roll up and slice into strips. Set aside.

For the sweet pork, heat 2 tablespoons water in a wok over medium heat, add the pork, fish sauce, and sugar, and stir until the sugar has dissolved. Add the soy sauce and shallot, and stir-fry for 1 minute or until cooked, then remove from the heat.

Place the rice on a serving plate, then arrange the sweet pork, shallots, fried dried shrimp, sliced chiles, mango, yard-long beans, and fried dried chiles on the side. Sprinkle with the sliced omelet and serve with the lime.

ข้าวคลุกกะปิ

Shrimp Paste Fried Rice

Origin Central
Preparation time 20–25 minutes
Cooking time 15 minutes
Serves 2–3

For the crispy shrimp
7 tablespoons vegetable oil
½ cup (2¼ oz/60 g) dried shrimp

For the omelet
vegetable oil, for frying
3 eggs, beaten

For the rice
scant 3 cups (1 lb 2 oz/500 g) Steamed Jasmine Rice
  (see p. 378), warm
1 tablespoon shrimp paste
3 tablespoons vegetable oil
5 cloves garlic, chopped
½ shallot, chopped

To serve
5 red and green bird's eye chiles, chopped
Sweet Stir-Fried Pork (see p. 346)
1 sour green mango or sour green apple, shredded
2 shallots, sliced
lime wedges

To make the crispy shrimp, heat the oil in a wok over low-medium heat. Add the dried shrimp and fry for 2–3 minutes until golden brown. Remove from the wok with a slotted spoon and set aside on paper towels.

In a clean wok, make the omelet. Add 1 teaspoon of oil, and roll around the wok. Add ⅓ cup (2½ fl oz/75 ml) of the beaten egg and roll around the wok to create a thin crepe. Cook for about 2 minutes until set. Put the omelet on a plate and set aside. Repeat this process with another teaspoon of oil and the remaining egg until all the egg is used, adding a teaspoon of oil at a time. Stack the omelets, then cut them into quarters and slice them into ½-inch/1-cm-thick strips. Set aside.

Put the cooked rice in a large bowl. Mix ½ tablespoon water with the shrimp paste until combined, then add to the rice. Using your hands, gently mix until the rice is well coated with shrimp paste.

Heat the oil in a wok over medium heat, add the garlic and shallot, and sauté until fragrant. Add the rice, stir, and toss the mixture for 2–3 minutes until the rice is hot and a slightly darker color.

To serve, fill a small bowl to the rim with the rice and turn upside down in the middle of a serving plate. Top the rice with the chiles, then place the omelete strips, crispy shrimp, pork, mango, sliced shallots, and lime wedges to the side of the rice.

Photo p. 382

ข้าวกล้องผัดสมุนไพร

Fried Brown Rice
with Shrimp

Origin Central
Preparation time 5 minutes
Cooking time 7 minutes
Serves 2

4 tablespoons vegetable oil
6 cloves garlic, finely chopped
11 oz/300 g shrimp (prawns), peeled, deveined,
  and tails intact
2 eggs, beaten
2 cups (12 oz/350 g) steamed brown rice
2 tablespoons diced fried tofu
4 teaspoons granulated sugar
2 tablespoons soy sauce
2 tablespoons peas
2 tablespoons diced carrot
2 tablespoons diced onion

To garnish
½ Lebanese cucumber, peeled and sliced
1 tomato, sliced
2 teaspoons chopped cilantro (coriander)
1 scallion (spring onion), chopped
2 tablespoons corn kernels

Heat the oil in a wok over medium heat.
Add the garlic and stir-fry for 1 minute until
fragrant. Add the shrimp (prawns) and stir-fry
for 1–2 minutes until they turn pink. Add the
eggs and cook for 1 minute until cooked. Add
the rice and stir-fry for 2 minutes. Add the tofu,
sugar, and soy sauce and stir-fry for another
1 minute until fragrant. Add the peas, carrot,
and onion and stir-fry for another 1 minute.
Garnish with the cucumber, tomato, cilantro
(coriander), scallion (spring onion), and corn
kernels and serve.

ข้าวหนุกงา

Rice with Black
Sesame Seeds

Origin North
Preparation time 5 minutes
Cooking time 5 minutes
Serves 2–3

4 tablespoons black sesame seeds
1¾ cups (11 oz/300 g) cooked Glutinous Rice
  (see p. 378)
½ teaspoon salt
¼ cup (2 oz/50 g) superfine (caster) sugar (optional)

Toast the black sesame seeds in a pan over
medium heat for 2–3 minutes or until fragrant.
Remove from the heat and pound in a mortar
with a pestle until a fine powder. Add the rice
and pound together. Add the salt and sugar,
and continue to pound until combined. Serve.

ข้าวผัดพริกขี้หนูกุ้งสด

Spicy Shrimp Fried Rice

Origin Central
Preparation time 10 minutes
Cooking time 5 minutes
Serves 2

3 tablespoons vegetable oil
3 cloves garlic, finely chopped
10 shrimp (prawns), peeled and deveined, with tails
  still intact
3 cups (1 lb 3 oz/525 g) Steamed Jasmine Rice
  (see p. 378)
2 tablespoons soy sauce
2 teaspoons oyster sauce
½ teaspoon granulated sugar
10 red and green bird's eye chiles, finely chopped
2 scallions (spring onions), chopped
1 small cucumber, peeled and sliced

Heat the oil in a wok over medium heat, add
the garlic and sauté for 30 seconds. Add the
shrimp (prawns) and cook for 1 minute. Add
the rice, soy sauce, oyster sauce, and sugar
and stir-fry for 1–2 minutes, then add the chiles
and stir-fry for another 30 seconds or until
thoroughly combined. Serve with the scallions
(spring onions) and cucumber.

ข้าวหมกไก่

Thai Chicken with Seasoned Fried Rice

Origin Central
Preparation time 15 minutes
Cooking time 50 minutes
Serves 8–10

1 cilantro (coriander) root, chopped
7 cloves garlic, chopped
30 white peppercorns
1-inch/2.5-cm piece fresh ginger, peeled and chopped
5 shallots, chopped
1 cup (9 fl oz/250 ml) Fried Shallots oil (see p. 64)
2¼ lb/1 kg boneless chicken breast
scant 1 cup (7 oz/200 g) evaporated milk
juice of 2 limes
5 tomatoes, coarsely chopped
1 cilantro (coriander) stem
5 pandan leaves
2 tablespoons granulated sugar
1½ teaspoons salt
5 cups (2¼ lb/1 kg) jasmine rice
1 tablespoon masala powder
¾ teaspoon saffron threads
1 tablespoon butter
6 tablespoons Fried Shallots (see p. 64), to garnish

For the dipping sauce
1 cilantro (coriander) root
1 teaspoon pickled garlic
1 garlic bulb, cloves separated
1¼ tablespoons peppermint leaves (about 40 leaves)
1 small scallion (spring onion), about 3 inches/
  7.5 cm long
15 bird's eye chiles
1 handful of salt
½ cup (3½ oz/100 g) jaggery, palm sugar, or soft light
  brown sugar
2 tablespoons Tamarind Puree (see p. 63)

To serve
raw vegetables, such as lettuce and cucumber
1 small bunch of cilantro (coriander)

For the dipping sauce, pound the cilantro (coriander) root, pickled garlic, and garlic together in a mortar with a pestle until smooth. Remove from the mortar and set aside.

Pound the peppermint leaves, scallion (spring onion), and chiles together in the mortar with a pestle. Set aside.

Pour 1 cup (9 fl oz/250 ml) water into a large wok or pan, add the salt, sugar, and tamarind, and cook, stirring, over medium heat. Stir in the pounded garlic mixture and the peppermint leaves mixture and cook for another 5 minutes, stirring continuously. Transfer to a small serving bowl and set aside.

Pound the cilantro (coriander) root, garlic, and peppercorns in a mortar with a pestle. Remove from the mortar and set aside. Pound the ginger and shallots in the mortar with a pestle.

Heat the fried shallot oil in a wok over medium heat, add the cilantro root mixture, and sauté for 2 minutes. Add the pounded ginger and shallots to the wok and sauté for 2 minutes until fragrant. Add the chicken, evaporated milk, lime juice, tomatoes, cilantro (coriander) stem, pandan leaves, sugar, and salt and stir until combined.

Transfer to a large pan and add 4¼ cups (1¾ pints/1 liter) water. Bring to a boil, then add the rice, masala powder, and saffron. Stir well, then cover with a lid and cook over medium heat for about 30 minutes. Add the butter and stir until thoroughly combined. Garnish with the fried shallots and serve with the dipping sauce, raw vegetables, and cilantro (coriander).

แหนมคลุก

Crispy Curry Rice with Fermented Pork

Origin Northeast
Preparation time 20 minutes
Cooking time 15 minutes
Serves 4

5 oz/150 g pork skin
2 cups (12 oz/350 g) Steamed Jasmine Rice (see p. 378)
1 tablespoon Red Curry Paste (see p. 38)
1 egg
½ teaspoon salt
5 cups (2 pints/1.2 liters) vegetable oil, for deep-frying
6 dried red chiles
7 oz/200g fermented pork
3 shallots, sliced
4-inch/10-cm piece fresh ginger, peeled and very
  finely sliced
5 scallions (spring onions), finely sliced
1 tablespoon lime juice
1½ teaspoons fish sauce
½ cup (2¾ oz/75 g) roasted peanuts
green lettuce, to serve

Bring a pan of water to a boil over medium heat. Add the pork skin and cook for 20–25 minutes. Drain and trim off the extra fat underneath the skin. The skin should be ¼ inch/7 mm thick. Slice into thin strips about ⅛ inch/2.5 mm thick and about 2 inches/5 cm long. Set aside.

Put the steamed rice and curry paste into a large bowl and mix well. Break in the egg, add the salt, and knead by hand until combined, then mold into egg-size balls.

Heat the oil for deep-frying in a wok or deep fryer to 350°F/180°C, or until a cube of bread browns in 30 seconds. Deep-fry the rice balls for 7–9 minutes until brown and crispy, then remove with a slotted spoon, drain on paper towels, and set aside.

Deep-fry the dried chiles for 10 seconds, then remove with a slotted spoon, drain on paper towels, and set aside

Put the crispy rice balls into a large bowl. Break into small pieces, then add the fermented pork, shallots, ginger, and three-quarters of the scallions (spring onions) and mix until combined.

Season to taste with the lime juice and fish sauce. Add the peanuts and fried chiles and mix again. Garnish with the remaining chopped scallions and serve with lettuce.

Photo p. 387

ส่วนผสม

Thai Pork Fried Rice with Fried Eggs

Origin Central
Preparation time 5 minutes
Cooking time 10 minutes
Serves 2

½ cup (4 fl oz/125 ml) vegetable oil
3 eggs
2 cloves garlic, chopped
5 oz/150 g pork loin or shoulder, cut into thin slices
3 cups (1 lb 3 oz/525 g) cooked jasmine rice
1½ tablespoons soy sauce
1 tablespoon oyster sauce
½ teaspoon granulated sugar
1 cup (2½ oz/70 g) coarsely chopped Chinese kale
⅓ cup (1½ oz/40 g) sliced onions
1 tomato, cut into small wedges

To serve
1 cucumber, peeled and sliced
lime wedges

Heat the oil in a wok over high heat, add 2 of the eggs, one at a time, and fry for 2 minutes. Remove, cover to keep warm, and set aside.

Drain all but 2 tablespoons oil from the wok and reduce the heat to medium. Add the garlic and stir-fry for 1 minute until fragrant, then add the pork and stir-fry for 2–3 minutes until cooked. Add the remaining egg, gently beat, and cook for 40–50 seconds until the egg is lightly cooked. Add the rice and stir-fry for another 1 minute or until well mixed, then season with the soy sauce, oyster sauce, and sugar and stir-fry for another 2 minutes until well combined. Add the kale, onions, and tomato wedges and stir fry for 1–2 minutes.

To serve, place the rice on serving plates, top with a fried egg, and arrange the cucumber and lime wedges on the side.

Photo p. 388

ข้าวมันกะทิ

Rice with Coconut Milk

Origin Central
Preparation time 5 minutes
Cooking time 35–40 minutes
Serves 2

1 cup (7 oz/200 g) jasmine rice
1⅔ cups (14 fl oz/400 ml) coconut milk
2 tablespoons superfine (caster) sugar
1 teaspoon salt

Wash the rice and drain through a strainer (sieve).

Heat the coconut milk, scant 1 cup (8 fl oz/230 ml) water, sugar, and salt in a large nonstick pan over medium heat and stir until the sugar and salt have dissolved. Reduce the heat to low and add the rice. Cover with a lid and cook for 30–35 minutes, stirring occasionally, until the rice is soft. Serve.

ข้าวน้ำมะพร้าวอ่อน

Rice with Coconut Water

Origin Central
Preparation time 5 minutes
Serves 2

1 cup (6 oz/175 g) Steamed Jasmine Rice (see p. 378)
1 cup (9 fl oz/250 ml) young coconut water
1 cup (3½ oz/100 g) shredded young coconut meat, plus extra to garnish
salt, to taste
granulated sugar, to taste (optional)

Put the cooked rice into a large bowl and pour over the coconut water. Add the coconut meat and salt to taste and mix well. Add sugar if you prefer a sweeter taste. Serve garnished with coconut flesh.

ขนมจาก

Glutinous Coconut Rice in Palm Leaves

Origin Central
Preparation time 15 minutes
Cooking time 20 minutes
Serves 8

scant 3¼ cups (1 lb 2 oz/500 g) black glutinous
  (sticky) rice flour
1½ cups (9 oz/250 g) rice flour
2½ cups (1 lb 2 oz/500 g) jaggery, palm sugar, or soft
  light brown sugar
1¼ cups (9 oz/250 g) granulated sugar
3 cups (9 oz/250 g) grated fresh coconut flesh
1 teaspoon salt
palm leaves, about 10–20 inches/25–50 cm long

Before you begin cooking, check that your
charcoal is glowing white hot, or your gas
grill (barbecue) is preheated to 400°F/200°C.
Alternatively, heat a conventional indoor broiler
(grill) to medium.

Mix the flours, sugars, coconut, and salt
together in a large bowl.

Lay a palm leaf out on a work surface and put
1 tablespoon of the rice mixture lengthwise
onto the leaf and cover with another palm leaf.
Pin with small bamboo pins or toothpicks at
the top, middle, and bottom of the palm leaves
to secure. Repeat until all the mixture is used.
Chargrill or broil (grill) over medium-low heat
for 10 minutes on each side. Serve.

ข้าวต้มมัด

Glutinous Rice in a Banana Leaf

Origin Northeast
Preparation time 5 minutes, plus soaking time
Cooking time 1½ hours
Serves 10

2 cups (11 oz/300 g) dried red beans
5 cups (2¼ lb/1 kg) glutinous (sticky) rice
2 teaspoons chopped cilantro (coriander) root
2 teaspoons ground black pepper
1½ cups (12 fl oz/350 ml) coconut milk
3¾ cups (1 lb 10 oz/750 g) granulated sugar
2 teaspoons salt
2 cups (16 fl oz/475 ml) coconut cream
banana leaves, cut into 6 x 7-inch/15 x 18-cm rectangles
1 bunch of ripe bananas

Soak the beans and glutinous (sticky) rice in
separate bowls of cold water overnight. The
next day, drain the rice and beans.

Bring 4¼ cups (1¾ pints/1 liter) water to a boil
in a large pan, add the beans, and cook for
25 minutes, then drain.

Meanwhile, pound the cilantro (coriander)
roots and pepper in a mortar with a pestle.
Set aside.

Put the beans and the cilantro root mixture in
a wok and stir-fry over medium heat for about
3 minutes. Remove from the heat and set aside.

Combine the coconut milk, sugar, and salt in
another wok and cook over medium heat for
2–3 minutes, stirring occasionally, until the
sugar and salt have dissolved. Add the drained
rice and cook for another 7 minutes, stirring
continuously. Stir until the rice absorbs all the
liquid, then slowly add the coconut cream. Mix
well and cook for another 20 minutes. Let cool.

Lay a banana leaf on a work surface. Put
1½ tablespoons of the rice mixture in the
center of the leaf and flatten. Place one-quarter
of a banana and 1 tablespoon of beans on top.
Fold the banana leaf over the filling, tucking
in the side to form a package and secure
with string. Steam the packages in a steamer
for 45–60 minutes or until the rice has
softened. Serve.

Photo p. 390

ข้าวอบสับปะรด

Baked Pineapple and Rice

Origin Central
Preparation time 15 minutes
Cooking time 20 minutes
Serves 2

1 pineapple
2–3 tablespoons vegetable oil
2¾ oz/70 g chicken breast, cut into ⅝-inch/
  1.5-cm cubes
5 uncooked shrimp (prawns), peeled and deveined
1½ cups (9½ oz/270 g) Steamed Jasmine Rice
  (see p. 378)
¼ cup (1½ oz/40 g) diced red bell pepper
2 teaspoons curry powder
1 tablespoon soy sauce
½ teaspoon granulated sugar
¼ teaspoon salt
½ cup (1½ oz/40 g) pork floss (dried shredded pork)
¼ cup (1½ oz/40 g) roasted cashew nuts

To prepare the pineapple, cut off the stem, then cut across the top, about 1¼ inches/3 cm from the crown and set aside. This will be the "lid." Use a long thin knife to cut along the inside of the pineapple to loosen the pineapple flesh, then scoop out the flesh to leave a hollowed-out pineapple "bowl." Set ½ cup (3 oz/80 g) of the pineapple flesh aside and cut the remaining flesh into small chunks and set aside.

Preheat the oven to 350°F/180°C/Gas Mark 4. Heat the oil in a wok over medium heat, add the chicken, and stir-fry for 1 minute. Add the shrimp (prawns) and cook for another minute or until the chicken and shrimp are cooked. Add the rice, pineapple chunks, and red bell pepper and stir-fry for 1 minute to combine. Add the curry powder, soy sauce, sugar, and salt and stir-fry for another 1 minute or until thoroughly combined. Spoon the mixture into the pineapple bowl and bake in the oven for 10 minutes. Remove from the oven and top with the pork floss and cashew nuts. Cover with the pineapple lid and serve.

Photo p. 393

ข้าวผัดสับปะรด

Fried Rice with Pineapple

Origin Central
Preparation time 10 minutes
Cooking time 8 minutes
Serves 2

3 tablespoons vegetable oil
2 cloves garlic, sliced
4 oz/120 g shrimp (prawns), peeled and deveined,
  with tails still intact
2½ cups (1 lb/450 g) Steamed Jasmine Rice (see p. 378)
1½ tablespoons soy sauce
1 teaspoon granulated sugar
1½ cups (9 oz/250 g) diced pineapple (cut into ¾-inch/
  2-cm dice)
½ cup (2¾ oz/75 g) roasted cashew nuts
2 scallions (spring onions), thinly sliced, to garnish
2 lime wedges, to serve

Heat the oil in a wok over medium heat, add the garlic, and stir-fry for about 1 minute or until fragrant. Add the shrimp (prawns) and stir-fry for 1–2 minutes until the shrimp turn pink. Remove the shrimp from the wok and set aside.

Add the steamed rice to the wok and stir for about 1 minute or until the rice is well coated with the oil. Add the soy sauce, sugar, and shrimp and stir-fry for 1–2 minutes. Add the pineapple and cashew nuts and cook for another 1 minute, stirring gently. Transfer to a serving bowl and garnish with the scallions (spring onions). Serve with the lime wedges.

Photo p. 394

ผัดหมี่ฮกเกี้ยน

Phuket Style Stir-Fried Hokkien Noodles

Origin South
Preparation time 10 minutes
Cooking time 5–7 minutes
Serves 2

2 tablespoons vegetable oil
2 shallots, finely chopped
2 oz/50 g shoulder pork, sliced
2 oz/50 g fresh squid, cleaned and tentacles set aside
5 uncooked shrimp (prawns), peeled and deveined
2 oz/50 g sea bass, cut into pieces
8 small oysters, shucked
12 oz/350 g Hokkien egg noodles
1½ teaspoons dark soy sauce
2 tablespoons soy sauce
7 oz/200 g napa (Chinese) cabbage, cut into
  2-inch/5-cm lengths
½ cup (4 fl oz/125 ml) chicken or pork broth (stock)
2 eggs, poached

Heat the oil in a wok over high heat, add the shallots, and quickly stir-fry for 2 minutes or until soft and starting to brown. Add the pork and stir-fry for 30 seconds, then add the squid tubes and tentacles, shrimp (prawns), fish, and oysters, and stir-fry for 2–3 minutes until cooked. Add the noodles and stir-fry for another 1 minute or until the noodles have softened. Season with the soy sauces and stir until thoroughly combined. Add the napa (Chinese) cabbage and broth (stock) and stir-fry for another 1 minute. Remove the wok from the heat and serve with the poached eggs on top.

ยำกุ้นเส้นแคปหมูทรงเครื่อง

Glass Noodle and Fried Pork Spicy Salad

Origin Central
Preparation time 10 minutes, plus soaking time
Cooking time 5 minutes
Serves 2

3½ oz/100 g dried glass noodles
10 uncooked shrimp (prawns), peeled and deveined,
  tails still intact
⅓ cup (2 oz/50 g) cooked chicken breast pieces
2 oz/50 g ground (minced) pork
2 tablespoons dried shrimp
2 tablespoons Fried Garlic (see p. 64)
2 scallions (spring onions), cut into 1-inch/2.5-cm slices
2 Chinese celery stalks, 1-inch/2.5-cm slices
10 pieces crispy pork skin, crushed

For the dressing
2 tablespoons Chili Jam (see p. 35)
2 tablespoons lime juice
2 tablespoons fish sauce
1 teaspoon granulated sugar

Soak the noodles in a bowl of water for 10 minutes, then drain and cook in a pan of boiling water for 1 minute or prepare according to package directions, until cooked. Drain and set aside.

Bring a pan of water to a boil over medium heat. Add the shrimp (prawns) and cook for 2–3 minutes, then remove with a slotted spoon and drain. Set aside.

Return the water to a boil, add the pork and cook for 2–3 minutes, then remove with a slotted spoon and drain. Set aside.

For the dressing, mix the chili jam, lime juice, fish sauce, and sugar together in a bowl.

Put the noodles, shrimp, chicken, pork, dried shrimp, and garlic in a serving bowl, add the dressing, and mix well. Add the scallions (spring onions), Chinese celery, and pork skin, and mix well. Serve.

ยำวุ้นเส้น

Spicy Noodles, Pork, and Seafood Salad

Origin Central
Preparation time 15 minutes, plus soaking time
Cooking time 10 minutes
Serves 2

3½ oz/100 g dried glass noodles
3½ oz/100 g ground (minced) pork
2 small squid, sliced into rings
6 uncooked shrimp (prawns), peeled and deveined
1 small onion, sliced lengthwise
1 handful of cilantro (coriander), coarsely chopped
1 cup (2 oz/50 g) chopped Chinese celery, cut into
  1½-inch/4-cm length pieces
1 tomato, sliced
¼ cup (1½ oz/40 g) roasted peanuts

For the spicy sauce
2 tablespoons fish sauce
2 tablespoons lime juice
1½ teaspoons granulated sugar
4 red bird's eye chiles, chopped
1½ teaspoons pickled garlic juice (optional)

Soak the noodles in a bowl of water for
10 minutes, or prepare according to package
directions. Drain, cut, and set aside.

Cook the pork in a pan of boiling water for
1–2 minutes until cooked, then drain and
set aside.

Cook the squid in another pan of boiling water
for 2–3 minutes until cooked, then drain and
set aside.

Cook the shrimp (prawns) in another pan of
boiling water for 1–2 minutes until the shrimp
change color, then drain and set aside.

To make the spicy sauce, mix the fish sauce,
lime juice, sugar, chiles, and pickled garlic
juice, if using, together in a bowl until the sugar
has dissolved. Set aside.

Cook the noodles in a pan of boiling water for
1–2 minutes until soft and cooked. Drain and
rinse in cold water and drain again. Transfer
to a bowl, add the shrimp (prawns), squid,
pork, onion, cilantro (coriander), celery, tomato,
and the sauce and mix well. Sprinkle with the
peanuts and serve.

หมี่กรอบสมุนไพร

Crispy Rice Noodles with Herbs

Origin South
Preparation time 10 minutes, plus soaking time
Cooking time 20 minutes
Serves 3

11 oz/300 g dried rice noodles
4 cups (1⅔ pints/950 ml) vegetable oil, for deep-frying
10 kaffir lime leaves
3½ oz/100 g dried red chiles
3 lemongrass stalks, finely sliced
2 tablespoons Tamarind Puree (see p. 63)
2 tablespoons dried chili flakes
1 teaspoon salt
2 tablespoons jaggery, palm sugar, or soft light
  brown sugar
¼ cup (2 fl oz/60 ml) glucose syrup

Soak the noodles in a bowl of water for
10 minutes, or according to package directions,
then drain and set aside.

Heat the oil for deep-frying in a wok or deep
fryer to 350°F/180°C or until a cube of bread
browns in 30 seconds. Fry the rice noodles in
batches for 1 minute, then remove and drain
on paper towels.

Deep-fry the kaffir lime leaves, dried chiles,
and sliced lemongrass in the same oil for
30 seconds until crispy. Remove from the wok
and drain on paper towels.

Bring the tamarind, chili flakes, salt, sugar,
and glucose syrup to a boil in a clean wok.
Stir continuously. Keep boiling for 5 minutes.
Slowly pour the tamarind sauce over the
fried rice noodles and stir until thoroughly
combined. Serve.

Alternatively, let cool, transfer to in an airtight
container, and store in the refrigerator for up
to 15 days.

ผัดไทยไข่ห่อ

Phat Thai Wrapped in Eggs

Origin Central
Preparation time 10–15 minutes, plus soaking time
Cooking time 15–20 minutes
Serves 3

7 oz/200 g dried rice noodles
2 tablespoons fish sauce
3 tablespoons granulated sugar
1½ tablespoon lime juice
1 tablespoon Tamarind Puree (see p. 63)
3½ tablespoons vegetable oil
2 tablespoons finely chopped shallots
3 cloves garlic, finely chopped
1½ tablespoons finely chopped sweet fermented radish
½ cup (¾ oz/20 g) dried shrimp
2 oz/50 g fresh extra-firm tofu, cut into ½-inch/
   1-cm cubes
3 oz/80 g uncooked jumbo shrimp (king prawns),
   peeled and deveined, tails still intact
1–2 tablespoons chicken or vegetable broth (stock)
1 cup (3½ oz/100 g) bean sprouts, plus extra to serve
½ cup (¾ oz/20 g) chopped Chinese chives, cut into
   1½-inch/4-cm lengths
scant ¼ cup (1¼ oz/30 g) unsalted peanuts, roasted
   and crushed
5 eggs, beaten
1 handful of cilantro (coriander) sprigs, to garnish
lime wedges, to serve

Soak the dried noodles in a bowl of water for 10 minutes or according to package directions, until soft. Drain and set aside.

Mix the fish sauce, sugar, lime juice, and tamarind in a small bowl and set aside.

Heat a large skillet or frying pan over medium heat. Add 3 tablespoons oil, the shallots, garlic, and fermented radish, and sauté for 1 minute. Add the dried shrimp and fry for another 1 minute. Add the tofu and cook for another 1 minute. Add the shrimp (prawns) and sauté for 1–2 minutes until the shrimp turn pink and are cooked. Push everything to one side of the pan.

Add the noodles and the broth (stock) to the pan and stir-fry for 1 minute without mixing with the rest of the food in the pan, then add the sauce. Continue to stir-fry the noodles for another 2 minutes or until cooked and the sauce starts to dry out. Mix everything in the pan together, then add the bean sprouts, chives, and roasted peanuts. Stir well. Remove the pan from the heat, divide the noodles into serving portions, and set aside.

Heat 1½ teaspoons oil in a wok over medium heat. Roll the oil around the wok and when the wok is hot, add ⅓ cup (2½ fl oz/75 ml) beaten egg. Roll the eggs in a circular motion to create a thin crepelike omelet, about 10 inches/25 cm diameter. When the omelet is cooked, remove from the wok and place in a 6½-inch/16-cm bowl. Put one portion of noodles into the omelet and fold the omelet over to wrap around the noodles. Turn the bowl upside down onto a serving plate. Repeat until all the portions of noodles are used. Garnish with cilantro (coriander) and serve with lime wedges and raw bean sprouts.

Fried Noodles in Coconut Milk with Shrimp

Origin South
Preparation time 10 minutes, plus soaking time
Cooking time 10 minutes
Serves 2

5 oz/150 g dried rice noodles
3–4 small shallots, finely chopped
15 dried red bird's eye chiles, seeded
½ teaspoon shrimp paste
1 cup (9 fl oz/250 ml) coconut milk
1 tablespoon jaggery, palm sugar, or soft light
  brown sugar
1½ teaspoons Tamarind Puree (see p. 63)
¼ teaspoon salt
10 uncooked shrimp (prawns), peeled and deveined
black pepper

To serve
raw or steamed vegetables, such as cucumber,
  bean sprouts, and yard-long beans

Soak the noodles in a bowl of water for
10 minutes or according to package directions,
until soft. Drain and set aside.

Pound the shallots and chiles together in a
mortar with a pestle until smooth, then add the
shrimp paste and pound until combined.

Bring the coconut milk to a boil in a pan over
medium heat. Add the chili paste, stir, and boil
for about 2 minutes. Add the sugar, tamarind,
salt, and a pinch of black pepper, and stir
until combined and begining to boil. Add the
shrimp (prawns) and cook for 1–2 minutes
until the shrimp turn pink and are cooked.
Add the noodles and stir for 3–4 minutes until
thoroughly combined and the noodles are soft,
and the sauce has dried out. Add a little water
if the sauce has dried out but the noodles are
still not soft enough to serve. Serve with raw
or steamed vegetables.

Photo p. 398

Drunken Noodles with Pork

Origin Central
Preparation time 5 minutes
Cooking time 7 minutes
Serves 2

7 oz/200 g flat rice noodles
2 tablespoons vegetable oil
3–4 cloves garlic, pounded
7 red and green bird's eye chiles, pounded
3½ oz/100 g pork tenderloin, thinly sliced
5 oz/150 g Chinese broccoli, chopped into 1½-inch/
  4-cm lengths
7 baby corn, halved lengthwise
5 straw mushrooms, halved
2 tablespoons soy sauce
1½ teaspoons granulated sugar
1 handful of holy basil leaves

Separate the strips of noodles from each
other. If the noodles have been kept in the
refrigerator, wrap them in cheesecloth (muslin)
and steam in a steamer for 2–3 minutes until
warmed through. Alternatively, heat in a
microwave for 1 minute or prepare according
to package directions. Set aside.

Heat the oil in a wok over medium-high
heat. Add the garlic and chiles and quickly
stir-fry for 30 seconds or until fragrant. Add the
pork and stir-fry for 1 minute or until cooked.
Add the broccoli and baby corn and stir-fry
for another 1–2 minutes. Add the noodles,
mushrooms, soy sauce, and sugar and stir-fry
for 1–2 minutes or until the noodles are soft
and fully flavored. Add the basil leaves and
stir 2–3 times. Serve.

บะหมี่ราดหน้าไก่

Fried Noodles with Chicken and Gravy

Origin Central
Preparation time 15 minutes
Cooking time 13 minutes
Serves 4–5

2 teaspoons soy sauce
⅓ cup (1½ fl oz/45 g) tapioca flour
1 x 14-oz/400-g chicken breast, cut into
 ¼-inch/½-cm strips
11 oz/300 g Chinese egg noodles
¼ cup (2 fl oz/60 ml) vegetable oil, plus extra
 for drizzling
4 cloves garlic, crushed
6 cups (2½ pints/1.4 liters) chicken broth (stock)
1½ tablespoons salted soybeans
1 tablespoon soy sauce
⅓ cup (2½ fl oz/75 ml) oyster sauce
1 tablespoon granulated sugar
1 teaspoon ground black pepper
9 oz/250 g bamboo shoots in brine, drained
 and cut into ½-inch/1-cm batons
1 x 5-oz/150-g can champignon or white button
 mushrooms

To garnish
2 scallions (spring onions), cut into ½-inch/1-cm batons
4–5 red chiles, seeded

To serve
a selection of condiments, such as granulated sugar,
 dried chili flakes, fish sauce, and white vinegar

Put the soy sauce and 1 tablespoon tapioca flour into a shallow bowl, add the chicken and mix to coat. Cover the bowl with plastic wrap (clingfilm) and leave for at least 10 minutes.

Fill a pan halfway with water and bring to a boil. Add the noodles in batches and cook for 2–3 minutes at a time or according to package directions. Remove with a slotted spoon and place on a serving plate. Drizzle with oil to prevent the noodles from sticking together or drying out, and set aside.

Heat the oil in a wok over medium heat, add the garlic, and stir-fry for 1 minute until golden and fragrant. Add the chicken, increase the heat slightly, and stir-fry for 2–3 minutes until the chicken starts to cook.

To make the gravy, pour in the broth (stock) and bring to a boil. Add the salted soybeans, soy sauce, oyster sauce, sugar, and black pepper. Reduce the heat and simmer, stirring occasionally for 5 minutes or until the chicken is cooked.

Meanwhile, put the selection of condiments in separate bowls and set aside.

Put the rest of the tapioca flour in a bowl, add ⅓ cup (2½ fl oz/75 ml) water, and stir well until smooth.

Increase the heat under the wok to medium and add the tapioca flour mixture in small amounts to thicken the gravy. The texture of the gravy should be thick but not gloopy. Add the bamboo shoots and mushrooms, then bring to a boil and cook for 2–3 minutes.

Spoon the chicken and gravy over the noodles and garnish with the scallions (spring onions) and chiles. Serve with the sugar, chili flakes, fish sauce, and white vinegar.

Photo p. 401

ผัดหมี่โคราช

Korat-Style Fried Noodles

Origin Northeast
Preparation time 10 minutes
Cooking time 7–10 minutes
Serves 2

3 tablespoons vegetable oil
2 shallots, chopped
3 garlic cloves, chopped
1½ cups (12 fl oz/350 ml) chicken broth (stock)
1 tablespoon fish sauce
1½ tablespoons granulated sugar
2 tablespoons Tamarind Puree (see p. 63)
1 tablespoon chili powder
1½ teaspoons salted soybeans
3½-oz/100-g dried rice noodles
4 scallions (spring onions), chopped into 1½-inch/
  4-cm pieces
1 cup (3½ oz/100 g) bean sprouts
4 Chinese chives, snipped into 1½-inch/4-cm pieces

Heat the oil in a wok over medium heat, add the shallots and garlic, and stir-fry for about 1 minute until golden brown. Add the chicken broth (stock), season with fish sauce, sugar, tamarind, chili powder, and salted soybeans, and bring to a boil.

Quickly rinse the noodles under cold running water, then add to the wok and stir-fry for 5–7 minutes, or according to package directions, until the noodles are soft, cooked, and have almost dried out. If the stock dries out before the noodles are cooked, add a little water to the wok. Reduce the heat, then add the scallions (spring onions), bean sprouts, and chives. Mix well and stir-fry for another 30 seconds. Serve.

ผัดซีอิ๊วเส้นใหญ่

Rice Noodles with Pork

Origin Central
Preparation time 10 minutes
Cooking time 8 minutes
Serves 2

7 oz/200 g fresh wide rice noodles
2 tablespoons vegetable oil
4–5 cloves garlic, finely sliced
3½ oz/100 g pork shoulder or tenderloin, thinly sliced
2 tablespoons soy sauce
1½ teaspoons cane sugar
7 oz/200 g Chinese broccoli, cut into 1½-inch/
  4-cm lengths
1 egg

Separate the strips of noodles from each other. If they have been in the refrigerator, wrap in cheesecloth (muslin) and steam for 3–5 minutes to warm through, or put them in the microwave for 1 minute. Set aside.

Heat the oil in a wok over medium-high heat. Add the garlic and quickly stir-fry for 30 seconds or until fragrant. Add the pork and stir-fry for 1 minute or until cooked. Add the rice noodles and stir-fry for another 1 minute or until the noodles have softened. Season with the soy sauce and sugar, stir, then add the broccoli and stir-fry for another 1–2 minutes.

Move the noodle mixture to one side of the wok, then break the egg into the wok. Beat and let cook a little before moving the noodles back into the center. Stir-fry for another minute or until throroughly thoroughly combined. Serve.

Crispy Rice Vermicelli with Calamansi Sauce

Origin Central
Preparation time 10 minutes, plus soaking time
Cooking time 25 minutes
Serves 3–4

3½ oz/100 g dried rice vermicelli
4 cups (1⅔ pints/950 ml) vegetable oil, for deep-frying
1 egg, beaten
2¼ oz/60 g extra firm tofu, cubed
3½ oz/100 g uncooked shrimp (prawns), peeled, deveined, and coarsely chopped

For the paste
½ shallot, chopped
1 clove garlic, chopped
1 teaspoon chopped pickled garlic

For the sauce
1 tablespoon vegetable oil
1½ teaspoons Tamarind Puree (see p. 63)
1 tablespoon calamansi (Chinese orange) or white passion fruit juice
1½ tablespoons calamansi (Chinese orange) or passion fruit zest, julienned
1 tablespoon lime juice
1½ tablespoons superfine (caster) sugar
½ cup (3½ oz/100 g) jaggery, palm sugar, or soft light brown sugar
pinch of salt
1 teaspoon white vinegar
1½ teaspoons ketchup (optional)
1 tablespoon fish sauce

To garnish
½ cup (1 oz/25 g) chopped scallions (spring onions)
scant ½ cup (1½ oz/40 g) bean sprouts
1 red spur chile, seeded and sliced
1 small handful of cilantro (coriander) sprigs
4 tablespoons Fried Shallots (see p. 64)

To serve
raw or steamed vegetables, such as yard-long beans, bean sprouts, and cucumbers

Soak the vermicelli in a bowl of water for 5 minutes or according to package directions. Drain and set aside.

Heat the oil for deep-frying in a wok or deep fryer to 350°F/180°C or until a cube of bread browns in 30 seconds. Spread 1¼-oz/30-g portions of the vermicelli around the wok and deep-fry for 1 minute at a time or until golden brown and crispy on both sides. Remove with a slotted spoon and drain on paper towels. Repeat until all the vermicelli are used.

In the same wok, pour the beaten egg through a fine strainer (sieve) and drizzle around the wok (about 8 inches/20 cm away from the wok) to create an egg "mesh." Remove and drain on paper towels. Add the tofu to the wok and deep-fry for 2 minutes or until golden brown. Remove and drain on paper towels. Deep-fry the shrimp (prawns) for 1–2 minutes, then remove and drain on paper towels.

Pound all the ingredients for the paste in a mortar with a pestle.

For the sauce, heat the oil in a clean wok over medium heat, add the paste, and stir-fry for 1–2 minutes until fragrant. Add the tamarind, calamansi (Chinese orange) or passion fruit juice and zest, the lime juice, both sugars, salt, vinegar, ketchup, and fish sauce and stir for 4–5 minutes until thickened. Add the deep-fried shrimp and tofu and stir-fry for another 1–2 minutes. Add the crispy noodles and stir until the noodles are completely coated in the sauce.

Transfer to a serving plate and garnish with the egg "mesh," scallions (spring onions), bean sprouts, chiles, cilantro (coriander), and fried shallots. Serve with raw or steamed vegetables.

ขนมจีนน้ำยาป่า

Rice Noodles with Spicy Sauce

Origin Northeast
Preparation time 10 minutes
Cooking time 30 minutes
Serves 4

4 cups (1⅔ pints/950 ml) fish or chicken broth (stock)
10 dried chiles, chopped
7 cloves garlic, chopped
6 shallots, chopped
5 thin slices galangal, chopped
2 lemongrass stalks, chopped
6 fingerroots, chopped
2 tablespoons fermented fish sauce
1 x 1 lb 2-oz/500-g snakehead fish, sea bass, or sea
  bream, filleted, and cut into bite-size pieces
1½ tablespoons fish sauce
½ teaspoon granulated sugar
20 fish balls
2 cups (3½ oz/100 g) chopped spring onions (scallions)

To serve
2¼ lb/1 kg cooked rice noodles
1½ cups (5 oz/150 g) bean sprouts
1 cup (2 oz/50 g) basil
3 cups (10 oz/270 g) chopped yard-long beans
2 handfuls water mimosa, coarsely chopped
¼ cup (2¾ oz/20 g) dried chili flakes
4 hard-boiled eggs, halved

Bring 1 cup (9 fl oz/250 ml) water and the broth (stock) to a boil in a large pan. Add the chiles, garlic, shallots, galangal, lemongrass, fingerroots, and fermented fish sauce and boil for about 7 minutes. Add the fish, reduce the heat, and simmer for 10 minutes or until softened. Strain through cheesecloth (muslin) into a bowl and reserve the broth. Set aside.

Separate the fish meat and set side. Pound the cooked chiles, garlic, galangal, lemongrass, fingerroot, and shallots in a mortar with a pestle. Add the fish meat and pound until combined. Set aside.

Return the stock to the pan and bring to boil over medium heat. Add the paste, fish sauce, sugar, and fish balls and boil for 2-3 minutes. Add the scallions (spring onions) and cook for about 2 minutes. Remove from the heat and set aside.

Divide the noodles and fish balls among serving bowls and pour the broth over them. Top with bean sprouts, basil, yard-long beans, water mimosa, chili flakes, and eggs. Serve.

ผัดเส้นจันทร์

Fried Noodles

Origin Central
Preparation time 10 minutes, plus soaking time
Cooking time 5 minutes
Serves 10

2¼ lb/1 kg dried rice noodles
3 tablespoons vegetable oil
1¼ cups (10 fl oz/300 ml) Tamarind Puree (see p. 63)
1½ cups (11 oz/300 g) jaggery, palm sugar, or soft light
　brown sugar
2¼ lb/1 kg blue crabs, stir-fried and cut into small
　pieces (see p. 338)
1 lb 2 oz/500 g uncooked shrimp (prawns), peeled
　and deveined

For the chili paste
3½ oz/100 g dried red chiles, seeded
10 shallots, chopped
2 garlic bulbs, cloves separated and chopped
1 tablespoon salt

To serve
5 cups (7 oz/200 g) chopped Chinese chives
1½ cucumbers, peeled and sliced lengthwise
　into chunks
5 cups (1 lb 2 oz/500 g) bean sprouts

Soak the noodles in a bowl of water for
10 minutes, or according to package directions,
until soft, then drain, rinse, and set aside.

For the chili paste, soak the dried chiles in
a bowl of hot water for 15 minutes or until
rehydrated, then drain and chop.

Pound the chiles, shallots, garlic, and salt in
a mortar with a pestle until smooth.

Heat the oil in a wok over medium heat, add
the chili paste, and stir-fry for 1 minute until
fragrant. Add the tamarind and sugar and
simmer for about 3 minutes, stirring until the
sugar has dissolved. Add the crab pieces and
stir-fry for 2 minutes. Add the shrimp (prawns),
noodles, and a few snipped chives, then reduce
the heat to low and cook for 3–4 minutes. Serve
with the remaining chives, the cucumber, and
bean sprouts.

Photo p. 405

บะหมี่ลูกชิ้นเนื้อเปื่อย

Stewed Beef Noodles

Origin Central
Preparation time 10 minutes, plus soaking time
Cooking time 2 hours
Serves 4

11 oz/300 g dried rice noodles
1 cup (3½ oz/100 g) bean sprouts
½ cup (1 oz/25 g) shredded lettuce
1 tablespoon sliced Chinese celery (cut into 1-inch/
　2.5-cm slices)
2 tablespoons sliced scallions (spring onions)
2 tablespoons sliced cilantro (coriander)

For the beef broth (stock)
4½ lb/2 kg beef sirloin, cut into 1¼-inch/3-cm pieces
2 star anises
2 cinnamon sticks
¼ cup (2 fl oz/60 ml) soy sauce
2 teaspoons salt
scant ¼ cup (1½ oz/40 g) granulated sugar
1 tablespoon coriander seeds
1 tablespoon dark soy sauce
2 tablespoons oyster sauce

Soak the noodles in a bowl of water for
10 minutes, or according to package directions,
until soft, then drain, rinse, and set aside.

To make the beef broth (stock), bring 8½ cups
(3½ pints/2 liters) water to a boil in a large pan.
Add all the ingredients and return to a boil. Use
a slotted spoon to remove any scum. Cover
with a lid, reduce the heat to low, and simmer
for 1–2 hours until the beef is tender. Remove
the beef from the pan and set aside.

Blanch the rice noodles and bean sprouts
in a pan of boiling water for 1 minute, then
drain and divide among serving bowls. Add
the lettuce, Chinese celery, scallions (spring
onions), cilantro (coriander), and ⅓ cup (2 oz/
50 g) stewed beef. Add 1 ladleful of beef broth
to each bowl and serve.

Photo p. 407

Rice Noodles with Shredded Chicken p. 409

ขนมจีนไก่ฉีก

Rice Noodles with Shredded Chicken

Origin Central
Preparation time 15 minutes, plus cooling time
Cooking time 25 minutes
Serves 4

2 cups (16 fl oz/475 ml) coconut milk
2 skinless, boneless chicken breasts, cut in
  half lengthwise
¼ teaspoon salt
2¼ lb/1 kg fresh rice noodles or 14 oz/400 g dried
  rice noodles

To serve
1 cup (9 fl oz/250 ml) Chili Jam (see p. 35)
1 bunch of cilantro (coriander), half the stems removed
1 cucumber, cut into ¼-inch/7-mm-thick slices
1 head lettuce, leaves separated

Bring the coconut milk to a boil in a large pan over medium heat. Add the chicken and salt, reduce the heat to low-medium, and simmer for 10 minutes. Remove from the heat and let the chicken cool in the pan for 10 minutes.

Remove the chicken with a slotted spoon and transfer to a cutting (chopping) board. Use a fork to shred the chicken, then return to the pan and set aside.

Cook the noodles according to the package directions. If using dried noodles, first soak them in a bowl of water for 10 minutes, or according to package directions, until soft. Drain and rinse under cold water, then leave in the strainer (sieve) to drain completely. Use your hand or a fork to roll the vermicelli into small rolls and place on a serving plate.

To serve, divide the rolls of noodles among serving plates and top with 2–3 tablespoons of the chili jam and 3–4 tablespoons of the chicken and coconut milk. Serve with the cilantro (coriander), cucumber slices, and lettuce leaves.

Photo p. 408

เส้นใหญ่ราดหน้า

Rice Noodles with Pork and Gravy

Origin Central
Preparation time 10 minutes
Cooking time 10 minutes
Serves 4

3 tablespoons vegetable oil
14 oz/400 g flat wide rice noodles
1 tablespoon dark soy sauce
5 cloves garlic, finely chopped
9 oz/250 g pork tenderloin or shoulder, thinly sliced
6 cups (2½ pints/1.4 liters) chicken broth (stock)
3 tablespoons soy sauce
½ teaspoon salt
1 tablespoon granulated sugar
1 tablespoon salted soybeans
2 tablespoons tapioca flour
7 oz/200 g Chinese broccoli, cut into 2-inch/
  5-cm-long pieces

Heat 2 tablespoons oil in a wok over medium heat. Add the rice noodles and dark soy sauce and stir-fry for 1–2 minutes until the noodles have softened. Remove from the wok and set aside.

Heat 1 tablespoon oil in the wok over medium-high heat, add the garlic, and quickly stir-fry for 1 minute or until fragrant. Add the pork and stir-fry for 1 minute. Add the broth (stock) and bring to a boil. Season with the soy sauce, salt, sugar, and salted soybeans and return to a boil.

Dissolve the tapioca flour in ¼ cup (2 fl oz/ 50 ml) water and slowly add to the wok, stirring continuously, until the mixture has thickened into a gravy. Add the broccoli and cook for about 2 minutes or until the broccoli is tender.

Transfer the noodles to a deep serving plate or bowl and pour the gravy, pork, and vegetables over the noodles. Serve.

ก๋วยเตี๋ยวคั่วไก่

Fried Rice Noodles with Chicken

Origin Central
Preparation time 25 minutes, plus standing time
Cooking time 10 minutes
Serves 2

7 oz/200 g skinless, boneless chicken breast, sliced
1 teaspoon ground white pepper
½ teaspoon sesame oil
1½ tablespoons soy sauce
14 oz/400 g large fresh rice noodles
3 tablespoons vegetable oil
3 cloves garlic, crushed
1 tablespoon finely chopped sweet preserved turnip
1 tablespoon oyster sauce
1 tablespoon granulated sugar
2 eggs
1 cup (3⅛ oz/100 g) bean sprouts
4–5 leaves round or curly lettuce
2 scallions (spring onions), finely chopped

Put the chicken, ground white pepper, sesame oil, and 1 teaspoon soy sauce in a bowl, mix well, and let stand for 10–15 minutes.

Separate the strips of noodles from each other. If the noodles have been kept in the refrigerator, wrap them in cheesecloth (muslin) and steam in a steamer for 2–3 minutes until warmed through. Alternatively, heat in a microwave for 1 minute. Set aside.

Heat 2 tablespoons oil in a wok over low-medium heat, add the garlic and preserved turnip, and stir-fry for 10 seconds or until fragrant. Add the chicken, increase the heat to medium, and stir-fry for 2–3 minutes until cooked. Add the noodles and stir-fry for 1–2 minutes, then season with 2 teaspoons soy sauce, the oyster sauce, and sugar. Stir until combined, then move to one side of the wok.

Add 1 tablespoon oil, break in the eggs, and let the egg whites become lightly cooked before scrambling. When the eggs are cooked halfway, mix with the noodles and stir-fry for about 1 minute or until the eggs are fully cooked. Add the bean sprouts and stir-fry for 20 seconds. Remove from the heat. Let cool for 1 minute, then add the lettuce and scallions (spring onions) and stir. Serve.

Photo p. 411

ขนมจีนซาวน้ำ

Rice Vermicelli with Pineapple and Coconut Milk

Origin Central
Preparation time 20 minutes
Cooking time 10 minutes
Serves 4

2¼ lb/1 kg fresh rice vermicelli or 14 oz/400 g
  dried rice vermicelli
3 cups (4 oz/120 g) dried shrimp
2 cups (16 fl oz/475 ml) coconut milk
3 tablespoons granulated sugar
1 teaspoon salt

For the chili sauce
10 red and green bird's eye chiles, chopped
½ cup (4 fl oz/125ml) fish sauce
1 lime, thinly sliced

To serve
½ cup (1 oz/25 g) chopped fresh ginger
10 cloves garlic, thinly sliced
2 cups (11½ oz/330 g) diced pineapple

Cook the vermicelli according to the package directions. If using dried vermicelli, first soak them in a bowl of water for 10 minutes, or according to package directions, until soft. Drain and rinse under cold water, then leave in the strainer (sieve) to drain completely.

Process the dried shrimp in a food processor into fine flakes, then set aside.

For the chili sauce, put the chiles, fish sauce, and lime slices in a small serving bowl and mix well. Set aside.

Simmer the coconut milk, sugar, and salt in a pan over low-medium heat for 2–3 minutes until the sugar and salt have dissolved. Remove from the heat and set aside.

To serve, divide the vermicelli among serving bowls and pour over the coconut milk mixture. Top with the ginger, garlic, dried shrimp flakes, diced pineapple, and the chili sauce.

Desserts

ข้าวโพดคลุก

Corn with Young Coconut

Origin Northeast
Preparation time 3 minutes
Cooking time 15 minutes
Serves 2

1 cup (3 oz/80 g) shredded fresh coconut, or ½ cup
 (1½ oz/40 g) dry unsweetened (desiccated) coconut
2 corn cobs, husks removed
1½ tablespoons granulated sugar
¼ teaspoon salt

If using the dry unsweetened (desiccated) coconut, wrap in cheesecloth (muslin) and steam in a steamer for 10 minutes or until hydrated and softened. Remove from the heat and let cool.

Boil the corn in a pan of water for 10–12 minutes then drain and slice the corn kernels from the cob. Discard the cob. Mix the corn kernels and coconut (leave some for decorating) together in a bowl, then add the sugar and salt, and coarsely stir the mixture together. Serve decorated with the remaining coconut.

แกงบวดข้าวโพด

Corn in Coconut Milk

Origin Central
Preparation time 10 minutes
Cooking time 10 minutes
Serves 2–3

1⅔ cups (14 fl oz/400 ml) coconut milk
scant ½ cup (3½ oz/100 g) jaggery, palm sugar, or soft
 light brown sugar
½ teaspoon salt
2⅔ cups (14 oz/400 g) corn kernels

Bring the coconut milk to a boil in a pan over medium heat. Add the sugar and salt, and stir until the sugar has dissolved. Add the corn, gently stir, then return to a boil. Reduce the heat and simmer for 4–5 minutes, stirring occasionally. Serve hot or cold.

ตะโก้ข้าวโพด

Corn and Pandan Pudding

Origin South
Preparation time 10 minutes
Cooking time 25 minutes
Makes 15–20

2¼ lb/1 kg banana leaves, cut into 6-inch/15-cm
  diameter circles
½ cup (2 oz/50 g) mung bean flour
1 cup (7 oz/200 g) superfine (caster) sugar
1 cup (6 oz/175 g) cooked corn kernels
1 cup (9 fl oz/250 ml) Pandan Extract (see p. 63)

For coconut topping
1⅔ cups (14 fl oz/400 ml) coconut milk
½ cup (3 oz/80 g) rice flour
½ teaspoon salt
2 tablespoons superfine (caster) sugar

Prepare 15–20 banana-leaf cups. For each cup, place 2 banana leaf circles back to back with the shiny surface face outward on both sides. From the outside of the circle, fold up about 1¼ inches/3 cm of banana leaf and then fold in on itself to create a corner. Secure with toothpick or use a stapler. Repeat until there are 4 corners.

For the filling, mix the mung bean flour, sugar, corn, pandan extract, and 1 cup (9 fl oz/250 ml) water together in a pan. Heat over low-medium heat, stirring continuously for 7–8 minutes until thick and transparent.

Fill each banana cup with about 1 tablespoon of the mixture or leave ¼-inch/5-mm head space from the top of the banana cup. Repeat until all the cups are filled. Set aside.

For the topping, mix the coconut milk, rice flour, salt, and sugar together in a pan and heat over medium heat, stirring constantly for 6–7 minutes until cooked. Top each filled banana cup with about ½ tablespoon of the topping, let cool, and serve.

ขนมขุยหนู

Steamed Rice Flour Topped with Coconut Flesh

Origin Central
Preparation time 5 minutes, plus soaking time
Cooking time 15 minutes
Serves 4

2½ cups (1 lb 2 oz/500 g) superfine (caster) sugar
generous 3 cups (1 lb 2 oz/500 g) rice flour
meat of 2 coconuts, cut into thin strips
¼ cup (2 oz/50 g) salt
jasmine flowers, to garnish

Bring 2 cups (16 fl oz/475 ml) water and the sugar to a boil in a pan over medium heat. Stir until the sugar has dissolved and the mixture is syrupy, then remove from the heat and let cool.

Sprinkle ½ cup (4 fl oz/120 ml) water onto the rice flour to dampen it, then sift this wet rice flour through a strainer (sieve) into a bowl. Wrap the powdered rice flour in cheesecloth (muslin) and steam in a steamer for 10 minutes, then transfer to a large bowl and let cool.

Gradually add the cold sugar syrup to the cold steamed rice flour and mix well with a spatula.

Mix the coconut flesh and salt together in a bowl, then stir into the rice flour mixture until combined. Transfer to a serving bowl and garnish with jasmine flowers. Serve.

Golden Egg Teardrops

Origin Central
Preparation time 30 minutes, plus steeping time
Cooking time 20 minutes
Serves 4

10–12 jasmine flowers or 1½ teaspoons jasmine essence
5 cups (2¼ lb/1 kg) superfine (caster) sugar
1 pandan leaf, knotted
7 duck egg yolks
3 tablespoons rice flour

To make the jasmine water, bring 4 cups (1⅔ pints/950 ml) water to a boil in a large pan over medium heat. Let cool and transfer to a large bowl. Add the jasmine flowers to the water, cover the bowl with plastic wrap (clingfilm) and let steep overnight.

The next day, remove the flowers with a slotted spoon and discard.

For the syrup, mix the sugar with the jasmine water or jasmine essence and pandan leaf in a pan over medium-low heat, then bring to a boil.

Meanwhile, strain the egg yolks through cheesecloth (muslin) into a bowl. Whisk until thick, smooth, and pale yellow. Be careful not to overwhisk. Add the flour and gently fold the mixture until well mixed.

When the sugar and jasmine water has started boiling, remove the pandan leaf with a slotted spoon. Discard the leaf.

Use the narrow grooved handle of a noodle spoon or a teaspoon to scrape ½ teaspoon of the egg mixture onto another spoon, then use your thumb to push the egg mixture out of the spoon and into the syrup, making sure that the syrup is still boiling (with bubbles breaking on the surface). Repeat until all the egg mixture is used or until there is no room on the surface of the syrup. The egg mixture should be teardrop shaped. Let the egg mixture cook in the syrup for 4–5 minutes, then remove with a slotted spoon and transfer to a bowl.

Pour about ½ cup (4 fl oz/120 ml) of the syrup mixture over the egg droplets. Let cool, then remove the droplets from the syrup with a slotted spoon and serve.

Photo p. 423

ขนมหม้อแกง

Coconut Custard with Fried Shallots

Origin Central
Preparation time 15 minutes
Cooking time 25 minutes
Serves 8–10

8½ cups (3½ pints/2 liters) coconut milk
scant 1 cup (5 oz/150 g) rice flour
6⅔ cups (3¼ lb/1.5 kg) jaggery, palm sugar, or soft
  light brown sugar
13 duck eggs or 15 hen eggs, beaten
5 tablespoons Fried Shallots (see p. 64)

Preheat the oven to 350°F/180°C/Gas Mark 4.
Grease a 12-inch/30-cm square baking pan.

Mix the coconut milk, flour, sugar, and eggs
together in a bowl until thoroughly combined.
Pour the mixture into a pan and cook over
medium heat for 7 minutes, stirring frequently.
Pour the batter into the prepared baking
pan and bake for 15 minutes or until golden
brown. Sprinkle with the fried shallots, cut into
squares, and serve.

Photo p. 424

ลูกเดือยมะพร้าวอ่อน

Job's Tears and Young Coconut Porridge

Origin Central
Preparation time 10 minutes, plus soaking time
Cooking time 1 hour 20 minutes
Serves 4

1 cup (7 oz/215 g) Job's tear seeds (Chinese
  pearl barley)
5 cups (2 pints/1.2 liters) coconut water
½ cup (1½ oz/40 g) sliced fresh coconut
½ cup (3½ oz/100 g) granulated sugar
½ teaspoon salt
2 tablespoons cornstarch (cornflour)
2 tablespoons arrowroot starch
½ cup (4 fl oz/120 ml) coconut cream

Rinse and soak the Job's tear seeds in a bowl
of water overnight. The next day, drain and
rinse. Transfer to a large pan, add 4 cups
(1⅔ pints/950 ml) water, cover with a lid, and
cook over low heat for about 1 hour or until
cooked. Drain and rinse the Job's tears again
and return to the pan. Add the coconut water
and bring to a boil over medium heat. Add the
sliced coconut, sugar, and half the salt, and stir
until the sugar and salt have dissolved.

Dissolve the cornstarch (cornflour) and the
arrowroot starch in ¼ cup (2 fl oz/60 ml) water.
Stir half of the mixture into the pan and cook
until thick. Remove from the heat.

Bring the coconut cream to a boil in another
pan over medium heat. Add the remaining
salt and stir for about 2 minutes or until the salt
has dissolved. Add the rest of the cornstarch
mixture and stir until thickened. Remove
from the heat.

Put the Job's tears into small serving bowls
and pour over the coconut cream. Serve.

ข้าวเหนียวเหลืองหน้ากุ้ง

Sweet Glutinous Rice with Dried Shrimp

Origin Central
Preparation time 15 minutes, plus soaking time
Cooking time 30 minutes
Serves 10

2 turmeric roots, peeled and chopped
5 cups (2¼ lb/1 kg) glutinous (sticky) rice
2¼ lb/1 kg banana leaves, cut into 6-inch/15-cm
   diameter circles
4¼ cups (1¾ pints/1 liter) coconut milk
1 tablespoon salt
1 cup (7 oz/200 g) superfine (caster) sugar

For the topping
2½ cups (7 oz/200 g) shredded fresh coconut
scant 1 cup (3½ oz/100 g) dried shrimp, pounded
1 cup (7 oz/200 g) superfine (caster) sugar
7 oz/200 g Fried Shallots (see p. 64)

Pound the turmeric in a large mortar with a pestle. Add 8½ cups (3½ pints/2 liters) water, mix, then strain through cheesecloth (muslin) into a large bowl. Discard the residue left in the cheesecloth. Add the rice to the turmeric juice and mix well, then cover and let soak overnight or for at least 3 hours.

Wrap the soaked rice in cheesecloth and steam in a steamer for 30–35 minutes, stirring the rice every 10 minutes until cooked through. The rice will look transparent when cooked.

Prepare the banana-leaf cups. For each cup, place 2 banana leaf circles back to back with the shiny surface face outward on both sides. From the outside of the circle, fold up about 1¼ inches/3 cm of banana leaf and then fold in on itself to create a corner. Secure with a toothpick or use a stapler. Repeat until there are 4 corners.

Bring the coconut milk to a boil in a pan over low-medium heat. Add the salt and sugar and stir until the sugar has dissolved. Add the rice and cook for 3–4 minutes until thoroughly combined. Remove from the heat, cover with a lid, and leave for 10 minutes.

For the topping, dry-fry the shredded coconut in a wok over medium heat for 1–2 minutes, stirring continuously, until just starting to color, Add the dried shrimp, superfine (caster) sugar, and fried shallots and stir until combined.

Spoon the rice into the banana-leaf cups and sprinkle with the topping. Serve.

Photo p. 427

Caramel

Origin Central
Preparation time 5 minutes, plus soaking time
Cooking time 3½ hours
Makes 25–30 squares

1¼ cups (9 oz/250 g) glutinous (sticky) rice
scant ⅓ cup (2 oz/50 g) rice flour
6¼ cups (2½ pints/1.5 liters) coconut milk
scant 4½ cups (2¼ lb/1 kg) jaggery, palm sugar, or soft
  light brown sugar

Soak the rice in a large bowl of water overnight
or for at least 3 hours. Wash and drain. Wrap
the rice in cheesecloth (muslin) and steam in
a steamer for 30–35 minutes, stirring the rice
every 10 minutes until cooked through. The
rice will look transparent when cooked.

Mix the rice flour with the steamed rice in
another pan, then add the coconut milk and
sugar and cook over low heat for 2–3 hours or
until sticky. Let cool in a casserole dish, then
cut into 1½-inch/4-cm squares and serve.

Sweet Coconut Balls

Origin Central
Preparation time 10 minutes
Cooking time 30 minutes
Serves 5

½ cup (2¾ oz/70 g) glutinous (sticky) rice flour
½ cup (4 fl oz/120 ml) coconut milk
½ teaspoon salt, plus extra for rolling
1⅓ cups (11 oz/300 g) jaggery, palm sugar, or soft light
  brown sugar
1 cup (3 oz/80 g) shredded fresh coconut, plus ½ cup
  (1½ oz/40 g) for rolling

Mix the flour, coconut milk, and salt together
in a bowl, then use your hands to knead the
dough until sticky. Cover with plastic wrap
(clingfilm) and set aside.

Bring the sugar to a simmer in a wok over
low heat for 2–3 minutes until softened. Add
the shredded coconut and stir-fry until dry.
Remove from the heat and set aside.

Spread the extra coconut and salt out on
a plate. Set aside.

Roll out the dough on a work surface. Use
a cookie cutter to cut out small circles from
the dough. Put a teaspoon of the filling in the
center of a circle and mold the dough around
the filling to enclose it in a ball. Repeat until
all the filling is used.

Bring a large pan of water to a boil over
medium heat, carefully drop the balls into
the water, and cook for 4–5 minutes or until
they float to the surface. Drain and roll in the
shredded coconut and salt. Serve.

ข้าวเหนียวถั่วดำ

Sweet Glutinous Rice with Black Beans

Origin Central
Preparation time 5 minutes, plus soaking time
Cooking time 45 minutes
Serves 4

1 cup (7 oz/200 g) dried black beans
1⅔ cups (14 fl oz/400 ml) coconut milk
⅓ cup (2¾ oz/75 g) jaggery, palm sugar, or soft light
  brown sugar
¼ cup (2 oz/50 g) granulated sugar
¼ teaspoon salt

For the glutinous rice
2½ cups (1 lb 2 oz/500 g) glutinous (sticky) rice
2 cups (16 fl oz/475 ml) coconut milk
1 tablespoon salt
¾ cup (5 oz/150 g) granulated sugar

For the rice, soak the rice in a bowl of water overnight or for at least 3 hours. Drain and rinse, then put in cheesecloth (muslin) and steam in a steamer for 20 minutes.

Pour the coconut milk into a pan, add the salt and granulated sugar, and gradually bring to a boil. Remove from the heat and set three-quarters of this sweet coconut milk aside for the topping.

Put the rice and remaining sweet coconut milk into another pan, mix well, cover with a lid, and cook over medium heat for 5 minutes. Pour the reserved sweet coconut milk over the rice.

For the beans, rinse the black beans under cold running water, then put into a pan and cover with 4 cups (1⅔ pints/950 ml) water. Bring to a boil and boil for about 20 minutes until soft.

Bring the coconut milk to a boil in another pan over low heat, add the salt and sugars, and stir, then add the black beans and stir until mixed. Pour on top of the rice and serve.

ข้าวเหนียวหัวหงอก

Coconut Rice Balls

Origin Central
Preparation time 5 minutes
Serves 4

2 cups (12 oz/350 g) Glutinous Rice (see p. 378)
1 cup (3 oz/80 g) shredded fresh coconut
3 tablespoons superfine (caster) sugar
¾ teaspoon salt

Mix the cooked rice, three-quarters of the coconut, the sugar, and salt together in a large bowl. Scoop a teaspoon of the mixture and roll it into a ball, then place on a plate. Repeat until all the mixture is used. Sprinkle with the remaining coconut and serve.

ถั่วดำต้มน้ำตาลกะทิ

Black Beans in Coconut Milk

Origin Central
Preparation time 5 minutes, plus soaking time
Cooking time 1½ hours
Serves 4

1 cup (7 oz/200 g) dried black beans
1⅔ cups (14 fl oz/400 ml) coconut milk
⅓ cup (2¾ oz/75 g) jaggery, palm sugar, or soft
  light brown sugar
¼ cup (2 oz/50 g) superfine (caster) sugar
¼ teaspoon salt

Soak the beans in a bowl of water for 2 hours, then drain, rinse, and put into a pan. Pour in enough water to cover and bring to a boil over medium heat. Boil for 50–60 minutes or until softened. Drain and transfer to a clean pan. Add the coconut milk and ⅓ cup (2½ fl oz/75 ml) water and bring to a boil over medium heat. When the mixture is boiling, add both sugars and the salt and stir until the sugars have dissolved. Reduce the heat to low and simmer for 30 minutes or until the beans are fully flavored. Remove from the heat and serve.

Photo p. 430

ข้าวหลามมะพร้าวอ่อน

Glutinous Rice in Coconut Shell

Origin South
Preparation time 10 minutes, plus soaking time and resting time
Cooking time 45 minutes
Serves 5

2½ cups (1 lb 2 oz/500 g) glutinous (sticky) rice
2½ cups (1 pint/600 ml) coconut milk
2¼ cups (1 lb/450 g) granulated sugar
¼ tablespoon salt
¼ cup (2 oz/50 g) cooked black beans or red beans
5 young coconuts
2 oz/50 g arrowroot starch or tapioca flour

Soak the rice in a large bowl of cold water overnight or for at least 3 hours. Wash and drain. Wrap the rice in cheesecloth (muslin) and steam in a steamer for 30–35 minutes, stirring the rice every 10 minutes until cooked through. The rice will look transparent when cooked. Set aside.

Heat the coconut milk, sugar, and salt in a pan over medium heat and simmer, stirring, until the sugar has dissolved.

Put the steamed rice into a bowl and add the black or red beans. Sprinkle with half the sweetened coconut milk and stir until thoroughly combined. Let rest for 10 minutes.

Open the young coconuts, remove the flesh with a spoon, keeping the shells intact. Set the shells aside. Shred the coconut flesh, add to the rice and bean mixture, and stir until well mixed. Set aside.

Preheat the oven to 425°F/220°C/Gas Mark 7.

Mix the starch or flour with the remaining sweetened coconut milk in a pan and simmer over low heat for a few minutes or until thickened. Add the mixture to the rice and coconut mixture, then pour into the coconut shells and bake for 10–15 minutes. Serve.

ข้าวหลาม

Glutinous Rice Roasted in Bamboo

Origin Central
Preparation time 15 minutes, plus soaking time
Cooking time 3–3½ hours
Makes 12

2½ cups (1 lb 2 oz/500 g) glutinous (sticky) rice
½ cup (3½ oz/100 g) dried black beans
1 cup (9 fl oz/250 ml) coconut milk
1 cup (7 oz/200 g) superfine (caster) sugar
1 teaspoon salt
bamboo stalks, about 2 inches/5 cm in diameter, and cut into 12-inch/30-cm long pieces
1 banana leaf, to cover

Soak the rice in a bowl of water for about 2 hours, then drain and set aside.

Soak the beans in a bowl of water for 2 hours, then drain, rinse, and put into a pan. Pour in enough water to cover and bring to a boil over medium heat. Reduce the heat and simmer for about 30 minutes. Remove from the heat and mix with the rice. Spoon the mixture into the bamboo stalks until three-quarters full.

Before you begin cooking, check that your charcoal is glowing white hot.

Bring the coconut milk, sugar, and salt to a boil over medium heat and stir until the sugar has dissolved. Remove from the heat and carefully pour into the bamboo stalks. Cover with the banana leaf and cook over the charcoal fire for 2½–3 hours. Remove from the heat, carefully split the bamboo stalks open, and serve.

Sweet Glutinous Rice in Banana Leaf

Origin Central
Preparation time 30 minutes, plus soaking time
Cooking time 1 hour 40 minutes
Makes 20

2½ cups (1 lb 2 oz/500 g) glutinous (sticky) rice
½ cup (3½ oz/100 g) dried black beans
2 cups (18 oz/500 ml) coconut milk
½ cup (3½ oz/100 g) granulated sugar
2 teaspoons salt
10 ripe small bananas
banana leaves, cut into 7–8-inch/18–20-cm-wide strips

Soak the rice in a bowl of water overnight or for at least 3 hours, then drain, rinse under cold running water, and drain again.

Soak the beans in another bowl of water for 2 hours, then drain, rinse, and put into a pan. Pour in enough water to cover and bring to a boil over medium heat. Boil for 50–60 minutes or until softened.

Meanwhile, mix the coconut milk, sugar, and salt together in a bowl, then strain through cheesecloth (muslin) into a clean bowl.

Combine the rice and sweetened coconut milk in a wok over medium heat and stir continuously for about 10 minutes until the rice starts to cook. Remove from the heat and set aside.

Peel the bananas and cut in half lengthwise.

Lay a banana leaf on a flat work surface. Place a tablespoon of rice and 10 black beans in the center of the leaf. Cover with 2 halves of banana and top with a final spoonful of rice. Cover the filling with the sides of the leaf, fold over the ends, and secure with string to form a package. Repeat until all the filling has been used. Steam the packages in a steamer for 40–45 minutes, then serve.

Photo p. 433

Glutinous Rice in Tiger Grass Leaf

Origin North
Preparation time 20 minutes, plus soaking time
Cooking time 1½ hours
Makes 20

2½ cups (1 lb 2 oz/500 g) glutinous (sticky) rice
½ cup (3½ oz/100 g) dried kidney beans
½ cup (3½ oz/200 g) granulated sugar
1 teaspoon salt
tiger grass leaves, for wrapping

Soak the rice in a bowl of water overnight or for at least 3 hours, then drain, rinse under cold running water, and drain again. Transfer to a bowl and set aside.

Soak the beans in another bowl of water for 2 hours, then drain, rinse, and put into a pan. Pour in enough water to cover and bring to a boil over medium heat. Boil for 50–60 minutes or until softened.

Add the beans to the rice and mix together thoroughly, then add the sugar and salt.

Lay a tiger grass leaf on a flat work surface. Put an ½-inch/1-cm mound of the rice and bean mixture into the center of the leaf. Fold the leaf into a triangular shape and secure with a bamboo strip. Repeat until all the filling is used.

Bring 12⅔ cups (5¼ pints/3 liters) water to a boil in a large pan, add the packages, reduce the heat, and simmer for 30 minutes. Remove the packages with a slotted spoon, let cool slightly, then serve.

Photo p. 434

ชาลาเปากรอบ

Crispy Stuffed Buns

Origin Central
Preparation time 15 minutes, plus soaking time
Cooking time 40–45 minutes
Serves 6

2 cups (10 oz/275 g) glutinous (sticky) rice flour
1 cup (5¾ oz/160 g) rice flour
½ cup (1½ oz/40 g) shredded fresh coconut
scant ½ cup (3½ oz/100 g) jaggery, palm sugar, or
  soft light brown sugar

For the filling
½ cup (3½ oz/100 g) split mung beans
⅔ cup (5 oz/150 g) jaggery, palm sugar, or soft light
  brown sugar
½ cup (1½ oz/40 g) shredded fresh coconut
2–3 cups (18–25 fl oz/500–700 ml) vegetable oil,
  for deep-frying

For the filling, soak the mung beans in a bowl of water for 2 hours.

Meanwhile, to make the dough, mix the flours together in a bowl. Gradually add ½–¾ cup (4–6 fl oz/120–175 ml) water, a little at a time, and mix until a dough starts to form. Use your hands to knead the dough and continue to add the remaining water. Add the shredded coconut and sugar and knead until the dough is sticky and can be shaped into a ball.

Drain the mung beans, then wrap in a piece of cheesecloth (muslin) and steam in a steamer for 25 minutes or until cooked.

Melt the sugar in a wok over low heat for 2–3 minutes until softened. Add the shredded coconut and mung beans and continue to cook until dry enough to mold into 1-inch/2.5-cm balls. Set aside.

Roll the dough out on a work surface to a thickness of ⅟₁₆ inch/2 mm and cut into circles with a 2½-inch/6-cm-diameter cookie cutter. Put a ball of filling into the center of a circle and fold over the dough to enclose the filling into a ball. Continue until all the filling is used.

Heat the oil for deep-frying in a large wok or deep fryer to 350°F/180°C or until a cube of bread browns in 30 seconds. Deep-fry the balls in batches for 7–8 minutes until crispy and golden brown, then remove with a slotted spoon and drain on paper towels. Serve.

ขนมไข่หงส์

Sugar-Coated Stuffed Dough Balls

Origin Central
Preparation time 10–15 minutes, plus soaking and resting times
Cooking time 1 hour 30 minutes
Serves 6

¼ cup (1½ oz/40 g) rice flour
1½ cups (8 oz/220 g) glutinous (sticky) rice flour
¼ teaspoon salt
1 tablespoon jaggery, palm sugar, or soft light brown sugar
2 tablespoons coconut milk
vegetable oil, for deep-frying
½ cup (3½ oz/100 g) superfine (caster) sugar

For the filling
½ cup (4 oz/120 g) split mung beans
1 tablespoon vegetable oil
1 shallot, finely chopped
1 tablespoon jaggery, palm sugar, or soft light brown sugar
¼ teaspoon salt
¼ teaspoon ground white pepper

For the filling, soak the mung beans in a bowl of water for 30 minutes. Drain, rinse, and drain again. Wrap the mung beans in cheesecloth (muslin) and steam in a steamer over medium heat for 20 minutes or until cooked. Remove from the cheesecloth and let cool. Process the mung beans in a food processor and set aside.

Heat the 1 tablespoon oil in a wok over medium heat. Add the shallot and stir-fry for 1 minute or until softened. Add the mung beans, sugar, salt, and white pepper, reduce the heat to medium-low, then stir until the sugar has dissolved and the mixture is thoroughly combined. Remove from the heat and set aside.

To make the dough, mix the rice flour, glutinous rice flour, and salt together in a large bowl. Add the sugar and crumble into the flour mixture. Gradually pour in the coconut milk and ½ cup (4 fl oz/120 ml) water, a little at a time, while using your other hand to crumble and mix the flour mixture in the water. Keep kneading the mixture until a smooth dough forms. Add a little more water if the dough is too dry. Cover with plastic wrap (clingfilm) and rest for 20 minutes.

Once the filling is cool, roll just under a tablespoon of the mixture into a ball and set aside. Repeat until all the filling is used.

Divide the dough into small portions and gently roll into balls and set aside. Repeat until all the dough is used. Take one dough ball at time, and flatten it by holding the ball in one hand and using your thumb to gently press down from the center of the ball, working your way outward until you have a dough circle that is about ⅛-inch/3-mm thick and 2½ inches/6 cm in diameter. Put a ball of filling in the middle of the circle and gently wrap the dough up to enclose the filling. Use your fingers to squeeze and tap to seal the dough together. Gently roll into a ball and set aside. Repeat until all the dough and filling are used.

Heat the oil for deep-frying in a wok or deep fryer to 350°F/180°C or until a cube of bread browns in 30 seconds. Deep-fry the dough balls, in batches, for about 8 minutes or until golden brown and crispy. Remove with a slotted spoon and drain on paper towels.

Bring the superfine (caster) sugar and ½ cup (4 fl oz/120 ml) water to a boil in a clean wok over medium heat. Let the sugar mixture boil for about 2½ minutes or until thickened. Remove from the heat and immediately add the deep-fried dough balls and stir until they are coated in the sugar syrup. Remove with a slotted spoon and let cool slightly. Serve.

Photo p. 437

ขนมถั่วแปบ

Sweet Mung Bean Packages

Origin Central
Preparation time 10 minutes, plus soaking time
Cooking time 45 minutes
Serves 4

⅔ cup (4 oz/120 g) split mung beans
⅔ cup (1½ oz/45 g) shredded fresh or dry unsweetened
  (desiccated) coconut
3 tablespoons granulated sugar
¼ teaspoon salt
2 tablespoons sesame seeds, toasted
1 cup (5oz /140 g) glutinous (sticky) rice flour

Soak the mung beans in a bowl of water for
2 hours, then drain and rinse. Wrap the beans
and coconut in separate pieces of cheesecloth
(muslin) and steam in a steamer for 25 minutes.

Meanwhile, mix the sugar, salt, and sesame
seeds together in a small bowl and set aside.

Mix the flour and 1 cup (9 fl oz/250 ml) water
together in a bowl until a dough forms. Knead
the dough until soft and smooth. Pinch off
pieces of dough and shape into small balls.

Bring a large pan of water to a boil over high
heat. Carefully place the dough balls into the
pan one by one. Boil for 5 minutes until cooked
and the balls float to the surface. Remove with
a slotted spoon and transfer to a large bowl.
Add a small amount of water to prevent the
balls from sticking together.

Spread the steamed mung beans and coconut
out on separate plates.

On a clean work surface, flatten the balls into
½-inch/1-cm-thick patties. Place 1–2 teaspoons
mung beans in the center of the patty and wrap
the edges over it to create an oval package.
Squeeze the edges to seal, roll in the steamed
mung beans, then place on a serving plate.
Repeat with each dough patty. Cover with the
steamed coconut, sprinkle with the sugar and
sesame seed mixture, and serve.

เต้าส่วน

Mung Bean Porridge with Coconut Milk

Origin Central
Preparation time 5 minutes, plus soaking time
Cooking time 30 minutes
Serves 2–3

½ cup (4 oz/120 g) split mung beans
½ cup (4 fl oz/120 ml) coconut cream
¼ teaspoon rice flour
a pinch of salt
½ cup (3½ oz/100 g) granulated sugar
1½ tablespoons tapioca flour
1 tablespoon arrowroot flour

Soak the mung beans in a bowl of water for
2 hours, then drain and rinse. Put the beans
in cheesecloth (muslin) and steam in a steamer
for 25 minutes or until cooked. Set aside.

Mix the coconut cream, rice flour, and salt
together in a pan and cook over low heat for
3–4 minutes or until thickened. Set aside.

Bring 3 cups (1¼ pints/750 ml) water to a boil
in another pan. Add the sugar and stir until
dissolved. Mix the tapioca flour, arrowroot
flour, and ¼ cup (2 fl oz/60 ml) water together
in a bowl. Continue to stir the sugar mixture
in the pan and gradually pour in the flour
mixture. Stir and cook for 1–2 minutes or until
thickened. Add the mung beans, then stir and
cook for another 3–4 minutes or until the mung
beans are fully flavored. Transfer to serving
bowls, pour over the coconut cream mixture,
and serve.

ซ่าหริ่ม

Colorful Mung Bean Noodles in Coconut Milk

Origin Central
Preparation time 10 minutes
Cooking time 30 minutes
Serves 4

1½ cups (7 oz/195 g) mung bean starch
  (mung bean flour)
1½ cups (12 fl oz/350 ml) Pandan Extract (see p. 63)
5–7 drops red food coloring
1 cup (8 oz/225 g) jaggery, palm sugar, or soft light
  brown sugar
1 cup (7 oz/200 g) granulated sugar
1 teaspoon salt
2 cups (16 fl oz/475 ml) coconut milk
Thai scented dessert candle, for smoking
ice cubes, to serve

Divide the mung bean starch (flour) into 3 equal portions to make *sa-lim* noodles in different colors. For the green noodles, mix ½ cup (2½ oz/65 g) starch, the pandan juice, and 1 cup (9 fl oz/250 ml) water together until thoroughly combined. For red noodles, mix ½ cup (2½ oz/65 g) starch, the red food coloring, and 2½ cups (1 pint/600 ml) water together until thoroughly combined. For white noodles, mix ½ cup (2½ oz/65 g) starch and 2½ cups (1 pint/600 ml) water together until thoroughly combined.

Fill a large pan with cold water and set aside.

Heat the first portion of starch in a separate pan over low heat for 7–9 minutes, stirring until translucent and shiny. When cooked, pour the mixture into a sa-lim mold or a potato ricer and slowly press the mixture through the mold, letting it drop into the pan of cold water. The mixture should resemble noodles. Let soak in the cold water for at least 10 minutes, then drain and wrap in cheesecloth (muslin). Transfer to a plate and set aside. Repeat with the second and third starch portions.

Heat the sugars, salt, and coconut milk in another pan over low heat, stirring, for about 5 minutes or until the sugars have dissolved.

Place the candle in a small bowl on a plate. Light both ends of the candle and let stand for 2 minutes. Blow out the candle and wait until the black smoke disappears and you can smell the aroma, then quickly put the candle (still in the bowl on a plate) into the pan of coconut milk syrup, cover with a lid, and let smoke for 10–15 minutes. This process can be repeated as many as 5–6 times for a more intense aroma. The candle can be used again if there is still some left after the dessert has been scented.

To serve, divide the different color mung bean noodles among serving bowls, pour the aromatic coconut milk over them, and add ice cubes.

Mung Bean Custard with Fried Shallots

Origin Central / South
Preparation time 45 minutes, plus soaking time
Cooking time 40 minutes
Serves 8

1¼ cups (7 oz/200 g) split mung beans
¾ cup (6 fl oz/175 ml) vegetable oil
10 shallots, halved lengthwise and finely sliced
4 eggs
1 cup (8 oz/225 g) jaggery, palm sugar, or soft light
  brown sugar
¼ teaspoon salt
¼ cup (1½ oz/40 g) rice flour
2½ cups (1 pint/600 ml) coconut milk

Soak the mung beans in a bowl of water for 2 hours, then drain and rinse. Put the beans in cheesecloth (muslin) and steam in a steamer for 25 minutes or until cooked. Pound the beans in a mortar with a pestle until fine, then transfer to a bowl and set aside.

For the crispy shallots, heat the oil in a wok over medium heat, add the shallots, and fry for 10–12 minutes or until golden brown. Set aside and reserve 2 tablespoons of the fried oil.

Preheat the oven to 400°F/200°C/Gas Mark 6. Grease a 12-inch/30-cm round baking pan with butter or oil.

Beat the eggs in a large bowl, then add the sugar, salt, and rice flour and mix well until the sugar has dissolved. Add the coconut milk, all but 1 tablespoon of the crispy shallots, and the reserved fried oil and mix well. Pour into the bowl containing the mung beans and mix well.

Heat the mixture in a pan over low heat for about 5 minutes stirring continuously until smooth. Pour the mixture into the greased pan. Bake for 30 minutes or until the mixture has risen and turned golden brown on top. Let cool slightly, then remove from the pan and sprinkle with the reserved crispy shallots. Serve.

Mung Bean Pudding with Ginkgo

Origin Central
Preparation time 10 minutes, plus soaking time
Cooking time 25 minutes
Serves 4

1¼ cups (8 oz/225 g) split mung beans
¾ cup (5oz/150 g) granulated sugar
2 cups (12 oz/350 g) shelled ginkgo nuts
1 cup (9 fl oz/250 ml) coconut cream
½ teaspoon salt

Soak the mung beans in a bowl of water for 2 hours, then drain and rinse.

Bring 3 cups (1¼ pints/750 ml) water in a pan to a boil, add the mung beans, and cook for 15 minutes or until softened. Add the sugar and ginkgo nuts, cook for another 10 minutes, then remove from the heat and transfer to a serving bowl.

Bring the coconut cream and salt to a boil in another pan over low-medium heat, then pour over the mung bean pudding and serve.

ขนมครองแครงกะทิ

Tapioca Balls in Coconut Milk

Origin Central
Preparation time 5 minutes
Cooking time 15 minutes
Serves 4

1 cup (4 oz/120 g) tapioca flour, plus extra for coating
1½ cups (9 oz/250 g) rice flour
½ cup (3½ oz/100 g) granulated sugar
½ teaspoon salt
1 cup (9 fl oz/250 ml) coconut cream
1 tablespoon white sesame seeds

Sift the tapioca flour and rice flour into a bowl, add about ½ cup (4 fl oz/120 ml) tepid water, and stir until doughlike. Remove from the heat and let cool. Knead the dough and then pinch off small pieces and roll into balls. Press each ball onto a krong krang press, gnocchi press, or use a fork. Coat in a little tapioca flour to prevent them from sticking together.

Bring 8½ cups (3½ pints/2 liters) water to a boil in a large pan. Add the tapioca balls and cook for 3 minutes or until transparent. Remove with a slotted spoon and put into a large bowl of cold water for 4–5 minutes. Transfer to a plate and set aside.

Bring the sugar, salt, and coconut cream to a boil in another pan, stirring occasionally. Add the dough balls and cook for 4–5 minutes. Transfer to serving bowls and sprinkle with sesame seeds. Serve.

ขนมมันถั่ก

Tapioca Dessert with Peanuts

Origin Central
Preparation time 5 minutes
Cooking time 15 minutes
Serves 4

vegetable oil, for greasing
1 cup (5¾ oz/160 g) rice flour
¼ cup (1 oz/30 g) tapioca flour

For the syrup
1 packed cup (8 oz/225 g) soft light brown sugar
2 tablespoons roasted peanuts, ground

Grease a shallow, square baking pan with oil.

Mix the flours and 2 cups (16 fl oz/475 ml) water together in a large bowl. Pour the batter into a pan and simmer for 10 minutes over low heat, stirring frequently. Transfer to the greased baking pan and let cool. Cut into 1-inch/2.5-cm squares and place on a serving plate.

For the syrup, mix the sugar and ½ cup (4 fl oz/120 ml) water together in a pan over medium heat and simmer, stirring, for 5 minutes or until syrupy. Pour the syrup over the squares, sprinkle with the ground peanuts, and serve.

ข้าวเหนียวแดง

Red Glutinous Rice with Sesame Seeds

Origin Central
Preparation time 5 minutes, plus soaking time
Cooking time 45–50 minutes
Serves 6

1⅔ cups (11 oz/300 g) glutinous (sticky) rice
1 cup (9 fl oz/250 ml) coconut milk
1⅓ cups (9¾ oz/275 g) jaggery, palm sugar, or soft light
  brown sugar
1 heaping tablespoon white sesame seeds, roasted
banana leaves, cut into 6-inch/15-cm diameter circles

Soak the rice in a large bowl of cold water
overnight or for at least 3 hours. Wash and
drain. Wrap the rice in cheesecloth (muslin)
and steam in a steamer for 30 minutes, stirring
the rice every 10 minutes, until cooked
through. Dry the steamed rice and let cool.

Prepare the banana-leaf cups. For each cup,
place 2 banana leaf circles back to back with
the shiny surface face outward on both sides.
From the outside of the circle, fold up about
1¼ inches/3 cm of banana leaf and then fold
in on itself to create a corner. Secure with a
toothpick or use a stapler. Repeat until there
are 4 corners.

Simmer the coconut milk and sugar in a wok
over medium heat until it begins to thicken.
Add the rice and stir until the rice becomes
light, dry, and crispy, about 15–20 minutes.

Carefully spoon the mixture into the banana
leaf cups and let cool. Sprinkle with the sesame
seeds and serve.

Photo p. 443

ข้าวตู

Dried Rice Balls

Origin South
Preparation time 10 minutes, plus cooling time
Cooking time 10 minutes
Serves 50 rice balls

scant ½ cup (3½ oz/100 g) packed brown sugar
¾ cup (6 fl oz/175 ml) jasmine water
3¾ cups (11 oz/300 g) shredded coconut
1⅓ cups (11 oz/300 g) jaggery, palm sugar, or soft light
  brown sugar
3½ cups (1 lb 8½ oz/700 g) Ground Toasted Rice
  (see p. 64)

Put the sugar and jasmine water in a bowl
and mix well. Transfer to a pan and put over
medium heat. Stir continuously for 3–5 minutes
until the sugar mixture begins to thicken. Add
the shredded coconut and stir continuously
until all the sugar has been absorbed and the
coconut has become sticky. Remove from the
heat and let cool.

Spread the rice out on a plate. Use a tablespoon
or damp hands to shape the cold coconut
mixture into bite-size balls, then roll the balls
in the ground rice.

Glutinous Rice Balls in Coconut Milk

Origin Central
Preparation time 10 minutes
Cooking time 30 minutes
Serves 7–10

For the green rice flour balls
10 pandan leaves, finely sliced
1 cup (5 oz/140 g) glutinous (sticky) rice flour

For the yellow rice flour balls
1 cup (4 oz/120 g) diced Thai pumpkin
1 cup (5 oz/140 g) glutinous (sticky) rice flour

For the purple rice flour balls
½ cup (2 oz/50 g) diced taro
1 cup (5 oz/140 g) glutinous (sticky) rice flour

For the coconut milk
3 cups (1¼ pints/750 ml) coconut milk
¾ cup (5 oz/150 g) granulated sugar
¼ cup (2 oz/50 g) jaggery, palm sugar, or soft
  light brown sugar
1 teaspoon salt
2 knotted pandan leaves
meat from 2 coconuts
1 cup (8 fl oz/250 ml) coconut cream

To make the green rice balls, smash the pandan leaves in a mortar with a pestle, then pound to a paste. Add 1 cup (9 fl oz/250 ml) water and instantly squeeze with your hands to get 3 tablespoons thick pandan juice. Mix the glutinous (sticky) rice flour and pandan juice together in a bowl to form a sticky dough, then knead. Gradually add ½ cup (4 fl oz/120 ml) water to the dough until no longer sticky. Divide the dough into small portions and roll into balls. Set aside.

For the yellow rice balls, steam the pumpkin in a steamer for 3 minutes or until soft, let cool, then pound in a mortar with a pestle. Mix the rice flour and pounded pumpkin together in a bowl, then knead. Gradually add ½ cup (4 fl oz/ 120 ml) water to the dough until no longer sticky. Divide the dough into small portions and roll into balls. Set aside.

For the purple rice balls, steam the taro in a steamer for 3–4 minutes or until soft, let cool, then pound in a mortar with a pestle. Mix the rice flour and the pounded taro in a bowl, then knead. Gradually add ½ cup (4 fl oz/120 ml) water to the dough until no longer sticky. Divide the dough into small portions and roll into balls. Set aside.

Bring a large pan of water to a boil over medium heat, add the rice balls, and cook for 4–5 minutes or until they float to the surface. Remove with a slotted spoon and set aside.

For the coconut milk, bring the coconut milk, sugars, salt, pandan leaves, and coconut meat to a boil in a pan. Reduce the heat and cook, stirring continuously, for 3–4 minutes. Add the rice flour balls and return to a boil. Remove from the heat and stir in the coconut cream. Serve hot or cold.

Ginkgo Nuts and Dates in Longan Syrup

Origin Central
Preparation time 10 minutes
Cooking time 15 minutes
Serves 8–10

1 cup (7 oz/200 g) dried longans, rinsed
1 cup (5 oz/150 g) dried jujube (Chinese dates), rinsed
1 cup (6 oz/175 g) shelled ginkgo nuts
1 packed cup (8 oz/225 g) soft light brown sugar

Put 12⅔ cups (5¼ pints/3 liters) water, the dried longans, dried jujube, and ginkgo in a large pan and bring to a boil over medium heat. Reduce the heat to low and simmer for about 15 minutes, adding more water if necessary. Add the sugar to taste, then transfer to a heatproof serving bowl and serve.

Ginkgo Nuts, Taro, and Coconut Dessert

Origin Central
Preparation time 10 minutes
Cooking time 25 minutes
Serves 10–15

1½ cups (11 oz/300 g) granulated sugar
5¾ cups 2¼ lb/1 kg shelled ginkgo nuts
2 cups (7 oz/200 g) diced taro
water and meat of 2 young coconuts
2 tablespoons tapioca flour
1 cup (9 fl oz/250 ml) coconut cream
1 teaspoon salt

Bring 8½ cups (3½ pints/2 liters) water and the sugar to a boil in a pan over medium heat. Add the ginkgo nuts and taro, reduce the heat, and simmer for about 15 minutes, until softened. Add the coconut water and meat and continue to simmer for 5 minutes.

Dissolve the tapioca flour in 2 tablespoons water, then gradually pour into the pan, stirring continuously. Bring to a boil, then remove from the heat and set aside.

Bring the coconut cream to a boil in another pan, add the salt, stir, and return to a boil. Remove from the heat.

Put the ginkgo nuts and coconut meat in small serving bowls and pour the coconut cream over them. Serve.

ข้าวต้มหัวหงอก

Glutinous Rice with Coconut and Black Sesame

Origin North
Preparation time 30 minutes, plus soaking time
Cooking time 1 hour
Serves 8–10

2½ cups (1 lb 2 oz/500 g) glutinous (sticky) rice
5 banana leaves, cut into 2 x 6-inch/5 x 15-cm
  long strips
4¼ cups (11 oz/300 g) dry unsweetened
  (desiccated) coconut
¾ cup (3½ oz/100 g) black sesame seeds
1 cup (7 oz/200 g) granulated sugar

Soak the rice in a large bowl of water overnight or for at least 3 hours, then drain.

Lay a banana leaf on a flat work surface. Place a little of the rice at one end of the leaf, leaving a 2½-inch/1-cm border. Carefully fold the leaf and the filling diagonally to create a triangle. Continue to fold, creating triangles until the end of the leaf is reached. Secure with toothpicks. Repeat until all the rice is used.

Bring 4 cups (1⅔ pints/950 ml) water to a boil in a large pan over medium heat. Carefully drop the packages into the water, return to a boil, and reduce the heat. Cover with a lid and simmer for 1 hour. Remove the packages with a slotted spoon, drain, and let cool.

Put the the coconut, sesame seeds, and sugar in a small bowl and mix well. Set aside.

Unwrap the packages and discard the banana leaves. Roll the rice in the coconut, sesame seeds, and sugar mixture. Serve.

ถั่วเคลือบ

Sesame and Sugar-Coated Peanuts

Origin Central
Preparation time 5 minutes
Cooking time 35 minutes
Serves 4

2 cups (11 oz/300 g) raw peanuts
1¼ cups (9 oz/250 g) granulated sugar
¼ teaspoon salt
2 tablespoons white sesame seeds

Rinse the peanuts in plenty of cold water, then drain and set aside.

Put ½ cup (4 fl oz/120 ml) water, the peanuts, and sugar in a wok over medium heat and bring to a boil. Reduce the heat to medium-low and simmer, stirring continuously for about 20 minutes or until thickened. Be careful not to let the sugar boil and caramelize. Remove from the heat and continue stirring until the sugar cools, dries, and coats the peanuts.

Sprinkle with the salt, and put the pan back over medium heat. Stir continuously for about 10 minutes until the sugar coating the peanuts starts to melt again. Add the sesame seeds and stir until the peanuts are well coated, then remove from the heat. Transfer to a large tray and use a spatula to separate the peanuts. Let cool, then serve.

Photo p. 446

มันเทศต้มน้ำขิง
Sweet Potato in Ginger Syrup

Origin South
Preparation time 10 minutes
Cooking time 15 minutes
Serves 10

1 cup (7 oz/200 g) granulated sugar
¼ teaspoon salt
3 sweet potatoes, cut into 1½-inch/4-cm cubes
1 cup (3¼ oz/90 g) peeled and sliced fresh ginger
  (1¼-inch/3-cm-thick pieces)

Bring 4 cups (1⅔ pints/950 ml) water to a boil in a large pan over medium heat. Add the sugar and salt and return to a boil for 1–2 minutes. Add the sweet potatoes and ginger and continue to boil for another 10–12 minutes. Remove from the heat and let cool for 10 minutes. Serve hot or cold.

สังขยาไข่ขยาฟักทอง
Pumpkin Custard

Origin Central
Preparation time 15 minutes
Cooking time 20 minutes
Serves 16

11 duck eggs
1⅔ cups (14 fl oz/400 ml) coconut milk
2 cups (1 lb/450 g) jaggery, palm sugar, or soft light
  brown sugar
3 cups (12 oz/350 g) peeled, seeded, and sliced
  pumpkin batons (about 1½ inches/4 cm long and
  ½ inch/1 cm wide)

Beat the eggs in a bowl until lightly foamy.

Mix the coconut milk and sugar together in another bowl until well blended, then pour into the beaten egg and mix well. Strain the mixture through a strainer (sieve) into an 8-inch/20-cm square baking pan, 2 inches/ 5 cm deep. Sprinkle with the pumpkin batons and steam in a steamer over high heat for about 20 minutes or until firm. Let cool, then cut the custard into 16 squares and serve.

Photo p. 449

สังขยาฟักทอง
Coconut Custard in Pumpkin

Origin Central
Preparation time 15 minutes
Cooking time 30–40 minutes
Serves 4

1 small pumpkin, about 5 inches/12 cm in diameter
4 duck eggs, beaten
⅔ cup (5 fl oz/150 ml) coconut cream
¾ cup (6 oz/175 g) jaggery, palm sugar, or soft light
  brown sugar
½ teaspoon salt
2 pandan leaves

Remove the top of the Thai pumpkin by cutting around the stem to create a "lid" about 3½ inches/8 cm in diameter. Set the lid aside. Scoop out the seeds with a spoon. Set aside.

Whisk the eggs and coconut cream together in a bowl, add the sugar, salt, and pandan leaves, and mix well. Use your hand to squeeze the mixture until the pandan leaves are soft and aromatic and the sugar has dissolved. Strain through cheesecloth (muslin) or a fine strainer (sieve) and pour into the pumpkin. Fill to just under the top of the pumpkin.

Carefully place the pumpkin and its lid (on the side), into a large steamer, at least twice the size of the pumpkin. Steam over medium heat for 35–40 minutes or until the custard is firm and cooked and the pumpkin is soft. Let cool slightly, then serve whole with the reserved lid on top.

Pumpkin in Syrup

ฟักทองเชื่อม

Origin Central
Preparation time 10 minutes, plus soaking time
Cooking time 15–20 minutes
Serves 10

3¼-lb/1.5-kg pumpkin, peeled and cut into
  bite-size pieces
8½ cups (3½ pints/2 liters) limewater (see p. 509)
½ cup (4 fl oz/120 ml) coconut cream
½ teaspoon salt
1 tablespoon rice flour
1½ cups (11 oz/300 g) granulated sugar
½ teaspoon lime juice

Soak the pumpkin in the limewater for about
30 minutes, then rinse and drain.

Bring the coconut cream to a boil in a pan
over low heat and add the salt. Add the rice
flour and stir occasionally until the coconut
milk has thickened.

Bring 1½ cups (12 fl oz/350 ml) water, the sugar,
and lime juice to a boil in another pan over
medium heat. Boil, stirring occasionally until
the sugar has dissolved, then add the pumpkin.
Cook for about 10 minutes until the pumpkin
is glossy. Transfer to a serving bowl, pour the
coconut milk over the top, and serve.

Wax Gourd Dessert

ขนมฟัก

Origin South
Preparation time 10 minutes
Cooking time 30 minutes
Serves 5–6

2 cups (9¼ oz/260 g) peeled and grated wax gourd
1⅓ cups (7 oz/190 g) tapioca flour
1 cup (8 oz/225 g) jaggery, palm sugar, or soft light
  brown sugar
1 cup (3 oz/80 g) peeled and grated overripe coconut
1 teaspoon salt
banana leaves, cut into 8-inch/20-cm wide strips

Put the grated wax gourd in cheesecloth
(muslin) and squeeze into a bowl to remove
any excess liquid. Discard the liquid and put
the damp wax gourd flesh in a bowl. Sprinkle
with the tapioca flour and mix well. Add the
sugar, grated coconut, and salt and mix again.
The mixture should be neither too thick nor
too dry.

Lay a banana leaf on a work surface. Put
2 tablespoons of the wax gourd mixture in
the center of the leaf. Cover the filling with the
sides of the leaf and fold over the ends to make
a package. Secure with toothpicks. Repeat until
all the wax gourd mixture is used.

Place the packages in a steamer and steam
over over high heat for 30 minutes or until
cooked. Let cool, then serve.

ขนมครก

Coconut Cakes
with Herbs

Origin Central
Preparation time 10 minutes,
Cooking time 30 minutes
Serves 10

scant 3¼ cups (1 lb 2 oz/500 g) rice flour
10½ cups (4½ pints/2.5 liters) coconut milk
1 tablespoon salt
1½ cups (11 oz/300 g) granulated sugar
½ cup (4 fl oz/120 ml) vegetable oil, for coating
2 cilantro (coriander) sprigs, chopped
2 scallions (spring onions), chopped

For the batter, mix the rice flour with 2 cups
(16 fl oz/475 ml) tepid water in a bowl.

Mix the coconut milk, salt, sugar, cilantro
(coriander), and scallions (spring onions)
together in another bowl.

Coat the *khanom krok* pan or pancake puff pan
with oil and place over medium heat. The pan
is ready when a small drop of batter sizzles.
Stir the batter and carefully pour a little into the
molds until about two-thirds full, then carefully
pour the coconut milk mixture on top to fill the
molds. Cover with a lid and cook for about
5 minutes before removing the desserts from
the molds with a spoon or fork. Serve.

วุ้นในลูกมะพร้าว

Gelatin in Young Coconut

Origin Central
Preparation time 35 minutes, plus setting and
chilling time
Cooking time 5 minutes
Serves 3

3 fresh young coconuts
⅓ cup (2¾ oz/65 g) granulated sugar
1½ tablespoons gelatin powder

Open the coconuts, pour out the water into a
bowl, and set aside. Scrape out the flesh in thin
layers with a spoon. Distribute the flesh evenly
among the coconut shells.

Strain the water through cheesecloth (muslin)
and bring to a boil in a pan. Add the gelatin
powder, reduce the heat, and simmer for
5 minutes. Pour the coconut water mixture back
into the coconuts and let set for 30 minutes.
Chill in the refrigerator until ready to serve.

ขนมถ้วย

Coconut Milk Custard

Origin North
Preparation time 15 minutes
Cooking time 20 minutes
Makes 40 custards in talai cups

1 cup (9 fl oz/250 ml) unshaken can coconut milk,
   cream and milk separated
½ teaspoon salt
1½ cups (9 oz/250 g) rice flour
½ cup plus 2 tablespoons (4½ oz/125 g) jaggery, palm
   sugar, or soft light brown sugar

Season the coconut cream with salt. Set aside.

Mix the coconut milk and the rice flour together
in a large bowl, add the sugar, and stir well.

Pour the mixture into small talai cups or small
heatproof cups or bowls about three-quarters
full and steam in a steamer for 10 minutes
until cooked.

Pour the coconut cream over the rice mixture
and continue to steam for another 10 minutes
until the coconut cream is cooked. Serve.

สาคูมะพร้าวอ่อน

Tapioca and Young Coconut in Coconut Milk

Origin Central
Preparation time 5 minutes
Cooking time 15 minutes
Serves 4

1 cup (5 oz/150 g) small tapioca pearls
½ cup (3½ oz/100 g) superfine (caster) sugar
1½ cups (3½ oz/100 g) shredded fresh coconut
1¼ cups (½ pint/300 ml) coconut milk
¼ teaspoon salt

Bring about 5 cups (2 pints/1.2 liters) water to a boil in a pan over medium-high heat.

Put the tapioca pearls in a strainer (sieve) and dip in water, then shake once. Add to the pan of boiling water and cook for about 7 minutes, stirring occasionally until the tapioca pearls are cooked and translucent. Add the sugar and coconut meat and gently stir until the sugar has dissolved, then remove from the heat.

Heat the coconut milk and salt in another pan over low heat for about 5 minutes. Transfer the tapioca to small serving bowls with the coconut milk on the side.

กล้วยทอด

Fried Bananas

Origin Central
Preparation time 15 minutes
Cooking time 15 minutes
Serves 6

1 tablespoon superfine (caster) sugar
¾ cup (4 oz/120 g) rice flour`
¼ cup (1 oz/30 g) all-purpose (plain) flour
⅔ cup (1½ oz/45 g) dry unsweetened (desiccated) coconut
1 cup (9 fl oz/250 ml) coconut milk
2 tablespoons white sesame seeds
1 teaspoons salt
6–8 semi-ripe small bananas, peeled and sliced into ½-inch/1-cm lengths
5 cups (2 pints/1.2 liters) vegetable oil, for deep-frying

Mix the sugar, flours, coconut, coconut milk, sesame seeds, salt, and ¼ cup (2 fl oz/60 ml) water together in a large bowl until the sugar and flour have dissolved.

Dip the bananas into the batter and make sure they are well coated.

Heat the oil for deep-frying in a wok or deep fryer to 350°F/180°C or until a cube of bread browns in 30 seconds. Deep-fry the bananas for 6–7 minutes or until golden and crispy, then remove with a slotted spoon and drain on paper towels. Serve.

ข้าวต้มมัดใบกระพ้อ

Glutinous Rice, Beans, and Banana in Palm Leaves

Origin South
Preparation time 10 minutes, plus soaking time
Cooking time 50 minutes
Serves 6

2½ cups (1 lb 2 oz/500 g) glutinous (sticky) rice
1⅔ cups (14 fl oz/400 ml) coconut milk
1 teaspoon salt
1 cup (7 oz/200 g) superfine (caster) sugar
⅔ cup (3½ oz/100 g) cooked black beans
10 small ripe bananas, cut lengthwise into 3 slices
palm leaves, for wrapping

Soak the rice in a bowl of water for about
1 hour, then drain and set aside.

Bring the coconut milk and salt to a boil in
a wok or pan over medium heat. Add the
rice and cook, stirring constantly, for about
5 minutes until dry. Add the sugar and stir-fry
for another 5 minutes. Remove from the heat,
add the black beans, and stir. Let cool.

Lay a palm leaf on a work surface, then put a
tablespoon of the rice mixture between 2 thin
slices of banana on top of the leaf. Fold the leaf
to make a package and secure with toothpicks.
Repeat until all the filling is used. Steam in a
steamer for about 40 minutes until the rice
becomes sticky. Serve.

กล้วยต้มคลุกมะพร้าว

Banana with Shredded Coconut and Sesame Seeds

Origin Central
Preparation time 5 minutes
Cooking time 20 minutes
Serves 8

1 cup (3 oz/80 g) shredded coconut
1 teaspoon salt
10 semi-ripe small bananas, peeled
1 teaspoon sesame seeds, roasted
2 tablespoons granulated sugar

Mix the shredded coconut and salt together
in a small bowl and set aside.

Bring a medium pan of water to a boil, add the
bananas, and cook for 20 minutes. Drain the
bananas in a colander and cool under cold
running water, then slice lengthwise. Put the
banana slices into the coconut mixture and roll
to coat. Place on a serving plate and sprinkle
with sesame seeds and sugar. Serve.

กล้วยน้ำว้าเชื่อม

Bananas in Syrup

Origin Central
Preparation time 5 minutes
Cooking time 40 minutes
Serves 8

10 semi-ripe small bananas, peeled
2½ cups (1 lb 2 oz/500 g) granulated sugar

Bring a medium pan of water to a boil, add
the bananas, reduce the heat, and simmer for
10 minutes until tender. Remove with a slotted
spoon and cut into 1-inch/2.5-cm-thick slices.
Set aside.

Bring the sugar and 1½ cups (12 fl oz/350 ml)
water to a boil in another pan and boil for
3–4 minutes, stirring, until the sugar has
dissolved. Add the banana pieces, reduce the
heat, and cook for 30 minutes or until the syrup
thickens and the bananas turn red. Serve.

กล้วยคลุกมะพร้าว

Banana with Shredded Coconut

Origin Central
Preparation time 5 minutes
Cooking time 10 minutes
Serves 5

1 cup (3 oz/80 g) shredded young coconut meat
10 ripe small bananas
2 tablespoons granulated sugar
½ teaspoon salt

Spread the shredded coconut out in a shallow bowl or plate.

Steam the unpeeled bananas in a steamer for about 10 minutes or until soft and tender. Peel the bananas, then cut into 1-inch/2.5-cm pieces and roll in the shredded coconut until coated.

Mix the sugar and salt together in a small bowl and sprinkle over the bananas. Serve.

ขนมกล้วย

Sweet Banana

Origin Central
Preparation time 5 minutes
Cooking time 30 minutes
Serves 5

1¼ cups (3½ oz/100 g) shredded fresh coconut
½ teaspoon salt
10 ripe small bananas, peeled and mashed
1 cup (5¾ oz/160 g) rice flour
1 cup (7 oz/200 g) jaggery, palm sugar, or soft light brown sugar
1 cup (9 fl oz/250 ml) coconut milk

Mix the shredded coconut and the salt together in a small bowl. Reserve half for the garnish.

Put the bananas, rice flour, sugar, the mixed shredded coconut and salt, and the coconut milk into a large bowl and mix well. Pour into small talal cups or heatproof cups or bowls and sprinkle with the reserved shredded coconut. Steam in a steamer for 30 minutes, then serve.

Photo p. 454

กล้วยไข่เชื่อม

Caramelized Bananas

Origin Central
Preparation time 10 minutes
Cooking time 30–35 minutes
Serves 4

1½ cups (11 oz/300 g) superfine (caster) sugar
2 pandan leaves, sliced
8 semi-ripe small bananas, peeled, or 4 ordinary bananas, halved crosswise
1 teaspoon lime juice
½ cup (4 fl oz/120 ml) coconut milk
1 teaspoon all-purpose (plain) flour
a pinch of salt

Bring 2 cups (16 fl oz/475 ml) water to a boil in a wok over medium heat, add the sugar, then reduce the heat and simmer for 5 minutes. Add the pandan leaves, return to a boil, then remove from the heat.

Strain the syrup through a fine strainer (sieve) into a pan and discard the pandan leaves. Add the bananas to the pan, put over medium-low heat, and simmer for 12–15 minutes on each side or until the bananas turn glossy and have fully absorbed the syrup. Sprinkle over the lime juice and remove from the heat. Transfer to a serving plate and set aside.

Mix the coconut milk, flour, and salt together in a small pan, then put over medium-low heat for 2–3 minutes or until thickened. Remove from the heat and drizzle over the caramelized bananas. Serve immediately.

กล้วยบวชชี

Bananas in Coconut Milk

Origin Central
Preparation time 5 minutes
Cooking time 25 minutes
Serves 5

1 tablespoon split mung beans
10 small bananas, peeled
2 cups (16 fl oz/475 ml) coconut milk
1 teaspoon salt
1½ cups (11 oz/300 g) granulated sugar

Dry-fry the mung beans in a wok over low heat
for 5 minutes until roasted, shaking and stirring
to prevent the beans from burning. Meanwhile,
bring a small pan of water to a boil, then add
the mung beans and cook for 5 minutes.

Bring another pan of water to a boil, add the
bananas, and boil for 10 minutes. Drain and
transfer to a bowl of cold water for 3–4 minutes.
Drain, then cut the bananas in half lengthwise
and then into 1-inch/2.5-cm slices.

Bring the coconut milk to a simmer in a wok
over low heat, add the mung beans, and cook
for 10 minutes. Add the salt, sugar, and bananas
and cook for another 5 minutes. Serve.

กล้วยน้ำว้าเชื่อม

Jackfruit and Tapioca Threads in Coconut Milk

Origin Central
Preparation time 20 minutes
Cooking time 5 minutes
Serves 4

1 cup (7 oz/200 g) granulated sugar
generous ¾ cup (3½ oz/100 g) tapioca flour, plus extra
  for sprinkling
1 teaspoon red food coloring
1 teaspoon green food coloring
1⅔ cups (14 fl oz/400ml) coconut milk
1½ cups (9 oz/250 g) sliced jackfruit
ice cubes, to serve
1 teaspoon salt

To make the sugar syrup, bring ¾ cup (6 fl oz/
175 ml) water and the sugar to a boil in a pan
over medium heat. Stir until the sugar has
dissolved and the mixture is syrupy.

Put the tapioca flour into a large bowl and
gradually add scant ½ cup (3½ fl oz/100 ml)
hot water, stirring quickly. Knead for 5 minutes
until a dough forms.

Divide the dough into 3 portions. Mix one
portion with the green food coloring, another
with the red, and leave the third portion
uncolored. Knead each portion separately on
a lightly dusted work surface.

Have a bowl of cold water ready. Bring a pan
of water to a boil.

Using a rolling pin, roll the 3 portions of dough
into thin sheets, then slice into thin threads.
Sprinkle with a little tapioca flour to prevent
them from sticking together. Put the threads
into the pan of boiling water and cook for
3–4 minutes or until transparent. Remove
with a slotted spoon and transfer to the bowl
of cold water.

Bring the coconut milk and salt to a boil in
another pan over medium heat, then remove
from the heat.

Divide the tapioca threads and sliced jackfruit
among small serving bowls, pour the coconut
milk and sugar syrup over them, and add a few
ice cubes. Serve.

ข้าวเหนียวเปียกลำไยดอกอัญชัญ

Rice Pudding with Longans and Butterfly Pea Flowers

Origin Central
Preparation time 15 minutes, plus soaking time
Cooking time 20 minutes
Serves 4

1 cup (7 oz/200 g) glutinous (sticky) rice
1 small handful fresh butterfly pea flowers
¾ cup (5 oz/150 g) granulated sugar
2 cups (14 oz/400 g) seeded longans
1 cup (9 fl oz/250 ml) coconut cream
1 teaspoon salt

Soak the rice in a bowl of water overnight. The next day, drain and rinse under cold running water.

Bring 3 cups (1¼ pints/750 ml) water to a boil in a pan. Add the rice and butterfly pea flowers and cook for about 15 minutes or until the rice is softened. Add the sugar and longans, then remove the pan from the heat and set aside.

Bring the coconut cream to a boil in another pan over low-medium heat, then stir in the salt.

Put the rice mixture into a serving bowl and pour the coconut cream over it. Serve.

สาคูเปียกลำไย

Tapioca with Longan

Origin Central
Preparation time 5 minutes
Cooking time 12 minutes
Serves 4

1 cup (5 oz/150 g) small tapioca pearls
½ cup (3½ oz/100 g) superfine (caster) sugar
1 cup (7 oz/200 g) peeled and seeded longans
1¼ cups (10 fl oz/300 ml) coconut milk
¼ teaspoon salt

Bring about 5 cups (2 pints/1.2 liters) water to a boil in a pan over medium-high heat.

Put the tapioca pearls in a strainer (sieve) and dip in water, then shake once. Add to the pan of boiling water and cook for about 7 minutes, stirring occasionally, until the tapioca pearls are cooked and translucent. Remove from the heat and drain. Return to the pan, add the sugar, and longans, and gently stir until the sugar has dissolved.

Heat the coconut milk and salt in another pan over low heat for about 5 minutes. Transfer the tapioca and longan mixture to a serving bowl and pour the coconut milk over it. Serve.

Photo p. 458

ข้าวเหนียวมะม่วง

Glutinous Rice with Mango

Origin Central
Preparation time 10 minutes, plus soaking
and standing times
Cooking time 35 minutes
Serves 6

1½ cups (11 oz/300 g) glutinous (sticky) rice
¼ cup (2 oz/50 g) split mung beans
½ cup (4 fl oz/120 ml) coconut milk
½ cup (3½ oz/100 g) superfine (caster) sugar
¼ teaspoon salt
2 ripe mangoes, peeled and cut to 1¼-inch/
  3-cm-wide slices

Soak the rice in a bowl of water for at least
3 hours, or preferably overnight, then rinse
and drain.

Soak the beans in a bowl of water for 1 hour.
Drain and pat dry with paper towels.

Wrap the rice in cheesecloth (muslin) and
steam in a steamer for 30–35 minutes. Stir
every 10 minutes. The rice will look transparent
when cooked.

Put the coconut milk, sugar, and salt in a small
pan over low-medium heat and stir until the
sugar has dissolved. Remove from the heat and
set aside. Reserve about ⅓ cup (2½ fl oz/75 ml)
for the topping.

Toast the mung beans in a dry skillet or frying
pan over low-medium heat, stirring frequently,
for 5 minutes, or until they turn dark yellow and
have completely dried.

Once the rice is cooked, transfer to a bowl
and add the sweet coconut milk. Mix together
well, cover with plastic wrap (clingfilm), and let
stand for 10–15 minutes.

Top the sweet rice with the toasted mung
beans and serve with mango slices.

Photo p. 460

มังคุดลอยแก้ว

Mangosteen in Syrup

Origin Central
Preparation time 5 minutes, plus marinating time
Serves 4

2½ cups (1 lb 2 oz/500 g) superfine (caster) sugar
½ teaspoon salt
1 lb 2 oz/500 g mangosteen, peeled and seeded
crushed ice, to serve

Bring 4 cups (1⅔ pints/950 ml) water to a
boil in a large pan over medium heat. Add
the sugar and salt and return to a boil for
1–2 minutes or until the sugar has dissolved.
Add the mangosteen and continue to boil over
low heat until softened. Remove from the heat
and let cool. Transfer to a bowl, cover with
plastic wrap (clingfilm), and let marinate in
the refrigerator for 24 hours.

Remove the mangosteen from the refrigerator,
add crushed ice, and serve cold.

ลอดช่องกะทิสด

Pandan Leaf Noodles in Coconut Milk Syrup

Origin Northeast
Preparation time 10 minutes
Cooking time 25 minutes
Serves 6

1 cup (9 fl oz/250 ml) limewater (see p.509) or
   club soda (soda water)
3½ oz/100 g pandan leaves, finely sliced
1½ cups (9 oz/250 g) rice flour
¼ cup (1 oz/25 g) arrowroot flour
1 tablespoon mung bean flour
ice cubes, to serve

For the coconut milk syrup
2 cups (16 fl oz/475 ml) coconut milk
1 cup (8 oz/225 g) jaggery, palm sugar, or soft
   light brown sugar
½ teaspoon salt

Process the pandan leaves with 3 cups (1¼ pints/750 ml) water in a food processor until thoroughly combined. Pour the blended mixture through a very fine strainer (sieve) or cheesecloth (muslin) into another bowl. Set aside only the extract.

Mix the flours together well in a large bowl, then gradually stir in the limewater or club soda (soda water) until a dough forms. Knead the dough for 4–5 minutes, then add the pandan extract and use your hands to mix until smooth.

Prepare a large bowl of ice-cold water.

Put the flour mixture into a nonstick pan or wok over medium heat and stir for 6–7 minutes until the mixture starts to thicken. Reduce the heat to low and stir for another 4–5 minutes until the mixture is thick, dark green, and glossy, with a gooey syrupy consistency. The mixture should not be too watery or too thick. If the batter is too thick add a little more water and stir until mixed. Transfer to a potato ricer and let drip into the bowl of ice-cold water. Let stand in the ice-cold water for 5–7 minutes until firm and set. Transfer to a clean bowl, using a slotted spoon, and set aside.

Put the coconut milk, sugar, and salt into a pan over low heat, and stir for about 5 minutes or until the sugar has dissolved. Remove from the heat and let cool.

Divide the dough strands among serving bowls and pour over the cooled coconut milk syrup. Top with ice cubes, then serve.

Candied Sugar Palm Fruit

จาวตาลเชื่อม

Origin Central
Preparation time: 10 minutes, plus soaking time
Cooking time 1–2 hours
Serves 7–8

25 mature sugar palm fruit
1 shredded banana leaf
¼ oz/10 g ground alum
5 cups (2¼ lb/1 kg) granulated sugar

To serve
1 banana leaf

Rinse the sugar palm fruit and scrub its skin with the shredded banana leaf to remove its grease, then rinse again under cold running water.

Mix the ground alum and 4¼ cups (1¾ pints/ 1 liter) water together in a large bowl. Soak the sugar palm fruit in the alum water for 30 minutes, then remove and rinse under cold running water.

Bring a pan of water to a boil, add the sugar palm fruit, and boil for 5 minutes. Remove with a slotted spoon and set aside.

To prepare the sugar syrup, mix 6¼ cups (2½ pints/1.5 liters) water and 3 cups (1 lb 5 oz/ 600 g) of the sugar together in a pan and bring to a boil. Add the sugar palm fruit, reduce the heat, and simmer over medium heat for 1–2 hours. Add more water if necessary. Gradually add the remaining sugar until the fruit has absorbed the sugar and become shiny. Let cool, then serve the candied fruit on the whole banana leaf.

Photo p. 463

Muskmelon in Coconut Milk

น้ำกะทิแตงไทย

Origin Central
Preparation time 5 minutes
Cooking time 10 minutes
Serves 7

scant 1 cup (7 fl oz/200 ml) coconut milk
1 cup (8 oz/225 g) jaggery, palm sugar, or soft light
  brown sugar
1 teaspoon salt
1 muskmelon or cantaloupe, peeled, seeded,
  and cut into bite-size pieces
crushed ice cubes, to serve

Heat the coconut milk in a pan over low heat. Add the sugar and salt and stir continuously until it reaches a gentle boil. Remove from the heat and let cool.

Put about 7 cubes of muskmelon or cantaloupe into a serving bowl. Add the coconut milk syrup and some crushed ice cubes and serve.

ขนมเปียกปูนใบเตย

Pandan Pudding

Origin Central
Preparation time 10 minutes
Cooking time 10 minutes
Serves 4

vegetable oil, for greasing
10 pandan leaves
½ cup (3 oz/80 g) rice flour (ground flour)
1 tablespoon mung bean flour
½ tablespoon tapioca flour
1 cup (9 fl oz/250 ml) limewater (see p.509) or
  club soda (soda water)
1½ tablespoons granulated sugar
⅓ cup (2¾ oz/75 g) jaggery, palm sugar, or soft light
  brown sugar
1 cup (3 oz/80 g) grated fresh coconut

Grease a baking sheet with oil and set aside.

Put the pandan leaves and 1 cup (9 fl oz/
250 ml) water in a food processor and blend
until smooth.

Mix the flours together in a wok or pan, then
gradually add the red limewater or club
soda (soda water), stirring constantly. Add
the pandan juice and stir until smooth. Add
the sugars and stir again until thoroughly
combined. Put over medium heat and stir
constantly until the mixture begins to cook.
Reduce the heat slightly and stir until shiny,
solid, and dark green in color. This will take
7–8 minutes in total.

Pour the mixture onto the prepared baking
sheet. Use a spatula to spread the mixture
over the surface of the baking sheet. Let cool.
Cut into 2½-inch/6-cm squares, then remove
from the tray. Sprinkle with the grated coconut
and serve.

Photo p. 464

วุ้นกะทิใบเตย

Pandan and Coconut Milk Gelatin

Origin Central
Preparation time 8 minutes, plus setting and
chilling time
Cooking time 10 minutes
Serves 6

For the coconut gelatin (jelly)
2 cups (16 fl oz/475 ml) coconut milk
1 tablespoon gelatin powder
½ teaspoon salt
½ cup (3½ oz/100 g) granulated sugar

For the pandan gelatin (jelly)
1½ tablespoons gelatin powder
1 cup (7 oz/200 g) plus 1 tablespoon granulated sugar
1 cup (9 fl oz/250 ml) pandan juice

To make the coconut gelatin (jelly), heat the
coconut milk in a pan to 104–122°F/40–50°C,
then add the gelatin powder. Stir until the
gelatin melts, then add the salt. Stir and bring
to a boil. Reduce the heat, add the sugar, and
stir until the sugar has dissolved. Fill a shallow
tray halfway with the mixture and let cool at
room temperature for about 25 minutes.

To make the pandan gelatin, heat 3 cups
(1¼ pints/750 ml) water in a pan to 104–122°F/
40–50°C and add the gelatin powder. Stir until
the gelatin melts, then bring to a boil over low
heat and continue to stir. Reduce the heat, add
the sugar, and stir until the sugar has dissolved.
Pour in the pandan juice and stir to combine.

When the coconut gelatin starts to set, pour
the pandan gelatin on top, and set aside at
room temperature for about 25 minutes or
until set, then chill in the refrigerator for
about 30 minutes or until firm. To serve, cut
the gelatin into squares with a serrated knife
and transfer to serving plates.

Guest Chefs

Ty Bellingham
Sailors Thai, Sydney

Amy Chanta
Chat Thai, Sydney

Harold Dieterle
Kin Shop, New York

Ian Kittichai
Issaya Siamese Club, Bangkok

Saiphin Moore
Rosa's Thai Cafe, London

Ann Redding & Matt Danzer
Uncle Boons, New York

Duangporn (Bo) Songvisava & Dylan Jones
Bo.lan, Bangkok

Henrik Yde-Andersen
Sra Bua by Kiin Kiin, Bangkok

Ty Bellingham
Sailors Thai

106 George Street
The Rocks
Sydney 2000

Born and raised in Australia, Ty Bellingham first joined iconic Sydney eating house Sailors Thai in 1996. It was here that he fell in love with the sophistication required to achieve the Thai flavor profile, the commitment to painstaking preparation and to using fresh, but hard to source ingredients found in original recipes. Passionate about using time-honored techniques and serving Thai food in the traditional shared plates style, Bellingham has traveled extensively in Thailand to refine his skills. In 2006, under his watch, Sailors Thai was "hatted" for the first time by *The Sydney Morning Herald*'s Good Food Awards. In 2010 Bellingham moved to New York to run Thai restaurant Kittichai before returning to Sailors Thai as Executive Chef in 2013.

ยำปลาอินทรีย์
King Fish and Young Coconut Salad

Preparation time 30 minutes, plus soaking time
Serves 4

For the salad
3 oz/80 g king fish fillets, skinned and thinly sliced
3 oz/80 g young coconut meat, thinly sliced
1 red shallot, thinly sliced
1 big pinch round leaf mint
1 big pinch cilantro (coriander) leaves
½ lemongrass stalk, thinly sliced
3 kaffir lime leaves, thinly sliced
1 teaspoon roasted ground jasmine rice, to garnish

For the dressing
1 large clove garlic
1 lemongrass stalk
1½-inch/4-cm piece fresh ginger, peeled
1 cup (9 fl oz/250 ml) lime juice
⅓ cup (3 oz/80 g) granulated sugar
2 teaspoons fish sauce
2 teaspoons sea salt

To make the dressing, finely grate the garlic, lemongrass, and ginger, then put in a bowl. Add the lime juice, sugar, fish sauce, and sea salt and mix well. It should be a little sweet and salty but mostly sour. Set aside.

Add the fish to the dressing, cover with plastic wrap (clingfilm), and let marinate for 3 minutes. When the fish has cured, add all the other salad ingredients to the bowl and toss well but lightly so as not to break up the fish. Serve sprinkled with the ground rice.

หมูพะโล้

Parlow of Pork Side

Preparation time 1¼ hours
Cooking time 2 hours
Serves 4

2¼ lb/1 kg pork side (belly)

For the paste
3½ oz/100 g cilantro (coriander) root
1 teaspoon white peppercorns
6 star anise
2 cloves, pounded
3 cinnamon sticks
2 cups (6 oz/175 g) peeled and chopped fresh ginger
10 oz/275 g cloves garlic

For the master broth (stock)
⅓ cup (2½ fl oz/75 ml) vegetable oil
⅓ cup (3½ oz/100 g) rock candy (rock sugar)
generous 1 cup (9 oz/250 g) jaggery, palm sugar,
  or soft light brown sugar
1½ cups (12 fl oz/350 ml) soy sauce
1½ cups (12 fl oz/350 ml) dark soy sauce
1½ cups (12 fl oz/350 ml) oyster sauce
4 pandan leaves

For the salad
1 bunch scallions (spring onions), finely sliced
1 long red chile, seeded and thinly sliced
11 oz/300 g pickled mustard greens, thinly sliced
1 bunch cilantro (coriander) leaves

For the dressing
3 cloves garlic
½-inch/1-cm galangal
1 long red chile
1 long green chile
2 tablespoons salt
¼ teaspoon granulated sugar
⅔ cup (5 fl oz/150 ml) white vinegar

For the paste, pound all the ingredients in a mortar with a pestle until smooth.

Heat the oil in a large pan over medium heat, add the paste, and stir-fry for 1 minute until golden. Add the sugars and sauté for 5 minutes until slightly caramelized. Add the sauces, pandan leaves, and 21 cups (8¾ pints/5 liters) water. Bring to a boil, then reduce the heat and simmer for 30 minutes. Strain through a strainer (sieve) into a large bowl. This stock can be stored in an airtight container in the refrigerator for up to 2 weeks. To reuse, top off with the sugars and soy sauces.

Preheat the oven to 400°F/200°C/Gas Mark 6. Braise the pork side (belly) for 2 hours or until ready. Rest for 10–15 minutes, then cut into 4 portions. Cut each portion into quarters and divide among serving bowls.

Reheat ⅔ cup (5 fl oz/150 ml) of the stock in a pan and check the seasoning. It should taste rich, salty, and a little sweet. Pour over the pork.

Mix all the salad ingredients together in a bowl.

For the dressing, pound the garlic, galangal, and chiles in a mortar with a pestle until smooth. Add the salt, sugar, and vinegar and stir. The dressing should taste sour and salty with a hint of chile. Add a tablespoon of the dressing to the salad and mix well, then place on top of the pork and serve.

แกงมัสมั่นเนื้อ

Southern Massaman Curry of Beef Cheeks and Dutch Cream Potatoes

Preparation time 1 hour, plus marinating and resting time
Cooking time 3½ hours
Serves 4

2 beef cheeks (salted for 24 hours)
generous 2 cups (18 fl oz/500 ml) soy sauce
½ cup (3½ oz/100 g) superfine (caster) sugar
½ cup (2 oz/50 g) white pepper
4¼ cups (1¾ pints/1 liter) coconut cream
1 lemongrass stalk, sliced
3-inch/7.5-cm galangal, sliced
10 kaffir lime leaves
1 red onion

For the paste
5 dried red chiles, soaked for 1 hour and roasted
3 oz/80 g red onions, roasted
3 garlic bulbs, cloves separated, peeled, and roasted
2¼ oz/60 g lemongrass stalks, roasted
2-inch/5-cm piece of galangal, peeled and roasted
2-inch/5-cm piece of fresh ginger, roasted
a pinch of salt
2 teaspoons coriander seeds, roasted and strained
  (sieved)
1 teaspoon cumin seeds, roasted and strained (sieved)

For the curry
1 cup (9 fl oz/250 ml) vegetable oil
1 cup (9 fl oz/250 ml) separated coconut cream
½ cup (3½ oz/100 g jaggery, palm sugar, or soft light
  brown sugar
scant ½ cup (3½ fl oz/100 ml) tamarind puree
generous 2 cups (18 fl oz/500 ml) coconut cream
¼ teaspoon cardamom, roasted
2 cloves, roasted
1 piece cassia bark, roasted
1 bay leaf
4 Dutch cream, russet, or King Edwards potatoes,
  quartered
4 red shallots
scant ½ cup (3½ fl oz/100 ml) mandarin juice and
  pineapple juice (blend the pineapple with a knob
  of fresh ginger)
deep-fried red shallots, to garnish

Remove any sinew from the beef cheeks, then put into a large bowl, add the soy sauce, sugar, and white pepper, cover with plastic wrap (clingfilm), and let marinate in the refrigerator for 24 hours.

Put the beef cheeks into a large pan, add generous 2 cups (18 fl oz/500 ml) water, the coconut cream, lemongrass, galangal, lime leaves, and red onion, and braise for about 3 hours over low heat until tender. Let cool, then strain and cut into bite-size pieces. Reserve the braising liquid.

For the paste, pound all the ingredients in a mortar with a pestle until smooth.

Heat the oil, curry paste, and the separated coconut cream in a wok or large pan over medium heat for about 10 minutes until fragrant. Season with the sugar and tamarind. Add some of the braising liquid (remembering that it is quite salty) with the generous 2 cups (18 fl oz/500 ml) coconut cream, about half and half, then add the roasted cardamom, cloves, cassia bark, and bay leaf. Add the potatoes and red shallots and simmer for about 5 minutes or until the potatoes are cooked. Check the seasoning and thickness of the curry.

Add the beef cheeks to the curry and simmer for 5 minutes. Remove from the heat and set aside for a while to rest and let the flavor develop.

To serve, add a splash of the mandarin and pineapple juice, and serve sprinkled with deep-fried red shallots.

ขนมโค

Caramelized Coconut and Pandan Pastry Dumplings

Preparation time 40 minutes
Cooking time 25–30 minutes
Serves 4

For the dumplings
1 cup (7 oz/200 g) jaggery, palm sugar, or soft light
  brown sugar
1 cup (7 oz/200 g) coconut sugar
5 cups (12 oz/350 g) shredded fresh coconut
2 cups (5 oz/150 g) shredded toasted coconut
scant ½ cup (3½ oz/100 g) maltose
white sesame seeds, roasted, to garnish

For the pandan dough
5 pandan leaves, chopped
1½ cups (9 oz/250 g) glutinous (sticky) rice flour

For the sweet cream
generous 2 cups (18 fl oz/500 ml) coconut cream
1 pandan leaf
2 tablespoons (¾ oz/20 g) glutinous (sticky) rice flour
½ cup (3½ oz/100 g) granulated sugar
¼ teaspoon sea salt

For the dumplings, put both sugars in a pan, add a splash of water, and warm over medium-low heat, stirring, for 2 minutes until a syrup. Add the coconuts, stir, and cook for about 10 minutes or until semidry. Add the maltose and stir for about 5 minutes until completely dry. Remove from the heat and let cool slightly.

Use damp hands to roll the mixture into ½-inch/1-cm balls, then let cool in the refrigerator. This will provide a number of coconut balls, which can be stored in a freezer in an airtight container for up to 1 month.

For the dough, put the pandan leaves into a food processor with 1 cup (9 fl oz/250 ml) water and process until smooth. Strain through a fine strainer (sieve) into a bowl. Press all of the water out of the paste to achieve 1 cup (9 fl oz/250 ml) pandan juice. Add the rice flour and mix until firm and semidry.

For the sweet cream, bring the coconut cream, scant 1 cup (7 fl oz/200 ml) water, and the pandan leaf to a boil in a large pan. Remove from the heat. Put the rice flour in a bowl, add a little of the coconut cream mixture, and whisk until smooth. Add the remaining cream mixture, then transfer back to the pan. Simmer over low heat for 10 minutes, then let cool slightly. When warm, remove the pandan leaf and add the sugar and salt, then strain the mixture through a fine strainer into another pan and set aside.

Roll out the dough on a work surface and cut into circles larger than the dumplings. Put a dumpling in the middle and fold over the dough to enclose. Repeat until all the dumplings are used.

Bring a large pan of water to a boil over medium heat. Add the dumplings and boil for about 10 minutes or until they float to the surface. Remove with a slotted spoon and transfer to a serving bowl. Pour over the warm sweet cream, sprinkle with sesame seeds, and serve.

Amy Chanta
Chat Thai

20 Campbell Street
Haymarket
Sydney 2000

Born in Bangkok Amy Chanta left Thailand in her early twenties to pursue a life of adventure in Sydney. What she found was a city with only one Thai restaurant and endless possibilities. She opened the first Chat Thai in 1994, and since then she has opened six more restaurants. She frequently visits Thailand and the surrounding Asian region for inspiration and to constantly expand her knowledge of Thai cuisine and its evolution. Her fascination with food and the market place is boundless and her appreciation of the complexities and contrasts in Thai cuisine from every region has only deepened over the years.

ยำหัวปลี

Warm Salad of Banana Blossom, Jumbo Shrimp, and Chicken

Preparation time 20 minutes
Cooking time 15 minutes
Serves 6

2 cups (16 fl oz/475 ml) chicken broth (stock)
1 chicken breast
1 banana blossom
juice of 1 lemon
1 tablespoon grated mature coconut
1 x 14 fl oz/400 ml unshaken can of coconut milk, cream and milk separated
3 jumbo shrimp (king prawns)
1½ tablespoons thinly sliced shallots
1 tablespoon sliced and deep-fried red shallots
1 tablespoon finely julienned kaffir lime leaves
5 cashew nuts, to garnish

For the dressing
2 tablespoons lime juice
1½ tablespoons fish sauce
1½ tablespoons palm sugar, liquidized or soft brown sugar
1 tablespoon Chili Jam (see p. 35)
1 tablespoon coconut cream (from the top of the unshaken can, see above)

Bring the chicken broth (stock) to boil in a pan over medium heat. Reduce the heat, add the chicken breast and cook for 5 minutes or until cooked. Remove with a slotted spoon and let cool. Hand shred the chicken into ¼-inch/5-mm-thick strips. Set aside

Prepare a bowl of iced water and add the lemon jucie. Thinly slice the inner part of the banana blossom and put the rest in the bowl of iced water. Set aside.

Dry fry the grated coconut in a small skillet or frying pan for 1 minute until golden brown, then set aside.

Bring the coconut milk to a simmer in a pan over medium heat. Add the shrimp (prawns) and poach for 1–2 minutes or until the shrimp are still slightly translucent.

Make the dressing by mixing the lime juice, fish sauce, sugar, chili jam, and the coconut cream together in a bowl. Set aside.

Put all the salad ingredients into a large bowl, add the dressing, and toss everything together until well coated. Garnish with the cashew nuts and shrimp, then serve.

ขนมจีนแกงเขียวหวานไก่

Green Curry Chicken with Fermented Rice Noodles

Preparation time 30 minutes
Cooking time 30 minutes
Serves 6

3 tablespoons sunflower oil
1 x 14 fl oz/400 ml unshaken can of coconut milk,
  cream and milk separated
1 x 2¼—21.2-lb/1–1.2 kg chicken, you can ask your
  butcher to chop the chicken into 12 pieces (or more,
  depending how large or small you like it) to include
  the bones, kidney, and liver
1 cup (9 fl oz/250 ml) chicken broth (stock)
⅓ cup (2½ oz/75 ml) fish sauce
2 tablespoons softened jaggery, palm sugar, or soft
  light brown sugar
10 apple eggplants (aubergines) quartered
½ cup (1¼ oz/30 g) pea eggplants (aubergines),
  stems removed
15 kaffir lime leaves, tough inner stems removed
  and coarsely torn
4 long red chiles, diagonally, sliced
2 cups (3½ oz/100 g) sweet basil leaves, leaves
  and flowering tops only
11 oz/300 g fermented rice noodles or somen, to serve

For the curry paste
1 large lemongrass stalk, sliced into small disks
5 Thai shallots, coarsely chopped
2 garlic bulbs, cloves separated and peeled
peel of ½ kaffir lime, coarsely chopped
1 small finger of galangal, sliced into small disks
1 tablespoon shrimp paste
15 green bird's eye chiles
handful of bird's eye chile leaves (optional)

For the curry paste, pound all the ingredients in a mortar with a pestle until smooth, then set aside. It can be stored in an airtight container in the refrigerator for up 3 days or in the freezer for up to a month.

Heat the oil, curry paste and the coconut cream in a large heavy pan over medium heat, stirring continuously for about 10 minutes until the green oil starts to ooze and you get a heady fragrance. Add the coconut milk, bring to a boil, and cook for 10 minutes.

Increase the heat to high, add the chicken and broth (stock), then cover with a lid and cook for 20 minutes until the chicken is cooked through. After 10 minutes season with the fish sauce and sugar, then add the eggplants (aubergines) and slow boil for the remaining 10 minutes. Remove from the heat and add the kaffir lime leaves, sliced red chiles, and basil. Don't put the lid on immediately because the steam will blacken the leaves.

Add the noodles to boiling water and cook for about 1 minute or according to package directions until cooked. Drain and serve with the green curry.

Stir-Fried Fish with Holy Basil, Wild Ginger, and Green Peppercorns

Preparation time 20 minutes
Cooking time 20 minutes
Serves 6

all-purpose (plain) flour, for coating
7 oz/200 g king mackerel fillets, sliced
2 cups (16 fl oz/475 ml) vegetable oil, for pan-frying
3 tablespoons sunflower oil
4 round eggplants (aubergines), quartered
⅓ cup (¼ oz/10 g) pea eggplants (aubergines)
2 tablespoons wild ginger, julienned
3 strips young green peppercorns
1½ oz/40 g king brown mushrooms
1½ oz/40 g young coconut tips or heart of palm, sliced
1 tablespoon fish sauce
1 tablespoon soy sauce
1 teaspoon granulated sugar
¼ cup (2 fl oz/60 ml) chicken broth (stock)
1 packed cup (2 oz/50 g) holy basil
2 kaffir limes leaves, stripped
1 long red chile, sliced

For the curry paste
2 long yellow chiles
5 red bird's eye chiles, chopped
5 garlic cloves
1 tablespoon sliced galangal
1 tablespoon sliced yellow galangal
1 tablespoon sliced lemongrass
1 tablespoon wild ginger
10 black peppercorns

For the curry paste, pound all the ingredients in a mortar with a pestle until smooth, then set aside. This paste can be stored in an airtight container in the refrigerator for up to 3 days or in the freezer for up to a month.

Spread the flour on a large plate and coat the fish in the flour.

Heat the oil for pan-frying in a pan over medium heat, add the coated fish in small batches, and pan-fry for about 5 minutes until golden brown. Set aside.

Heat the sunflower oil in a wok over medium heat, add the curry paste, and sauté for 1 minute until fragrant. Increase the heat to high, add all the vegetables, and stir-fry quickly for 3–5 minutes. Add the fish sauce, soy sauce, sugar, and broth (stock), then add the fried fish, basil, kaffir lime leaves, and red chile and toss until evenly coated. Serve.

ปลาราดพริก

Crispy Fried Whole Fish with Roasted Chile and Garlic Sauce

Preparation time 20 minutes
Cooking time 20 minutes
Serves 6

4 cups (1¾ pints/1 liter) vegetable oil, for deep-frying
1 x 1 lb 8½ oz/700 g red snapper
4 tablespoons sunflower oil
1⅓ cups (7 oz/200 g) finely diced shallots
¼ cup (1¼ oz/35 g) garlic, finely chopped
¼ cup (1¼ oz/35 g) long red chile, finely chopped
¾ cup (6 fl oz/175 ml) chicken broth (stock)
4 cherry tomatoes, halved
3½ tablespoons tamarind puree
¼ cup (2 fl oz/60 ml) fish sauce
3½ tablespoons superfine (caster) sugar

To garnish
2 long red chiles, finely sliced
4 kaffir lime leaves, finely sliced

Heat the oil for deep-frying in a wok or deep fryer to 350°F/180°C or until a cube of bread browns in 30 seconds. Deep-fry the snapper for 7 minutes until golden brown, then remove with a slotted spoon and drain on paper towels before setting aside on a serving plate.

Heat the sunflower oil in a wok over medium heat, add the shallots, and stir-fry for 5 minutes until fragrant and reduced by about half. Add the garlic and stir-fry for 3–5 minutes until soft. Add the chile and stir for a minute, then add the broth (stock), cherry tomatoes, tamarind, fish sauce, and sugar. Stir briefly and pour over the fish. Garnish with the chiles and kaffir lime leaves and serve.

ส้มตำไทย

Green Papaya Salad

Preparation time 15–20 minutes
Serves 6

5 oz/150 g green papaya, peeled
2 tablespoons grated jaggery, palm sugar, or soft light brown sugar
3 large cloves garlic
2 red bird's eye chiles
1 handful of green beans
1½ teaspoons roasted peanuts
1 tablespoon dried shrimp
4 grape or cherry tomatoes, halved
2 tablespoons fish sauce
2 tablespoons lime juice

Shred the green papaya, then immediately soak in a bowl of iced water for 5 minutes. Drain and store in the refrigerator until ready to use.

Pound the sugar, garlic, and chile in a mortar with a pestle until almost paste like. Use a large spoon to help scoop and toss the ingredients until thoroughly combined. Add the green beans, peanuts, and dried shrimp and pound until slightly flat and crushed. Add the tomatoes and gently crush until squashed and the juices ooze but are not completely broken. Add the fish sauce and lime juice, then pound and toss until the sugar has dissolved. Add the shredded green papaya, toss until well mixed, and serve.

Harold Dieterle
Kin Shop

469 6th Avenue
New York
NY, 10011

Harold Dieterle's first kitchen memories are of learning to prepare traditional Sicilian Sunday suppers with his mother while growing up on Long Island. He went on to become the inaugural winner of Bravo's Top Chef series in 2005. Today, together with his business partner, Alicia Nosenzo, Dieterle owns and operates three critically acclaimed restaurants in New York City's West Village. Kin Shop is devoted to contemporary Thai cuisine. Dieterle spent time in Thailand learning about the cuisine and culture. It was an unforgettable experience and he continues to travel there to extend his knowledge of the cuisine. Kin Shop is inspired by these trips and the menu features both reinterpretations of traditional Thai dishes and new creations inspired by Thai ingredients.

เมี่ยงคำ

Miang of Dungeness Crab with Lychee

Preparation time 15 minutes, plus cooling time
Cooking time 12 minutes
Serves 4

1 tablespoon fried shallots
1 tablespoon fried ginger
1 tablespoon fried garlic
4 oz/120 g Dungeness crabmeat
2 tablespoons finely chopped fresh lychee
1 tablespoon finely chopped shallot
1 tablespoon finely chopped chives
16 betel leaves
salt and freshly ground black pepper

For the fish sauce caramel
1 cup (8 oz/225 g) jaggery, palm sugar, or soft light
  brown sugar
¼ cup (2 fl oz/60 ml) fish sauce
¼ cup (2 fl oz/60 ml) tamarind puree
2 tablespoons lime juice

For the ginger vinaigrette
1 tablespoon finely chopped ginger
2 teaspoons fish sauce
1 tablespoon lime juice
3 tablespoons olive oil
salt and freshly ground black pepper

For the fish sauce caramel, put the sugar and 2 tablespoons water in a pan and heat over high heat for 5 minutes until caramelized. Add the fish sauce and tamarind and cook for about 7 minutes until reduced by one-quarter. Add the lime juice, then let cool to room temperature and set aside.

For the vinaigrette, put the ginger, fish sauce, and lime juice into a blender and process until combined. While the blender is still running, slowly drizzle in the oil through the feeder tube to form an emulsion, then season to taste. Strain the dressing through a chinois (fine mesh sieve). Set aside.

To assemble the dish, put the fried shallots, garlic, and ginger in a bowl and mix well. Set aside. Put the crabmeat, lychee, shallots, and chives into another bowl and gently toss together, then dress with 3 tablespoons vinaigrette. Smear some of the fish sauce caramel on top of each betel leaf, then place a spoonful of the crab salad on each leaf. Garnish the top of each leaf with some fried shallot, ginger, and garlic mixture and season with salt and pepper, and serve.

Steamed Arctic Char with Glutinous Rice and Gaeng Som Curry

Preparation time 40 minutes, plus soaking time
Cooking time 1¾ hours
Serves 4

1 cup (1¼ oz/30 g) chopped Siamese watercress
1 cup (5 oz/150 g) bamboo shoots
1 cup (3½ oz/100 g) baby Romanesco cauliflower, blanched
4 tablespoons fried shallots, to garnish

For the curry paste
5 shallots
6 cloves garlic
2 teaspoons shrimp paste, roasted
2 teaspoons coriander seeds
2 tablespoons chopped galangal
1 lemongrass stalk, chopped
2 green chiles, seeded
2 red chiles, seeded
2 dried red bird's eye chiles, seeded
2 teaspoons salt

For the gaeng som curry
1 tablespoon vegetable oil
8½ cups (3½ pints/2 liters) vegetable broth (stock)
3 star anise
1 cassia stick
1 cup (9 fl oz/250 ml) pickled green peppercorns brine

For the glutinous rice
1 cup (7 oz/200 g) glutinous (sticky) rice
½ cup (4 fl oz/120 ml) coconut milk
2 tablespoons fish sauce
4 pieces banana leaf

For the fish
2 limes
1 onion, sliced
1 x 2-inch/ 5-cm piece fresh ginger, sliced
1 lemongrass stalk, sliced
2 cups (16 fl oz/475 ml) white wine
4 x 6 oz/175 g Arctic char or salmon fillets, skinned
4 teaspoons vegetable oil
salt and freshly ground black pepper

First make the curry paste. Place all the ingredients in a blender, add 3 tablespoons water, and process until smooth.

For the gaeng som curry, heat the oil in a pan over medium heat. Add the curry paste and cook for 2 minutes. Add the remaining ingredients and simmer for 30 minutes. Strain and set aside.

For the glutinous (sticky) rice, soak the rice in a bowl of water overnight. Next day, drain the rice, put in a steamer, and cook for 30 minutes, or until done. Put the rice into a bowl and stir in the coconut milk. Season with the fish sauce. Wrap the rice mixture in banana leaves, secure with toothpicks, and reheat in the steamer for 15 minutes. Meanwhile, check that your charcoal is glowing white hot, or your gas grill (barbecue) is preheated to 400°F/200°C. When the rice is hot, remove the banana leaves and place the rice mixture on the grill. Grill for about 3 minutes on each side, then set aside.

Put 4 cups (1¾ pints/1 liter) gaeng som curry in a large pan, add the watercress, bamboo shoots, and cauliflower and cook over medium heat for 30 minutes. When hot, set aside while the fish cooks.

To cook the fish, put the lime, onion, ginger, lemongrass, white wine, and about 4 quarts (7 pints/4 liters) water in the steamer, check the seasoning, and simmer for 15 minutes. Brush the bottom of each fish with the oil and season generously. Place the fish in the steamer basket and cook for 5 minutes.

To assemble the dish, place the glutinous rice in a bowl, add the vegetables, and pour the gaeng som curry around the rice. Place the steamed fish on top and garnish with fried shallots. Serve.

โรตี

Fried Roti with Kaffir Lime Sugar and Calamansi Curd

Preparation time 40 minutes, plus chilling, freezing, and resting time
Cooking time 1¼ hours
Serves 4

For the kaffir lime sugar
10 kaffir lime leaves
1 cup (7 oz/200 g) granulated sugar

For the calamansi curd
juice and zest of 2 calamansi (Chinese oranges) or
   of 1 orange and 1 lime
½ cup (3½ oz/100 g) granulated sugar
4½ oz/130 g egg yolks
scant 2 sticks (7½ oz/215 g) unsalted butter, cubed

For the roti
1 ⅔ cups (6½ oz/180 g) all-purpose (plain) flour
1 teaspoon salt
3 tablespoons margarine, melted, plus extra for oiling
½ cup (4 fl oz/120 ml) milk, warmed
vegetable oil, for deep-frying

Preheat the oven to 325°F/160°C/Gas Mark 3. Place the kaffir lime leaves on a baking sheet then dry in the oven for about 1 hour. Remove from the oven, put in a spice grinder with the sugar and mix together. Set aside.

Meanwhile, make the calamansi curd. Line a baking sheet with plastic wrap (clingfilm) and set aside. Put the juice, sugar, and zest in a heatproof bowl and whisk together until combined. Place the bowl on top of a pan of gently simmering water and slowly whisk in the yolks to temper. Cook, whisking the curd frequently, until thick and the whisk leaves a mark in the curd. Remove from the heat and whisk in the butter until melted. Pass the curd through a chinois (fine mesh sieve) onto the lined baking sheet, cover with plastic wrap, and let cool in the refrigerator.

For the roti, sift the flour and salt into a bowl. Add the margarine and stir until crumbly. Slowly pour in the milk and stir until a dough forms. Knead the dough without adding any extra flour until it comes away from the bowl and forms a ball. Continue kneading for about 10 minutes until slightly sticky. Cut into 4 pieces and roll each portion into a ball, then flatten slightly with the palm of your hand. Place the flattened dough balls on a baking sheet, cover with a damp cloth, and let rest for 30 minutes.

Oil a rolling pin and work surface with margarine. Roll each ball out into a paper-thin circle, about 9 inches/23 cm in diameter. Place on a baking sheet, cover with plastic wrap, and freeze for about 15 minutes until firm, then cut into 4 wedges.

Heat enough oil for deep-frying in a heavy-bottom pan or deep fryer to 350°F/180°C, or until a cube of bread browns in 30 seconds. Fry the roti for about 3 minutes on each side until golden brown, then remove with a slotted spoon and drain on paper towels.

To assemble the dish, put the roti into a bowl, add the kaffir lime sugar, and gently toss until coated. Smear some curd on the bottom of a plate, place the roti on top, and serve.

ย่าหมูกรอบกับหอยนางรมทอด

Crispy Pork and Oyster Salad

Preparation time 20 minutes, plus curing and cooling time
Cooking time 4 hours 10 minutes
Serves 4

vegetable oil, for deep-frying
2 cups (9 oz/240 g) all-purpose (plain) flour
8 large oysters, shucked
2 cups (7 oz/200 g) sliced celery
¼ cup (2 oz/50 g) pickled red onions
2 tablespoons mint leaves
½ cup (½ oz/15 g) baby celery greens (leaves)
salt and freshly ground black pepper
4 tablespoons crushed toasted peanuts, to garnish

For the braised pork side
1 x 1 lb 2 oz/500 g Hampshire pork side (belly)
1 cup (8 oz/225 g) kosher salt
½ cup (3½ oz/100 g) granulated sugar
1 tablespoon chopped kaffir lime leaves
1 tablespoon coriander seeds
8½ cup s (3½ pints/2 liters) chicken broth (stock)

For the chili-lime vinaigrette
½ cup (4 fl oz/120 ml) lime juice
¼ cup (2 fl oz/60 ml) vegetable oil
2 bird's eye chiles
1 clove garlic
2 tablespoons jaggery, palm sugar, or soft light
  brown sugar
3 tablespoons fish sauce

For the braised pork, put the pork side (belly) in a large bowl or dish, then add the salt, sugar, kaffir lime leaves, and coriander seeds, and cover with plastic wrap (clingfilm). Let cure in the refrigerator for 24 hours.

Preheat the oven to 300°F/150°C/Gas Mark 2. Rinse the pork with water, then put in a large casserole dish, add the chicken broth (stock), and braise in the oven for 4 hours or until tender. Remove the pork from the chicken broth and let cool. Slice the pork into 12 slices, about 2 inches/5 cm wide by 1 inch/2.5 cm thick, and set aside.

For the vinaigrette, place all the ingredients in a blender and process until combined. Strain through a chinois and set aside.

Heat enough oil for deep-frying in a deep, heavy-bottom pan or deep fryer to 350°F/180°C, or until a cube of bread browns in 30 seconds. Deep-fry the pork slices for 2 minutes. Meanwhile, put the flour in a bowl, add the oysters, and coat generously. Deep-fry the coated oysters for 4 minutes until the oysters and pork are golden brown and crispy. Remove with a slotted spoon and drain on paper towels. Season generously.

Place the oysters on a serving plate and put the pork in a bowl. Add the celery, pickled red onions, mint, and 1 cup (9 fl oz/250 ml) vinaigrette to the pork, check for seasoning, and mix to combine. Place the pork mixture on the serving plate with the oysters, top the salad with baby celery greens, and garnish with the peanuts.

Ian Kittichai
Issaya Siamese Club

4 Soi Sri Aksorn
Chua Ploeng Road
Sathorn, Bangkok

Internationally renowned Thai chef, Ian Kittichai started out pushing a food cart through his Bangkok neighborhood. He has since founded an international food and beverage consultancy company, Cuisine Concept Co., authored multiple cookbooks, and established restaurants in New York, Barcelona, Mumbai, and Bangkok. Thanks to his weekly television cooking show, *Chef Mue Thong* (Chef Golden Hands)—aired all over the world—and his role of Iron Chef in Iron Chef Thailand, Kittichai has gained a truly global audience. Issaya Siamese Club is Kittichai's flagship Thai restaurant located in the heart of Bangkok. At Issaya, Kittichai combines traditional Thai ingredients and flavors with the finest international cooking methods and techniques.

ย่าเป็ดกรอบ
Crispy Duck Salad

Preparation time 30 minutes
Cooking time 3–3½ hours
Serves 4

4¼ cups (1¾ pints/1 liter) duck fat oil or vegetable oil
2 duck legs, with thighs and drums
4¼ cups (1¾ pints/1 liter) vegetable oil, for deep-frying
1 red bird's eye chile, finely sliced
2 tablespoons fish sauce
1 tablespoon lime juice
½ teaspoon salt
1 teaspoon superfine (caster) sugar
2 tablespoons julienned green papaya
5 red radishes, sliced
¼ cup (1¼ oz/30 g) cubed mangosteen, cut into
  ¾-inch/2-cm pieces (optional)
¾ oz/20 g lemongrass, thinly sliced
¼ cup (¼ oz/10 g) fresh mint leaves, torn into halves
¼ cup (¼ oz/10 g) fresh cilantro (coriander) leaves,
  separated
1¼ oz/30 g carambola (star fruit), sliced into
  ½-inch/1-cm pieces
¼ cup (1¼ oz/30 g) cubed ripe mango, cut into
  ½-inch/1-cm cubes

Heat the duck fat or vegetable oil to 185°F/85°C in a large pan. Add the duck thighs, keeping the heat constant at 185°F/85°C, and simmer for 3–3½ hours until cooked. If the bone is twisted, it should come away from the meat easily. Set aside.

Heat the oil for deep-frying in a large pan or deep fryer to 350°F/180°C or until a cube of bread browns in 30 seconds. Deep-fry the slow-cooked duck thighs for about 5 minutes until golden brown and crispy, then remove with a slotted spoon and drain on paper towels. Remove the bones and cut each thigh into 4–6 pieces.

Mix the chiles, fish sauce, lime juice, salt, and sugar together in a large bowl. Add the papaya, radishes, mangosteen, lemongrass, mint, cilantro (coriander), carambola (star fruit), and mango and gently toss until well mixed. Place the salad on a serving plate with the duck and serve.

กระดูกหมูอบซอส
Red Curry-Glazed Baby Back Ribs

Preparation time 15 minutes, plus soaking time
Cooking time 2¼ hours
Serves 4

For the red curry paste
½ oz/15 g dried red finger chiles
½ teaspoon coriander seeds
½ teaspoon cumin seeds
2 teaspoons coarse sea salt
4 white peppercorns
1½ lemongrass stalks, finely sliced
¾ oz/20 g finely chopped shallots
5 cloves garlic
¼ oz/10 g galangal, finely sliced
grated zest of ½ lime
1 kaffir lime leaf, vein removed and finely chopped
1 tablespoon shrimp paste
1 section banana leaf or a piece of kitchen foil

For the sauce
2½ cups (1 lb 2 oz/500 g) jaggery, palm sugar, or soft
   light brown sugar
5½ oz/160 g salted yellow bean paste

For the baby back ribs
2 oz/50 g galangal, smashed and thickly sliced
1 lemongrass, smashed and cut into ¾-inch/
   2-cm pieces
5 kaffir lime leaves, veins removed and finely chopped
½ teaspoon black pepper
½ teaspoon salt
1 lb 2 oz/500 g baby back ribs

Steamed Jasmine Rice (see p. 378), to serve

For the curry paste, soak the dried chiles in a bowl of hot water for 15 minutes or until rehydrated, then drain and chop. Set aside.

Dry-fry the coriander seeds, cumin seeds, sea salt, and white peppercorns in a pan over medium heat for 2–3 minutes. Finely grind the spices in a mortar with a pestle until smooth or use a food processor. Add the dried chiles, lemongrass, shallots, garlic, galangal, lime zest, and kaffir lime leaves and finely grind again until smooth. This paste can be stored in an airtight container in the refrigerator for up to 5 days.

Wrap the shrimp paste in the banana leaf or kitchen foil and roast the package in a skillet or frying pan for 1 minute on each side. Remove the paste from the package and let cool, then add the paste to the mortar or food processor and grind or process until smooth. Set aside.

For the sauce, melt the sugar in a pan over low heat. Add the yellow bean paste and red curry paste and stir until well combined. Set aside.

For the ribs, pour 8½ cups (3½ pints/2 liters) water into a large pan, add all the remaining ingredients, and bring to a boil. Cover with kitchen foil, reduce the heat to low, and simmer for 2 hours.

Preheat the broiler (grill) if using. Remove the ribs from the pan and pour over the sauce, then place under a salamander or broiler for 5–8 minutes. Serve with steamed rice.

ย่าหัวปลีกับยอดมะพร้าว

Banana Blossom Salad

Preparation time 30 minutes
Cooking time 15 minutes
Serves 4

For the dressing
generous 2 cups (18 fl oz/500 ml) tamarind puree
¼ cup (2 fl oz/60 ml) coconut cream
scant ¼ cup (1½ oz/40 g) jaggery, palm sugar, or soft
 light brown sugar
3½ oz/100 g Chili Jam (see p. 35)
1 tablespoon soy sauce

For the turmeric cream
scant ½ cup (3½ fl oz/100 ml) fresh coconut cream
½ teaspoon ground turmeric
½ teaspoon cornstarch (cornflour)

For the salad
2 tablespoons lime juice
3½ oz/100 g banana blossom
2 oz/50 g heart of palm, diced into ¾-inch/2-cm pieces
¼ cup (1¼ oz/30 g) deep-fried, thinly sliced shallots
scant ⅓ cup (1¼ oz/30 g) toasted shredded coconut or
 toasted coconut flakes
½ teaspoon dried chili flakes
¼ cup (1¼ oz/30 g) roasted peanuts, chopped
4 kaffir lime leaves, veins removed and finely chopped

To garnish
1 butterfly pea flower, torn (optional)
2 small Chinese broccoli flowers (optional)
½ red finger chile, seeded and julienned

For the dressing, bring all the ingredients to a boil in a pan over medium heat, then remove and set aside.

For the turmeric cream, bring all the ingredients to a boil in a pan over medium heat, until thickened, stirring constantly. Remove and set aside.

To clean and prepare banana blossoms, pour 4¼ cups (1¾ pints/1 liter) cold water into a large bowl and add the lime juice. Peel away and discard the outer red petals from the banana blossom and also the small white strips of banana flower. Cut off the tip and the end of the blossom, then split the blossom in half lengthwise and cut the pieces in half again. Put the quarters into the bowl of water. Peel and clean each layer of the blossom, and discard the small white strips of banana flower inside. Dice the cleaned leaves into ¾-inch/ 2-cm cubes and return to the water. Repeat until all the leaves have been chopped, then drain the excess water, and set aside.

Put the heart of palm into a pan, add the diced banana blossom and the dressing, and heat until warm. Remove from heat, add the shallots, coconut, chili flakes, peanuts, and half the kaffir lime leaves and mix together. Transfer to a serving plate, drizzle over some turmeric cream, and garnish with the flowers, chile, and the remaining kaffir lime leaves. Serve.

ต้มโคล้งทะเล

Market Fish in a Spicy Lemongrass-Tamarind Broth

Preparation time 15 minutes
Cooking time 20 minutes
Serves 4

2¼ oz/60 g lemongrass stalks, thinly sliced
2 kaffir lime leaves, veins removed and finely chopped
1 x ⅜-inch/7.5-mm piece galangal, thinly sliced
½ teaspoon crushed dried red finger chiles
⅓ cup (2¾ fl oz/80 ml) tamarind puree
¼ cup (2 fl oz/60 ml) fish sauce
a pinch of superfine (caster) sugar
3½ oz/100 g uncooked shrimp (prawns), peeled and
  deveined
¼ oz/10 g squid, sliced into ½-inch/1-cm pieces
3½ oz/100 g skinless sea bass, cut into ¾-inch/2-cm
  pieces
¼ cup (¼ oz/10 g) fresh holy basil leaves
1 sprig cilantro (coriander)

For the lemongrass-tamarind broth
1 dried red finger chile
1 lemongrass stalk, halved and smashed
⅓ cup (1¼ oz/40 g) halved small shallots
1-inch/2.5-cm piece galangal, thickly sliced
1 kaffir lime leaf, vein removed and finely chopped
1 oz/25 g smoked and dried whisker sheatfish or
  smoked catfish or smoked trout

For the broth, heat a griddle (grill) pan over low heat. Add the dried chile, lemongrass, shallots, galangal, lime leaves, and dried fish and grill each side of the fish for 5 minutes until colored. Remove from the heat and set aside.

Bring 4¼ cups (1¾ pints/1 liter) water to a boil in a large pan and add the grilled chiles, lemongrass, shallots, galangal, and kaffir lime leaves and return to a boil.

Meanwhile, break the fish flesh into large chunks. Discard all the innards but keep the remaining parts of the fish. Add the fish flesh and remaining parts of the fish to the boiling broth and boil for 10 minutes until the broth has reduced by half. The broth should now have color. Remove from the heat and strain through a fine-meshed strainer (sieve) into a clean large pan. Discard the solids.

Bring the broth to a boil over high heat. Add the lemongrass, lime leaves, galangal, dried chiles, tamarind juice, fish sauce, and sugar. Cover the pan until it begins to boil. Add the shrimp (prawns), squid, and white fish, and boil for 1–2 minutes or until cooked. Add the basil leaves and stir. Remove from the heat, transfer to a serving bowl and garnish with the cilantro (coriander) leaves. Serve.

หอยเชลล์กับหมูหวาน

Seared Scallops with Pork Side Relish

Preparation time 30 minutes
Cooking time 1 hour
Serves 4

For the green seafood dipping sauce
4 cloves garlic
2 cilantro (corriander) roots
3 sprigs cilantro (coriander)
2 green finger chiles
1 green bird's eye chile
⅓ cup (2½ fl oz/75 ml) fish sauce
scant ½ cup (3½ fl oz/100 ml) lime juice
1 tablespoon jaggery, palm sugar, or soft light
  brown sugar
1 tablespoon pickled garlic
scant ½ cup (3 ½ fl oz/100 ml) pickled garlic juice

For the salad
2 tablespoons vegetable oil
3 large scallops
2 lemongrass stalks, thinly sliced
1 tablespoon Ceylon spinach, torn (optional)
10 mint leaves, torn into halves
4 shallots, thinly sliced
4–6 scallop shells, to serve

To garnish
vegetable oil, for deep-frying
6 pieces of salmon skin, thinly sliced
1 red finger chile, seeded and julienned
2 tablespoons cabbage, cut into 2-inch/5-cm pieces
⅓ cup (1¼ oz/30 g) long green bean pieces, 2-inch/
  5-cm long
¼ cup (1¼ oz/30 g) long cucumber pieces, 2-inch/
  5-cm long

For the sweetened pork
1 lb 2 oz/500 g pork side (belly), cut into ¾-inch/
  2-cm pieces
generous 1 cup (9 oz/250 g) jaggery, palm sugar, or soft
  light brown sugar
1 teaspoon dark soy sauce
1 garlic bulb, cloves separated and chopped
¼ cup (1 oz/25 g) black pepper
2 teaspoons salt

For the dipping suce, put all the ingredients in
a food processor and blend until smooth. Set
aside. This sauce can be stored in an airtight
container in the refrigerator for up to 1 week.

For the salad, heat the oil in a nonstick skillet
or frying pan until hot, add the scallops, and
sear for 4 minutes on both sides or until
nicely brown. Cut each scallop into half and
keep warm.

Toss the lemongrass, Ceylon spinach, mint
leaves, and shallots with ¼ cup (2 fl oz/60 ml)
dipping sauce in a large bowl. Spoon the salad
mixture into the scallop shells or use small
plates and top with the scallops.

For the garnish, heat the oil for deep-frying in
a large wok or deep fryer to 350°F/180°C or
until a cube of bread browns in 30 seconds.
Deep-fry the salmon skin for 5 minutes until
golden brown and crispy, then remove with
a slotted spoon and drain on paper towels.

Garnish the salad with the chile, cabbage,
green beans, cucumbers, and salmon skin.

For the sweetened pork, sauté the pork side
(belly) in a large skillet or frying pan for about
10 minutes. Add the sugar, dark soy sauce,
garlic, black pepper, and salt, then pour in
about 4¼ cups (1¾ pints/1 liter) water until the
pork is covered and cook for 50 minutes until
the fat separates. Discard the fat and transfer
the pork to a serving plate. Serve with the
scallop shells.

ขนมดอกมะลิ

Jasmine Flower Flan

Preparation time 1 hour, plus chilling and churning time
Cooking time 30 minutes
Makes 10–20 tuiles and 4¼ cups (1¾ pints/1 liter)
ice cream

For the flan
3 tablespoons agar-agar powder or 3 gelatin leaves
scant 3 cups (23 fl oz/690 ml) heavy (double) cream
⅓ cup (2½ oz/60 g) superfine (caster) sugar
2–3 drops jasmine essence
mixed citrus fruit salad or mixed berry salad,
   to serve (optional)

For the rice tuile
scant ½ cup (2¾ oz/75 g) jasmine rice, cooked
¼ cup (2 fl oz/60 ml) coconut milk
1 tablespoon superfine (caster) sugar
a pinch of salt
1 tablespoon egg whites
2–3 drops jasmine essence
vegetable oil cooking spray, for greasing

For the jasmine rice ice cream
1 cup (9 fl oz/250 ml) coconut milk
scant ¾ cup (4 oz/120 g) jasmine rice, cooked
scant ⅔ cup (4 oz/120 g) superfine (caster) sugar
5 egg yolks
a pinch of salt
2–3 drops jasmine essence
scant 2 cups (15 fl oz/450 ml) heavy (double) cream

For the flan, bring the agar-agar and cream to a boil in a pan over medium heat. Add the sugar and stir until it is completely dissolved, then remove from the heat and stir in the essence. Divide the mixture equally among 4 ramekins, about ⅓ cup (2¾ fl oz/80 ml) size. Chill in the refrigerator for at least 2 hours or until the flan has set.

For the tuile, process all the ingredients in a blender. Grease a pizzelle maker with oil, then drop a tablespoon of the batter onto the bottom and press the top down tightly. Cook until golden and crispy. Remove and let cool. Alternatively, preheat the oven to 340°F/170°C/Gas Mark 3. Spread a tablespoon of the batter into a 3¼–4-inch/8–10-cm-diameter circle on a nonstick silicone baking mat and bake for 10–15 minutes or until golden brown and crispy. Remove and let cool. Set aside 8 tuiles to use for this dessert. The remaining tuiles can be stored in an airtight container at room temperature for up to a week.

For the ice cream, bring the coconut milk and cooked jasmine rice to a boil in a pan over medium heat, then transfer to a blender and process until smooth. Return to the pan and bring to a boil over medium heat.

Whisk the sugar, egg yolks, salt, and jasmine essence together in a large heatproof bowl. Gradually add the boiling coconut milk mixture, whisking continuously, until thoroughly combined and smooth. Add the cream and chill in the refrigerator overnight.

The next day, churn the mixture according to the ice cream maker machine's instructions.

To serve, unmold the flans onto serving plates. Break the tuiles into pieces, place 2 scoops of ice cream onto each plate, and top with a piece of tuile. Serve with fruit salad.

Saiphin Moore
Rosa's Thai Cafe

12 Hanbury Street
London, E1 6QR

Saiphin Moore's career as a chef began at secondary school, when she opened up a grocery store in her small hometown, Phetchabun, in northern Thailand. The store soon became a success and Moore decided to open a small restaurant selling homemade favorites to the locals. In 2001, she travelled to Hong Kong, where she met her husband and business partner, Alex, and together they launched their first Thai restaurant. In 2006, the couple moved to London and set up a humble street stall on Brick Lane, offering a takeaway service of home-cooked Thai food. This led to the opening of Rosa's Thai Café in an archetypal British "caff" in Spitalfields in 2008. Demand for Moore's authentic Thai food has led to the opening of three more sites across London.

เนื้อสะเต๊ะ
Beef Satay

Preparation time 20 minutes, plus marinating time
Cooking time 10 minutes
Serves 2

3 lemongrass stalks
7-inch/18-cm piece galangal, peeled
4–5 kaffir lime leaves
1 teaspoon granulated sugar
2 teaspoons curry powder
2 teaspoons coriander powder
4–5 cilantro (coriander) roots
1 teaspoon turmeric
1 teaspoon caraway powder
½ teaspoon salt
¼ cup (2 fl oz/60 ml) coconut milk
14 oz/400 g beef, very thinly sliced

For the sauce, put the lemongrass, galangal, lime leaves, sugar, and spices in a blender and process until smooth. Transfer to a bowl, add the coconut milk, and mix well until combined. Put the beef in the marinade and turn until well coated. Cover with plastic wrap (clingfilm) and let marinate in the refrigerator for 2 hours.

Preheat the broiler (grill). Thread the marinated beef onto skewers and broil (grill) for 5 minutes on each side until cooked. Serve.

ผัดกระเพราหมู
Spaghetti with Pork, Chile, and Basil

Preparation time 10 minutes
Cooking time 10 minutes
Serves 4

3 tablespoons hot chiles
3 cloves garlic
3 tablespoons vegetable oil
1 lb 2 oz/500 g ground (minced) pork
1½ tablespoons fish sauce
1 tablespoons soy sauce
1 teaspoon granulated sugar
14 oz/400 g spaghetti, cooked
½ cup (1 oz/25 g) holy or sweet basil leaves
3 kaffir lime leaves, chopped

Put the chiles and garlic in a mortar and crush with a pestle.

Heat the oil in a pan over medium heat, add the crushed garlic and chile, and stir-fry for 1 minute or until golden brown. Add the pork and stir-fry for about 5 minutes until cooked. Season with the fish sauce, soy sauce, and sugar to taste, then toss to mix well. Add the cooked spaghetti, sweet basil, and lime leaves and serve.

ผัดปลาหมึก

Thai Calamari

Preparation time 5 minutes
Cooking time 15 minutes
Serves 2

3–4 cilantro (coriander) roots
1 lemongrass stalk
1 tablespoon cornstarch (cornflour)
1 tablespoon egg yolk
pinch of salt
7 oz/200 g squid, cut into small strips
vegetable oil, for deep-frying

To garnish
1 teaspoon vegetable oil
1 teaspoon chopped green and red (bell) pepper
1 teaspoon chopped white onion
2–3 red chiles, sliced
1 lemongrass stalk, finely sliced
1 teaspoon torn lime leaves

Put the lemongrass and cilantro (coriander) root into a blender and process until combined, then put in a bowl and set aside.

Put the cornstarch (cornflour), egg yolk, and the salt into a bowl and stir to make a batter.

Add the squid to the cilantro (coriander) root and lemongrass mixture and stir until the squid is coated.

Heat the oil for deep-frying in a wok or deep fryer to 350°F/180°C or until a cube of bread browns in 30 seconds. Dip the coated squid into the batter, then carefully drop into the hot oil and deep-fry in batches for 2–3 minutes until crispy and golden brown. Remove with a slotted spoon and drain on paper towels.

For the garnish, heat the oil in a pan over medium heat, add the vegetables, and stir-fry for 2–3 minutes. Place the squid on a serving plate, garnish with the stir-fried vegetables, and serve.

ผัดเส้นหมี่

Stir-Fried Rice Noodles with Northern Thailand Chili Paste

Preparation time 10 minutes, plus soaking time
Cooking time 15 minutes
Serves 2

11 oz/300 g dried rice noodles
10 dried chiles (if you want less spicy, add less chiles)
5 shallots
5 cloves garlic, crushed
2 tablespoons vegetable or sunflower oil
9 oz/250 g ground (minced) chicken
20 cherry tomatoes, chopped
1 teaspoon shrimp paste
1 tablespoon granulated sugar
2 tablespoons fish sauce

To garnish
chopped cilantro (coriander)
scallion (spring onion)

Soak the noodles in a bowl of water for about 10 minutes, or according to package directions until soft, then drain and set aside.

Put the dried chiles, shallots, and garlic in a blender and process until smooth.

Heat the oil in a skillet or frying pan over high heat for 10 seconds. Add the chile, shallot, and garlic mixture and stir-fry for 1–2 minutes. Add the chicken and stir-fry for 3 minutes until cooked through. Then add the cherry tomatoes and the remaining ingredients and stir to combine.

Pat the noodles with paper towels to remove excess moisture, then add to the pan and stir-fry for 2–3 minutes until soft.

Garnish with chopped cilantro (coriander) and scallion (spring onion) and serve.

Ann Redding &
Matt Danzer
Uncle Boons

7 Spring Street
New York
NY 10012

Chefs Ann Redding and Matt Danzer are the husband and wife team behind Uncle Boons in New York's Nolita neighborhood. The couple first met in 2004 while working at Thomas Keller's restaurant Per Se and went on to open a grocery store—Reddings Market—in Shelter Island. They now share the kitchen at Uncle Boons as owners and co-chefs serving traditional Thai home cooking. Redding grew up in Ubon Ratchathani Province in Northeast Thailand and the restaurant is named after her real life Uncle Boon. The fun and eclectic menu is inspired by Redding's upbringing in Thailand and features family recipes as well as the couple's favorite Thai dishes.

น้ำพริกปลาดุก

Charcoal Smoked
Catfish & Pork Chili Dip

Preparation time 20 minutes
Cooking time 55 minutes
Serves 4

½ cup (4 fl oz/120 ml) coconut milk
8 oz/225 g ground (minced) pork
11 oz/300 g smoked catfish, flaked

For the tomato nam prik base
2 oz/50 g banana chiles, sliced
12 oz/350 g onions, cut into medium dice
3 oz/80 g cloves garlic
1 oz/25 g red bird's eye chiles
2 tablespoons canola (rapeseed) oil, for roasting
11¼ oz/320 g plum tomatoes, cut into large dice
2 tablespoons fish sauce
½ cup (4 fl oz/120 ml) lime juice
¾ cup (1¼ oz/35 g) chopped cilantro (coriander) leaves
¼ teaspoon jaggery, palm sugar, or soft light
  brown sugar
salt

To serve
seasonal vegetables, such as green mango, round
  (aubergine), radishes, and sugar snap peas
crispy pork rinds
lime wedges

For the tomato nam prik base, preheat the oven to 375°F (190°C/Gas Mark 5).

Toss the banana chiles, onions, garlic, and bird's eye chiles in oil and season with salt. Roast in the oven for about 30 minutes until dark and charred.

Toss the tomatoes in oil and season with salt. Roast in the oven for about 10 minutes or until the skin is colored but the flesh is still juicy—about half the time of other vegetables. Remove the vegetables from the oven and put in a food processor and pulse together until fine but not a paste. Add the remaining ingredients and a pinch of salt, and pulse a few more times to incorporate. You will need scant 2 cups (1 lb/450 g) of the tomato base for this recipe.

Heat the coconut milk in pan over medium heat. Add the pork and cook for 8–10 minutes or until cooked through. Add the tomato base and the catfish, mix well, and heat for 5–6 minutes until just warmed through. Serve as a dip with raw vegetables, crispy pork rinds, and lime wedges.

Sour Orange Curry with Shrimp, Fish, and Little Neck Clams

Preparation time 20 minutes, plus standing time
Cooking time 1 hour
Serves 2

1½ tablespoons olive oil, for cooking
6 jumbo shrimp (king prawns), peeled with the heads
   and tails intact
2 x 5 oz/140 g hake or cod fillets, cut into 5-inch/
   2-cm pieces
10 little neck clams
5 oz/150 g betel leaves, julienned
5 oz/150 g chayote, julienned
1 salted duck egg yolk
½ cup (¾ oz/20 g) cilantro (coriander) leaves

For the orange chili vinegar
1 cup (9 fl oz/250 ml) white vinegar
5 bird's eye chiles, sliced
1 teaspoon granulated sugar
zest and juice of 1 orange
pinch of salt

For the sour curry
olive oil, for stir-frying
⅓ cup (4 oz/113 g) red curry paste
1 tablespoon peeled and chopped fingerroot
1 cup (9 fl oz/250 ml) white wine
8 cups (3⅕ pint/1.9 liters) fish or seafood broth (stock)
1 x 4 oz/113 g hake or cod fillet
1 tablespoon fish sauce
1 teaspoon jaggery, palm sugar, or soft light
   brown sugar
¾ cup (3¼ oz/80 g) tamarind puree
salt

For the vinegar, put all the ingredients in a bowl or pitcher (jug) and stir together until combined. Let stand for at least 2 hours.

For the sour curry, heat a little olive oil in a pan over medium-low heat, add the curry paste and fingerroot, and sauté for about 3 minutes until aromatic. Pour in the white wine, scrape all the sediment from the bottom of the pan, and stir into the curry paste. Add the seafood stock and fish and simmer for 15 minutes. Turn off the heat and add the fish sauce, sugar, and tamarind. Season to taste with salt then puree with an immersion (stick) blender until all the fish meat has broken down.

Heat a little olive oil in a large pan over medium heat. Once hot, add the shrimp (prawns) and fish. Lightly sear the shrimp for 1½ minutes on each side and the fish for about 2 minutes on each side until a light golden color. Add the sour curry and clams, then bring to a simmer and cover with a lid.

As soon as the clam shells open, remove from the heat. Add the betel leaves and chayote and taste for seasoning. Put into a large serving bowl, microplane the salted duck egg yolk over the top, and garnish with cilantro (coriander) leaves. Serve with the orange chili vinegar on the side so guests can add at the last minute.

Charcoal Grilled Blowfish Tails with Seafood Nam Prik

Preparation time 15 minutes, plus marinating time
Cooking time 10 minutes
Serves 4

1 lb/450 g blowfish tails, cleaned

For the marinade
scant 1 cup (8 fl oz/240 ml) coconut milk
¼ lemongrass stalk, sliced
½ cup (¾ oz/20 g) sliced cilantro (coriander) stems
¼ oz/10 g kaffir lime leaves

For the seafood dipping sauce
1 small clove garlic, chopped
1 tablespoon chopped cilantro (coriander) leaves
  and stems
2 green bird's eye chiles, sliced
2½ teaspoons jaggery, palm sugar, or soft light brown
  sugar, softened
in a microwave
¼ cup (2 fl oz/60 ml) lime juice
2 tablespoons white vinegar
2 tablespoons fish sauce
1 heaping teaspoon olive oil
zest of 1 lime
pinch of salt

Put all the marinade ingredients in a blender and process well. Pour into a bowl, add the blowfish tails, cover with plastic wrap (clingfilm), and let marinate for at least 45 minutes.

Meanwhile, make the dipping sauce. Put the garlic, cilantro (coriander), chiles, and softened sugar in a bowl and mix well until combined. Add the remaining ingredients and whisk until thoroughly combined. Set aside.

Before you begin cooking, check that your charcoal is glowing white hot, or your gas grill (barbecue) is preheated to 375°F/190°C. Grill the fish over medium-high heat for about 4 minutes on each side or until lightly charred and cooked through. Serve with the seafood dipping sauce.

Coconut Sundae with Palm Sugar Whipped Cream and Sweet and Salty Peanuts

Preparation time 20 minutes, plus cooling time
Cooking time 15 minutes
Serves 4

4 large scoops coconut ice cream
4 tablespoons freshly grated coconut meat, toasted
4 coconut butter cookie wafers

For the palm sugar whipped cream
⅓ cup (3¼ oz/85 g) jaggery, palm sugar, or soft light
  brown sugar
2 cups (16 fl oz/475 ml) heavy (double) cream
canola (rapeseed) oil, for deep-frying

For the candied peanuts
5 cups (2¼ lb/1 kg) granulated sugar
2 cups (11 oz/300 g) peanuts
flaky sea salt

For the palm sugar whipped cream, put the sugar in a heatproof bowl and briefly heat in the microwave to melt. Put the cream in a pan and heat gently over low heat until warm. Whisk in the melted sugar until thoroughly combined. Remove from the heat and let cool quickly. Put the sweetened cream in a food mixer and whip to soft peaks. Set aside.

For the candied peanuts, bring scant 4 cups (1⅔ pints/950 ml) water and 4 cups (1¾ lb/ 800 g) sugar to a boil in a pan over medium heat. Add the peanuts and boil for 4 minutes. Drain, then toss in the remaining sugar.

Heat enough oil for deep-frying in a wok or deep fryer to 350°F/180°C or until a cube of bread browns in 30 seconds. Shake off the excess sugar from the peanuts and deep-fry for 2 minutes or until golden brown. Remove with a slotted spoon and lay flat in a single layer on a baking sheet. Season with sea salt.

To assemble the sundae, put 1 scoop of the coconut ice cream into individual sundae dishes. Top with the whipped cream, toasted coconut, and candied peanuts. Decorate with a wafer and serve.

Duangporn (Bo) Songvisava & Dylan Jones
Bo.lan

42 Soi Pichai Ronnarong
Songkram Sukhumvit 26
Klongteoy, Bangkok 10110

Husband-and-wife team, Duangporn Songvisava and Dylan Jones met while working at chef David Thompson's restaurant, Nahm, in London. Together they decided it was time to open a truly remarkable Thai restaurant in Bangkok and in 2009 they opened Bo.lan. Working closely with local farmers Songvisava and Jones feel a strong social responsibility to the local community. They are passionate about campaigning to raise awareness of important issues regarding Thai food and food security, whether it is through teaching at several leading Thai universities or on their weekly Thai PBS Television program, *Eat Am Are*. In 2013 Bo.lan was voted 15 in the San Pellegrino 50 Best Restaurants in Asia awards, while Songvisava won the inaugural award for Asia's best female chef.

หลนไข่เค็มใส่กุ้งสับแนมกับปลาหมึกย่าง
Relish of Salty Duck Egg and Minced Shrimp in Coconut Cream

Preparation time 20 minutes
Cooking time 15 minutes
Serves 4 as part of a shared Thai meal with rice

½ cup (4 fl oz/120 ml) coconut cream
a dash of light chicken broth (stock)
1 boiled salted duck egg
1½ teaspoons seasoned shrimp (prawn) tomalley
pinch of jaggery, palm sugar, or soft light brown sugar
fish sauce, to taste
a pinch of ground white pepper
tamarind water, to taste
4 oz/120 g ground (minced) shrimp (prawns)
3–5 Thai shallots, sliced
1–2 teaspoons finely sliced lemongrass
1 teaspoon julienned ginger
1 teaspoon julienned white turmeric root
1 furry eggplant (aubergine), sliced
1 long red chile, cut into rings
2 tablespoons chopped cilantro (coriander)

To serve
grilled squid
raw or steamed vegetables, such as ivy gourd, young pumpkin, okra, wing beans, and cucumber

Bring the coconut cream and broth (stock) to a simmer in a large pan. Crumble in the salted duck egg, then add the shrimp (prawn) tomalley, sugar, and a dash of fish sauce and simmer for until thickened slightly. Season with white pepper and tamarind. Add a little more fish sauce and palm sugar if needed. Add the shrimp (prawns), then add the shallots, lemongrass, ginger, tumeric, eggplant (aubergine), and red chile. Finish with the cilantro (coriander). Check the seasoning. It should be rich from the coconut, salty from the duck eggs, and slightly fragrant of white pepper with just a hint of sourness. Serve with grilled squid and raw or steamed vegetables.

Red Curry of Grilled Fish and Cassia Leaf

Preparation time 45 minutes, plus soaking and standing time
Cooking time 10–15 minutes
Serves 4

For the curry paste
½ cup (2 oz/50 g) large dried red chiles, seeded
½ teaspoon coriander seeds, toasted
½ teaspoon cumin seeds, toasted
1 cilantro (coriander) root
grated zest of ½ kaffir lime
3–5 red bird's eye chiles
⅓ cup (1¼ oz/30 g) dried and smoked freshwater fish
2-inch/5-cm piece galangal, chopped
2 lemongrass stalks, chopped
¼ cup (1¼ oz/30 g) cloves garlic
⅓ cup (1 oz/30 g) sliced shallots
shrimp paste, to taste
salt

For the fermented fish sauce
7 oz/200 g fermented fish
5–10 shallots, bruised
1 kaffir lime leaf, cut in half
about 5 kaffir lime leaves, bruised
about 2 lemongrass stalks, bruised
7 oz/200 g pork skin
light chicken broth (stock) or water, to cover

For the pickled mustard green salad
½ cup (2¾ oz/70 g) diced pickled mustard greens, cut
  into ½-inch/1-cm squares
¼ cup (¾ oz/20 g) sliced shallots
10 red bird's eye chiles, thinly sliced
2 tablespoons golden superfine (caster) sugar
fish sauce, to taste (optional)

For the curry
2 oz/50 g fermented cassia leaves, chopped
¾ cup (6 fl oz/175 ml) coconut cream, plus 1 tablespoon
  to garnish
1–2 tablespoons jaggery, palm sugar, or soft light
  brown sugar
1 tablespoon fish sauce, to taste
½ cup (4 fl oz/120 ml) coconut milk
2 kaffir lime leaves, bruised and torn
1 each long red and green chiles, seeded and cut
  lengthwise into 1-inch/2.5-cm pieces
1 tablespoon shredded lesser galangal
4–5 oz/120–150 g grilled ocean fish, such as snapper,
  grouper, red grouper, or skate
1½ teaspoons julienned lime leaf

For the curry paste, soak the dried chiles in a bowl of water for 15 minutes or until rehydrated, then drain and set aside. Put a pinch of salt into a mortar and add one ingedient at a time starting from the hardest most fibrous through to the softest and wettest. Pound each ingredient finely before adding the next. Taste before adding the shrimp paste and add a small amount at a time until the desired saltiness is achieved. Set aside.

For the fermented fish sauce, place all the ingredients in a pan and simmer for 30 minutes until the fish has broken up and the liquid has reduced by half. Strain through cheesecloth (muslin) while hot into a large heatproof bowl and let cool. Transfer to an airtight container and store in the refrigerator for up to 3 months. Use sparingly for the best results.

For the salad, mix all the ingredients together in a large bowl and let stand for at least 1 hour. It should be sour, salty, spicy, and slightly sweet.

For the curry, put the cassia leaves into a pan of cold water and bring to a boil. Strain the leaves in a strainer (sieve) and squeeze them of excess liquid, then repeat the process. Transfer to a pan of cold water and bring to a boil. Reduce the heat and simmer for 15–30 minutes until cooked and only very slightly bitter. Strain and set aside.

Bring ½ cup (4 fl oz/120 ml) coconut cream to a boil in a large wok, then reduce the heat and simmer for 6 minutes, stirring gently occasionally until the fat begins to separate. Add the curry paste and cook, stirring regularly, for 7–10 minutes until fragrant. Add 1–2 tablespoons of the fermented fish sauce, if using, then add the sugar and fish sauce and stir-fry for another minute. Add the coconut milk, ¼ cup (2 fl oz/60 ml) cream, the bruised lime leaves, and chopped cassia leaves. Bring to a boil, then reduce the heat and simmer for 5 minutes until the oil begins to separate and the curry is infused with the flavor of the cassia leaves. Adjust the seasoning—it should be rich, smoky, and fragrant. To finish, add the cut chiles, galangal, and grilled fish. Garnish with a splash of coconut cream and the julienned lime leaves and serve with the pickled mustard greens salad.

Broiled Beef Salad with Mangosteen and Chili Mint Dressing

Preparation time 10 minutes
Cooking time 15–20 minutes
Serves 4

about 4–5 oz/120–150 g beef strip loin
3 tablespoons mint leaves
3 tablespoons picked cilantro (coriander)
2 tablespoons finely sliced shallots
1 tablespoon finely sliced lemongrass
4–5 mangosteens, with the larger segments containing the seeds removed
1½ teaspoons chiffonaded kaffir lime leaves

For the dressing
4 cloves garlic
½ cup (1 oz/25 g) fresh mint
6–10 small red scud chiles
1–2 teaspoons grilled shrimp paste
1½ teaspoons jaggery, palm sugar, or soft light brown sugar
1 teaspoon unrefined superfine (caster) sugar
fish sauce, to taste
1–2 tablespoons lime juice
2–3 tablespoons coconut cream
fresh fruits and vegetables, such as cabbage, mint sprigs, green beans, small purple apple eggplants (aubergines), to serve

For the dressing, pound the garlic, mint, chiles, and the shrimp paste together in a mortar with a pestle until a very fine paste. Add both sugars and fish sauce to taste followed by the lime juice and coconut cream. Taste the dressing, it should be hot, sour, and salty with a pleasing sweetness and a strong fragrance of mint. Set aside.

For the salad preheat the broiler (grill) to high heat and broil (grill) the beef for 3–5 minutes on both sides or until medium rare, then let rest. Slice and set aside.

Put the mint, cilantro (coriander), shallots, lemongrass, and mangosteen in a bowl, add a generous amount of the dressing, and toss lightly together. Add the beef, then drizzle a small amount of the remaining dressing over the top. Finish with a little of the julienned lime leaves and serve with fruits and vegetables and a sprig of mint.

Stir-Fried Pork with Santol

Preparation time 5–10 minutes
Cooking time 7 minutes
Serves 4

2 tablespoons vegetable oil
7 oz/200 g pork neck, sliced
1½ teaspoons jaggery, palm sugar, or soft light brown sugar
fish sauce, to taste
¼–scant ½ cup (2–3½ fl oz/50–100 ml) light chicken broth (stock)
5 oz/150 g santol
4 kaffir lime leaves, torn
4 red and green chiles, seeded and sliced lengthwise
a squeeze of lime juice

For the paste
2 cilantro (coriander) roots
5–10 red bird's eye chiles
5 Thai shallots
5 garlic bulbs
½–1 tablespoon shrimp paste

For the paste, pound all the ingredients together in a mortar with a pestle until a coarse paste is achieved, then set aside.

Heat the oil in a wok over medium-low heat, add the paste, and stir-fry for 1–2 minutes until fragrant. Add the sliced pork, then increase the heat slightly, and cook for 1–2 minutes until almost cooked. Season with the sugar and a small amount of fish sauce, then add a little of the broth (stock) to loosen the mixture. Add the santol, lime leaves, and chiles and stir-fry for 1–2 minutes until the sauce is thick and a coating consistency. Finish with a squeeze of lime and taste. It should be hot, sour, and equally sweet and salty. Adjust the seasoning, if necessary, then serve.

Henrik Yde-Andersen
Sra Bua by Kiin Kiin

Siam Kempinski Hotel Bangkok
991/9 Rama 1 Road
Pathumwan
Bangkok 10330

Danish chef Henrik Yde-Andersen and his business partner Thai-Danish Lertchai Treetawatchaiwong run a string of highly acclaimed restaurants, from the Michelin-starred Kiin Kiin, to gourmet takeout restaurant Aroii. The two first met in 2005 and together they set out to introduce Thai haute cuisine to Copenhagen's restaurant scene. They achieved this goal when they opened Kiin Kiin in 2006. Two years later the restaurant was awarded a Michelin star. In 2010 the pair opened Sra Bua by Kiin Kiin in Bangkok. Like Kiin Kiin, the restaurant offers a modern interpretation of Thai cuisine, deconstructing the classics but retaining the traditional flavors. In 2013 it was voted 29 in the San Pellegrino 50 Best Restaurants in Asia awards.

เนื้อบนเมนูสน้ำย่าและสมุนไพร
"Yam" Meringue with Beef Tartare and Herbs

Preparation time 15 minutes
Cooking time 15 minutes
Serves 4

For the meringue
2 egg whites
1¾ cups (7 oz/200 g) confectioners' (icing) sugar
fish sauce, to taste
lime juice, to taste
2 large green chiles, seeded

For the tartare
fish sauce, to taste
7 oz/200 g very fresh beef tenderloin or mignon fillet, finely chopped
2 shallots, finely chopped
8 cilantro (coriander) stems
8 Thai cilantro (coriander) stems
8 mint leaves

Beat the egg whites in a large bowl, slowly adding the confectioners' (icing) sugar, fish sauce, and lime juice until it is a balance of sweet and sour and stiff peaks form.

Process the chile in a small food processor or spice grinder until smooth, then add to the meringue. Set aside.

For the tartare, put the fish sauce and beef into a bowl, cover with plastic wrap (clingfilm), and let marinate for 5 minutes.

Arrange the meringue in a bowl, add the beef on the side, and sprinkle with the shallot and herbs. Serve.

Frozen Red Curry with Lobster Salad and Lychee

Preparation time 30 minutes, plus soaking time
Cooking time 15 minutes
Serves 4

For the pickled lychee
sugar syrup, to cover
12 lychees, peeled, pitted, and chopped into
 small pieces

For the red curry paste
3½ oz/100 g large red chiles, seeded
5 small red shallots
10 cloves garlic
4-inch/10-cm piece galangal, peeled and chopped
2½ lemongrass stalks
11 black peppercorns
20 cilantro (coriander) roots
30 kaffir lime leaves
1 handful of coriander seeds
2 tablespoons dried shrimp
⅓ cup (2¼ oz/60 g) shrimp paste
zest and juice of 2 limes

For the lobster salad
baby lobsters
4 teaspoons ginger juice
fish sauce, to taste
4 teaspoons superfine (caster) sugar

For the frozen red curry
1 tablespoon vegetable oil
1¼ cups (10 fl oz/300 ml) coconut milk
⅓ cup (2¾ fl oz/80 ml) condensed milk or palm sugar
1½ tablespoons fish sauce
lime juice, to taste
1 handful of Thai basil, with stems

To garnish
12 fresh coriander seeds
scallions (spring onions), finely chopped
Thai basil

Heat the sugar syrup in a pan over medium heat. Put the lychees in a large heatproof bowl, pour over the hot syrup, and let soak for 24 hours.

For the red curry paste, pound all the ingredients in a mortar with a pestle until smooth, then set aside.

For the lobster salad, boil as many lobsters as your budget allows in a large pan of boiling water for 4–6 minutes. Drain, let cool slightly, then remove and discard the shell and chop the flesh into pieces. Transfer to a bowl, add the ginger juice, fish sauce, and sugar to taste, and cover with plastic wrap (clingfilm). Let marinate in the refrigerator for 10 minutes.

Heat the oil in a wok over medium heat, add 2 tablespoons red curry paste, and sauté for 1 minute. Add the coconut milk and season to taste with the condensed milk or sugar, fish sauce, and lime juice. Add the Thai basil and mix to a soft paste. The basil stems provide a slight liquorice flavor to the curry. Bring to a boil, then transfer to a sorbetière or ice cream machine and churn the mixture according to the machine's instructions.

Remove the soaked lychees with a slotted spoon and transfer to a small bowl. Set aside. Blend the lychee syrup with a handheld blender or an electric mixer to create a foam. Set aside.

Scoop the ice cream onto a plate and decorate with the lobster salad, drained lychees, and fresh coriander seeds. Spoon the lychee foam over the dish, garnish with the scallions (spring onions) and basil, and serve.

Banana Cake with Salted Ice Cream and Fluffy Coconut Milk

Preparation time 6 hours
Cooking time 1 hour
Serves 4

For the cake
5½ tablespoons (2¾ oz/70 g) butter
2 tablespoons honey
¾ cup (3½ oz/100 g) cashew flour
½ cup (3½ oz/100 g) superfine (caster) sugar
1¼ tablespoons potato starch
1 tablespoon coconut flakes
1 teaspoon baking powder
1 teaspoon five-spice powder
1 vanilla bean (pod)
2 egg whites
1 ripe banana, peeled and mashed

For the fluffy coconut milk
4¼ cups (1¾ pints/1 liter) coconut milk
1¼ cups (9 oz/250 g) superfine (caster) sugar
4 gelatin leaves
1 vanilla bean (pod)

For the salted coconut ice cream
4¼ cups (1¾ pints/1 liter) coconut milk
generous 1 cup (9 oz/250 g) brown sugar
1 heaping teaspoon salt

For the crispy coconut
2 tablespoons confectioners' (icing) sugar
1 egg white
1½ cups coconut flakes

To serve
1 x 14 fl oz/400 ml can condensed milk, simmered for
  6 hours (allow can to cool completely before opening)
meat of 1 fresh coconut, finely sliced

For the cake, preheat the oven to 350°F/180°C/Gas Mark 4. Melt the butter and honey in a pan over low heat. Put all the dry ingredients into a large bowl and stir in the melted butter mixture, followed by the egg whites and mashed banana. Spoon the dough into a cake pan and bake in the oven for 15 minutes.

For the fluffy coconut milk, warm the coconut milk in a pan over low heat with the sugar for 5 minutes until the sugar has dissolved. Stir in the gelatin, then transfer to a siphon, seal the top, and charge with a cartridge. Shake vigorously and set aside.

For the ice cream, bring the coconut milk to a boil in a pan over medium heat. Add the sugar and salt and stir until the sugar and salt have dissolved, then transfer to an ice cream machine. Churn according to the machine's instructions.

For the crispy coconut, preheat the oven to 300°F/150°C/Gas Mark 2. Beat the confectioners' (icing) sugar and egg white lightly in a large bowl, then add the coconut flakes and stir until combined. Transfer to a baking pan and bake in the oven for about 20 minutes until golden and crisp.

Arrange the cake on a serving plate, spray over the fluffy coconut (it should be a gravel-like consistency), and decorate with the crispy coconut. Spoon over the ice cream and boiled condensed milk, sprinkle with the sliced coconut, and serve.

ไข่สไตล์กินกิน

Egg Kiin Kiin

Preparation time 1 day
Cooking time 1 hour
Serves 4

First layer
10 cloves garlic
heavy (double) cream

Second layer
1 tablespoon vegetable oil
8 green beans or 2 green asparagus (if in season),
  finely chopped
soy sauce, to taste
fish sauce, to taste
oyster sauce, to taste
1 red bird's eye chile, finely chopped
2 cloves garlic

Third layer
4 egg yolks or 4 whole eggs

Fourth layer
7 tablespoons or scant 1 stick (3½ oz/100 g) butter
1 egg yolk
1 tablespoon lime juice
12 holy basil leaves

To garnish
deep-fried holy basil leaves

For the first layer, boil the garlic cloves in a pan of boiling water. Repeat 5 times using fresh water each time. To make a puree, add a splash of cream and stir until smooth.

For the second layer, heat the oil in a pan over medium heat, add the beans or asparagus, soy sauce, fish sauce, oyster sauce, chile, and garlic and sauté for 10 minutes.

For the third layer, put the egg yolks in a sealed plastic food bag and poach in a bain-marie at 133°F/56°C for 2 hours. Alternatively, boil the whole eggs in a pan of water for about 3 minutes. Scoop out the runny egg yolks and discard the shell and egg whites.

For the fourth layer, melt the butter in a pan. Beat the remaining egg yolk with the lime juice in a bowl. Slowly stir in the melted butter to emulsify. Blend the basil in a small food processor with a splash of water and add to the egg yolk mixture. Transfer to a siphon, seal the top, and charge with a cartridge. Shake vigorously and set aside.

To serve, arrange the layers in egg shells or small glasses. Start with the garlic puree, followed by the fried beans and the poached egg yolks. Finish by dispensing the basil cream on top. Garnish with deep-fried basil leaves.

Glossary

Acacia leaves
The immature, feathery leaves of the *Acacia pennata*, they are cooked in soups, curries, omelets, and stir fries, and are also added raw to green mango salads.

Amaranth
An exotic plant, also known as pigweed, the leaves and grains of which are edible and highly nutritious. The leaves are eaten as a vegetable in many areas of the world. Use spinach instead if you can't find them.

Asiatic pennywort leaves
The scalloped, green leaves of the Asiatic pennywort plant (*Centella asiatica*) are used in the preparation of drinks as well as being included raw in salads and cold rolls.

Bamboo shoots
Quite a few species of bamboo are edible, mostly from the botanical genera *Phyllostachys* or *Bambusa*. *Thyrsostachys siamensis* is one of the most common in Thailand. Its edible shoots are either collected in the wild or cultivated. Boiling them in water destroys the toxicity of the prussic acid that they contain. Bamboo shoots can be fresh, canned, or pickled in brine. Dried shoots are also available.

Banana
Banana leaves, blossoms, and fruits are widely used in Thai cuisine. The leaves are traditionally used as wrappers, for display, or as containers for steaming or grilling food. They can be bought frozen and thawed under warm running water. If you cannot buy them, use foil instead, although the subtle flavor of the banana leaf will be absent from the finished dish.

Banana blossom, the purple bud of the banana plant is used both raw, in salads, and cooked in curries, or as a side dish.

There are more than twenty varieties of banana used in Thai cooking, mostly for desserts, sometimes very locally grown. Bananas are also popular as street food, either grilled or deep-fried.

Basil
There are three main types of basil used in Thai cooking: Thai sweet basil (*Ocimum basilicum*), hairy or hoary basil (*Ocimum americanum*), and holy basil (*Ocimum tenuiflorum* or *sanctum*.) Thai sweet basil has a quite intense taste with an anise or licorice flavor. Often used for curries, soups, and stir fries, it doesn't like a long cooking time, so it is best sprinkled on just before serving.

Hairy basil, also called lemon basil, has a lime flavor that goes well with fish.

Used mostly in fish and seafood dishes, holy basil has a clove-like or allspice fragrance and needs to be cooked to develop its flavor.

Tree basil (*Ocimum gratissimum*) is a strong-flavored herb. It is a variety of sweet basil and is often used as an ingredient in stir fries. The seeds of tree basil are often used as a spice in Northern Thailand.

Beans
Winged beans (*Psophocarpus tetragonolobus*) are the most common beans in Thailand whose taste is very similar to green beans and asparagus. The leaves, flowers, and roots are also edible. The leaves are similar to spinach and the roots to potato.

Yard-long beans (*Vigna unguiculata*), also called snake beans, have pods more than 1 foot/30 cm long. Young and freshly picked, they are eaten raw with chili paste or cooked in stir fries and fish cakes.

Stink beans (*Parkia speciosa*), also called bitter beans, have a strong smell that disappears with cooking. Stink beans are eaten raw or roasted in the pod. The peeled beans are often stir-fried with curry paste, shrimp (prawns), or pork.

Betel leaves
The traditional wrapper for the popular *miang* snacks, these shiny leaves are collected on the *Piper sarmentosum* plant. They are often confused with the true betel leaves of *Piper betle*, a perennial creeper, which are very similar but wider and stronger in taste. Napa (Chinese) cabbage, lettuce, and Chinese kale are also used for *miang*.

Bilimbi
A fruit of the cucumber tree (*Averrhoa bilimbi*), it is short, light green, and sour. It contains citric acid so is often found pickled in Asia. Related to the carambola (star fruit), it is often added to sour curries.

Butterfly-pea flower
A deep blue flower with yellow markings from the plant *Clitoria ternatea*, it is used in the preparation of sweet drinks and can also be battered and deep-fried.

Cabbages
Most of the cabbages or related leafy greens belong to the same botanical genus: *Brassica*. Mustard greens (*Brassica juncea*), napa (Chinese) cabbage (*Brassica rapa* subsp. *pekinensis* and *chinensis*), and Chinese kale or Chinese broccoli (*Brassica oleracea*) are usually stir-fried with garlic fish sauce and served as a side dish. They can also be preserved and pickled.

Chayote shoots
The young shoots and leaves of the chayote plant (*Sechium edule*) are eaten raw in Thai salads as well as cooked in stir fries and soups.

Chiles
The fruits of certain varieties of capsicum plant, with a unique hot flavor, there are many types of fresh and dried chiles used in Thailand. The most common fresh chiles used are the spur chile (2½ in/6 cm) and the smaller bird's eye chile (1¼ in/3 cm). The spur chile can be green, red, or orange. It is larger and spicier than the bird's eye chile, and it is often used decoratively or simply as a vegetable in stir fries and curries. Bird's eye chiles may be green or red in color, according to their ripeness. Always used in abundance, fresh chiles are either raw or roasted.

Sundried chiles are also available in different sizes. The larger ones are a key ingredient for curry paste, after being soaked in water, while the smallest—bird's eye chiles—are ground to a powder after roasting. The hottest parts of the chile are the seeds, which can be discarded before use. Local Thai people, however, do not remove the seeds, thereby increasing the strength and heat of their pastes.

Chinese celery

The celery used in Thailand is much smaller in size and stronger in taste than the regular leaf one. In Thai cuisine it is commonly used in soups.

Chinese fish cake

A fish cake in the shape of a long tube, it is also known as a fish slice. In Thai cuisine they are often sliced and used in noodle soups. They are available from most Asian markets.

Cilantro (coriander)

There are three different types of herb called cilantro used in Thai cooking and they belong to three different plant genera: sawtooth cilantro (*Eryngium foetidum*), Vietnamese cilantro (*Polygonum odoratum*), and the ordinary cilantro (*Coriandrum sativum*). The latter, sometimes called Chinese parsley, is the most popular. The roots and seeds are used in most Thai curry pastes, while the leaves and stems (including the flowers) are always used as a garnish (together with mint or scallions/spring onions), in order to bring freshness.

As suggested by one of its vernacular names, the sawtooth cilantro leaf has serrated edges and the taste is stronger than the classic cilantro.

Mostly used in Southeast Asian cuisine and virtually unknown outside this part of the world, the stems and leaves of the Vietnamese cilantro have a cilantro-like smell with a lemony note.

Citrus fruits

The juice of the small Thai lime brings sourness and freshness to many dishes. If used during cooking, the juice is added at the very end before serving, to retain the fragile aroma. Always use lime juice to flavor fried rice.

A small, very sour, green citrus fruit with orange flesh, calamansi is another type of citrus fruit—a hybrid unknown in the wild. More popular in other Southeast Asian countries, it is used in the same way as lime, mostly for its sour taste.

The zest of the wrinkled green citrus known as the kaffir lime (*Citrus hystrix*) is mostly used in curries. The aromatic oil in the leaves is the most fragrant part, and is used to flavor soups, curries, and steamed fish dishes. Kaffir lime leaves are almost always very finely sliced before being eaten.

Coconut

An oily nut grown on a coconut palm, with a coarse brown exterior and white flesh. The flesh can be used fresh or dried in large or small pieces, or grated and dried (desiccated), and is added to dishes to give flavor and texture. The liquid inside the fruit is called coconut water and is typically a street food drink that is drunk straight from the fruit, using a plastic straw. Alternatively, liquid can be extracted from the coconut meat to make coconut milk, or a slightly thicker version, coconut cream. Along with chili or curry pastes, coconut milk is an essential ingredient in many curries.

To make fresh coconut milk, grate the flesh of a fresh coconut into a bowl. Cover with water and leave.to soak for 30 minutes. Pour the mixture through a clean piece of cheesecloth (muslin) or into a clean bowl. This first extract is thick, and is used like coconut cream. It requires careful handling when cooking, and should be added to dishes slowly after reducing the heat, otherwise it will curdle.

To make a thinner coconut milk, return the soaked coconut to the bowl, cover with water, and repeat the soaking and straining process. This coconut milk can be boiled for longer periods.

The coconut terminal bud—called heart of palm—is much appreciated for its delicate aroma and slightly sweet flavor, which is very different to other palm species. Usually the terminal buds are collected from old trees since their removal accelerates the death of the plant. Heart of palm is often finely chopped and used in salads.

Corn

Boiled corn cobs are a very popular street food in Central Thailand. They are sold in markets and in small stalls along the road. Corn kernels are often used in Thai desserts.

Cow tree leaves

The leaves of the cow tree (*Garcinia cowa*), which can be found across Thailand in most lowland forest areas, are used in a local pork curry from Chanthaburi Province. The leaves can be substituted with any sour leaves, such as tamarind leaves.

Crab

Two main types of crabs are available in Thailand, and they are both seawater crabs: the soft-shell crab and the rice field crab (considered a pest because it eats the young rice stems.) The soft-shell crab is harvested shortly after it has shed its hard shell and before it has formed another. The rice field crab is often pickled with salt and included in a variation of Thai papaya salad.

Curry pastes

There are many curry pastes in Thailand. Every home has its own interpretation, but the basic ingredients do not vary: chiles, cilantro (coriander), salt, pepper, garlic, shallot, and shrimp paste. Made using a mortar and pestle, they have the texture of a slightly moist paste, more or less coarsely ground. The most common are classified by their color: green using fresh green chiles, red using dried rehydrated red chiles, and yellow, which gets its distinctive color from the inclusion of turmeric, a root commonly used in southern Thailand. This broad classification does not cover all variations: fresh or dried peppers can be roasted before pounding, some traditional northern recipes do not use shrimp paste, and other regions incorporate fingerroot. However, the most famous Thai curry paste, Massaman, is milder and contains a number of ground spices, such as coriander, cumin, and cardamom.

Curry powder

Mainly used in dishes with Muslim origins, this mix also reflects the Indian influence.

Daikon (mooli)

A giant, white radish, it has a peppery taste, similar to watercress, and can be eaten raw or cooked.

Dill

Mostly used as a fresh herb in North and Northeast Thailand in the same way as cilantro (coriander), mint, or scallions (spring onions).

Durian

A native fruit to Southeast Asia and regarded by many as the "king of the fruits" the durian can weigh up to 6½ lb/3 kg and is mostly grown in Eastern Thailand. The yellowish and soft flesh of this round, spiky fruit is sweet and creamy with little juice. While it is mostly eaten raw, ripe or unripe durian can be cooked in curries or soups. It is at its best when just ripened and has the dubious reputation of a bad and intrusive smell.

Eggplant (aubergine)

Several kinds of eggplants of different shapes and sizes are used in Thai cuisine: small, long, and round. Pea eggplants (*Solanum torvum*) are the smallest ones, found in clusters. They have a slightly bitter taste and can be eaten raw or cooked in curries.

Round eggplants (*Solanum xanthocarpum*) come in a variety of colors, such as green, white, and yellow. Slightly bitter, they are eaten raw. Like other vegetables, they help to reduce the burning sensation in the mouth from spicy dishes. The unripe ones are often used in curries.

Long green eggplants have a denser texture than the purple variety and are often broiled (grilled) or stir-fried.

Eggs and salted eggs

Chicken and duck eggs are both sold in Thai markets, nevertheless, the salted preserved ones are mostly made from duck eggs. The thickness of their shell makes it possible to keep them longer in the brine. Eggs and egg yolks are also the central ingredient of specific desserts inherited from the Portuguese, typically prepared in the Central Plains region.

Fingerroot

Often called lesser galangal or Chinese ginger, this root is mainly used in fish dishes to reduce the strong taste of freshwater fish.

Fish

Seawater and freshwater fish are part of everyday meals all around Thailand. Fish are caught both in the sea and rivers in the eastern and southern part of the country, but they are also widely raised in aquaculture farms located along the coast as well as in inland areas. Most of the fish used in the Thai recipes are white fish, such as tilapia, sea bass, snakehead, and catfish.

Among the most popular, is the short mackerel, which is found in almost every market, displayed in small bamboo baskets, after having been steamed. Its closest "relatives" are horse mackerel and sardines.

Sun-drying is the most effective way of preserving fish for a long time. It occurs near the seaside, riverside, canals, or ponds. Fish—mostly of small or medium size—are open and gutted before being dried. Dried fish is used in soups, sauces, salads, and curries.

Fish sauce and fermented fish

A source of salt and a flavor enhancer, fish sauce is obtained by fermenting small fish, such as anchovies, with salt, for several months. The salt content of the fish sauce can easily exceed 30 percent. In Thailand, another type of fish sauce, *tai pla,* is common. It is obtained by the same method but it uses fish guts. In southern Thailand, the less common fish sauce, called *budu*, is prepared in the same way.

Originating from Northeast Thailand, fermented fish is the result of the fermentation of freshwater fish (snakehead, for instance) with salt and roasted rice flour. Fermented fish sauce is the juice that exudes from this process of fermentation.

Galangal

The greater galangal (also called Siamese ginger) is a pale rhizome of the plant (*Alpinia galangal*), and is similar to ginger, with reddish root tips. More pungent than ginger, fresh galangal is used in curry pastes, but also gives a very specific taste to some Thai soups.

Garcinia

A small, segmented, thin-skinned green fruit, its rind and extract are often used as a souring agent in curries.

Garlic and shallots

Probably the most basic ingredients of Thai cuisine, Thai garlic and shallots are used in almost every savory dish. They are smaller than other varieties around the world and have a more delicate fragrance. Take this into account when measuring the recipe quantities, which are based on small garlic and shallots being used.

Garlic is often cooked with the skin still on when deep-fried. Freshly made garlic or shallot oil is a very interesting by-product. As well as being deep-fried, shallots are often served raw, especially in salads, sauces, and dips.

Ginger

Thai cooks prefer the fresh ginger rhizomes, young or mature. Used in many curries, soups, and salads, ginger is also the prominent ingredient in popular dishes like Chicken with Ginger. It has a strong pungent flavor and, when grated or pounded, gives a warm, citrus flavor to dishes. Mature ginger is fibrous, and less moist than fresh, young ginger. It also has a stronger taste.

Gourds

Angled gourd is a long, dark green, ridged fruit, with a thick skin and a soft interior. The gourd must be harvested at an early stage of its development to be edible, before it becomes too fibrous. The young fruit's spongy flesh has a subtle, sweet flavor and can be used in salads, stir-fries, and sauces.

Bitter gourd is a bitter vegetable with a knobbly green skin. It comes in many varieties ranging from short to long, dark green and pale green and is commonly used in Thai soups. It can be found in Asian grocery stores.

Bottle gourd is a bottle-shaped pale green fruit, with a nutty flavor. Squash can be used as an alternative.

Great morinda (*Morinda citrifolia*)

A tree in the coffee family, native to Southeast Asia, the juice of which has a neutral taste and is used to give a green color to rice dishes. The leaves may be replaced by pandan leaves or Chinese kale leaves. Also known as noni.

Indian trumpet flower pod

This is the large seed pod of the Indian trumpet flower (*Oroxylum indicum*) that somewhat resembles an enormous string (runner) bean. In Thailand the young pods are grilled over an open fire, then the outer layer is scraped off, and the rest is sliced and served with chili sauce, added to curries, or fried with shrimp paste.

Insects

Because they are very good sources of protein, insects are eaten in many provinces of Thailand and especially in the North and Northeast. Often collected in the countryside, some insects, such as crickets, palm weevils, and bamboo caterpillars are now produced in specialized farms. While the insects themselves are eaten, so too are the larvae of silkworms and the eggs of red ants.

Jackfruit

The largest fruit that you can find on a tree, jackfruit can reach a weight of more than 66 lb/30 kg. Inside this oblong, spiky-skinned fruit is a shiny orange to yellow meat—arranged in lobe shaped segments—that is edible when ripe. Unripe jackfruit requires cooking. Used mainly for desserts, it has a neutral sweetness. Jackfruit contains a white substance that numbs the hands, so some Asian stores sell already cleaned and cut jackfruit. If you buy a whole fruit you might like to wear gloves when handling it.

Job's tear seeds
Also called Chinese pearl barley, it belongs to the grass family, but not to the same genus as barley. Job's tear has long been used in traditional Chinese medicine and as a nourishing cereal. It is added to soups and broths in the form of flour or whole grain. In Japan and Thailand, a non-dairy drink from Job's tears is available in the market as an alternative health food. Job's tears are often served in Thai drinks, such as tea and soymilk.

Julienne
To cut food into tiny strips.

Khanom krok pan
A round pan containing about thirty small round molds, it can be substituted with a pancake puff pan.

Knead
To fold, press, and stretch dough until it becomes smooth and elastic.

Lead tree seeds
The seeds of the lead tree (*Leucaena leucocephala*) are eaten raw as a side dish with other hot and spicy dishes.

Lemongrass
Together with lime and kaffir lime, lemongrass is one of the three components of the lemony taste of Thai cuisine. The hard stems of this perennial grass need to be freed from their fibrous outer leaves and finely chopped or crushed to release the essential oils and sweet, subtle citrus flavor.

Limewater
A natural mineral water made with pink or red limestone paste is widely used in Thai cuisine. It is used to make soft fruit and vegetables firm before pickling or long cooking. The fruit or vegetable is peeled, cut, and left to soak in the limewater. It can also be used to make pastry crispy. The paste can be found in Asian grocery stores.

To make limewater, mix 1 tablespoon of pink or red limestone paste with 3 cups (1¼ pints/750 ml) water in a large bowl. Stir well, then transfer to a sterilized jar, cover, seal, and let stand for at least 3–4 hours or until the limestone has completely precipitated and the water is clear. Only the clear water must be used. Shake the jar about an hour before using. The water should be discarded when the clay solids settle in under 30 minutes. Use club soda (soda water) as an alternative, but not if soaking.

Lotus stems
The long green stems (more than 6 ft/2 m) of the lotus (*Nelumbo nucifera*) are grown in ponds and need to be peeled before cooking. They have a mild sweet flavor and can be eaten either raw in salads or cooked.

Lychee
A fruit with a rough pinkish red rind, which surrounds a delicate whitish flesh and stone, the flesh has a floral smell and fragrant, sweet flavor.

Madan leaves
The young leaves or the madan tree (*Garcinia schomburgkiana*)—a close relative of the mangosteen tree—can be eaten raw but are often cooked with pork curry in Southern Thailand. They can also be cooked with fish or served as a vegetable accompaniment to many Thai dishes.

Mango
One can find mangoes throughout the year in the markets in Thailand. Dozens of varieties are grown. Ripe mangoes are delicious served with sticky rice. Green sour mangoes can be eaten raw and they are often used in place of, or in combination with, lime to bring a sour note to savory dishes. The horse mango (*Mangifera foetida*) is a large green relative of the mango. The sap of the young fruit causes skin irritation; the mature fruit has orange yellow fibrous flesh and a strong aroma.

Mangosteen
A small, round fruit, with a thick, dark purple inedible "shell" surrounding edible white flesh, it is creamy in texture and has a sweet, slightly tart flavor.

Mangrove trumpet tree flowers
The long, trumpet-shaped flowers of the mangrove trumpet tree (*Dolichandrone spathacea*) are very fragrant and edible. When eaten in Thai cuisine, the flowers are either stir-fried or used as an ingredient in curries and fish soups. They can also be stuffed with curry. These flowers can be hard to find so zucchini (courgette) flowers are a good substitute.

Mekong river seaweed
A seaweed that grows on underwater rocks and thrives in clear water. It is cleaned, flattened into sheets and then sundried.

Melinjo leaves
The young leaves of the small tropical Melinjo tree (*Gnetum gnemon*) are eaten raw or cooked in soups. These leaves can be hard to find and can be replaced by other leafy vegetables, such as spinach, Chinese kale, bok choy (pak choi), or ivy gourd.

Mortar and pestle
The universal tool of Thai cuisine, the most common duo consists of a clay mortar and a wooden pestle. Depending on the size, they can be used to pound curry pastes, dips, and even some salads. In some areas, they are carved out of stone and very occasionally made entirely of wood. It is advisable to use a heavy stone mortar and pestle to pound ingredients to a paste. The ingredients should be added to the mortar in small amounts to make it easier to pound. Alternatively, a food processor may be used.

Mung Beans
Most of the beans like mung beans, kidney beans, or black beans are used in Thailand for desserts. However, mung beans have many more uses. Green when unpeeled, they become yellow when they are skinned and "split." Mung bean flour is made from these split beans and is used to create the very thin, transparent, glass noodles (see Noodles). By letting mung beans germinate, one gets bean sprouts, which are often used in Thai stir fries and salads.

Mushrooms
The cloud ear mushroom (*Auricularia polytricha*) is a gray-brown fungus, it has little flavor itself but possesses a distinctive crunchy texture and is used in stir fries, soups, and salads.

The termite mushroom (*Termitomyces fuliginosus*) is typically from Kanchanaburi Province and is a wild mushroom with a very refined taste. It is available in Thailand during the hot season.

Lentinula is a genus of wood-inhabiting mushrooms common to tropical regions. The most well known is the shiitake mushroom (*Lentinula edodes*), which is often steamed or fried in Thai cuisine.

Neem or sadao (*Azadirachta indica*)
A tree mainly found in the Northeast region, neem is one of the most popular indigenous vegetables. The young shoots and flowers are bitter when eaten raw. When steamed, they can be dipped into sauces. It is hard to replace neem with another vegetable, due to its distinctive taste.

Noodles
Several types of noodles are commonly available in Thailand: rice noodles, fermented rice noodles, egg noodles, and glass noodles.

Made from rice flour, rice noodles are available in different thicknesses including very thin vermicelli. They can be found dried but most often they are sold fresh in Thai markets.

Fermented rice noodles are made from rice that has been left to ferment for a couple of days before being converted into starch, which is then kneaded and passed through a strainer (sieve) to form noodles.

Egg noodles are made from wheat flour and eggs, and are popular in Northern Thailand.

Dried glass or cellophane noodles are made from mung bean starch (flour) and have a transparent appearance.

Oyster sauce
An authentic oyster sauce is prepared by caramelizing oyster broth until it becomes viscous and dark brown. No other addition is needed, not even salt. Modern oyster sauce, used in the same way as fish or soy sauce, is made from sugar, salt, and water thickened with starch and flavored with oyster essence.

Pandan leaves
The long and narrow leaves of the pandan plant *(Pandanus amaryllifolius)* are mostly used in desserts and drinks to impart a pleasant, nutty taste, reminiscent of fresh hay. They are also used for the green color of their juice.

Papaya
Very popular for the green papaya salad, unripe papaya has a green skin that needs to be removed. The latex of the green fruit contains papain, an enzyme used to tenderize meat.

Pink mempat leaves
The young leaves of the pink mempat tree *(Cratoxylum formosum)* are eaten raw or boiled. They can be substituted with tamarind leaves.

Pomelo
When in season in Thailand—around August and September—pomelo is eaten fresh, as it is valued for its sweet-and-sour taste. It is also the main ingredient of the Thai pomelo salad.

Pork floss
A variety of dried pork, it has a light and fluffy texture and is made from stewing pork in a sweetened soy sauce mixture until it begins to break into strands. It is then strained and dried before being mashed and beaten while frying until the pork is almost completely dry.

Pound
To grind ingredients in a mortar with a pestle to make a powder or paste.

Rambutan
A small round fruit, covered in a leathery, spiny red skin, surrounding a pale flesh, slightly tart in flavor.

Rice
When they ask for alms at dawn, Buddhist monks in Thailand often receive a portion of cooked rice. When they return to their monastery, these portions are left to dry on the ground to preserve them. This gives some indication of how fundamental rice is to everyday life in Thailand—a country that boasts the fifth largest acreage under rice cultivation in the world. Rice is part of every Thai meal and is the most important source of carbohydrates. Rice is cropped right across the country, with the Central and Northeast regions being the most important areas of rice production.

There are, however, differences in the type of rice produced and eaten in these regions. While glutinous (sticky) rice is mainly eaten in the North and Northeast regions, in the Central Plains long-grain rice is predominant. There are significant differences between these two types of rice. Glutinous rice has thick, opaque grains and contains more amylopectin, which causes it to become sticky when cooked. As such, it is less digestible than long-grain rice. Jasmine rice, which originates from Thailand, is the most famous of all long-grain rice. Known for its delicate nutty taste, jasmine rice is steamed, while glutinous rice is soaked, then steamed.

Ground and roasted, white glutinous rice is used in the preparation of fermented fish.

Freshly ground rice is used as a flour in desserts as a thickening agent.

Roselle leaves
The green, tripart leaves of the roselle plant (*Hibiscus sabdariffa*), a species of hibiscus, have a distinctive sour flavor, and can be eaten in soups and stir fries. The plant's fleshy, bright red fruit is also used, fresh or dried, to make a drink.

Salacca (snake fruit)
This fruit, with dark reddish, scaly skin grows in clusters at the base of the palm *Salacca zalacca*, a very large spiny shrub. Its white flesh surrounds a large kernel. Salacca is available to buy fresh or canned in sugar syrup.

Sesame seeds
The seed of the sesame plant, found in black and white varieties, they have an oily, nutty flavor and are used in small quantities as a thickening agent, and for making sweet dishes and snacks.

Shrimp (prawns)
In addition to the caught shrimp (prawns), Thailand is a major producer of farmed shrimp (prawns). These are eaten in many dishes such as salads, soups, curries, and stir fries.

Dried shrimp are used as a condiment. They are first boiled before being sundried and freed from their shells. They have a unique taste and are frequently used in curry pastes. When pounded they should have the consistency of fine flakes.

Shrimp paste
Prepared in the southern part of the country during the fishing season, this is a pungent pink paste made from very small shrimp that have been fermented with sea salt. It is a universal Thai seasoning or condiment present in many dishes.

Skin (from animal)
The skin of two animals, pork and buffalo, is used in everyday cuisine. Boiled pork skin and—mostly in the Northeast—buffalo skin, are included in some savory dishes. After being boiled and cleared of its fat, deep-fried pork skin—crackling—is a very popular snack.

Soybeans

These are small round legumes (pulses) that can be eaten fresh (green) or dried (yellow and black), and also be made into a variety of products, including tofu, pastes, and sauces. Two key ingredients of Thai cuisine are produced from soybeans: tofu (see Tofu) and soy sauce.

Soy sauce is obtained by fermenting soybeans and rice or wheat flour with the help of a starter based on a mold (*Aspergillus oryzae*). Dark soy sauce is thickened with starch and sugar. In Thai cuisine soy sauce is often used as a salty condiment and natural flavor enhancer in a similar way as is fish sauce and—less often—oyster sauce.

The fermentation of soybeans leads to two other important ingredients of Thai cuisine: fermented soybean paste and dehydrated round soybean sheets. Both are mainly used in Northern Thailand as a source of protein and as a flavor enhancer.

Star gooseberry

The small, sour, pale yellow fruits of the Star gooseberry tree (*Phyllanthus acidus*), found throughout Southeast Asia, are used in salads, while the young leaves are often included in Thai papaya salad. The young shoots are eaten raw or cooked (boiled or fried) in many Thai dishes as they lend a spicy peppery flavor to the dish. They can be replaced by yard-long beans (see Beans).

Sterilizing jars

To sterilize jars, wash the jars and lids thoroughly in hot, soapy water. Rinse well, then place the jars and lids open-side up, without touching, on a baking sheet. Transfer to an oven preheated to 250°F/120°C/Gas mark ½, and leave for at least 30 minutes. Alternatively, boil the jars and lids in a large pan of water for 15 minutes. Take care to ensure that the jars are already warmed before placing them in a hot oven.

Sugar

Although granulated white sugar is widely used in Thai cuisine, there are two other major types of sugar processed in Thailand: cane sugar and palm sugar. Unlike the first, which is produced in large factories, palm sugar is often produced in small artisan workshops. The sap is collected from various palm trees and then cooked and concentrated to form a granular paste. Used in both savory and sweet dishes, it brings both a deep color and a unique flavor.

Sugar palm fruit

A dark round fruit of the sugar palm tree (*Borassus flabellifer*), which has a thick black husk. The inner part of the young fruit contains three sweet jelly seed-sockets that are edible. These are translucent and have a crunchy texture similar to lychees (see Lychee) but with a milder flavor. They are often candied in sugar.

Tamarind

There are two ways of using tamarind in Thai cuisine. The very young leaves, which have a sour taste similar to sorrel, are used in soups and curries. The inside of the pods (the flesh around the seeds) is a key seasoning ingredient of Thai cuisine, bringing acidity to dishes and providing an interesting balance between sweet and sour. It can be bought dried. The dried fruit is ground and pulped or soaked in water to extract its flavor. A sweet variety of tamarind is also available, although some acidity is still noticeable.

Tapioca flour

A starch extracted from the yucca root (cassava), it is used in a variety of Thai desserts and as a thickening agent.

Taro roots and leaves

The stems of some types of taro or elephant ear plants are edible, though they require boiling. Their texture absorbs the liquid of curries like a sponge. Boiled leaves are also eaten in some parts of the country particularly in curries.

Thai scented dessert candle

Scented candles allow dessert vendors to create an aroma trail for their special desserts. This type of candle can be bought at any morning market in Thailand or from a specific dessert shop owner. Light both ends of the u-shaped candle and place it onto a small plate or bowl. Let it burn for 2 minutes, then blow out the candle and wait until the black smoke disappears and you can smell the aroma. Put the smoking candle in the pan or bowl you are using, cover with a lid, and let smoke for 10–15 minutes. This process can be repeated 5–6 times. The candle can be used another time if there is still some left after you have finished smoking the dessert.

Tiger grass leaves

The leaves of the bamboo-like clumping tiger grass (*Thysanolaena maxima*) are used to wrap foods, particularly glutinous (sticky) rice (see Rice), when cooking.

Tofu

There are various forms of tofu, with different textures that range from soft to firm. Often developed in small workshops, soymilk—made from ground soybeans—is heated and curdled by coagulants agents, mostly salts like calcium sulfate or chloride. The resulting curds are then pressed into white blocks.

Egg tofu mostly has a soft texture and is obtained by adding whole beaten eggs to soymilk, before adding the coagulant. Egg tofu is shaped in the form of a cylinders and it is wrapped in plastic. It is a pale yellow color, which is mostly due to the addition of food colorants.

Bubble tofu or tofu skin is the dried thin film that forms on the surface of concentrated soymilk as it boils.

Turmeric

The rhizome of the south, with its distinct orange color, turmeric is mostly used as a dry powder all around the world. In Southern Thailand, turmeric is used fresh as an ingredient of chili pastes, for instance, bringing an earthy and peppery flavor and a distinctive yellow color.

Vegetable hummingbird flowers

The white and red flowers of the *Sesbania grandiflora* tree, they are cooked in curries as well as being included raw in chili pastes.

Vinegar

White vinegar is mostly used in Thailand. In some areas, the sap of palm trees (the same as for palm sugar) is fermented in order to obtain palm vinegar.

Water Spinach

A semi-aquatic leaf vegetable with thin, hollow stems and long, arrow-head shaped leaves. Its leaves are eaten raw in salads and are included in many stir fries, soups, and curries.

Yucca Root (Cassava)

Obtained from palm roots, like sago, yucca root is the edible root of a tropical plant enclosing a white starchy flesh within a brown rind. Originally from Brazil, yucca root was brought to Southeast Asia by European colonists. It is often used in Thai desserts.

Index

Captions

Thai Cook Contributors

**Cooks who contributed
traditional recipes for
inclusion in the book:**

Amnuai Sa-Labphet
Amnuan Jeemook
Ampa Phongaksorn
Ampai Aim-Um
Ampai Pangsawad
Ampai Sornkleng
Ampawan Korrateeratada
Amphon Kongkune
Amporn Bantaowong
Amporn Cheilomkhome
Amporn Jairoon
Anchalee Limchootrakol
Aniwat Bootwilai
Aphisit Saema
Ar-Phirom Nukulkij
Ar-Ranya Chaimongkol
Ar-Ranya Sriyakhum
Ardisorn Chiethai
Arlew Saema
Arpaporn Phetkamhang
Arporn Boonthum
Arporn Phak-Sar
Arree Hutsayee
Arreewan Hutsayee
Arroom Boonthum
Au-Krit Wongthongsalee
Bang-On Karin
Bang-On Parisitthinava
Bang-Orn Rakkwamsuk
Benjarat Wanthongsook
Boadang Boonyo
Boakhew Sornvai
Boalai Puttichard
Boaman Tapook
Boaphun Pongnara
Boonchoen Phokaew
Boonchoie Nontathi
Boonlevt Changyoo
Boonnone Sangrayap
Boonnow Tarnsombat
Boonsoa Maiprakhon
Boonsowl Maiprakhon
Boontan Yoddannone
Boy Suitisantisakul
Bussaba Chankhumnera
Cha-Lhom Khemkhon
Chabar Sangrit
Chad Majang
Chaiwat Intarasit
Chalernpon Nitikulvorawong
Chaloae Si-Ondee
Chaloaw Virogjana
Chamaiporn Sanglung
Chankhom Uthikom
Chayaporn Manee-Sutham
Chittra Veerathong

Chittravadee Deethon
Choiejoo Akkavasakulpinyo
Chonnaphat Borriboon
Choochard Limchootrakol
Choom Noomporn Praditthane
Chunchom Porjapore
Chunmanee Kapong
Chunphit Porjapore
Chutichai Singhakraipa
Coamchalawe Wanthongsook
Daecha Meesuwan
Dang Natesangkhew
Daranee Kittivanit
Darin Ar-Runnart
Dootdao Chanchai
Duangdao Wongpunya
Duangduan Jamesiri
Duangnate Saekowe
Fong Att-Suwan
Gean Thaiprakhon
Hatairat Jewma
Hemm Yampew
Jaideaw Pankhum
Jamrus Jantasrikhum
Jaranya Srirak
Jaray Deat-U-Dom
Jaree Sookdee
Jaroon Toongparoo
Jarunee Chilimart
Jaruwan Hutsayee
Jeerasak Chantakom
Jintana Boonwatee
Jintana Chinsri
Jintana Namkorn
Jiranun Srisook
Jitssil Uitisantisakul
Jongdee Set
Joom Saya
Joon Thairum
Jumneain Surisanun
Kaesorn Horrasard
Kaewta Tassanamontain
Kanchana Yimkrib
Kanittha Ha-Klin
Kanjana Kantanon
Kankaew Poraha
Kankong Wongpracha
Kanokwan Deedoychart
Kanorkrat Wannarat
Kanyaporn Arson
Kasorn Horasatra
Kasorn Teera-Ampornphun
Kesirin Khongkhew
Ketnisa Nanawan
Khemthong Chanchaie
Khomphong Taprom
Khonenoot Khotirossaranee
Khumnoie Nuangnit
Kim Steppe
Koabkuae Lawnthavee
Komejee Khunsantad

Komfong Duang-On
Kompang Tomkaew
Kongkeaw Duangna
Kotchaporn Khongklowe
Krasae Saisawad
Krasaesin Pootubnoo
Kritsana Meepat
Kumpun Boonyoad
Kurab Poongsaka
Kurab Pradabsook
Lamom Kanbootdee
Lamphan Khemkhon
Lamyoung Naiesungnoen
Leaw Fongfune
Lumjeak Jangpai
Mana Sookklaw
Maneerat Limchootrakol
Mathurot Kevdthong
Mêm Somany
Mongkol Pladphl
Monta Loaiprakhon
Na Peu Nae Chaopongpai
Nab Sapathammakul
Naitakan Prathomkate
Napaporn Pradit
Narakorn Chama
Naree Chantakom
Narong Jakteerungkoon
Natcha Wiboonpin
Natji Toongparoo
Nattaya Kaevee
Nawaphumin Chaichompoo
Nicha Sriwong
Nillpat Wanchanaboon
Nipaporn Ak-Karath
Niphon Toonkomhong
Niyom Ubolphun
Niyom Chobsook
Noi Boa-Ban
Nongkran Mankong
Nonglux Kridsang
Nongnuch Doakboa
Nongyao Soabsai
Noo Phokaew
Noo Putphun
Noopin Sirivet
Noopin Wanthongsook
Nooror Somany
Nootchavee Marrawang
Nuansri Jairoon
Nujira Tantaisong
Numchai Punpued
Nun Noochun
Nuntaphong Janthana
Nunthisar Phangkool
Nutchaleeporn Supasiritananun
Oanjun Poomee
Ooyjai Saisamute
Ooyjoo Yeesan
Or-Rathai Hirun
Orratai Khongklowe

Pairin Klam-Phot
Paitoon Taranunthakul
Pakorn Amrungsakhorn
Palakorn Pandang
Panida Khewrum
Panjarat Sangrat
Pantipa Ouitekkeng
Parichad Intachote
Pathum Phunmangmee
Pattama Phetsuwan
Pattama Satavivawong
Pattra Warasit
Peeraya Loawhachot
Pha Singtee
Phaiboon Panpeng
Phayap Soaepan
Phisit Supasiritananun
Phongsri Suwannasut
Pikulthong Charhom
Pin Channane
Pipatpong Israsena Na Ayudhya
Piromrat Choo-Choie
Pitsamai Sintusuwan
Piyapat Srichana
Pong Surisa
Poongpayom Wattanapreedee
Poonyavee Hinkaie
Pornchai Suknirun
Pornthip Pengprakhon
Pornthipa Kiatpiriya
Porntip Nillakit
Potjana Loawhachot
Prajobe Prathomkate
Prakhong Kitimas
Prakob Hermsom
Pramoon Tubthong
Pranee Preesawang
Pranee Suksawat
Praneet Phosri
Pranorm Tassana
Prapai Phongaksorn
Prapaporn Sungtrisien
Prapit Oan-Ampai
Prasirt Wattanacharoen
Prasong Tubthong
Prathip Chompoonuch
Prathung Jaisookjai
Prathung Yampew
Prayard Lamoongtawai
Prayoung Komedee
Preecha Deetoe
Preecha Roata
Preechakieat Boonyakieat
Preeda Poonsawad
Preeyanuch Tatiyapunyalerd
Presirt Jaikrajang
Punnarai Rajavate
Ra-Ong Wongthongsalee
Rabeab Tanyahan
Ramduan Phonasamran
Ranoo Wongjantri
Raree Wongkhum
Ratanaporn Nuankoksung
Rattana Thongkune
Ream Prathomkate
Rin Sanboonsiri
Rooj Changtrakul

Rumyai Arphaisane
Rungrat Roata
Sa-Taine Sutthilux
Saeamg Sawanglab
Saiboa Yeaimsungnoen
Saichon Sukphiboon
Saiporn Porntrai
Saisamorn Suraphap
Saithong Jaieda
Saiyood Srisook
Sakultip Nitikulvorawong
Sakuna Benjawan
Salee Sawangchap
Sam-Muang Akkavasakulpinyo
Samai Poosrisoom
Samorn Jirarat
Samorn Somsub
Samran Sawangchap
Samril Phengsorn
Samrit Boonyoadn
Samroie Phetkamhang
Samrong Jaikra
Samroye Kaewsooksai
Sangwan Sawangrab
Sanit Sudjai
Sanong Sornjai
Saowanee Tipsawad
Sarinya Maiprakhon
Sarkorn Virayachai
Sasipen Chompoonuch
Sawang Doakboa
Sawang Verathumsarikul
Saweak Sintusuwan
Sawing Tubted
Sin Nawkoomuang
Sin Sridan
Siripen Santakorn
Soamkleang Soabwan
Soie Kosinpathompong
Somjai Pookngam
Somjai Vorrapinthong
Somjun Donsinpool
Somkid Hamarit
Somkid Srisook
Somkleang Suabwan
Somkuan Siripukdee
Somkwan Putphun
Sommai Kumboocha
Somphong Wichai
Sompit Somany
Somporn Katoong
Somporn Komsao
Somruie Boonphotong
Somtawin Rittiklang
Somwang Prajong
Somying Sophakorn
Sonthaya Mitmuang
Soomnook Pookaew
Soonboon Phermsin
Sorn Nakara
Srida Wanarat
Srimoon Apaikavee
Srinoun Inchirdchaie
Srisamorn Kongpem
Subin Keawtem
Sukanya Prannuttee
Sum Pookaew

Sumalai Sangsuwankul
Sumang Suwanta
Sumittra Treenon
Supa Wahalux
Supab Laddakul
Supawat
Supil Srithong
Surapat Wongpracha
Suwana Khoonmai
Suwapa Doakboa
Suwimol Kanbootdee
Tada Thungthong
Tanawat Poonsawad
Tanorn Suphanpayak
Tassanee Tarpunya
Thangchai Chanchai
Thavoran Ramphai
Theantawat Suka
Thippawan Verathumsarikul
Thongbai Klinkajorn
Thongbai Tubthong
Thongdee Kunathai
Thongin Khaoprapa
Thongkhom Lerdsom
Thongmone Kantanit
Thongsook Loaiprakhon
Thongyoi Srisamran
Tim Wadkhen
Tin Kornaoree
Tiraporn Doa-Krajaie
Toomthong Karin
Tuie Joomsin
Tukkata Boathong
Tunrudee Phonjang
Tussanee Phromboon
Ubon Sawatjoont
Uma Passawin
Unchaly Chulabutra
Upin Prompiman
Vallop Jitarree
Varee Lamoongtawai
Vasinee Santakorn
Vavdao Julabutra
Veenus Jirawong
Ven Rarin
Viangrat Srikwae
Vichid Tanasri
Virat Chanlen
Virat Wasutathip
Wanchi Jantasrikhum
Wanna Sanekhone
Wanna Mokthong
Wanna Treemake
Wanpen Eaim-Songkram
Wanpen Sornbunjong
Waree Somany
Wassana Moongkit
Watcharee Earbsapab
Wichid Komedee
Wikanda Soemai
Wilaiwan Earbsapab
Yaowaluck Kongprasert
Yint Roata
Yom Sricha-Em
Yont Surisa
Yugmeai Saema
Yungcheang Saema

Author's acknowledgments

First, I want to express my gratitude to the team that has always been in tune with my never-ending demands, namely Kanokrat Wannarat, Patama Phetsuwan, Chumrum Sahatchai and Suriya Yalor.

And this book would not have happened without the trust Emilia Terragni has given me from the earliest step. It would not be the book you have in your hands without the competence of the team at Phaidon who have led it to the end. I am thinking especially of Emma Robertson, Michelle Lo, Sophie Hodgkin, Julia Hasting, Kate Sclater, and Tim Balaam.

Benjamin Gaspart, for his part, looked after the thousands of images that are the source of the iconography of this book.

Hundreds and hundreds of people across Thailand have agreed to share their culture, ingredients, recipes, and much more. Their generosity and availability had no limits. In this context, more than being our translators, Nitiwadee Arunanurak and Pasinee Napombejra shared their extensive knowledge of Thai food culture.

Last, but by no means least, my deepest thoughts are for Nathalie Saverys, who encouraged me throughout all the crucial steps in the realization of this book.

Phaidon Press Limited
Regent's Wharf
All Saints Street
London N1 9PA

Phaidon Press Inc.
65 Bleecker Street
New York, NY 10012
www.phaidon.com

First published 2014
© 2014 Phaidon Press Limited
ISBN 978 0 7148 6529 4

A CIP catalogue record for this book is
available from the British Library.

Commissioning Editor: Emilia Terragni
Project Editor: Sophie Hodgkin
Production Controller: Vanessa Todd-Holmes

Designed by Hyperkit
Photographs & text by Jean-Pierre Gabriel
Recipe testing & development by Boe Dodds

The publisher would like to thank Sarah Boris,
Sam Gordon, Adam Jackman, Michelle Lo,
Louise Ramsey, Emma Robertson, and Kathy
Steer for their contributions to the book.